JavaServer Pages™

THE JAVA™ SERIES

Also from O'Reilly

JavaServer Pages™

Hans Bergsten

O'REILLY®

Beijing · Cambridge · Farnham · Köln · Paris · Sebastopol · Taipei · Tokyo

JavaServer Pages™
by Hans Bergsten

Copyright © 2001 O'Reilly & Associates, Inc. All rights reserved.
Printed in the United States of America.

Published by O'Reilly & Associates, Inc., 101 Morris Street, Sebastopol, CA 95472.

Editors: Robert Eckstein and Paula Ferguson

Production Editor: Nicole Arigo

Cover Designer: Pam Spremulli

Printing History:

          January 2001:   First Edition.

Library of Congress CIP Data is available at *http://www.oreilly.com/catalog/jserverpages/*.

ISBN: 1-56592-746-X

[M]

Table of Contents

Preface

JavaServer Pages™ (JSP) is a new technology for web application development that has received a great deal of attention since it was first announced.

Why is JSP so exciting? One reason is that JSP is Java-based, and Java is well-suited for enterprise computing. In fact, JSP is a key part of the Java™ 2 Enterprise Edition (J2EE) platform and can take advantage of the many Java Enterprise libraries, such as JDBC, JNDI, and Enterprise JavaBeans™.

Another reason is that JSP supports a powerful model for developing web applications that separates presentation from processing. Understanding why this is so important requires a bit of a history lesson. In the early days of the Web, the only tool for developing dynamic web content was the Common Gateway Interface (CGI). CGI outlined how a web server made user input available to a program, as well as how the program provided the web server with dynamically generated content to send back. CGI scripts were typically written in Perl. (In fact, CGI Perl scripts still drive numerous dynamic web sites.) However, CGI is not an efficient solution. For every request, the web server has to create a new operating-system process, load a Perl interpreter and the Perl script, execute the script, and then dispose of the entire process when it's done.

To provide a more efficient solution, various alternatives to CGI have been added to programmers' toolboxes over the last few years: FastCGI, for example, runs each CGI program in an external permanent process (or a pool of processes). In addition, mod_perl for Apache, NSAPI for Netscape, and ISAPI for Microsoft's IIS all run server-side programs in the same process as the web server itself. While these solutions offer better performance and scalability, each one is supported by only a subset of the popular web servers.

The Java Servlet API, introduced in early 1997, provides a solution to the portability issue. However, all these technologies suffer from a common problem: HTML code embedded inside programs. If you've ever looked at the code for a servlet, you've probably seen endless calls to `out.println()` that contain scores of HTML tags. For the individual developer working on a simple web site this approach may work fine, but it makes it very difficult for people with different skills to work together to develop a web application.

This is becoming a significant problem. As web sites become increasingly complex and are more and more critical to the success of an organization, the appearance and usability of the web interface becomes paramount. New client technologies, such as client-side scripts and DHTML, can develop more responsive and interactive user interfaces, stylesheets can make it easier to globally change fonts and colors, and images can make the interface more appealing. At the same time, server-side code is getting more complex, and demands for reliability, performance, and fault tolerance are increasing. The growing complexity of web applications requires a development model that allows people with different skills to cooperate efficiently.

JavaServer Pages provides just such a development model, allowing web page authors with skills in graphics, layout, and usability to work in tandem with programmers who are experienced in server-side technologies such as multithreading, resource pooling, databases, and caching. While there are other technologies, such as ASP, PHP, and ColdFusion, that support similar development models, none of them offers all the advantages of JSP.

What's in This Book

This book covers Version 1.1 of the JavaServer Pages specification, which was released in late 1999.

In this book, you will learn how to use all the standard JSP elements and features, including elements for accessing JavaBeans components, separating the processing over multiple pages to increase reusability and simplify maintenance, and sharing information between pages, requests, and users. You will also learn how to use and develop custom components. A rich set of custom components, for tasks such as integration of database data, internationalization, access control, and conditional processing, is described in detail. Many of these components are generic enough that you can reuse them directly in your own applications.

The examples in this book guide you through solutions to common JSP design problems, from basic issues such as retrieving and validating user input, to more advanced areas such as developing a database-driven site, authenticating users, providing personalized content, and implementing internationalization. The last part of the book describes how you can combine JSP with other Java technologies; in particular, I describe the combination of JSP and servlets and provide an overview of how JSP fits into the larger scope of J2EE.

Audience

This book is for anyone interested in using JSP technology to develop web applications. In particular, it is written to help the two types of people commonly involved in the development of a JSP-based application:

Page authors
> Page authors primarily develop the web interface to an application. This group uses HTML, stylesheets, and client-side code to develop a rich user interface, and wants to learn how to use JSP elements in web pages to interact with the server components of the application, such as databases and Enterprise JavaBeans (EJB).

Java programmers
> Java programmers are comfortable with the Java programming language and Java servlets. This group is interested in learning how to develop JSP components that page authors can use in web pages, such as JSP custom actions and JavaBeans, and how to combine JSP with other Java server-side technologies, such as servlets and EJB.

This book is structured into three parts, which I describe shortly, to make it easier to find the material you are most interested in.

What You Need to Know

It's always hard to assume how much you, as the reader, already know. For this book, it was even harder, since the material is intended for two audiences: page authors and programmers.

I have assumed that anyone reading this book has experience with HTML; consequently, I will not explain the HTML elements used in the examples. But even if you're an HTML wiz, this may be your first exposure to dynamic web content and web applications. A thorough introduction to the HTTP protocol that drives all web applications, as well as to the concepts and features specific to servlet and JSP-based web applications, is therefore included. If you want to learn more about HTML, I recommend *HTML and XHTML: The Definitive Guide*, by Chuck Musciano and Bill Kennedy (O'Reilly & Associates).

If you're a page author, I have assumed that you don't know anything about programming, although it doesn't hurt if you have played around with client-side scripting languages like VBScript or JavaScript (ECMAScript). This book contains a brief Java primer with enough information to allow you to use a modest amount of Java code in JSP pages. As you will see, I recommend that you use Java components developed by a Java programmer instead of putting your own Java code in the pages, so you don't have to know all the intricate details of the Java language to use JSP.

I have assumed that programmers reading this book are familiar with Java programming, object-oriented concepts, and Java servlets. If you plan to develop JSP components for page authors and are not familiar with Java programming, I recommend that you read an introductory Java book, such as *Exploring Java* by Patrick Niemeyer and Joshua Peck (O'Reilly). If you need to learn about servlets, I recommend *Java Servlet Programming* by Jason Hunter and William Crawford (O'Reilly) or another book that covers servlet technology.

The chapters dealing with database access require some knowledge of SQL and databases in general. I will explain all that you need to know to run the examples, but if you're hoping to develop database-driven applications, you will need to know more about databases than what's in this book.

Organization

This book is structured into three parts. The first part describes the fundamentals of HTTP (the protocol used by all web applications), how servlets and JSP are related, and how to set up a JSP development environment.

The focus of the second part is on developing JSP-based web applications using both standard JSP elements and custom components. Through practical examples, you will learn how to handle common tasks such as validating user input, accessing databases, authenticating users and protecting web pages, localizing your web site, and more. This portion of the book is geared more towards web content designers.

In the third part, you will learn how to develop your own custom actions and JavaBeans, and how to combine JSP with other Java server-side technologies, such as servlets and Enterprise JavaBeans (EJB). This portion of the book is targeted towards the programming community.

All in all, the book consists of 17 chapters and five appendixes as follows.

Part I, JSP Application Basics

Chapter 1, Introducing JavaServer Pages
Explains how JSP fits into the big picture of web applications and how it compares to alternative technologies.

Chapter 2, HTTP and Servlet Basics

    Describes the fundamental HTTP and servlet concepts you need to know to use JSP to its full potential.

Chapter 3, JSP Overview

    An overview of the JSP features, as well as the similarities and differences between JSP pages and servlets. Also introduces the Model-View-Controller design model and how it applies to JSP.

Chapter 4, Setting Up the JSP Environment

    Describes where to get the JSP reference implementation, Apache Tomcat, and how to set it up on your system. Also explains how to install the book examples.

Part II, JSP Application Development

Chapter 5, Generating Dynamic Content

    Explains how to use JSP to generate dynamic content and how to receive and validate user input.

Chapter 6, Using Scripting Elements

    A brief introduction to Java programming, followed by descriptions of all the JSP elements that let you embed Java code directly in your JSP pages.

Chapter 7, Error Handling and Debugging

    Describes the kinds of errors you may encounter during development of a JSP-based application, and strategies and JSP features that help you deal with them.

Chapter 8, Sharing Data Between JSP Pages, Requests, and Users

    Explains the JSP features that let you separate different types of processing in different pages to simplify maintenance and further development. Also describes how sessions can be used to build up information over a sequence of requests from the same user, and how information that applies to all users can be shared using the application scope.

Chapter 9, Database Access

    A quick overview of relational databases, JDBC, and SQL basics. Introduces a set of generic custom actions for reading, updating, and deleting database data.

Chapter 10, Authentication and Personalization

    Describes how authentication and access control can be implemented using container-provided and application-controlled mechanisms, and how to use information about the current user to personalize the web pages.

Chapter 11, Internationalization

Explains internationalization and localization, as well as the Java features available to implement an internationalized application. Describes a set of custom actions used to implement a web site with support for multiple languages.

Chapter 12, Bits and Pieces

Covers various areas not discussed in previous chapters, such as using XML and XSL with JSP, combining JSP with client-side code, reusing JSP fragments by including them in JSP pages, precompiling JSP pages, and more.

Part III, JSP in J2EE and JSP Component Development

Chapter 13, Web Application Models

An overview of J2EE and web application architectures using JSP in combination with other Java technologies.

Chapter 14, Combining Servlets and JSP

Describes in detail how JSP can be combined with servlets.

Chapter 15, Developing JavaBeans for JSP

Provides details about JavaBeans as they relate to JSP, including threading and synchronization concerns for session and application-scope JavaBeans, as well as how using JavaBeans can make it easier to eventually migrate to an EJB architecture. The beans used in previous chapters are reused as examples.

Chapter 16, Developing JSP Custom Actions

Describes the JSP Tag Extension mechanism and how it is used to develop custom actions, reusing many of the custom actions from previous chapters as examples.

Chapter 17, Developing Database Access Components

Describes the database-access custom actions used in the previous chapters and how to use them with both connection pools developed in-house and those provided by a third-party vendor. Also explains how you can reuse the database-access beans to develop your own application-specific database custom actions.

Part IV, Appendixes

Appendix A, JSP Elements Syntax Reference

Contains descriptions of all the standard JSP 1.1 elements.

Appendix B, JSP API Reference

Contains descriptions of all implicit objects available in a JSP page as defined by the servlet and JSP APIs, as well as the tag extension mechanism classes and interfaces.

Appendix C, Book Example Custom Actions and Classes Reference
> Contains descriptions of the custom actions, beans, and utility classes used in the examples.

Appendix D, Web-Application Structure and Deployment Descriptor Reference
> Contains descriptions of the standard web-application structure and all elements in the web-application deployment descriptor.

Appendix E, JSP Resource Reference
> Contains references to JSP-related products, web-hosting services, and sites where you can learn more about JSP and related technologies.

If you're a page author, I recommend that you focus on the chapters in Parts I and II. You may want to browse through Part III to get a feel for how things work behind the scenes, but don't expect to understand everything if you're not a Java programmer.

If you are a Java programmer, Part III is where the action is. If you're already familiar with HTTP and servlets, you may want to move quickly through Part I. However, this part does include information about the web application concept introduced in the Servlet 2.2 API that you may not be familiar with, even if you've worked with servlets for some time. I recommend that you read Part II to learn how JSP works, but you may want to skip ahead to the chapters in Part III from time to time to see how the components used in the examples are actually implemented.

About the Examples

This book contains over 50 examples that demonstrate useful techniques for database access, application-controlled authentication and access control, internationalization, XML processing, and more. The examples include complete applications, such as an online shopping site, an employee directory, and a personalized project billboard, as well as numerous smaller examples and page fragments. The included example tag library contains more than 20 custom actions that you can use directly in your application or as a starting point for your own development. The code for all the examples and most of the custom actions is contained within the text; you can also download all code from the O'Reilly web site at *http://www.oreilly.com/ catalog/jserverpages/*. In addition, you can see all the examples in action at *http:// www.TheJSPBook.com*.

All examples have been tested with the official JSP reference implementation, Apache Tomcat, on Windows (98 and NT 4.0) and Linux (Red Hat Linux 6.2) using Sun's Java 2 SDK (1.2.2 and 1.3). If you need more information on downloading and installing the Apache Tomcat server for use with the examples, see Chapter 4.

Conventions Used in This Book

Italic is used for:

- Pathnames, filenames, directories, and program names
- New terms where they are defined
- Internet addresses, such as domain names and URLs

Boldface is used for:

- Particular keys on a computer keyboard
- Names of user interface buttons and menus

`Constant Width` is used for:

- Anything that appears literally in a JSP page or a Java program, including keywords, datatypes, constants, method names, variables, class names, and interface names
- Command lines and options that should be typed verbatim on the screen
- All JSP and Java code listings
- HTML documents, tags, and attributes

`Constant Width Italic` is used for:

- General placeholders that indicate that an item should be replaced by some actual value in your own program

`Constant width bold` is used for:

- Text that is typed in code examples by the user

How to Contact Us

We have tested and verified all the information in this book to the best of our abilities, but you may find that features have changed or that we have let errors slip through the production of the book. Please let us know of any errors that you find, as well as suggestions for future editions, by writing to:

O'Reilly & Associates, Inc.
101 Morris St.
Sebastopol, CA 95472
1-800-998-9938 (in the U.S. or Canada)
1-707-829-0515 (international/local)
1-707-829-0104 (fax)

You can also send messages electronically. To be put on our mailing list or to request a catalog, send email to:

info@oreilly.com

To ask technical questions or to comment on the book, send email to:

bookquestions@oreilly.com

We have a web site for the book, where we'll list examples, errata, and any plans for future editions. You can access this page at:

http://www.oreilly.com/catalog/jserverpages/

For more information about this book and others, see the O'Reilly web site:

http://www.oreilly.com

Acknowledgments

I love to write and have always wanted to write a book someday. After getting a number of articles about Java servlets and a couple of chapters for a server-side Java book published, my confidence was so high that I sent an email to O'Reilly & Associates and asked if they wanted me to write a book about JSP. Much to my surprise (I guess my confidence was not so high after all), they said, "Yes!" I knew that it would be more work than I could imagine, and it turned out to be even more than that. But here I am, almost a year later, with 17 chapters and 5 appendixes in a nice stack on my desk, written and rewritten countless times. All that remains is to give thanks to everyone who helped me fulfill this dream.

First, I'd like to thank my editors, Paula Ferguson and Bob Eckstein. Paula was the one who accepted my book proposal in the first place, and then helped me through my stumbling steps of writing the first half of the book. Bob came aboard for the second half, and I'm really grateful to him for thoroughly reading everything and giving me helpful advice.

Thanks also to Rob Romano for doing the illustrations, to Christien Shangraw for helping out with the coordination, and to all the production people behind the scenes at O'Reilly who made sure the book got published.

Big thanks also go to the JSP and servlet specification leads, Eduardo Pelegri-Llopart and Danny Coward, for providing feedback, answering all my questions, and clarifying the vague and ambiguous areas of the specifications. You helped me more than I could ask for. I hope my contributions to the specifications repay my debt to some extent.

Thanks also to all of you who helped me improve the book in other ways: Jason Hunter for letting me borrow his connection pool code and Japanese examples;

Craig McClanahan, Larry Riedel, Steve Jung (Steve dedicates his effort to the memory of his father, Arthur H. Jung, who passed away March 17, 2000), Sean Rohead, Jerry Croce, Steve Piccolo, and Vikram David for reviewing the book and giving me many suggestions for how to make it better; all the Apache Tomcat developers for making a great JSP reference implementation; and the members of the *jsp-interest* mailing list for all the ideas about what to cover in this book.

Finally, thanks to everyone who encouraged me and kept my spirits high: Mom, Dad, and my sister, for their support and for teaching me to do what I believe in; all my old friends in Sweden, especially Janne Ek, Peter Hellström (and his dad, who helped me with the translation of the German example), Janne Andersson, Roger Bjärevall and Michael Rohdin; Anne Helgren, my writing teacher who convinced me I could do this; and all the guys in and around Vesica Pisces (*http:// www.vesicapisces.com*), Kelly, Brian, Adam, Bill, and James: I really enjoyed getting away from the writing now and then to hang with you and listen to you play.

—Hans Bergsten
September 2000

I

JSP APPLICATION BASICS

This part of the book describes the fundamentals of HTTP (the protocol used by all web applications), how servlets and JSP are related, and how to set up a JSP development environment and install the book examples.

Introducing
JavaServer Pages

The Java 2 Enterprise Edition (J2EE) has taken the once-chaotic task of building an Internet presence and transformed it to the point where developers can use Java to efficiently create multitier, server-side applications. Today, the Java Enterprise APIs have expanded to encompass a number of areas: RMI and CORBA for remote object handling, JDBC for database interaction, JNDI for accessing naming and directory services, Enterprise JavaBeans for creating reusable business components, JMS (Java Messaging Service) for message-oriented middleware, and JTA (Java Transaction API) for performing atomic transactions. In addition, J2EE supports *servlets*, an extremely popular Java substitute for CGI scripts. The combination of these technologies allows programmers to create distributed business solutions for a variety of tasks.

In late 1999, Sun Microsystems added a new element to the collection of Enterprise Java tools: JavaServer Pages (JSP). JavaServer Pages are built on top of Java servlets and are designed to increase the efficiency in which programmers, and even nonprogrammers, can create web content. This book is all about JavaServer Pages.

What Is JavaServer Pages?

Put succinctly, JavaServer Pages is a technology for developing web pages that include dynamic content. Unlike a plain HTML page, which contains static content that always remains the same, a JSP page can change its content based on any number of variable items, including the identity of the user, the user's browser type, information provided by the user, and selections made by the user. As you'll see later in the book, functionality such as this can be used to create web applications like shopping carts and employee directories.

A JSP page contains standard markup language elements, such as HTML tags, just like a regular web page. However, a JSP page also contains special JSP elements that allow the server to insert dynamic content in the page. JSP elements can be used for a wide variety of purposes, such as retrieving information from a database or registering user preferences. When a user asks for a JSP page, the server executes the JSP elements, merges the results with the static parts of the page, and sends the dynamically composed page back to the browser, as illustrated in Figure 1-1.

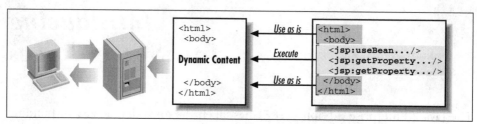

Figure 1-1. Generating dynamic content with JSP elements

JSP defines a number of standard elements useful for any web application, such as accessing JavaBeans components, passing control between pages, and sharing information between requests, pages, and users. Programmers can also extend the JSP syntax by implementing application-specific elements that perform tasks such as accessing databases and Enterprise JavaBeans, sending email, and generating HTML to present application-specific data. The combination of standard elements and custom elements allows for the creation of powerful web applications.

Why Use JSP?

In the early days of the Web, the Common Gateway Interface (CGI) was the only tool for developing dynamic web content. However, CGI is not an efficient solution. For every request that comes in, the web server has to create a new operating system process, load an interpreter and a script, execute the script, and then tear it all down again. This is very taxing for the server and doesn't scale well when the amount of traffic increases.

Numerous CGI alternatives and enhancements, such as FastCGI, mod_perl from Apache, NSAPI from Netscape, ISAPI from Microsoft, and Java Servlets from Sun Microsystems, have been created over the years. While these solutions offer better performance and scalability, all of these technologies suffer from a common problem: they generate web pages by embedding HTML directly in programming language code. This pushes the creation of dynamic web pages exclusively into the realm of programmers. JavaServer Pages, however, changes all that.

Embedding Elements in HTML Pages

JSP tackles the problem from the other direction. Instead of embedding HTML in programming code, JSP lets you embed specialized code (sometimes called scripting code) into HTML pages. Java is the default scripting language of JSP, but the JSP specification allows for other languages as well, such as JavaScript, Perl, and VBScript. We will begin looking at all the JSP elements in detail later, but at this point let's introduce you to a simple JSP page:

```
<html>
  <body bgcolor="white">

  <% java.util.Date clock = new java.util.Date(); %>
  <% if (clock.getHours() < 12) { %>
    <h1>Good morning!</h1>
  <% } else if (clock.getHours() < 18) { %>
    <h1>Good day!</h1>
  <% } else { %>
    <h1>Good evening!</h1>
  <% } %>
  Welcome to our site, open 24 hours a day.
  </body>
</html>
```

This page inserts a different message to the user based on the time of day: "Good morning!" if the local time is before 12:00 P.M., "Good day!" if between 12:00 P.M. and 6:00 P.M., and "Good evening!" if after 6:00 P.M. When a user asks for this page, the JSP-enabled web server executes all the highlighted Java code and creates a static page that is sent back to the user's browser. For example, if the current time is 8:53 P.M., the resulting page sent from the server to the browser looks like this:

```
<html>
  <body bgcolor="white">
  <h1>Good evening!</h1>
    Welcome to our site, open 24 hours a day.
  </body>
</html>
```

A screen shot of this result is shown in Figure 1-2. If you're not a programmer, don't worry if you didn't pick up what happened here. Everything will become clear as you progress through this book.

Of course, embedding too much code in a web page is no better than programming too many HTML tags in server-side code. Fortunately, JSP servers provide a number of reusable *action elements* that perform common tasks, as we'll see starting in Chapter 3, *JSP Overview*. These action elements look similar to HTML elements, but behind the scenes they are componentized Java programs that the server executes when the page is requested by a user. Action elements are a powerful feature

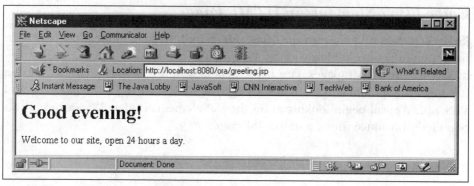

Figure 1-2. The output of a simple JSP page

of JSP, as they give web page authors the ability to perform complex tasks without
having to do any programming.

In addition to the standard action elements, in-house programmers and third parties can develop custom action elements (known as *custom actions* or *custom tags*,
and packaged in *custom tag libraries*) that web page authors can use to handle even
more complex and specialized tasks. This book includes a large set of custom
actions for conditional processing, database access, internationalization, and
more. Custom tag libraries are also available from various open source organizations and commercial companies.

Using the Right Person for Each Task

As I alluded to earlier, JSP allows you to separate the markup language code, such
as HTML, from the programming language code used to process user input,
access databases, and perform other application tasks. One way this separation
takes place is through the use of the JSP standard and custom action elements: the
elements are implemented with programming code and used the same way as
page markup elements in regular web pages. Another way is to combine JSP with
other Java Enterprise technologies. For example, Java servlets can handle input
processing, Enterprise JavaBeans (EJB) can take care of the application logic, and
JSP pages can provide the user interface.

This separation means that with JSP, a typical business can divide its efforts among
two camps that excel in their own areas of expertise, and comprise a JSP web development team with programmers who create the actions for the logic needed by the
application, and page authors who craft the specifics of the interface and use the
complex actions without having to do any programming. I'll talk more about this
benefit as we move through the book, although I should reiterate that the first half
of the book is devoted more to those without programming experience, while the
second half is for programmers who wish to use the JSP libraries to create their
own actions.

Precompilation

Another benefit that is important to mention is that a JSP page is always compiled before it's processed by the server. Remember that older technologies such as CGI/Perl require the server to load an interpreter and the target script each time the page is requested. JSP gets around this problem by compiling each JSP page into executable code the first time it is requested, and invoking the resulting code directly on all subsequent requests. When coupled with a persistent Java virtual machine on a JSP-enabled web server, this allows the server to handle JSP pages much faster.

Integration with Enterprise Java APIs

Finally, because JavaServer Pages is built on top of the Java Servlets API, JSP has access to all of the powerful Enterprise Java APIs, including:

- JDBC
- Remote Method Invocation (RMI) and OMG CORBA support
- JNDI (Java Naming and Directory Interface)
- Enterprise JavaBeans (EJB)
- JMS (Java Message Service)
- JTA (Java Transaction API)

This means that you can easily integrate JavaServer Pages with your existing Java Enterprise solutions, or take advantage of many aspects of enterprise computing if you're starting from scratch.

Other Solutions

At this point, let's digress and look at some other solutions for dynamic web content. Some of these solutions are similar to JSP, while others are descendants of older technologies. Many do not have the unique combination of features and portability offered by JavaServer Pages.

Active Server Pages (ASP)

Microsoft's Active Server Pages (ASP) is a popular technology for developing dynamic web sites. Just like JSP, ASP lets a page author include scripting code, such as VBScript and JScript, in regular web pages to generate the dynamic parts. For complex code, COM (ActiveX) components written in a programming language such as C++ can be invoked by the scripting code. The standard distribution includes components for database access and more, and other components are available from third parties. When an ASP page is requested, the code in the page is executed by the server. The result is inserted into the page and the combination of the static and dynamic content is sent to the browser.

ASP+, currently in beta, will add a number of new features to ASP. As an alternative to scripting, dynamic content can be generated by HTML/XML-like elements similar to JSP action elements. For improved performance, ASP+ pages will be compiled instead of interpreted, and compiled languages such as C++, C#, and VisualBasic will be added to the current list of scripting languages that can be embedded in a page.

ASP is bundled with Microsoft's Internet Information Server (IIS). Due to its reliance on native COM code as its component model, it's primarily a solution for the Windows platform. Limited support for other platforms, such as the Apache web server on Unix, is available through third-party products such as Chili!Soft (Chili!Soft), InstantASP (Halcyon Software), and OpenASP (ActiveScripting.org). You can read more about ASP and ASP+ on Microsoft's web site, *http://www. microsoft.com.*

PHP

PHP* is an open source web scripting language. Like JSP and ASP, PHP allows a page author to include scripting code in regular web pages to generate dynamic content. PHP has a C-like syntax with some features borrowed from Perl, C++, and Java. Complex code can be encapsulated in both functions and classes. A large number of predefined functions are available as part of PHP, such as accessing databases, LDAP directories, and mail servers, creating PDF documents and images, and encrypting and decrypting data. A PHP page is always interpreted by the server when it's requested, merging the result of executing the scripts with the static text in the page, before it's returned to the browser. The latest version is PHP 4, which uses compiled pages instead of interpreted pages to improve performance.

PHP is supported on a wide range of platforms, including all major web servers, on operating systems like Windows, Mac OS, and most Unix flavors, and with interfaces to a large number of database engines. More information about PHP is available at *http://www.php.net.*

ColdFusion

Allaire's ColdFusion product is another popular alternative for generating dynamic web content. The dynamic parts of a page are generated by inserting

---

* The precursor to PHP was a tool called Personal Home Page. Today PHP is not an acronym for anything; it's simply the name of the product.

HTML/XML-like elements, known as the ColdFusion Markup Language (CFML), into web pages. CFML includes a large set of elements for tasks like accessing databases, files, mail servers, and other web servers, as well as conditional processing elements like loops. The latest version of ColdFusion also includes elements for communication with Java servlets and Enterprise JavaBeans. Custom elements can be developed in C++ or Java to encapsulate application-specific functions, and CFML extensions are available from third parties. ColdFusion did not initially support scripting languages, but in ColdFusion 4.5, JavaScript-like code can be embedded in the web pages in addition to the CFML tags.

The ColdFusion 4.5 Enterprise Edition is supported on Windows, Solaris, HP/UX, and Linux for all major web servers and databases. For more information, visit Allaire's web site at *http://www.allaire.com*.

Java servlet template engines

A Java servlet template engine is another technology for separating presentation from processing. When servlets became popular, it didn't take long before developers realized how hard it was to maintain the presentation part when the HTML code was embedded directly in the servlet's Java code.

As a result, a number of so-called *template engines* have been developed as open source products to help get HTML out of the servlets. These template engines are intended to be used together with pure code components (servlets) and use only web pages with scripting code for the presentation part. Requests are sent to a servlet that processes the request, creates objects that represent the result, and calls on a web page template to generate the HTML to be sent to the browser. The template contains scripting code similar to the alternatives described earlier. The scripting languages used by these engines are less powerful, however, because scripting is intended only for reading data objects and generating HTML code to display their values. All the other products and technologies support general-purpose languages, which can (for better or for worse) be used to include business logic in the pages.

Two popular template engines are WebMacro (*http://www.webmacro.org*) and FreeMarker (*http://freemarker.sourceforge.net*).

The JSP Advantage

JSP 1.1 combines the most important features found in the alternatives:

- JSP supports both scripting and element-based dynamic content, and allows programmers to develop custom tag libraries to satisfy application-specific needs.

- JSP pages are precompiled for efficient server processing.

- JSP pages can be used in combination with servlets that handle the business logic, the model supported by Java servlet template engines.

In addition, JSP has a couple of unique advantages that make it stand out from the crowd:

- JSP is a specification, not a product. This means vendors can compete with different implementations, leading to better performance and quality.

- JSP is an integral part of J2EE, a complete platform for Enterprise class applications.

What You Need to Get Started

Before we begin, let's quickly look at what you need to run the examples and develop your own applications. You really need only three things:

- A PC or workstation with a connection to the Internet, so you can download the software you need

- A Java 2–compatible Java Software Development Kit (Java 2 SDK)

- A JSP 1.1–enabled web server, such as Apache Tomcat from the Jakarta Project

The Apache Tomcat server is the reference implementation for JSP 1.1. All the examples in this book were tested on Tomcat. In Chapter 4, *Setting Up the JSP Environment*, I'll show you how to download, install, and configure the Tomcat server, as well as all the examples from this book.

In addition, there are a wide variety of other tools and servers that support JSP, from both open source projects and commercial companies. Close to 30 different server products support JSP to date, and roughly 10 authoring tools with varying degrees of JSP support are listed on Sun's JSP web site (*http://java.sun.com/ products/jsp/*). Appendix E, *JSP Resource Reference*, also contains a collection of references to JSP-related products, web hosting services, and sites where you can learn more about JSP and related technologies. You may want to evaluate some of these products when you're ready to start developing your application, but all you really need to work with the examples in this book are a regular text editor, such as Notepad, vi, or Emacs, and of course the Tomcat server.

So let's get going and take a closer look at what JSP has to offer. We need a solid ground to stand on, though, so in the next chapter we will start with the foundations upon which JSP is built: HTTP and Java servlets.

2

HTTP and Servlet Basics

Let's start this chapter by defining the term *web application*. We've all seen regular client-side applications. But what exactly is a web application? Loosely, we could define it as an application running on a server that a user accesses through a thin, general-purpose client. Today, the most common client is a web browser on a PC or workstation, but soon all kinds of clients will be used, such as wireless PDAs, cellular phones, and other specialized devices.

The lofty goal here is to access all the information and services you need from any type of device you happen to have in front of you. This means that the same simple client program must be able to talk to many different server applications, and the applications must be able to work with many different types of clients. To satisfy this need, the protocol of how a client and a server talk to each other must be defined in detail. That's exactly what the HyperText Transport Protocol (HTTP) is for.

The communication model defined by HTTP forms the foundation for all web application design. You therefore need a basic understanding of HTTP to develop applications that fit within the constraints of the protocol, no matter which server-side technology you use. In this chapter, we look at the most important details of HTTP that you need to be aware of as a web application developer.

One other item. This book is about using JSP as the server-side technology, so that's what we'll primarily focus on. As we saw in Chapter 1, *Introducing JavaServer Pages*, JSP is based on the Java servlet technology. Both technologies share a lot of terminology and concepts, so knowing a bit about servlets will help you even when you develop pure JSP applications. And to really understand and use the full power of JSP, you need to know a fair bit about servlets. We will therefore take a quick look at servlet fundamentals in the last section of this chapter, including a programmer's introduction for those of you familiar with Java.

The HTTP Request/Response Model

HTTP and all extended protocols based on HTTP are based on a very simple but powerful communications model. Here's how it works: a client, typically a web browser, sends a *request* for a *resource* to a server, and the server sends back a *response* corresponding to the requested resource (or a response with an error message if it can't deliver the resource for some reason). A resource can be a simple HTML file, or it can be a program that stores the information sent in a database and generates a dynamic response. This request/response model is illustrated in Figure 2-1.

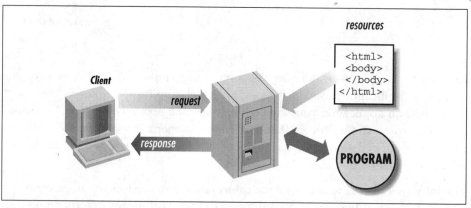

Figure 2-1. HTTP request/response with two resources.

This simple model implies three things you need to be aware of:

1. HTTP is a stateless protocol. This means that the server does not keep any information about the client after it sends its response, and therefore cannot recognize that multiple requests from the same client may be related.

2. Web applications cannot easily provide the kind of immediate feedback typically found in standalone GUI applications such as word processors or traditional client-server applications. Every interaction between the client and the server requires a request/response exchange. Performing a request/response exchange when a user selects an item in a list box or fills out a form element is usually too taxing on the bandwidth available to most Internet users.

3. There's nothing in the protocol that tells the server how a request is made; consequently, the server cannot distinguish between various methods of triggering the request on the client. For example, the HTTP protocol does not allow a web server to differentiate between an explicit request caused by clicking a link or submitting a form and an implicit request caused by resizing the browser window or using the browser's Back button. In addition, HTTP does

not allow the server to invoke client-specific functions, such as going back in
the browser history list or sending the response to a certain frame.

Over the years, people have come up with various tricks to overcome the first problem: HTTP's stateless nature. We'll look at them in general terms later in this
chapter. The other two problems are harder to deal with, but some amount of
interactivity can be achieved by generating a response that includes client-side
code (code executed by the browser), such as JavaScript or a Java applet. This
approach is discussed briefly in Chapter 12.

Requests in Detail

Let's take a closer look at requests. A user sends a request to the server by clicking
a link on a web page, submitting a form, or explicitly typing a web page address in
the browser's address field. To send a request, the browser needs to know which
server to talk to and which resource to ask for. This information is specified by the
Uniform Resource Identifier (URI), also commonly referred to as a *Uniform Resource
Locator* (URL). URI is the general term, while a URL is the specific type of URI
used to completely identify a web resource such as an HTML page. Here is an
example of a URL:

> *http://www.gefionsoftware.com/index.html*

The first part of this URL specifies that the HTTP protocol is used to request the
resource. This is followed by the name of the server, *www.gefionsoftware.com*. The
web server waits for requests to come in on a special TCP/IP port. Port number
80 is the standard port for HTTP requests. If the web server uses another port,
the URL must specify the port number in addition to the server name. For
example:

> *http://www.gefionsoftware.com:8080/index.html*

This URL is sent to a server that uses port 8080 instead of 80. The last part of the
URL, */index.html*, identifies the resource that the client is requesting. This is sometimes called the *URI path*.

The client browser always makes a request by sending a *request message*. An HTTP
request message consists of three things: a request line, request headers, and
sometimes a request body.

The request line starts with the request method name, followed by a resource identifier and the protocol version used by the browser:

```
GET /index.html HTTP/1.0
```

The most commonly used request method is named GET. As the name implies, a
GET request is used to retrieve a resource from the server. It's the default request

method, so if you type a URL in the browser's address field or click on a link, the request will be sent to the server as a GET request.

The request headers provide additional information the server may need to process the request. The message body is included only in some types of requests, like the POST request discussed later.

Here's an example of a valid HTTP request message:

```
GET /index.html HTTP/1.0
Host: www.gefionsoftware.com
User-Agent : Mozilla/4.5 [en] (WinNT; I)
Accept: image/gif, image/jpeg, image/pjpeg, image/png, */*
Accept-language : en
Accept-charset : iso-8859-1,*,utf-8
```

The request line specifies the GET method and asks for the resource */index.html* to be returned using the HTTP/1.0 protocol version. The various headers provide additional information the server can use to fulfill the request.

The Host header tells the server the hostname used in the URL. A server may have multiple names, so this information is used to distinguish between multiple virtual web servers sharing the same web server process.

The User-Agent header contains information about the type of browser making the request. The server can use this to send different types of responses to different types of browsers. For instance, if the server knows whether the request is sent by Internet Explorer or Netscape Navigator, it can send a response that takes advantage of each browser's unique features. It can also tell if a browser other than an HTML browser is used, such as a Wireless Markup Language (WML) browser on a cell phone or a PDA device, and generate an appropriate response.

The Accept headers provide information about the languages and file formats the browser accepts. These headers can be used to determine the capabilities of the browser and the user's preferences, and adjust the response to use a supported image format and the preferred language. These are just a few of the headers that can be included in a request message. The HTTP specification describes all of them.

The resource identifier (URI) doesn't necessarily correspond to a static file on the server. It can identify an executable program, a record in a database, or pretty much anything the web server knows about. That's why the generic term *resource* is used. In fact, there's no way to tell if the */index.html* URI corresponds to a file or to something else; it's just a name that means something to the server. The web server is configured to map these unique names to the real resources.

Responses in Detail

When the web server receives the request, it looks at the URI and decides, based on configuration information, how to handle it. It may handle it internally by simply reading an HTML file from the filesystem, or it may forward the request to some component that is responsible for the resource corresponding to the URI. This might be a program that uses a database to dynamically generate an appropriate response. To the client, it makes no difference how the request is handled; all it cares about is getting a response.

The response message looks similar to the request message. It consists of three things: a status line, response headers, and possibly a response body. Here's an example:

```
HTTP/1.0 200 OK
Last-Modified: Mon, 20 Dec 1999 23:26:42 GMT
Date: Tue, 11 Jan 2000 20:52:40 GMT
Status: 200
Content-Type: text/html
Servlet-Engine: Tomcat Web Server/3.2
Content-Length: 59

<html>
  <body>
    <h1>Hello World!</h1>
  </body>
</html>
```

The status line starts with the name of the protocol, followed by a result code and a short description of the result code. Here the result code is 200, meaning the request was executed successfully. The response message has headers just like the request message. In this example, the `Last-Modified` header gives the date and time that the resource was last modified. The client can use this information as a timestamp in a local cache; the next time the user asks for this resource, the client can ask the server to send it only if it's been updated since the last time it was requested. The `Content-Type` header tells the client what type of response data the body contains, and the `Content-Length` header shows how large it is. You can likely figure out what the other headers are for. A blank line separates the headers from the message body. Here, the body is a simple HTML page:

```
<html>
  <body>
    <h1>Hello World!</h1>
  </body>
</html>
```

Of course, the body can contain a more complex HTML page or any other type of content. For example, the request may return a page with <img> elements. When the browser reads the first response and finds the <img> elements, it sends a new request for the resource identified by each element, often in parallel. The server returns one response for each request, with a Content-Type header telling what type of image it is (for instance, image/gif) and the body containing the bytes that make up the image. All responses are then combined by the browser to render the complete page. This interaction is illustrated in Figure 2-2.

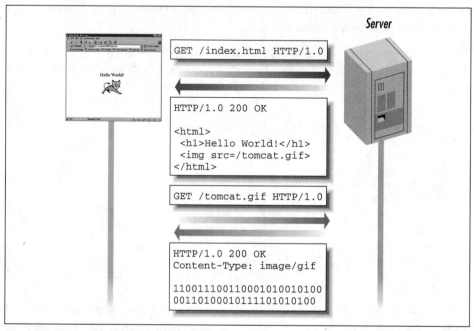

Figure 2-2. Interaction between a web client and a server

Request Parameters

Besides the URI and headers, a request message can contain additional information in the form of parameters. If the URI identifies a server-side program for displaying weather information, for example, request parameters can provide information about which city the user wants to see a forecast for. In an e-commerce application, the URI may identify a program that processes orders, with the user's customer number and the list of items to be purchased transferred as parameters.

Parameters can be sent in one of two ways: tacked on to the URI in the form of a *query string*, or sent as part of the request message body. Here is an example of a URI with a query string:

http://www.weather.com/forecast?city=Hermosa+Beach&state=CA

The query string starts with a question mark (?) and consists of name/value pairs separated by ampersands (&). These names and values must be *URL encoded*, meaning that special characters such as whitespace, question marks, ampersands, and all other nonalphanumeric characters are encoded so that they don't get confused with characters used to separate name/value pairs. In this example, the space between Hermosa and Beach is encoded as a plus sign. Other special characters are encoded as their corresponding hexadecimal ASCII value: for instance, a question mark is encoded as %3F. When parameters are sent as part of the request body, they follow the same syntax: URL-encoded name/value pairs separated by ampersands.

Request Methods

As described earlier, GET is the most commonly used request method, intended to retrieve a resource without causing anything else to happen on the server. The POST method is almost as common as GET. A POST request is intended to request some kind of processing on the server, for instance, updating a database or processing a purchase order.

The way parameters are transferred is one of the most obvious differences between the GET and POST request methods. A GET request always uses a query string to send parameter values, while a POST request always sends them as part of the body (additionally, it can send some parameters as a query string, just to make life interesting). If you code a link to a URI in an HTML page using an <a> element, clicking on the link results in a GET request being sent to the server. Since the GET request uses a query string to pass parameters, you can include hardcoded parameter values in the link URI:

```
<a href="/forecast?city=Hermosa+Beach&state=CA">
  Hermosa Beach weather forecast
</a>
```

When you use a form to send user input to the server, you can specify whether to use the GET or POST method with the method attribute, as shown below:

```
<form action="/forecast" method="POST">
  City: <input name="city" type="text">
  State: <input name="state" type="text">
  <p>
  <input type="SUBMIT">
</form>
```

If the user enters "Hermosa Beach" and "CA" in the form fields and clicks on the Submit button, the browser sends a request message like this to the server:

```
POST /forecast HTTP/1.0
Host: www.gefionsoftware.com
```

```
User-Agent : Mozilla/4.5 [en] (WinNT; I)
Accept: image/gif, image/jpeg, image/pjpeg, image/png, */*
Accept-language : en
Accept-charset : iso-8859-1,*,utf-8
```

```
city=Hermosa+Beach&state=CA
```

Due to the differences in how parameters are sent by GET and POST requests, as well as the differences in their intended purposes, browsers handle the requests in different ways. A GET request, parameters and all, can easily be saved as a bookmark, hardcoded as a link, and the response cached by the browser. Also, the browser knows that no damage is done if it sends a GET request again automatically, for instance if the user clicks the Reload or Back button.

A POST request, on the other hand, can not be bookmarked as easily; the browser would have to save both the URI and the request message body. Since a POST request is intended to perform some possibly irreversible action on the server, the browser must also ask the user if it's okay to send the request again. You have probably seen this type of confirmation dialog, shown in Figure 2-3, numerous times with your browser.

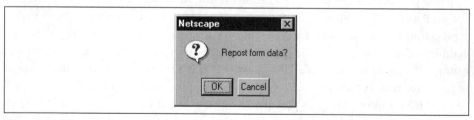

Figure 2-3. Repost confirmation dialog

Besides GET and POST, HTTP specifies the following methods:

OPTIONS

> The OPTIONS method is used to find out what options (e.g., methods) a server or resource offers.

HEAD

> The HEAD method is used to get a response with all headers that would be generated by a GET request, but without the body. It can be used to make sure a link is valid or to see when a resource was last modified.

PUT

> The PUT method is used to store the message body content on the server as a resource identified by the URI.

DELETE

> The DELETE method is used to delete the resource identified by the URI.

TRACE

> The TRACE method is used for testing the communication between the client and the server. The server sends back the request message, exactly as it was received, as the body of the response.

Note that these methods are not normally used in a web application.

State Management

As I touched on earlier, HTTP is a stateless protocol; when the server sends back the response corresponding to the request, it forgets all about the transaction. If a user sends a new request, the server has no way of knowing if it is related to the previous request.

This is fine for static content such as regular HTML files, but it's a problem for web applications where a number of requests may be needed to complete a transaction. Consider a shopping cart application: the server-side application needs to allow the user to select items in multiple steps, check the inventory when the user is ready to make the purchase, and finally process the order. In this scenario, the application needs to keep track of information provided by multiple requests from the same browser. In other words, it needs to remember the client's transaction state.

There are two ways to solve this problem, and both have been used extensively for web applications with a variety of server-side technologies. The server can either return the complete state with each response and let the browser send it back as part of the next request; or, it can save the state somewhere on the server and send back only an identifier that the browser returns with the next request. The identifier is then used to locate the state information saved on the server.

In both cases, the information can be sent to the browser in one of three ways:

- As a cookie
- Embedded as hidden fields in an HTML form
- Encoded in the URIs in the response body, typically as links to other application pages (this is known as *URL rewriting*)

Figure 2-4 outlines these methods.

A *cookie* is a name/value pair the server passes to the browser in a response header. The browser stores the cookie for the time specified by the cookie's expiration time attribute. When the browser sends a request to a server, it checks its "cookie jar" and includes all cookies it has received from the same server (that have not yet expired) in the request headers. Cookies used for state management don't have an expiration time, and expire as soon as the user closes the browser. Using cookies is the easiest way to deal with the state issue, but cookies are not supported by

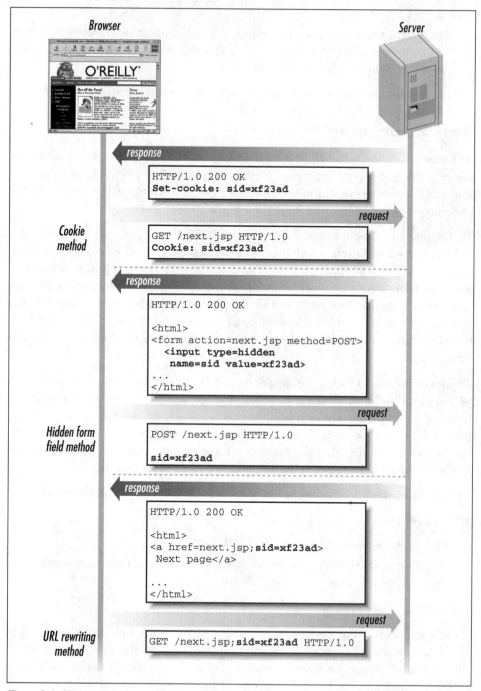

Figure 2-4. Client state information transportation methods

all browsers. In addition, a user may disable cookies in a browser that does support them because of privacy concerns. Hence, we cannot rely on cookies alone.

If hidden fields in an HTML form are used to send the state information to the browser, the browser returns the information to the server as regular HTTP parameters when the form is submitted. When the state information is encoded in URIs, it is returned to the server as part of the request URI, for instance when the user clicks on an encoded link.

Sending all state information back and forth between the browser and server is not efficient, so most modern server-side technologies employ the idea of keeping the information on the server and passing only an identifier between the browser and the server. This is called *session tracking*: all requests from a browser that contain the same identifier (session ID) belong to the same session, and the server keeps track of all information associated with the session. As you will see in the next section, the servlet specification hides the mechanisms used to implement session tracking to a large extent, making life easier for the application developer. You will learn how the JSP specification makes it even easier to use session tracking in Chapter 8, *Sharing Data Between JSP Pages, Requests, and Users*.

A session is valid until it's explicitly terminated (for instance, when the user logs out) or until it's automatically timed out by the server after a period of user inactivity (typically 30 minutes). Note that there's no way for the server to tell if the user closes the browser, since there's no permanent connection between the browser and the server, and no message is sent to the server when the browser disappears. Still, closing the browser usually means losing the session ID; the cookie expires or the encoded URIs are no longer available. So when the user opens a browser again, the server is unable to associate the new request with the previous session, and therefore creates a new session. However, all the session data associated with the previous session remains on the server until the session times out.

Servlets

The JSP specification is based on the Java servlet specification. In fact, JSP pages are often combined with servlets in the same application. So to use JSP effectively, it's important to understand the similarities and the concepts that apply to both technologies. In this section, we first take a brief look at what a servlet is, and then discuss the concepts shared by servlets and JSP pages. In Chapter 3, *JSP Overview*, we'll take a closer look at how JSP pages are actually turned into servlets automatically.

If you're already familiar with servlets, this is old news. You can safely skip the rest of this chapter. If you're not familiar with programming, don't worry about the details. The important thing is that you get familiar with the concepts described in the remainder of this chapter.

Advantages Over Other Server-Side Technologies

In simple terms, a servlet is a piece of code that adds new functionality to a server (typically a web server), just like CGI and proprietary server extensions such as NSAPI and ISAPI. But compared to other technologies, servlets have a number of advantages:

Platform and vendor independence

Servlets are supported by all the major web servers and application servers, so a servlet-based solution doesn't tie you to one specific vendor. And because servlets are written in the Java programming language, they can be used on any operating system with a Java runtime environment.

Integration

Servlets are developed in Java and can therefore take advantage of all the other Java technologies, such as JDBC for database access, JNDI for directory access, RMI for remote resource access, etc. Starting with Version 2.2, the servlet specification is part of the Java 2 Enterprise Edition (J2EE), making servlets an important ingredient of any large-scale enterprise application, with formalized relationships to other server-side technologies such as Enterprise JavaBeans (EJB).

Efficiency

Servlets execute in a process that runs until the servlet-based application is shut down. Each servlet request is executed as a separate thread in this permanent process. This is far more efficient than the CGI model, where a new process is created for each request. First of all (and most obviously), a servlet doesn't have the overhead of creating the process and loading the CGI script and possibly its interpreter. But another timesaver is that between requests, servlets can also access resources that remain loaded in the process memory, such as database connections and client state.

Scalability

By virtue of being written in Java and the broad support for servlets, a servlet-based application is extremely scalable. You can develop and test the application on a Windows 98 PC using the standalone servlet reference implementation, and deploy it on anything from a more powerful server running Linux and Apache to a cluster of high-end servers with an application server that supports loadbalancing and failover.

Robustness and security

Java is a strongly typed programming language. This means that you catch a lot of mistakes in the compilation phase that you would only catch during runtime if you used a scripting language like Perl. Java's error handling is also much more robust than C/C++, where an error like division by zero typically brings down the whole server.

In addition, servlets use specialized interfaces to server resources that are not vulnerable to the traditional security attacks. For instance, a CGI Perl script typically uses shell command strings composed of data received from the client to ask the server to do things like sending email. People with nothing better to do love to find ways to send data that will cause the server to crash, remove all files on the hard disk, or plant a virus or a backdoor when the server executes the command. A CGI script programmer must be very careful threats, but these problems are almost non- sn't communicate with the server in the same

ierits all these advantages by being based on

er, there are some fundamental points you t is a Java class that uses the Servlet Applica- The Servlet API consists of a number of classes nods that make it possible to process HTTP t manner.

st that should be handled by a servlet, it first servlet class exists. If it doesn't, it creates one. ervlet. It then asks the servlet to process the loaded, the same servlet instance (object) is ests. Eventually the web server needs to shut web server itself is shut down. It first informs is gives the objects a chance to do necessary base connection, before shutting down.

he web server and the servlet are defined by methods in the javax.servlet.Servlet interface, and are referred to as the servlet's *life-cycle methods*. Here are their formal definitions:

public void init(ServletConfig config)
> The init() method is called when the servlet is loaded so it can initialize its state: for instance, set up references to external resources such as a database and read configuration information.

public void service(ServletRequest req, ServletResponse res)
> The service() method is called to service a request. It's called zero or more times during the servlet's lifetime, and passes objects representing the request and response messages to the servlet.

```
public void destroy()
```
The destroy() method is called just before the servlet is taken out of service. It allows the servlet to release references to any external resources it has acquired during its lifetime.

Figure 2-5 illustrates how the web server uses the life-cycle methods.

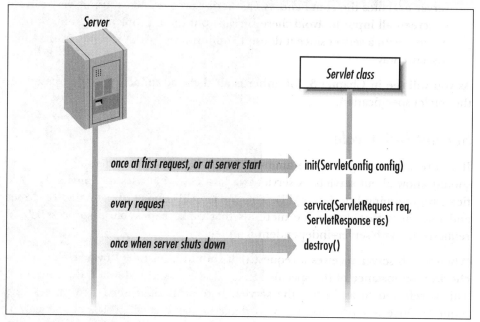

Figure 2-5. Servlet life cycle

Most interesting to us is the service() method. It gives the servlet access to two objects, which are passed as arguments to the method: a ServletRequest object and a ServletResponse object (when HTTP is used, specialized objects of type HttpServletRequest and HttpServletResponse are used instead). Through methods implemented by the ServletRequest object, the servlet can access all information known about the request message: parameter values, header values, authentication information, etc. The servlet uses methods of the Servlet-Response object to generate the response message. It can set headers, the status code, and the actual response body, which is typically a dynamically generated HTML page.

In Chapter 3, I discuss how a JSP page is turned into a servlet the first time it's requested, and then loaded, called, and shut down in exactly the same way as a regular servlet.

Servlet Containers

A servlet container is the connection between a web server and the servlets. It provides the runtime environment for all the servlets on the server as defined by the servlet specification, and is responsible for loading and invoking those servlets when the time is right.

There are many different types of servlet containers. Some containers are called add-ons, or plug-ins, and are used to add servlet support to web servers without native servlet support (such as Apache and IIS). They can run in the same operating-system process as the web server or in a separate process. Other containers are standalone servers. A standalone server includes web server functionality to provide full support for HTTP in addition to the servlet runtime environment. Containers can also be embedded in other servers, such as a climate-control system, to offer a web-based interface to the system. A container bundled as part of an application server can distribute the execution of servlets over multiple hosts. The server can balance the load evenly over all containers, and some servers can even provide failover capabilities in case a host crashes.

No matter what type it is, the servlet container is responsible for mapping incoming requests to a servlet registered to handle the resource identified by the URI and passing the request message to that servlet. After the request is processed, it is the container's responsibility to convert the response object created by the servlet into a response message and send it back to the client. This is illustrated in Figure 2-6.

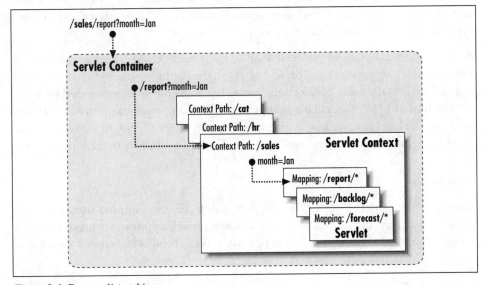

Figure 2-6. Request dispatching

Servlet Contexts

A servlet container implementing the Servlet 2.1 API (or later) can group servlets and other resources such as JSP pages, HTML pages, and image files into separate *servlet contexts*. Each servlet context represents a web application, and is associated with a unique URI path prefix called the *context path*, as shown in Figure 2-6. For instance, your human-resources application can be associated with the context path /hr and your sales-tracking system with the context path /sales. This allows one servlet container to distinguish between applications and dispatch requests like /sales/report?month=Jan to the sales tracking application and /hr/emplist to the human-resources application.

The remaining URI path is then used within the selected context to decide how to process the request by comparing it to path mapping rules. Such rules can be set up to send all requests starting with /report to one servlet and with /forecast to another. Another type of rule can be set up to let one servlet handle all requests with paths ending with a specific file extension, such as *.jsp*. Figure 2-6 shows how the different parts of the URI paths are used to direct the request processing to the right resource through the container and context.

Each context is self-contained and doesn't know anything about other applications running in the same container. All references between the servlets and JSP pages in the application are relative to the context path, and therefore referred to as *context-relative* paths. By using context-relative paths within the application, a web application can be deployed using any context path. The servlet specification defines a standard packaging format for web applications that all compliant containers know how to install and associate with a context. This is described in more detail in the last section of this chapter.

A web application can be more than just JSP pages, HTML pages, and images. Therefore, a context can hold on to objects shared by all components of the application,[*] such as database connections and other shared resources needed by multiple servlets and JSP pages. This is represented by the *application scope* in JSP, and we'll take a closer look at how to use it in Chapter 8. Each context also has its own set of configuration data, discussed in more detail in the last section of this chapter.

Sessions

Earlier, I mentioned that the Servlet API hides the mechanisms used to implement session tracking to a large extent. A servlet-based application doesn't need to know if the session ID is passed between the server and the browser as a cookie or

---

[*] There are special considerations for applications distributed over multiple servers. Chapter 13, *Web Application Models*, describes this in more detail.

encoded in the URIs. Instead, the servlet container looks at the information it receives with each request and decides which mechanism to use. If it receives a session ID cookie, it uses cookie-based tracking; if it receives an encoded URI, it uses URL rewriting. No matter which mechanism is used, the container gives the servlet access to the state information associated with the browser through the request object it passes to the servlet.

The state information is represented by a session object, which is an instance of a Servlet API class named `javax.servlet.http.HttpSession`. The session object acts as a container for other objects that make up the session state, with methods for adding, getting, and removing these objects. For instance, in an e-commerce application, the user picks items to buy from an online catalog. When the servlet receives a request to put an item in the shopping cart, it gets the session object from the request and places a Java object representing the item in the session by calling its `setAttribute()` method. Later, when the user checks out, another servlet picks up all items from the session using other methods, and processes the order.

Since a JSP page is turned into a servlet, it has access to the session in the same way, but JSP makes it even easier to work with session data through the concept of a *session scope*. We look at all aspects of sessions from a JSP perspective in Chapter 8.

Packaging Java Web Applications

A complete web application may consist of several different resources: JSP pages, servlets, applets, static HTML pages, custom tag libraries and other Java class files. Until very recently, different servers required an application with all these components to be installed and configured in different ways, making it very hard for web application developers to provide easy-to-use installation instructions and tools.

Version 2.2 of the servlet specification defines a portable way to package all these resources together, along with a *deployment descriptor*. A deployment descriptor is a file that outlines security requirements and describes how all the resources fit together. All files for the web application are placed in an archive file, called a Web Archive (WAR) file. A WAR file has a *.war* file extension and can be created with the Java *jar* command or a ZIP utility program such as *WinZip* (the same compression scheme is used).

All Servlet 2.2–compliant servers can install a WAR file and associate the application with a servlet context. During installation, a server is free to unpack the contents of the file and store it for runtime use in any way it sees fit, but the application developer needs to deal with only one delivery format. This standardized deployment format also enables server vendors to develop installation and configuration tools that make it easy to install a new web application.

The internal structure for a WAR file is defined by the JSP specification. During development, however, it's often more convenient to work with the web application files in an open filesystem instead of packaging and repackaging them into a WAR file every time you make a change. As a result, most containers support the WAR structure in an open filesystem as well.

The structure required for both is outlined here:

```
/index.html
/company/contact.html
/products/list.jsp
/images/banner.gif
/WEB-INF/web.xml
/WEB-INF/lib/bean.jar
/WEB-INF/lib/actions.jar
/WEB-INF/classes/com/mycorp/servlets/PurchaseServlet.class
/WEB-INF/classes/com/mycorp/util/MyUtils.class
/WEB-INF/...
```

The top-level in this structure is the document root for all web application files, such as HTML pages, JSP pages, and image files—in other words, all the files requested directly by the browser.

You're probably wondering about the *WEB-INF* directory. This directory contains the application deployment descriptor (*web.xml*) as well as subdirectories for other types of resources, such as Java class files and configuration files. A browser does not have access to the files under this directory, so it's safe to place files that you don't want public here.

The deployment descriptor file, *web.xml,* is a simple XML file. We will get much more familiar with the contents of this file as we proceed through the book. (Appendix D, *Web-Application Structure and Deployment Descriptor Reference,* also contains a complete reference of this file.) In addition, two *WEB-INF* subdirectories have special meaning if you're a programmer: *lib* and *classes.* The *lib* directory typically contains Java Archive (JAR) files (compressed archives of Java class files). As an alternative, class files can be stored in the *classes* directory without being compressed, which can be convenient during development. However, class files must be stored in subdirectories of the *classes* directory that mirror their package structure, and must follow standard Java conventions for how class files are organized in a directory tree.

3

JSP Overview

JSP is the latest Java technology for web application development, and is based on the servlet technology introduced in the previous chapter. While servlets are great in many ways, they are generally reserved for programmers. In this chapter, we look at the problems that JSP technology solves, the anatomy of a JSP page, the relationship between servlets and JSP, and how a JSP page is processed by the server.

In any web application, a program on the server processes requests and generates responses. In a simple one-page application, such as an online bulletin board, you don't need to be overly concerned about the design of this piece of code; all logic can be lumped together in a single program. But when the application grows into something bigger (spanning multiple pages, with more options and support for more types of clients) it's a different story. The way your site is designed is critical to how well it can be adapted to new requirements and continue to evolve. The good news is that JSP technology can be used in all kinds of web applications, from the simplest to the most complex. Therefore, this chapter also introduces the primary concepts in the design model recommended for web applications, and the different roles played by JSP and other Java technologies in this model.

The Problem with Servlets

In many Java servlet-based applications, processing the request and generating the response are both handled by a single servlet class. A example servlet looks like this:

```
public class OrderServlet extends HttpServlet {
    public void doGet(HttpServletRequest request,
        HttpServletResponse response)
        throws ServletException, IOException  {
```

```
response.setContentType("text/html");
PrintWriter out = response.getWriter();

if (isOrderInfoValid(request)) {
    saveOrderInfo(request);
    out.println("<html>");
    out.println("  <head>");
    out.println("    <title>Order Confirmation</title>");
    out.println("  </head>");
    out.println("  <body>");
    out.println("    <h1>Order Confirmation</h1>");
    renderOrderInfo(request);
    out.println("  </body>");
    out.println("</html>");
}
...
```

If you're not a programmer, don't worry about all the details in this code. The point is that the servlet contains request processing and business logic (implemented by methods such as isOrderInfoValid() and saveOrderInfo()) and also generates the response HTML code, embedded directly in the servlet code using println() calls. A more structured servlet application isolates different pieces of the processing in various reusable utility classes, and may also use a separate class library for generating the actual HTML elements in the response. But even so, the pure servlet-based approach still has a few problems:

- Detailed Java programming knowledge is needed to develop and maintain all aspects of the application, since the processing code and the HTML elements are lumped together.

- Changing the look and feel of the application, or adding support for a new type of client (such as a WML client), requires the servlet code to be updated and recompiled.

- It's hard to take advantage of web page development tools when designing the application interface. If such tools are used to develop the web page layout, the generated HTML must then be manually embedded into the servlet code, a process that is time-consuming, error-prone, and extremely boring.

Adding JSP to the puzzle lets you solve these problems by separating the request processing and business logic code from the presentation, as illustrated in Figure 3-1. Instead of embedding HTML in the code, you place all static HTML in JSP pages, just as in a regular web page, and add a few JSP elements to generate the dynamic parts of the page. The request processing can remain the domain of servlet programmers, and the business logic can be handled by JavaBeans and Enterprise JavaBeans (EJB) components.

As I mentioned before, separating the request processing and business logic from presentation makes it possible to divide the development tasks among people with

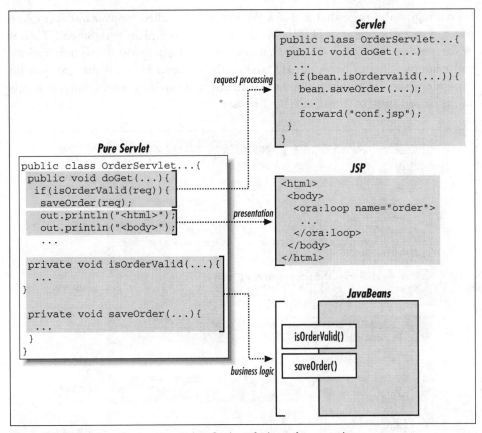

Figure 3-1. Separation of request processing, business logic, and presentation

different skills. Java programmers implement the request processing and business logic pieces, web page authors implement the user interface, and both groups can use best-of-breed development tools for the task at hand. The result is a much more productive development process. It also makes it possible to change different aspects of the application independently, such as changing the business rules without touching the user interface.

This model has clear benefits even for a web page author without programming skills who is working alone. A page author can develop web applications with many dynamic features, using generic Java components provided by open source projects or commercial companies.

The Anatomy of a JSP Page

A JSP page is simply a regular web page with JSP elements for generating the parts of the page that differ for each request, as shown in Figure 3-2.

Everything in the page that is not a JSP element is called *template text*. Template text can really be any text: HTML, WML, XML, or even plain text. Since HTML is by far the most common web page language in use today, most of the descriptions and examples in this book are HTML-based, but keep in mind that JSP has no dependency on HTML; it can be used with any markup language. Template text is always passed straight through to the browser.

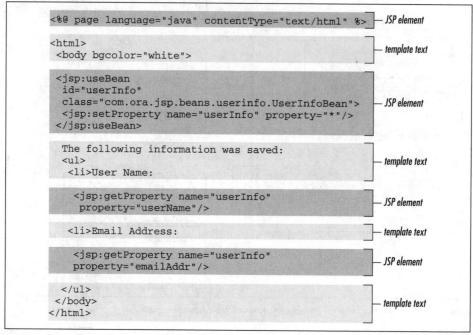

Figure 3-2. Template text and JSP elements

When a JSP page request is processed, the template text and the dynamic content generated by the JSP elements are merged, and the result is sent as the response to the browser.

JSP Elements

There are three types of elements with JavaServer Pages: *directive, action,* and *scripting* elements.

The directive elements, shown in Table 3-1, are used to specify information about the page itself that remains the same between page requests, for example, the scripting language used in the page, whether session tracking is required, and the name of a page that should be used to report errors, if any.

Table 3-1. Directive Elements

Element	Description
`<%@ page ... %>`	Defines page-dependent attributes, such as scripting language, error page, and buffering requirements
`<%@ include ... %>`	Includes a file during the translation phase
`<%@ taglib ... %>`	Declares a tag library, containing custom actions, used in the page

Action elements typically perform some action based on information that is required at the exact time the JSP page is requested by a client. An action element can, for instance, access parameters sent with the request to do a database lookup. It can also dynamically generate HTML, such as a table filled with information retrieved from an external system.

The JSP specification defines a few standard action elements, listed in Table 3-2, and includes a framework for developing custom action elements. A custom action element can be developed by a programmer to extend the JSP language. The examples in this book use custom actions for database access, internationalization, access control, and more.

Table 3-2. Standard Action Elements

Element	Description
`<jsp:useBean>`	Makes a JavaBeans component available in a page
`<jsp:getProperty>`	Gets a property value from a JavaBeans component and adds it to the response
`<jsp:setProperty>`	Sets a JavaBeans property value
`<jsp:include>`	Includes the response from a servlet or JSP page during the request processing phase
`<jsp:forward>`	Forwards the processing of a request to a servlet or JSP page
`<jsp:param>`	Adds a parameter value to a request handed off to another servlet or JSP page using `<jsp:include>` or `<jsp:forward>`
`<jsp:plugin>`	Generates HTML that contains the appropriate client browser-dependent elements (OBJECT or EMBED) needed to execute an Applet with the Java Plugin software

Scripting elements, shown in Table 3-3, allow you to add small pieces of code to a JSP page, such as an `if` statement to generate different HTML depending on a certain condition. Like actions, they are also executed when the page is requested. You should use scripting elements with extreme care: if you embed too much code in your JSP pages, you will end up with the same kind of maintenance problems as with servlets embedding HTML.

Table 3-3. Scripting Elements

Element	Description
`<% ... %>`	Scriptlet, used to embed scripting code.
`<%= ... %>`	Expression, used to embed Java expressions when the result shall be added to the response. Also used as runtime action attribute values.
`<%! ... %>`	Declaration, used to declare instance variables and methods in the JSP page implementation class.

JSP elements, such as action and scripting elements, are often used to work with *JavaBeans*. Put succinctly, a JavaBeans component is a Java class that complies with certain coding conventions. JavaBeans are typically used as containers for information that describes application entities, such as a customer or an order. We'll cover each of these element types, as well as JavaBeans, in the following chapters.

JSP Processing

A JSP page cannot be sent as-is to the browser; all JSP elements must first be processed by the server. This is done by turning the JSP page into a servlet, and then executing the servlet.

Just as a web server needs a servlet container to provide an interface to servlets, the server needs a JSP container to process JSP pages. The JSP container is often implemented as a servlet configured to handle all requests for JSP pages. In fact, these two containers—a servlet container and a JSP container—are often combined into one package under the name *web container* (as it is referred to in the J2EE documentation).

A JSP container is responsible for converting the JSP page into a servlet (known as the *JSP page implementation class*) and compiling the servlet. These two steps form the *translation phase*. The JSP container automatically initiates the translation phase for a page when the first request for the page is received. The translation phase takes a bit of time, of course, so a user notices a slight delay the first time a JSP page is requested. The translation phase can also be initiated explicitly; this is referred to as *precompilation* of a JSP page. Precompiling a JSP page avoids hitting the user with this delay, and is discussed in more detail in Chapter 12, *Bits and Pieces*.

The JSP container is also responsible for invoking the JSP page implementation class to process each request and generate the response. This is called the *request processing phase*. The two phases are illustrated in Figure 3-3.

As long as the JSP page remains unchanged, any subsequent processing goes straight to the request processing phase (i.e., it simply executes the class file).

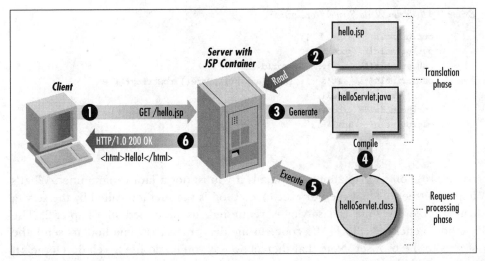

Figure 3-3. JSP page translation and processing phases

When the JSP page is modified, it goes through the translation phase again before entering the request processing phase.

So in a way, a JSP page is really just another way to write a servlet without having to be a Java programming wiz. And, except for the translation phase, a JSP page is handled exactly like a regular servlet: it's loaded once and called repeatedly, until the server is shut down. By virtue of being an automatically generated servlet, a JSP page inherits all of the advantages of servlets described in Chapter 2, *HTTP and Servlet Basics*: platform and vendor independence, integration, efficiency, scalability, robustness, and security.

Let's look at a simple example of a servlet. In the tradition of programming books for as far back as anyone cares to remember, we start with an application that just writes Hello World, but this time we will add a twist: our application will also show the current time on the server. Example 3-1 shows a hand-coded servlet with this functionality.

Example 3-1. Hello World Servlet

```
public class HelloWorldServlet implements Servlet {
    public void service(ServletRequest request,
        ServletResponse response)
        throws ServletException, IOException  {

        response.setContentType("text/html");
        PrintWriter out = response.getWriter();

        out.println("<html>");
        out.println("  <head>");
        out.println("    <title>Hello World</title>");
```

Example 3-1. Hello World Servlet (continued)

```
        out.println("  </head>");
        out.println("  <body>");
        out.println("    <h1>Hello World</h1>");
        out.println("    It's " + (new java.util.Date().toString()) +
            " and all is well.");
        out.println("  </body>");
        out.println("</html>");
    }
}
```

As before, don't worry about the details if you're not a Java programmer. What's important here is that the `service()` method is the method called by the servlet container every time the servlet is requested, as described in Chapter 2. The method generates all HTML code, using the `println()` method to send the strings to the browser. Note that there's no way you could use a web development tool to develop this type of embedded HTML, adjust the layout with immediate feedback, verify that links are intact, etc. This example is so simple that it doesn't really matter, but imagine a complex page with tables, aligned images, forms, some JavaScript code, etc., and you see the problem.

Also note the following lines, which add the current date and time to the response (shown in Figure 3-4):

```
        out.println("    It's " + (new java.util.Date().toString())
                + " and all is well.");
```

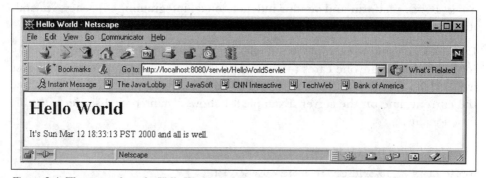

Figure 3-4. The output from the Hello World servlet

Example 3-2 shows a JSP page that produces the same result as the Hello World servlet.

Example 3-2. Hello World JSP Page

```
<html>
  <head>
    <title>Hello World</title>
  </head>
```

Example 3-2. Hello World JSP Page (continued)

```
  <body>
    <h1>Hello World</h1>
    It's <%= new java.util.Date().toString() %> and all is well.
  </body>
</html>
```

This is as simple as it gets. A JSP page is a regular HTML page, except that it may also contain JSP elements like the highlighted element in this example. This element inserts the same Java code in the page as was used in the servlet to add the current date and time. If you compare this JSP page to the corresponding servlet, you see that the JSP page can be developed using any web page editor that allows you to insert extra, non-HTML elements. And the same tool can later be used to easily modify the layout. This is a great advantage over a servlet with embedded HTML.

The JSP page is automatically turned into a servlet the first time it's requested, as described earlier. The generated servlet looks something like in Example 3-3.

Example 3-3. Servlet Generated from JSP Page

```
import javax.servlet.*;
import javax.servlet.http.*;
import javax.servlet.jsp.*;
import javax.servlet.jsp.tagext.*;
import java.io.*;
import org.apache.jasper.*;
import org.apache.jasper.runtime.*;

public class _0005chello_0002ejsphello_jsp_1 extends HttpJspBase {

    public void _jspService(HttpServletRequest request,
        HttpServletResponse  response)
        throws IOException, ServletException {

        JspFactory _jspxFactory = null;
        PageContext pageContext = null;
        HttpSession session = null;
        ServletContext application = null;
        ServletConfig config = null;
        JspWriter out = null;
        Object page = this;
        String  _value = null;
        try {

            _jspxFactory = JspFactory.getDefaultFactory();
            response.setContentType("text/html");
            pageContext = _jspxFactory.getPageContext(this, request,
```

Example 3-3. Servlet Generated from JSP Page (continued)

```
                    response,"", true, 8192, true);

            application = pageContext.getServletContext();
            config = pageContext.getServletConfig();
            session = pageContext.getSession();
            out = pageContext.getOut();

            out.write("<HTML>\r\n  <HEAD>\r\n    <TITLE>" +
                "Hello World</TITLE>\r\n  </HEAD>\r\n" +
                "  <BODY>\r\n    <H1>Hello World</H1>\r\n" +
                "    It's ");
            out.print( new java.util.Date().toString() );
            out.write(" and all is well.\r\n  </BODY>\r\n" +
                "</HTML>\r\n");

        } catch (Exception ex) {
            if (out.getBufferSize() != 0)
                out.clear();
            pageContext.handlePageException(ex);
        } finally {
            out.flush();
            _jspxFactory.releasePageContext(pageContext);
        }
    }
}
```

The generated servlet in Example 3-3 looks a lot more complex than the hand-coded version in Example 3-1. That's because a number of objects you can use in a JSP page must always be initialized (the hand-coded version doesn't need this generic initialization). These details are not important now; programming examples later in the book will show you how to use all objects of interest.

Instead, you should note that the servlet generated from the JSP page is a regular servlet. The _jspService() method corresponds to the service() method in the hand-coded servlet; it's called every time the page is requested. The request and response objects are passed as arguments to the method, so the JSP page has access to all the same information as does a regular servlet. This means it can read user input passed as request parameters, adjust the response based on header values (like the ones described in Chapter 2), get access to the session state, etc.—just like a regular servlet.

The highlighted code section in Example 3-3 shows how the static HTML from the JSP page in Example 3-2 has been embedded in the resulting code. Also note that the Java code to retrieve the current date and time has been inserted in the servlet as-is. By letting the JSP container convert the JSP page into a servlet that combines code for adding HTML to the response with small pieces of Java code for dynamic content, you get the best of both worlds. You can use familiar web page development tools to design the static parts of the web page, drop in JSP elements that generate the dynamic parts, and still enjoy all the benefits of servlets.

Client-Side Versus Server-Side Code

Page authors who have some experience developing client-side scripts using JavaScript (ECMAScript) or VBScript can sometimes get a bit confused when they start to use a server-side technology like JSP.

Client-side scripts, embedded in `<script>` elements, execute in the browser. These types of scripts are often linked to a form element such as a selection list. When the user selects an item in the list, the associated script is executed, perhaps populating another selection list with appropriate choices. Since all this code is executed by the browser, the client-side script provides immediate feedback to the user.

Server-side code, like action and scripting elements in a JSP page, executes on the server. Recall from Chapter 2 that the browser must make a request to the server to execute a JSP page. The corresponding JSP code is then used to produce a dynamic response.

This brings up an important point: there's no way a client-side script can directly call an individual Java code segment in the JSP page. A client-side script can ask the browser to make a request for the complete page, but it can't process the response and use it to do something such as populate a selection list with the data.

It is possible, although not very efficient, to link a user action to a client-side script, invoking an applet that in turn makes a request to a servlet or JSP page. The applet can then read the response and cause some dynamic action in the web browser. This approach may be reasonable on a fast intranet, but you probably won't be happy with the response times if you tried it on the Internet during peak hours. The reason is that the HTTP request/response model was never intended to be used for this type of incremental user interface update. Consequently, there's a great deal of overhead involved. If you still want to do this, be careful not to open up a security hole. For instance, if you develop an applet that can send any SQL statement to a servlet and get the query result back, you have made it possible for anyone to access all data in your database (that is accessible to the servlet), not just the data that your applet asks for.

—Continued—

Client-side and server-side code can, however, be combined with good results. You can embed client-side scripts as template text in your JSP pages, or generate it dynamically with actions or scripting elements. But keep in mind that it's still client-side code; the fact that it's generated by a JSP page doesn't change anything. A common use of client-side code is to validate user form input. Doing the validation with client-side code gives the user faster feedback about invalid input and reduces the load on the server. But don't forget that client-side scripting is not supported in all browsers, and even if it is, the user may have disabled the execution of scripts. Therefore, you should always perform input validation on the server as well.

Instead of using client-side scripts, you can of course use a Java applet to provide a more interactive user interface. Ideally the applet is self-contained; in other words, it doesn't have to talk to the server at all in order to present a user-friendly interface. If it needs to communicate with the server, however, it can do so using a far more efficient protocol than HTTP. *Java Servlet Programming* by Jason Hunter and William Crawford (O'Reilly) includes a chapter about different applet communication options.

JSP Application Design with MVC

JSP technology can play a part in everything from the simplest web application, such as an online phone list or an employee vacation planner, to full-fledged enterprise applications, such as a human resource application or a sophisticated online shopping site. How large a part JSP plays differs in each case, of course. In this section, we introduce a design model suitable for both simple and complex applications called Model-View-Controller (MVC).

MVC was first described by Xerox in a number of papers published in the late 1980s. The key point of using MVC is to separate components into three distinct units: the Model, the View, and the Controller. In a server application, we commonly classify the parts of the application as: business logic, presentation, and request processing. *Business logic* is the term used for the manipulation of an application's data, i.e., customer, product, and order information. *Presentation* refers to how the application is displayed to the user, i.e., the position, font, and size. And finally, *request processing* is what ties the business logic and presentation parts together. In MVC terms, the Model corresponds to business logic and data, the View to the presentation logic, and the Controller to the request processing.

Why use this design with JSP? The answer lies primarily in the first two elements. Remember that an application data structure and logic (the Model) is typically the most stable part of an application, while the presentation of that data (the View) changes fairly often. Just look at all the face-lifts that web sites have gone through to keep up with the latest fashion in web design. Yet, the data they present remains the same. Another common example of why presentation should be separated from the business logic is that you may want to present the data in different languages or present different subsets of the data to internal and external users. Access to the data through new types of devices, such as cell phones and Personal Digital Assistants (PDAs), is the latest trend. Each client type requires its own presentation format. It should come as no surprise, then, that separating business logic from presentation makes it easier to evolve an application as the requirements change; new presentation interfaces can be developed without touching the business logic.

This MVC model is used for most of the examples in this book. In Part II, JSP pages are used as both the Controller and the View, and JavaBeans components are used as the Model. The examples in Chapters 5 through 7 use a single JSP page that handles everything, while Chapters 8 through 11 show how you can use separate pages for Control and View to make the application easier to maintain. Many types of real-world applications can be developed this way, but what's more important is that this approach allows us to examine all the JSP features without getting distracted by other technologies. In Part III, we look at other possible role assignments when JSP is combined with servlets and Enterprise JavaBeans.

4

Setting Up the JSP Environment

This book contains plenty of examples to illustrate all the JSP features. All examples were developed and tested with the JSP reference implementation, known as the Apache Tomcat server, which is developed by the Apache Jakarta project. In this chapter you will learn how to install the Tomcat server and add a web application containing all the examples used in this book. You can, of course, use any web server that supports JSP 1.1, but Tomcat is a good server for development and test purposes. You can learn more about the Jakarta project and Tomcat, as well as how you can participate in the development, at the Jakarta web site: *http://jakarta.apache.org*.

Installing the Java Software Development Kit

Tomcat is a pure Java web server with support for the Servlet 2.2 and JSP 1.1 specifications. To use it, you must first install a Java runtime environment. If you don't already have one, you can download a Java SDK for Windows, Linux, and Solaris at *http://java.sun.com/j2se/*.

I recommend that you install the Java 2 SDK as opposed to the slimmed-down Runtime Environment (JRE) distribution. The reason is that JSP requires a Java compiler, which is included in the SDK but not in the JRE. Sun Microsystems has made the *javac* compiler from the SDK available separately for redistribution by the Apache Software Foundation. So technically, you could use the JRE and download the Java compiler as part of the Tomcat package, but even as I write this chapter, the exact legal conditions for distributing the compiler are changing.

Another alternative is to use the Jikes compiler from IBM (*http://www10.software.ibm.com/developerworks/opensource/jikes/*). Tomcat can be configured to use Jikes instead of the *javac* compiler from Sun; read the Tomcat documentation if you would like to try this. To make things simple, though, I suggest installing the Java 2 SDK from Sun. The examples were developed and tested with Java 2 SDK, Standard Edition, v1.2.2 and v1.3. I recommend that you use the latest version of the SDK available for your platform.

If you need an SDK for a platform other than Windows, Linux, or Solaris, there's a partial list of ports made by other companies at Sun's web site:

> *http://java.sun.com/cgi-bin/java-ports.cgi/*

Also check your operating system vendor's web site. Most operating system vendors have their own SDK implementation available for free.

Installation of the SDK varies depending on platform but is typically easy to do. Just follow the instructions on the web site where you download the SDK.

Before you install and run Tomcat, make sure that the JAVA_HOME environment variable is set to the installation directory of your Java environment, and that the Java *bin* directory is included in the PATH environment variable. On a Windows system, you can see if an environment variable is set by typing the following command in a Command Prompt window:

```
C:\> echo %JAVA_HOME%
C:\jdk1.1.2
```

If JAVA_HOME is not set, you can set it and include the *bin* directory in the PATH like this on a Windows system (assuming Java is installed in *C:\jdk1.2.2*):

```
C:\> set JAVA_HOME=C:\jdk1.2.2
C:\> set PATH=%JAVA_HOME%\bin;%PATH%
```

On a Windows 95/98 system, you can add these commands to the *C:\AUTOEXEC.BAT* file to set them permanently. Just use a text editor, such as Notepad, and add lines with the set commands. The next time you boot the PC, the environment variables will be set automatically. For Windows NT and 2000, you can set them permanently from the Environment tab in the System Properties tool.

If you use Linux or some other Unix platform, the exact commands depend on which shell you use. With *bash*, which is commonly the default for Linux, use the following commands (assuming Java is installed in */usr/local/jdk1.2.2*):

```
[hans@gefion /] export JAVA_HOME=/usr/local/jdk1.2.2
[hans@gefion /] export PATH=$JAVA_HOME/bin:$PATH
[hans@gefion /] echo $PATH
/usr/local/jdk1.2.2/bin:/usr/local/bin:/bin:/usr/bin
```

Installing the Tomcat Server

You can download the Tomcat Server either in binary format or as source code that you compile yourself. If you're primarily interested in learning about JSP, I recommend that you use the binary download to run the examples in this book and develop your own applications. If you're a Java programmer and interested in seeing how Tomcat is implemented, feel free to download the source and take a look at the internals.

The binary distribution is available at:

http://jakarta.apache.org/downloads/binindex.html

On this page you find three types of builds:

- Release builds
- Milestone builds
- Nightly builds

Release builds are stable releases that have been tested extensively and verified to comply with the servlet and JSP specifications. *Milestone builds* are created as intermediary steps towards a release build. They often contain new features that are not yet fully tested, but are generally known to work. A *nightly build,* however, may be very unstable. It's actually a snapshot of the latest source code and may have been tested only by the person who made the latest change. You should use a nightly build only if you're involved in the development of Tomcat.

You should download the latest release build. All examples in this book were developed and tested using the 3.2 (Beta 3) version, but any release later than 3.2 should work fine as well. When you click on the link for the latest release build and select the *bin* directory, you see a list of archive files in different formats, similar to Figure 4-1.

Pick a compression format that's appropriate for your platform. For Windows, select *jakarta-tomcat.zip* and save it to your hard drive, for instance in a directory named *C:\Jakarta.* You can unpack the package either with a ZIP utility program such as *WinZip,* or by using the *jar* command that's included in the Java distribution. Using the Command Prompt window where you set the JAVA_HOME and PATH environment variables earlier, change directory to the directory where you downloaded the ZIP file and unpack it:

```
C:\> cd Jakarta
C:\Jakarta> jar xvf jakarta-tomcat.zip
```

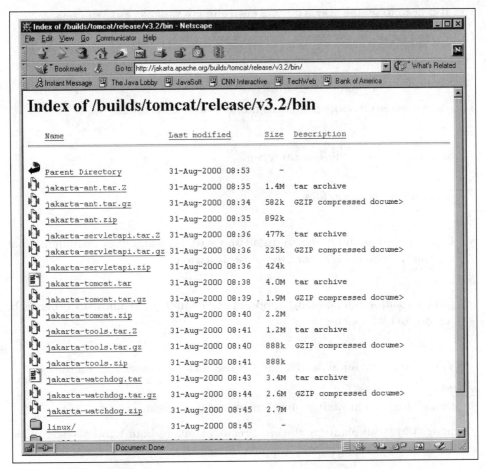

Figure 4-1. Release build packages

For Unix platforms, download the *jakarta-tomcat.tar.gz* file, for instance to */usr/ local*, and use these commands to unpack it (assuming you have GNU tar installed):

```
[hans@gefion /] cd /usr/local
[hans@gefion /usr/local] tar xzvf jakarta-tomcat.tar.gz
```

If you don't have GNU tar installed on your system, you can use this command:

```
[hans@gefion /usr/local] gunzip -c jakarta-tomcat.tar.gz | tar xvf -
```

This creates a directory structure with a top directory named *jakarta-tomcat* with a number of subdirectories. Like most software packages, the *doc* subdirectory contains a file named *Readme*; do exactly that. Software distributions change and if, for instance, the instructions in this chapter no longer apply when you download the software, the *Readme* file should contain information about how to get started.

You also need to set the TOMCAT_HOME environment variable. For Windows, use:

```
C:\Jakarta> set TOMCAT_HOME=C:\Jakarta\jakarta-tomcat
```

For Unix, use:

```
[hans@gefion /usr/local] export TOMCAT_HOME=/usr/local/jakarta-tomcat
```

The *jakarta-tomcat* directory contains a number of subdirectories:

bin

>   Scripts for starting the Tomcat server.

conf
>   Tomcat configuration files.

doc

>   Documents describing how to install and start Tomcat. Other documentation
>   is available as web pages once the server is started.

lib

>   Binary (platform-dependent) modules for connecting Tomcat to other web
>   servers such as Apache.

src

>   The source code for all servlet and JSP specification classes and interfaces.

webapps
>   Default location for web applications served by Tomcat.

No matter what your platform, the *bin* directory contains both Windows batch files
and Unix scripts for starting and stopping the server.

Windows Platforms

The Windows files are named *startup.bat*, *shutdown.bat*, and *tomcat.bat*. The *tomcat.bat*
file is the main script for controlling the server; it's called by the two other scripts
startup.bat and *shutdown.bat*. To start the server in a separate window, change directory to the *bin* directory and run the *startup.bat* file:

```
C:\Jakarta> cd jakarta-tomcat\bin
C:\Jakarta\jakarta-tomcat\bin> startup
```

A new Command Prompt window pops up and you see startup messages like this:

```
2000-09-01 09:27:10 - ContextManager: Adding context Ctx( /examples )
2000-09-01 09:27:10 - ContextManager: Adding context Ctx( /admin )
Starting tomcat. Check logs/tomcat.log for error messages
2000-09-01 09:27:10 - ContextManager: Adding context Ctx(  )
2000-09-01 09:27:10 - ContextManager: Adding context Ctx( /test )
```

```
2000-09-01 09:27:13 - PoolTcpConnector: Starting HttpConnectionHandler
  on 8080
2000-09-01 09:27:13 - PoolTcpConnector: Starting Ajp12ConnectionHandler
  on 8007
```

Just leave this window open; this is where the server process is running.

If you're running on a Windows 95 or 98 platform, you may see an error message about "Out of environment space" when you try to start the server. That's because the default amount of space allocated for environment variables is not enough. To change this default, run this command in the Command Prompt window before you run the *startup.bat* file again:

```
C:\Jakarta\jakarta-tomcat\bin> COMMAND.COM /E:4096 /P
```

This command sets the environment space to 4096 bytes (4 KB). That should be enough for the server. However, If you still get the same message, use a higher value.

For some installations, this command may not work. If it doesn't work, try this instead:

1. Close the Command Prompt window and open a new one.
2. Click on the MS-DOS icon at the top-left of the window.
3. Select the Properties option.
4. Click on the Memory tab.
5. Change the Initial Environment value from Auto to 4096.
6. Click on OK and try to start the server again.

At this point, the server may not start due to other problems. If so, the extra Command Prompt window may pop up and then disappear before you have a chance to read the error messages. If this happens, you can let the server run in the Command Prompt window with this command instead:

```
C:\Jakarta\jakarta-tomcat\bin> tomcat run
```

On Windows NT, first make sure that the Command Prompt window has a large enough screen buffer so that you can scroll back in case the error messages don't fit on one screen. Open the Properties window for the Command Prompt window (right mouse button in the upper-left corner), select Layout, and set the screen buffer size height to a large value (for instance 999). Unfortunately, the Command Prompt screen buffer cannot be enlarged for Windows 95/98, so scrolling back is not an option. If you run into problems on these platforms, double-check that you have installed the Java SDK correctly and that you have set the JAVA_HOME and PATH environment variables as described earlier.

Unix Platforms

For Unix, the corresponding scripts are named *startup.sh*, *shutdown.sh*, and *tomcat.sh*. Start the server with this command:

```
[hans@gefion /usr/local/jakarta-tomcat/bin] ./startup.sh
```

If you want Tomcat to start each time you boot the system, you can add the following commands to your */etc/rc.d/rc.local* (or equivalent) startup script:

```
export JAVA_HOME=/usr/local/jdk1.2.2
export TOMCAT_HOME=/usr/local/jakarta-tomcat
$TOMCAT_HOME/bin/startup.sh &
```

Two more subdirectories under the Tomcat home directory are then created the first time you start the server:

logs

> Server log files. If something doesn't work as expected, look at the files in this directory for clues as to what's wrong.

work

> A directory for temporary files that are created by the JSP container and other files. This directory is where the servlets generated from JSP pages are stored.

Testing Tomcat

To test the server—assuming you're running Tomcat on the same machine as the browser and that you're using the default port for Tomcat (8080)—open a browser and enter the following URL in the Location/Address field:

> *http://localhost:8080/*

The Tomcat main page is shown in the browser (see Figure 4-2), and you can now run all servlet and JSP examples bundled with Tomcat to make sure everything works.

When you're done testing Tomcat, stop the server like this:

```
C:\Jakarta\jakarta-tomcat\bin> shutdown
```

You should always stop the server this way, as opposed to killing the Command Prompt window the server is running in. Otherwise, the applications don't get a chance to close down gracefully, and when you start to connect external resources, like a database, various problems may occur.

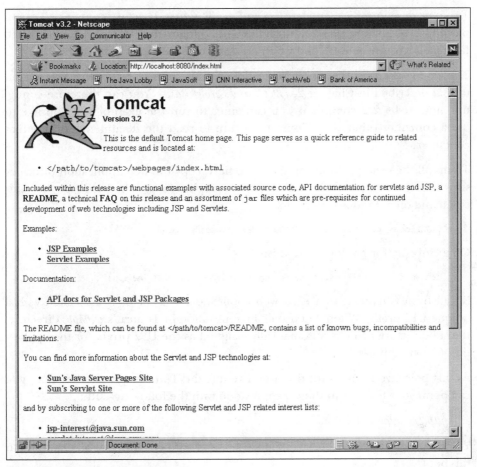

Figure 4-2. The Tomcat main page

Installing the Book Examples

All JSP pages, HTML pages, Java source code, and class files for the book examples can be downloaded directly from the O'Reilly web site:

http://www.oreilly.com/catalog/jserverpages/

They can also be downloaded from the book web site:

http://www.TheJSPBook.com

The file that contains all the examples is called *jspbook.zip*. Save the file on your hard drive, for instance in *C:\JSPBook* on a Windows platform, and unpack it:

```
C:\JSPBook> jar xvf jspbook.zip
```

You can use the same command on a Unix platform.

Two new directories are created: *ora* and *src*. The first directory contains all examples described in this book, and the second contains the Java source files for the JavaBeans, custom actions, and utility classes used in the examples.

The examples' directory structure complies to the standard Java web application format described in Chapter 2, *HTTP and Servlet Basics*. You can therefore configure any Servlet 2.2–compliant web container to run the examples. If you like to use a container other than Tomcat, be sure to read the documentation for that container.

To install the example application for Tomcat, copy the web application directory structure to Tomcat's default directory for applications, called *webapps*. Use this command on a Windows platform:

```
C:\JSPBook> xcopy /s /i ora %TOMCAT_HOME%\webapps\ora
```

On a Unix platform it looks like this:

```
[hans@gefion /usr/local/jspbook] cp -R ora $TOMCAT_HOME/webapps
```

Recall from Chapter 2 that each web application in a server is associated with a unique URI prefix. When you install an application in Tomcat's *webapps* directory, the subdirectory name is automatically assigned as the URI prefix for the application (*/ora* in this case).

At this point, you must shut down and restart the Tomcat server. After that, you can point your browser to the *ora* application with the following URL:

http://localhost:8080/ora/

You should see a start page, as in Figure 4-3, that contains links for all examples in this book.

Example Web Application Overview

The examples for this book are packaged as a standard Java web application, as described in Chapter 2. This file structure is supported by all Servlet 2.2–compliant servers, so you can use the example application as a guide when you create your own web applications. How a web application is installed is not defined by the specification, however, so it varies between servers. With Tomcat, you simply copy the file structure to the special *webapps* directory and restart the server. To modify the configuration information for an application, you need to edit the application's *WEB-INF/web.xml* file using a text editor. Other servers may offer special deployment tools that copy the files to where they belong and let you configure the application using a special tool, such as web-based forms.

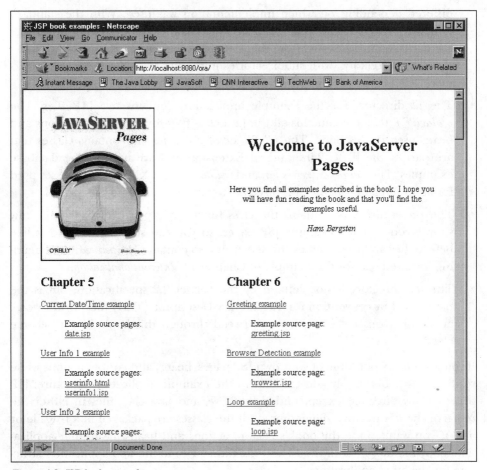

Figure 4-3. JSP book examples start page

If you look in the *ora* web application directory, you'll see that it contains an *index. html* file and a number of directories corresponding to chapters in this book. These directories contain all the example JSP and HTML pages.

There's also a *WEB-INF* directory with a *web.xml* file, a *lib* directory, a *classes* directory, and a *tlds* directory:

- The *web.xml* file contains configuration information for the example application in the format defined by the Servlet 2.2 specification. It's too early to look at the contents of this file now; we will return to parts of it when needed.

- The *lib* and *classes* directories are standard directories, also defined by the Servlet 2.2 specification. A common question asked by people new to servlets and JSP (prior to the standard web application format) was, "Where do I store my class files so that the server can find them?" The answer, unfortunately, differed depending on which implementation was used. With the standard web application format, however, it's easy to answer this question: if the classes are packaged in a JAR file, store the JAR file in the *lib* directory; otherwise, use the *classes* directory (with subdirectories mirroring the classes' package structure). The server will always look for Java class files in these two directories.

- The *lib* directory for the example application contains five JAR files. The *orataglib_1_0.jar* file contains all the Java class files for the custom actions and beans used in this book. The *jdbc20_stdext_classes.jar* file contains classes that are part of the JDBC 2.0 Standard Extension and are used in the database examples. The *xalan.jar, xerces.jar,* and *xsl.jar* contain XML parser classes used for an example in Chapter 12, *Bits and Pieces.*

- The *classes* directory contains the class for a servlet used to display the raw source code for the example JSP pages, so you can see what they look like before they are processed by the server. It also contains *.properties* files containing localized text for the example in Chapter 11, *Internationalization.*

- The *tlds* directory is not defined by the Servlet 2.2 specification, but is the name used by convention for Tag Library Descriptor (TLD) files. Don't worry about what this means now. As you read through this book, it will become clear.

If you want to try out some of your own JSP pages, beans, and custom actions while reading this book, simply add the files to the example application structure: JSP pages in any directory except under *WEB-INF*, and Java class files in either the *classes* or the *lib* directory, depending on if the classes are packaged in a JAR file or not. If you want to use the book's custom actions and beans in another application, copy the files in both the *lib* and *tlds* directories to the web application structure for the other application.

II

JSP APPLICATION DEVELOPMENT

The focus of this part of the book is on developing JSP-based web applications using both standard JSP elements and custom components. Through the use of practical examples, you will learn how to handle common tasks such as validating user input, accessing databases, authenticating users and protecting web pages, localizing your web site, and more.

- Chapter 5, *Generating Dynamic Content*
- Chapter 6, *Using Scripting Elements*
- Chapter 7, *Error Handling and Debugging*
- Chapter 8, *Sharing Data Between JSP Pages, Requests, and Users*
- Chapter 9, *Database Access*
- Chapter 10, *Authentication and Personalization*
- Chapter 11, *Internationalization*
- Chapter 12, *Bits and Pieces*

5

Generating Dynamic Content

JSP is all about generating dynamic content: content that differs based on user input, time of day, the state of an external system, or any other runtime conditions. JSP provides you with lots of tools for generating this content. In this book, you will learn about all of them—standard actions, custom actions, JavaBeans, and scripting elements. Before we do that, however, let's start with a few simple examples to get a feel for how the basic JSP elements work.

In this chapter, we develop a page for displaying the current date and time, and look at the JSP directive element and how to use JavaBeans in a JSP page along the way. Next, we look at how to process user input in your JSP pages and make sure it has the appropriate format. We also look at how you can convert special characters in the output, so they don't confuse the browser.

What Time Is It?

Recall from Chapter 3, *JSP Overview*, that a JSP page is just a regular HTML page with a few special elements. JSP pages should have the file extension *.jsp*, which tells the server that the page needs to be processed by the JSP container. Without this clue, the server is unable to distinguish a JSP page from any other type of file and sends it unprocessed to the browser.

When working with JSP pages, you really just need a regular text editor such as Notepad on Windows or Emacs on Unix. Appendix E, *JSP Resource Reference*, however, lists a number of tools that may make it easier for you, such as syntax-aware editors that color-code JSP and HTML elements. Some Interactive Development Environments (IDEs) include a small web container that allows you to easily execute and debug the page during development. There are also several web page authoring tools—the type of tools often used when developing regular HTML pages—that support JSP. I don't recommend that you use them initially; it's easier to learn how JSP works if you see the raw page elements before you use tools that hide them.

The first example JSP page, named *date.jsp*, is shown in Example 5-1.

Example 5-1. JSP Page Showing the Current Date and Time (date.jsp)

```
<%@ page language="java" contentType="text/html" %>
<html>
  <body bgcolor="white">

    <jsp:useBean id="clock" class="java.util.Date" />

    The current time at the server is:
    <ul>
      <li>Date: <jsp:getProperty name="clock" property="date" />
      <li>Month: <jsp:getProperty name="clock" property="month" />
      <li>Year: <jsp:getProperty name="clock" property="year" />
      <li>Hours: <jsp:getProperty name="clock" property="hours" />
      <li>Minutes: <jsp:getProperty name="clock" property="minutes" />
    </ul>

  </body>
</html>
```

The *date.jsp* page displays the current date and time. We'll look at all the different pieces soon, but first let's run the example to see how it works. Assuming you have installed all book examples as described in Chapter 4, *Setting Up the JSP Environment*, first start the Tomcat server and load the *http://localhost:8080/ora/* URL in a browser. You can then run Example 5-1 by clicking the "Current Date/Time example" link from the book examples main page, shown in Figure 5-1. You should see a result like the one shown in Figure 5-2.

Notice that the month seems to be off by one and the year is displayed as 100. That's because the `java.util.Date` class we use here numbers months from 0 to 11, so January is 0, February is 1, and so on, and it reports year as the current year minus 1900. That's just the way this example works. As you will see later, there are much better ways to display dates.

The page shown in Example 5-1 contains both regular HTML elements and JSP elements. The HTML elements are used as-is, defining the layout of the page. If you use the View Source function in your browser, you notice that none of the JSP elements are visible in the page source. That's because the JSP elements are processed by the server when the page is requested, and only the resulting output is sent to the browser. To see the unprocessed JSP page in a separate window, click on the source link for the *date.jsp* file in the book examples main page. The source

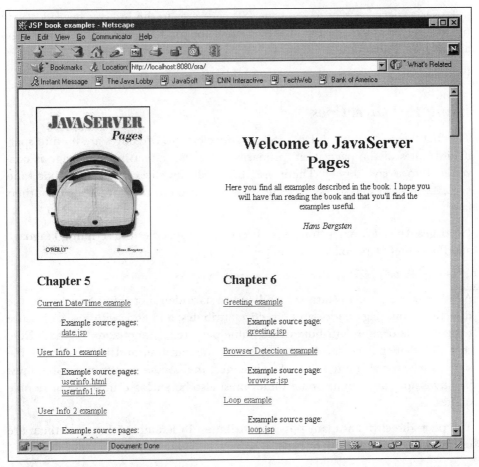

Figure 5-1. JSP book examples main page

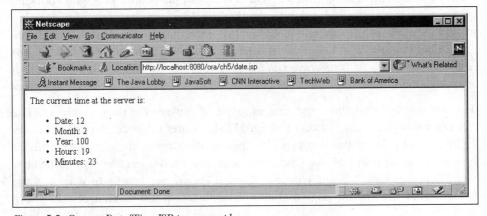

Figure 5-2. Current Date/Time JSP page example

link uses a special servlet to send the JSP page as-is to the browser instead of letting the server process it. This makes it easier for you to compare the source page and the processed result.

Let's look at each piece of Example 5-1 in detail.

Using JSP Directives

The first line in Example 5-1 is a JSP *directive* element. Directives are used to specify attributes of the page itself, primarily those that affect how the page is converted into a Java servlet. There are three JSP directives: page, include, and taglib. In this example, we're using only the page directive. We'll see the others later.

JSP pages typically start with a page directive that specifies the scripting language and the content type for the page:

```
<%@ page language="java" contentType="text/html" %>
```

A JSP directive element starts with a directive-start identifier (<%@) followed by the directive name (e.g., page) and directive attributes, and ends with %>. A directive contains one or more attribute name/value pairs (e.g., language="java"). Note that JSP element and attribute names are case-sensitive, and in most cases the same is true for attribute values. For instance, the language attribute value must be java, not Java. All attribute values must also be enclosed in single or double quotes.

The page directive has many possible attributes. In Example 5-1, two of them are used: language and contentType.

The language attribute specifies the scripting language used in the page. The JSP reference implementation (the Tomcat server) supports only Java as a scripting language.* java is also the default value for the language attribute, but for clarity you may still want to specify it. Other JSP implementations support other languages besides Java, and hence allow other values for the language attribute. For instance, both JRun (*http://www.allaire.com*) and Resin (*http://www.caucho.com*) support JavaScript in addition to Java.

The contentType attribute specifies the type of content the page produces. The most common values are text/html for HTML content and text/plain for preformatted, plain text. But you can also specify other types, such as text/xml for browsers that support XML or text/vnd.wap.wml for devices like cellular phones and PDAs that have built-in Wireless Markup Language (WML) browsers. If the content generated by the page includes characters requiring a charset other than

---

* In fact, Java is the only scripting language formally supported in the JSP specification, but the specification leaves room for other languages to be supported.

ISO-8859-1 (commonly known as Latin-1), you need to specify that charset with the `contentType` attribute. We'll look at the details of charsets in Chapter 11, *Internationalization.*

Using Template Text

Besides JSP elements, notice that the page shown in Example 5-1 contains mostly regular HTML:

```
...
<html>
  <body bgcolor="white">

...

    The current time at the server is:
    <ul>
      <li>Date: ...
      <li>Month: ...
      <li>Year: ...
      <li>Hours: ...
      <li>Minutes: ...
    </ul>

  </body>
</html>
```

In JSP parlance, this is called *template text*. Everything that's not a JSP element, such as a directive, action, or scripting element, is template text. Template text is sent to the browser as-is. This means you can use JSP to generate any type of text-based output, such as XML, WML, or even plain text. The JSP container doesn't care what the template text is.

Using JavaBeans

There is also some dynamic content in this example. Step back a moment and think about the type of dynamic content you see on the Web every day. Common examples might be a list of web sites matching a search criteria on a search engine site, the content of a shopping cart on an e-commerce site, a personalized news page, or messages on a bulletin board. Dynamic content is content generated by some server process, for instance the result of a database query. Before it is sent to the browser, the dynamic content needs to be combined with regular HTML elements into a page with the right layout, navigation bars, the company logo, and so forth. In a JSP page, the regular HTML is the template text described earlier. The result of the server processing—the dynamic content—is commonly represented by a *JavaBeans component.*

A JavaBeans component, or just a *bean* for short, is a Java class that follows certain coding conventions, so it can be used by tools as a component in a larger application. In this chapter, we discuss only how to use a bean, not how to develop one. (If you're a programmer and not already familiar with JavaBeans, you may want to skip ahead to Chapter 15, *Developing JavaBeans for JSP*, to learn about these coding conventions.) A bean is often used in JSP as the container for the dynamic content to be displayed by a web page. Typically, a bean represents something specific, such as a person, a product, or a shopping order. A bean is always created by a server process and given to the JSP page. The page then uses JSP elements to insert the bean's data into the HTML template text.

The type of element used to access a bean in a page is called a JSP *action element.* JSP action elements are executed when a JSP page is requested (this is called the request processing phase, as you may recall from Chapter 3). In other words, JSP actions represent dynamic actions that take place at runtime, as opposed to JSP directives, which are used only during the translation phase (when the JSP page is turned into Java servlet code). JSP defines a number of standard actions and also specifies how you can develop custom actions. For both standard and custom action elements, use the following notation:

```
<action_name attr1="value1" attr2="value2">
  action_body
</action_name>
```

Action elements, or tags as they are sometimes called,* are grouped into libraries (known as *tag libraries*). The action name is composed of two parts: a library prefix and the name of the action within the library, separated by a colon (i.e., jsp: useBean). All actions in the JSP standard library use the prefix jsp, while custom actions can use any prefix except jsp, jspx, java, javax, servlet, sun, or sunw. You specify input to the action through attribute/value pairs in the opening tag. The attribute names are case-sensitive, and the values must be enclosed in single or double quotes. For some actions, you can also enter data that the action should process in the action's body. It can be any text value, such as a SQL statement, or even other nested JSP action elements. You will see examples of action elements with a body later.

Before you use a bean in a page, you must tell the JSP container which type of bean it is and associate it with a name. The first JSP action in Example 5-1, <jsp: useBean>, is used for this purpose:

```
<jsp:useBean id="clock" class="java.util.Date" />
```

---

* An element is actually represented by a start tag and an end tag, but the term "tag" is often used to refer to what's formally known as an element.

The id attribute is used to give the bean a unique name. It must be a name that is a valid Java variable name: it must start with a letter and cannot contain special characters such as dots, plus signs, etc. The class attribute contains the fully qualified name of the bean's Java class. Here, the name clock is associated with an instance of the class java.util.Date. Note that we don't specify a body for this action. When you omit the body, you must end the opening tag with />, as in this example. In this case, when the JSP container encounters this directive, there is no bean currently available with the name clock, so the <jsp:useBean> action creates a bean as an instance of the specified class and makes it available to other actions in the same page. In Chapter 8, *Sharing Data Between JSP Pages, Requests, and Users*, you will see how <jsp:useBean> can also be used to locate a bean that has already been created.

Incidentally, the <jsp:useBean> action supports three additional attributes: scope, type, and beanName. The scope attribute is described in detail in Chapter 8, and the other two attributes are covered in Appendix A, *JSP Elements Syntax Reference*. We don't need to worry about those attributes here.

Accessing JavaBean Properties

The bean's data is represented by its *properties*. If you're a page author charged with developing a JSP page to display the content represented by a bean, you first need to know the names of all the bean's properties. This information should be available from the Java programmers on the team or from a third-party source. In this example, we use a standard Java class named java.util.Date as a bean with properties representing date and time information. Table 5-1 describes the properties used in this example. (If you're not a programmer, don't worry about the Java Type and Access columns at this point.)

Table 5-1. Properties for java.util.Date

Property Name	Java Type	Access	Description
date	int	read	The day of the month as a number between 1 and 31
hours	int	read	The hour as a number between 0 (midnight) and 23
minutes	int	read	The number of minutes past the hour as a number between 0 and 59
month	int	read	The month as a number from 0 to 11
year	int	read	The current year minus 1900

Once you have created a bean and given it a name, you can retrieve the values of the bean's properties in the response page with another JSP standard action, <jsp:getProperty>. This action obtains the current value of a bean property and inserts it directly into the response body.

To include the current date property value in the page, use the following tag:

```
<jsp:getProperty name="clock" property="date" />
```

The name attribute, set to clock, refers to the specific bean instance we defined with the <jsp:useBean> action previously. This action locates the bean and asks it for the value of the property specified by the property attribute. As documented in Table 5-1, the date property contains the day of the month as a number between 1 and 31. In Example 5-1, multiple <jsp:getProperty> actions are used to generate a list of all the clock bean's property values. The result is the page shown in Figure 5-2.

Input and Output

User input is a necessity in modern web pages. Most dynamic web sites generate pages based on user input. Unfortunately, users seldom enter information in exactly the format you need, so before you can use such input, you probably want to validate it.

And it's not only the input format that's important. Web browsers are also picky about the format of the HTML you send them. For instance, when you generate an HTML form with values taken from a database, a name such as O'Reilly can cause problems. The single quote character after the O can fool the browser into believing that it's at the end of the string, so you end up with just an O in your form.

Using JavaBeans to Process Input

As we saw earlier, a bean is often used as a container for data, created by some server process, and used in a JSP page that displays the data. But a bean can also be used to capture user input. The captured data can then be processed by the bean itself or used as input to some other server component (e.g., a component that stores the data in a database or picks an appropriate banner ad to display). The nice thing about using a bean this way is that all information is in one bundle. Say you have a bean that can contain information about a person, and it captures the name, birth date, and email address as entered by the person on a web form. You can then pass this bean to another component, providing all the information about the user in one shot. Now, if you want to add more information about the user, you just add properties to the bean, instead of having to add parameters all over the place in your code. Another benefit of using a bean to capture user input is that the bean can encapsulate all the rules about its properties. Thus, a bean representing a person can make sure the birthDate property is set to a valid date.

Using a bean to capture and validate user input is one aspect of building a web application that's easy to maintain and extend as requirements change. But it's not the only option. If you're a page author and intend to use JSP to develop sites using components from third parties, you may wonder how you can capture and validate input without access to a Java programmer who can develop the beans. Don't worry; we'll see another alternative in Chapter 9, *Database Access*.

Processing and validating input can also be performed by a servlet instead of a JSP page. If you're a programmer, you'll find examples of this approach in Chapter 14, *Combining Servlets and JSP*. In this part of the book, however, we use JSP pages for all aspects of the applications so we can focus on JSP features. And one JSP feature makes it very easy to capture user input, so let's see how it's done.

Setting JavaBeans properties from user input

In this next example, we capture information about web site users. It could be the frontend to a newsletter subscription site, for instance. In order to send the users information that might interest them, we register the birth date, sex, and lucky number, along with the full name and email address, for each person that signs up for the service.

To capture and validate the user input, the example uses a bean named `com.ora.jsp.beans.userinfo.UserInfoBean`, with the properties described in Table 5-2. If you're a programmer, you may want to skip ahead to peek at the source code for this bean class in Chapter 15.

Table 5-2. Properties for com.ora.jsp.beans.userinfo.UserInfoBean

Property Name	Java Type	Access	Description
userName	String	read/write	The user's full name
birthDate	String	read/write	The user's birth date in the format *yyyy-mm-dd* (e.g., 2000-07-07)
emailAddr	String	read/write	The user's email address in the format *name@company.com*
sex	String	read/write	The user's sex (`male` or `female`)
luckyNumber	String	read/write	The user's lucky number (between 1 and 100)
valid	boolean	read	`true` if the current values of all properties are valid, `false` otherwise

As shown in the Access column, all properties except `valid` are read/write properties. This means that, in addition to using the bean's properties to generate output (like in Example 5-1), the property values can be set based on user input.

The HTML form shown in Example 5-2 allows the user to enter information corresponding to the bean properties.

Example 5-2. An HTML Form that Sends User Input to a JSP Page (userinfo.html)

```html
<html>
  <head>
    <title>User Info Entry Form</title>
  </head>
  <body bgcolor="white">
    <form action="userinfo1.jsp" method="post">
      <table>
        <tr>
          <td>Name:</td>
          <td><input type="text" name="userName" >
          </td>
        </tr>
        <tr>
          <td>Birth Date:</td>
          <td><input type="text" name="birthDate" >
          </td>
          <td>(Use format yyyy-mm-dd)</td>
        </tr>
        <tr>
          <td>Email Address:</td>
          <td><input type="text" name="emailAddr" >
          </td>
          <td>(Use format name@company.com)</td>
        </tr>
        <tr>
          <td>Sex:</td>
          <td><input type="text" name="sex" >
          </td>
          <td>(Male or female)</td>
        </tr>
        <tr>
          <td>Lucky number:</td>
          <td><input type="text" name="luckyNumber" >
          </td>
          <td>(A number between 1 and 100)</td>
        </tr>
        <tr>
          <td colspan=2><input type="submit"></td>
        </tr>
      </table>
    </form>
  </body>
</html>
```

This is a regular HTML page that presents a form with a number of fields, as shown in Figure 5-3. There are a few things worth mentioning here. First, notice that each input field has a `name` attribute with a value that corresponds to a `UserInfoBean` property name. Matching the names lets us take advantage of a nice JSP feature that sets property values automatically, as you'll see shortly. Also note that the `action` attribute of the form specifies that a JSP page, *userinfo1.jsp*, is invoked when the user clicks the Submit button. Figure 5-3 shows what the form looks like in a browser.

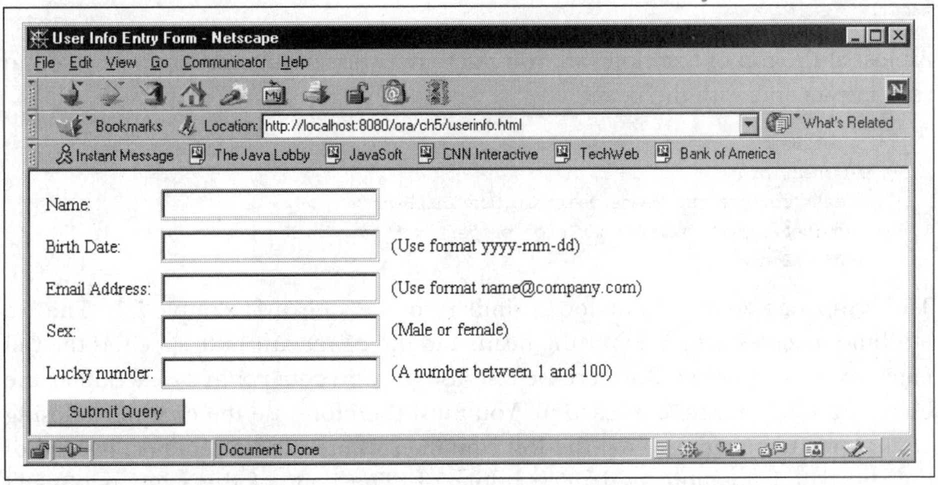

Figure 5-3. User input form

Example 5-3 shows the JSP page that is invoked when the user submits the form.

Example 5-3. A JSP Page that Validates User Input with a Bean (userinfo1.jsp)

```
<%@ page language="java" contentType="text/html" %>
<html>
  <body bgcolor="white">
    <jsp:useBean
      id="userInfo"
      class="com.ora.jsp.beans.userinfo.UserInfoBean">
      <jsp:setProperty name="userInfo" property="*" />
    </jsp:useBean>

    The following information was saved:
    <ul>
      <li>User Name: <jsp:getProperty
                        name="userInfo" property="userName" />
      <li>Birth Date: <jsp:getProperty
                         name="userInfo" property="birthDate" />
      <li>Email Address: <jsp:getProperty
```

Example 5-3. A JSP Page that Validates User Input with a Bean (userinfo1.jsp) (continued)

```
                      name="userInfo" property="emailAddr" />
    <li>Sex: <jsp:getProperty
                  name="userInfo" property="sex" />
    <li>Lucky number: <jsp:getProperty
                         name="userInfo" property="luckyNumber" />
    </ul>
    The user input is valid: <jsp:getProperty
                               name="userInfo" property="valid" />
  </body>
</html>
```

Almost at the top of Example 5-3, you see that a `<jsp:useBean>` action is used to associate a name with the bean:

```
<jsp:useBean
  id="userInfo"
  class="com.ora.jsp.beans.userinfo.UserInfoBean">
  <jsp:setProperty name="userInfo" property="*" />
</jsp:useBean>
```

The `<jsp:useBean>` action looks similar to the one in Example 5-1. The `id` attribute specifies the name for the bean, and the `class` attribute specifies the full name of the bean class. But here we also use a `<jsp:setProperty>` action as the body of the `<jsp:useBean>` action. You must therefore use the complete closing tag (`</jsp:useBean>`) to tell the JSP container where the action ends, instead of the shorthand notation used in Example 5-1. The body of the `<jsp:useBean>` action is executed only when a new bean is created. In this example, that's always the case, but as you will learn in Chapter 8, there are cases in which the bean already exists and the action is needed only to associate it with a name.

Now let's take a closer look at the `<jsp:setProperty>` action. As the name implies, this action is used to set the bean's property values. Like the `<jsp:getProperty>` action, it has a `name` attribute that must match the `id` attribute of a `<jsp:useBean>` action, and a `property` attribute that specifies which property to set.

When a form is submitted, the form field values are sent as request parameters with the same names as the form field elements. In Example 5-3, note that an asterisk (*) is used as the `property` attribute value of the `<jsp:setProperty>` action. This means that all bean properties with names that match request parameters sent to the page are set automatically. That's why it's important that the form element names match the bean property names, as they do here. Automatically setting all matching properties is a great feature; if you define more properties for your bean, you can set them simply by adding new matching fields in the form that invokes the JSP page.

Besides the `property` attribute, the `<jsp:setProperty>` action has two more optional attributes: `param` and `value`. If for some reason you can't use the same name for the parameters and the property names, you can use the `param` attribute to set a bean property to the value of any request parameter:

```
<jsp:setProperty
  name="userInfo"
  property="userName"
  param="someOtherParam"
/>
```

Here, the `userName` property is set to the value of a request parameter named `someOtherParam`.

You can also explicitly set a bean property to a value that is not sent as a request parameter with the `value` attribute:

```
<jsp:setProperty
  name="userInfo"
  property="luckyNumber"
  value="13"
/>
```

Here, the `luckyNumber` property is set to the value 13. You typically use the `value` attribute only when you set the bean properties based on something other than user input, for instance values collected from a database.

Validating user input

Never trust your users, at least not when it comes to entering information in the format you need. Often, you need to make sure the input is valid before you continue to process a request. A date, for instance, can be written in many different formats. If you don't live in the United States, you probably have had to fill out both an I-94 and a customs declaration form to be admitted by an immigration officer. You may have noticed that on one of the forms you need to write your birth date as *yyyy/mm/dd* and on the other you write it as *mm/dd/yyyy*. I always get it wrong.

Four of the `UserInfoBean`'s properties require a special format: `birthDate`, `emailAddr`, `sex`, and `luckyNumber`. A good place to make sure the input is valid is in the bean itself, which is exactly what the `UserInfoBean` does. With this bean, if you try to set any of the above properties to a value that isn't valid, the bean will leave the property unset. In addition, the bean has a true/false (Boolean) property named `valid`. This property has the value `false` unless all other properties have been set to valid values.

Let's see this in action. Example 5-3 displays the property values using the `<jsp:getProperty>` action:

```
<li>User Name: <jsp:getProperty
              name="userInfo" property="userName" />
```

Since a property is set only if the value is valid, no values are shown for improperly specified properties. Try it. Click on the "User Info 1 example" link under the Chapter 5 header in the book examples main page shown in Figure 5-1. Enter both valid and invalid values in the form and look at the result produced by the *userinfo1.jsp* page when you click Submit. A sample result is shown in Figure 5-4.

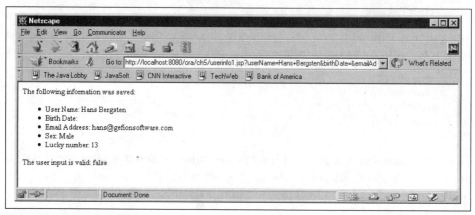

Figure 5-4. Output from userinfo1.jsp

Note that the Birth Date information is missing (at my age, you're not so eager to reveal your birth date), so the input is marked as invalid.

Keep On Doing It 'til You Get It Right

Okay, now you know how to set bean properties and you're aware that beans often validate their values. It would be nice if this technique could be used to display the same form over and over until all required input is correct. You can do that with just a few changes, as shown in Example 5-4, the *userinfo2.jsp* page.

Example 5-4. A JSP Page that Validates and Redisplays Until Correct (userinfo2.jsp)

```
<%@ page language="java" contentType="text/html" %>
<html>
  <head>
    <title>User Info Entry Form</title>
  </head>
  <body bgcolor="white">
    <jsp:useBean
      id="userInfo"
```

Example 5-4. A JSP Page that Validates and Redisplays Until Correct (userinfo2.jsp) (continued)

```
    class="com.ora.jsp.beans.userinfo.UserInfoBean">
    <jsp:setProperty name="userInfo" property="*" />
</jsp:useBean>

<%-- Output list of values with invalid format, if any --%>
<font color="red">
    <jsp:getProperty name="userInfo" property="propertyStatusMsg" />
</font>

<%-- Output form with submitted valid values --%>
<form action="userinfo2.jsp" method="post">
  <table>
    <tr>
      <td>Name:</td>
      <td><input type="text" name="userName"
        value="<jsp:getProperty
                  name="userInfo"
                  property="userName"
              />">
      </td>
    </tr>
    <tr>
      <td>Birth Date:</td>
      <td><input type="text" name="birthDate"
        value="<jsp:getProperty
                  name="userInfo"
                  property="birthDate"
              />">
      </td>
      <td>(Use format yyyy-mm-dd)</td>
    </tr>
    <tr>
      <td>Email Address:</td>
      <td><input type="text" name="emailAddr"
        value="<jsp:getProperty
                  name="userInfo"
                  property="emailAddr"
              />">
      </td>
      <td>(Use format name@company.com)</td>
    </tr>
    <tr>
      <td>Sex:</td>
      <td><input type="text" name="sex"
        value="<jsp:getProperty
                  name="userInfo"
                  property="sex"
              />">
```

Example 5-4. A JSP Page that Validates and Redisplays Until Correct (userinfo2.jsp) (continued)

```
            </td>
            <td>(Male or female)</td>
          </tr>
          <tr>
            <td>Lucky number:</td>
            <td><input type="text" name="luckyNumber"
              value="<jsp:getProperty
                       name="userInfo"
                       property="luckyNumber"
                    />">
            </td>
            <td>(A number between 1 and 100)</td>
          </tr>
          <tr>
            <td colspan=2><input type="submit"></td>
          </tr>
        </table>
      </form>
    </body>
</html>
```

Instead of using a static HTML page for the input form and a separate JSP page with the validation code, in this example we have combined them into a single JSP page. This page generates the form and provides an appropriate message based on whether or not the input is valid. The page also fills in the form with the valid values that have already been specified (if any) so the user needs to enter values only for missing or incorrect input.

Let's look at Example 5-4 from the top. The first thing to note is that the page generates a message using the `UserInfoBean` property named `propertyStatusMsg`. Here is the corresponding snippet:

```
<%-- Output list of values with invalid format, if any --%>
<font color="red">
  <jsp:getProperty name="userInfo" property="propertyStatusMsg" />
</font>
```

The first line here is a JSP comment. Text between `<%--` and `--%>` in a JSP page is treated as a comment and never appears in the result sent to the browser. For complex pages, it's always a good idea to include comments to explain things that are not obvious.

The `propertyStatusMsg` property can have three different values. If none of the properties have been set, the value is "Please enter values in all fields". If at least one value is missing or invalid, the message states "The following values are missing or invalid" and provides a list of the relevant properties. Finally, if all the values are valid, the `propertyStatusMsg` is "Thanks for telling us about yourself!"

Next we generate the form, filled out with all valid values. Here's the beginning of the form and the code for the `userName` property:

```
<%-- Output form with submitted valid values --%>
<form action="userinfo2.jsp" method="post">
  <table>
    <tr>
      <td>Name:</td>
      <td><input type="text" name="userName"
        value="<jsp:getProperty
              name="userInfo"
              property="userName"
            />">
      </td>
    </tr>
```

Most of this is plain HTML, which is treated as template text and passed on untouched to the browser. But note the use of a `<jsp:getProperty>` action as the HTML `<input>` element's `value` attribute. This is how the `userName` field in the form is filled in with the current value of the `userName` bean property. Also note how the form's `action` attribute points back to the JSP page itself.

Try this out by clicking on the "User Info 2 example" link on the book examples page. Enter both valid and invalid values in the form and look at the results. In Chapter 8, we'll expand on this example and look at how you can move on to another page when all input is valid.

One item may look a bit strange to you: an element (`<jsp:getProperty>`) is used as the value of another element's attribute (the `<input>` tag's `value` attribute). While this is not valid HTML syntax, it *is* valid JSP syntax. Remember that everything not recognized as a JSP element is treated as template text. Whether the template text is HTML, XML, WML, or just plain text doesn't matter. As far as the JSP container is concerned, the previous code is as valid as:

```
any old template text <jsp:getProperty
                    name="userInfo"
                    property="userName" /> more text
```

When the JSP page is processed, the action element is replaced with the value of the bean's property. The resulting HTML sent to the browser is therefore valid.

Formatting HTML Output

If you enter a value containing double quotes in the Name field of the *userinfo2.jsp* page, it doesn't work right. For example, try "Prince, "the artist"" and you'll see what I mean. Only "Prince," appears in the Name field, and the Birth Date field is not shown at all. What's going on here?

A look at the HTML code generated by the JSP page using your browser's View Source function reveals what's wrong:

```
<table>
  <tr>
    <td>Name:</td>
    <td><input type="text" name="userName"
      value="Prince, "the artist"">
    </td>
  </tr>
```

In the JSP file, double quotes are used to enclose the value of the `<input>` element's `value` attribute, so when the value itself includes a double quote, the browser gets confused. The first double quote in the value is interpreted as the end of the value. That's why you see only "Prince," in the field. Even worse, the rest of the value interferes with the interpretation of the rest of the form, causing the next input field to be ignored in most browsers.

One solution to this problem would be to use single quotes around the values instead, since HTML accepts either single quotes or double quotes. But then you would have the same problem if the user enters a value that includes a single quote. Fortunately, there's a better way.

What's needed is special treatment of all characters that can cause HTML interpretation problems when we generate HTML from dynamic strings. One way to handle this is to let the bean take care of the special treatment. The `UserInfoBean` can do this through another set of properties: `userNameFormatted`, `birthDateFormatted`, `emailAddrFormatted`, `sexFormatted`, and `luckyNumberFormatted`.

These are read-only properties that simply represent formatted versions of the corresponding real property values. The bean is designed so that when you use these property names, all troublesome characters in the real property values—such as single quotes, double quotes, less-than symbols, greater-than symbols, and ampersands—are converted to their corresponding HTML character entities (i.e., `&#39;`, `&#34;`, `&lt;`, `&gt;`, and `&amp;`). The browser handles the converted values with no problem. If you're curious about the Java code for the formatted properties, it's described in Chapter 15. Example 5-5 shows a JSP page that uses the new properties.

Example 5-5. A JSP Page with Validation and Formatting Using a Bean (userinfo3.jsp)

```
<%@ page language="java" contentType="text/html" %>
<html>
  <head>
    <title>User Info Entry Form</title>
  </head>
  <body bgcolor="white">
```

Example 5-5. A JSP Page with Validation and Formatting Using a Bean (userinfo3.jsp) (continued)

```
<jsp:useBean
  id="userInfo"
  class="com.ora.jsp.beans.userinfo.UserInfoBean">
  <jsp:setProperty name="userInfo" property="*" />
</jsp:useBean>

<%-- Output list of values with invalid format, if any --%>
<font color="red">
  <jsp:getProperty name="userInfo" property="propertyStatusMsg" />
</font>

<%-- Output form with submitted valid values --%>
<form action="userinfo3.jsp" method="post">
  <table>
    <tr>
      <td>Name:</td>
      <td><input type="text" name="userName"
        value="<jsp:getProperty
                name="userInfo"
                property="userNameFormatted"
              />">
      </td>
    </tr>
    <tr>
      <td>Birth Date:</td>
      <td><input type="text" name="birthDate"
        value="<jsp:getProperty
                name="userInfo"
                property="birthDateFormatted"
              />">
      </td>
      <td>(Use format yyyy-mm-dd)</td>
    </tr>
    <tr>
      <td>Email Address:</td>
      <td><input type="text" name="emailAddr"
        value="<jsp:getProperty
                name="userInfo"
                property="emailAddrFormatted"
              />">
      </td>
      <td>(Use format name@company.com)</td>
    </tr>
    <tr>
      <td>Sex:</td>
      <td><input type="text" name="sex"
        value="<jsp:getProperty
                name="userInfo"
```

Example 5-5. A JSP Page with Validation and Formatting Using a Bean (userinfo3.jsp) (continued)

```
                        property="sexFormatted"
                  />">
      </td>
      <td>(Male or female)</td>
    </tr>
    <tr>
      <td>Lucky number:</td>
      <td><input type="text" name="luckyNumber"
        value="<jsp:getProperty
                  name="userInfo"
                  property="luckyNumberFormatted"
                  />">
      </td>
      <td>(A number between 1 and 100)</td>
    </tr>
    <tr>
      <td colspan=2><input type="submit"></td>
    </tr>
  </table>
  </form>
  </body>
</html>
```

It's not always a good idea to have a bean handle this type of formatting, though. A bean is easier to reuse if it doesn't contain logic that is specific for one type of use, such as generating strings suitable for HTML. When we look at scripting elements and custom actions, we will revisit the subject of HTML formatting and look at other solutions to this problem.

Try the final version of this example by clicking on the "User Info 3 example" link. Now everything works fine, even if you happen to be Prince, "the artist."

6

Using Scripting Elements

When you develop a JSP-based application, I recommend that you try to place all Java code in JavaBeans, in custom actions, or in regular Java classes. However, to tie all these components together, you sometimes need additional code embedded in the JSP pages themselves. Recall from Chapter 3, *JSP Overview*, that JSP lets you put actual Java code in pages using a set of scripting elements. In this chapter we look at how you can use these scripting elements and when it makes sense to do so.

We start with a brief introduction to the Java language constructs you're likely to use in a JSP page. If you already know Java by heart you can safely skip the first section. But if you have never written a Java program, or are still a "newbie," you should read it carefully. Don't expect to become a Java guru after reading this introduction, of course. The Java language, combined with the standard libraries, provides many powerful features not covered here. To learn more about Java, I recommend that you read one of the many books dedicated to the language and its libraries, for instance *Java in a Nutshell* and *Java Examples in a Nutshell*, both by David Flanagan (O'Reilly).

Java Primer

You don't have to be a Java expert to develop JSP pages, but it helps to have an understanding of the basic concepts. This overview of the Java language and some of the standard classes should be enough to get you started.

Classes and Objects

Java is an object-oriented language. This means that everything in Java is an *object*, except for a few primitive types such as numbers, characters, and Boolean values.

An object is an instance of a *class*, which serves as a source code template describing how the object should behave. It's helpful to think of a class as a blueprint from which identical copies (objects) are created. Example 6-1 shows a simple Java class.

Example 6-1. Simple Java Class

```java
/**
 * This is just a simple example of a Java class
 * with two instance variables, a constructor, and
 * some methods.
 */

public class Rectangle {

  // Data
  private int width;
  private int height;

  // Constructor
  public Rectangle(int w, int h) {
    width = w;
    height = h;
  }

  // Methods
  public int getWidth() {
    return width;
  }

  public void setWidth(int w) {
    width = w;
  }

  public int getHeight() {
    return height;
  }

  public void setHeight(int h) {
    height = h;
  }

  public double getArea() {
    double area;

    area = width * height;
    return area;
  }

}
```

It's important to remember that a class always defines two items:

- *data*: a collection of information in an object
- *methods*: a set of functions that act on that data

Data

Data, often called variables, can consist of primitive datatypes such as integers, Booleans, and floating-point values (both the width and height in this example are integers, represented by the keyword `int`). In addition, data can also be objects. The type value that a variable holds must always be declared. The following example declares a variable of the object type `String`:

```
String title;
```

Until you give a variable a value, it contains a default value (0, `false`, or `null`). The name of the variable must start with a letter followed by a combination of letters and digits. There are many special characters, such as dots and plus signs, that are not allowed in a variable name. By convention, variable names often start with lowercase letters and do not have spaces:

```
String titleOfBook;
```

Methods

Methods are functions that take in zero or more primitive datatypes or objects, and perform some task on the object that may or may not result in a return value. If it does, the return value is also a primitive datatype or object. Here is an example of a method:

```
public void setHeight(int h) {
    height = h;
}
```

This method, called `setHeight()`, takes in a single integer, uses it to set the object variable `height`, and returns nothing (note the `void` keyword before the method name).

One special method that appears in Example 6-1 is the *constructor*. The constructor method always shares the same name as the class, and its return type is never declared. The constructor allows the object to initialize itself; it is invoked when the `new` keyword is used to create an instance of the class:

```
Rectangle rect1 = new Rectangle(28,72);
```

Here we create an instance of the class `Rectangle` and keep a reference to it in a variable called `rect1`. The new `Rectangle` object saves the value of the two integer constructor arguments, 28 and 72, in its internal variables, `width` and `height`.

Note that Java is a case-sensitive language: height and Height are not the same.
The standard naming convention for class names, unlike for variable names, is to
capitalize the first letter. For both class and variable names, the first letter in internal words is also capitalized; for instance:

```
aVeryLongNameForAVariable        // VARIABLE
ANameForAClass                   // CLASS
```

Statements

A statement is simply an instruction to do something. For example, the following
are statements in Java:

```
area = width * height;
return area;
```

The first statement takes the value of width and height, multiplies them
together, and places the result in the variable area. The second statement uses
the variable area as the return value for the current method. Statements almost
always appear inside of methods. In addition, all statements and variable declarations must end with a semicolon (;) in Java; this takes after other programming
languages, such as C and C++.

Inheritance

Java includes a number of standard classes. For a specific application, you can create your own classes, often based on the standard Java classes. Classes can be
arranged in a hierarchy, where one class extends the functionality of another class.
This is one of the fundamental attributes of an object-oriented language, called
inheritance. A class that extends another class, usually called a *subclass*, inherits
methods and variables from the class it extends, usually called the *superclass*. A subclass can add its own methods, or override the existing methods defined in the
superclass by creating identical methods in its own class. A typical example is a
class Vehicle with subclasses Car and Boat. The Vehicle class has a method
isLandBound(), returning true. The Car class uses the method as-is, but the
Boat class overrides it to return false. This is illustrated in Figure 6-1.

Inheritance lets you write code that works with objects on different levels of
abstraction. Let's say the Car class adds a method getDoors(), returning the
number of doors for a specific instance of the class. Code that works with Vehicle
objects can call the isLandBound() method and be ignorant about if an object is
a Car or a Boat, while code dealing exclusively with Car objects can call both the
isLandBound() and getDoors() methods: it inherits the former method from
Vehicle.

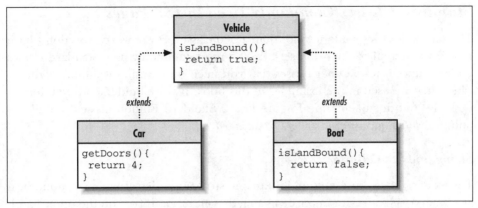

Figure 6-1. Class inheritance

Primitive Types

As we mentioned earlier, Java includes a number of primitive types for efficiency. These primitive types are listed in the following chart:

Type	Size	Values
int	4 bytes	–2,147,483,648 to 2,147,483,647
short	2 bytes	–32,768 to 32,767
long	8 bytes	–9,223,372,036,854,775,808 to 9,223,372,036,854,775,807
byte	1 byte	–128 to 127
float	4 bytes	32-bit IEEE 754 floating-point numbers
double	8 bytes	64-bit IEEE 754 floating-point numbers
char	2 bytes	Unicode characters
boolean	1 bit	true or false

Comments

Java supports two types of comments (Example 6-1 includes both types).

A comment that spans multiple lines, known as a *block comment*, starts with the characters /* and ends with the characters */:

```
/**
 * This is just a simple example of a Java class
 * with two instance variables, a constructor, and
 * some methods.
 */
```

Another type of comment is called an *end-of-line comment*. It starts with two slashes (//) and ends, as the name implies, at the end of the same line:

```
// Instance variable
```

Standard Classes Commonly Used in JSP Pages

The Java 2 libraries contain more than 1,500 classes. Don't worry, you don't have to learn about all of them to use JSP. The most commonly used standard classes are introduced here. Other classes that you need on occasion will be introduced when they are used in the examples in this book. If you would like more information, the full documentation for the Java 2 Standard Edition classes is available online at *http://java.sun.com/j2se/1.3/docs.html.*

String and StringBuffer

The `String` class represents an immutable string (a series of letters or numerical characters); its value can never be changed. A `StringBuffer`, on the other hand, is intended to be used when you build a string dynamically. Note that with the Java language, you can create a `String` object without using the new keyword; instead, just place the contents of the `String` in quotation marks.

For example, the following are equivalent:

```
String str1 = new String("The bright day");
String str1 = "The bright day";
```

`String` is the only object in Java where you can abbreviate its creation this way.

Some of the most commonly used `String` methods are:

`public boolean equals(Object anObject)`
> Returns `true` if the target and the argument represent exactly the same sequence of characters. For example:

```
String hello = new String("hello");
hello.equals("hello");  // Returns true
hello.equals("Hello");  // Returns false
```

`public boolean equalsIgnoreCase(String anotherString)`
> Returns `true` if the target and the argument represent exactly the same sequence of characters, ignoring case. For example:

```
String hello = new String("hello");
hello.equals("hello"); // Returns true
hello.equals("Hello"); // Returns true
```

`public String trim()`
> Returns a new `String` with all whitespace from both ends of the target `String` removed. For example:

```
String hello = " Hello ";
String trimmed = hello.trim();
trimmed.equals("Hello");    // Returns true
```

Some of the most commonly used `StringBuffer` methods are:

`public synchronized StringBuffer append(String str)`

Appends the argument to the target. For example:

```
StringBuffer buffer = new StringBuffer("Hello");
buffer.append(" JSP!");  // New value is "Hello JSP!"
```

`public String toString()`

Returns a `String` representing the data in the target. For example:

```
StringBuffer buffer = new StringBuffer("Hello");
buffer.append(" JSP!");  // New value is "Hello JSP!"
String hello = buffer.toString();
hello.equals("Hello JSP!");  // Returns true
```

Arrays

An array is a bundling of a number of variables of the same type (a class or a primitive type). In Java, arrays are also objects. You create a new array like this:

```
String[] myStrings = new String[4];
int[] myInts = new int[7];
```

The type of component in the array is the type specified before the empty brackets on the left side of the equals sign (=). The size of an array is fixed and must be specified within the brackets of the type definition following the new keyword.

You can access the individual components of an array by specifying the index of the component. The indexes always begin from 0 and count upward to the defined length minus one:

```
int i = myInts[0];
```

The number of components in an array is available in a variable of the array object named `length`. You can access it like this:

```
int myIntsLength = myInts.length;
```

Flow Control Statements

Flow control statements are used for situations such as testing conditions and looping. Let's briefly look at some examples.

To execute a piece of code only when a condition is true, use the `if` statement:

```
if ( hello.equals("Hello") ) {
  // Do something
} else {
  // Do something else
}
```

The code within parentheses following the `if` keyword is called an *expression*: it must be evaluated by the Java interpreter to some value, in this case a Boolean `true` or `false` value. Here we test if the `String` variable `hello` equals the string literal `"Hello"`. If it evaluates to `true`, the block of code between the first set of braces is executed. You can optionally use an `else` clause, like we do in this example, which is executed if it evaluates to `false`.

In some situations, you can use the *conditional operator* (`?`) as an alternative to the `if` statement:

```
String greeting = (clock.getHours() < 12) ?
    "Good morning" : "Good afternoon";
```

Here's how it works: first, the code before the `?` operator is evaluated. If the result is `true`, the value immediately after the `?` is returned. If it's `false`, the value after the colon is returned. This type of expression is more compact than an `if` statement when the only thing you want is to get one of two values depending on a simple condition.

Other common flow control statements are `while` and `for`. They are used to execute a block of code repeatedly. Let's look at the `while` statement first:

```
while (i < myArr.length) {
    // Do something
    i = i + 1;
}
```

Here, the expression following the `while` keyword is evaluated. If it is `true`, the code block within the braces is executed. After it completes, the expression is evaluated again. If it is still `true`, the code block is again executed. This looping repeats until the expression evalutes to `false`.

Here is an example of a `for` statement:

```
for (int i = 0; i < myArr.length; i++) {
    // Do something
}
```

The `for` statement has three expressions within the parentheses following the `for` keyword. The first expression is executed before anything else; it is typically used to initialize a variable used as an index. The expression in the middle must be a Boolean expression. If it evaluates to `true`, the block of code within braces is executed. After each code block iteration, the final statement is executed and the middle expression is evaluated again. If it's still `true`, the body is again executed and the third expression is tested, and so on. Note that the final expression is typically used to increment an index variable until the expression in the middle evaluates to `false`, at which point the loop will exit.

Operators

Operators are used to assign values to variables, perform numeric operations, and compare values, among other things. Java uses the usual operators for numeric addition, subtraction, multiplication, and division: +, −, *, and /. There are also shortcuts for some common expressions; for instance:

```
i += 3;
```

is the same as:

```
i = i + 3;
```

and:

```
i++;
```

is the same as:

```
i = i + 1;
```

The + operator can also be used to concatenate strings:

```
String hello = new String("Hello");
String helloWorld = hello + " World!";
```

This is not the most efficient way of concatenating strings though, so don't overuse it. Where performance is critical and you need to concatenate many strings together, it's more efficient to use a `StringBuffer`:

```
StringBuffer helloWorld = new StringBuffer("Hello");
helloWorld.append(" World!");
```

The operators for equal (==), not equal (!=), greater than (>), greater than or equal (>=), less than (<), and less than or equal (<=) are the same as in many other languages.

```
if (anInt > 2) {
    // Do something if an int variable value is greater than 2
}
```

Note that you cannot use the == operator to test if two `String` objects have the same value. That's because the == operator, when used with objects, tests if the variables are referencing the same `String` object, not if the values of two `String` objects are the same. (== works only when comparing the values of two primitive datatypes.) To compare objects with one another you must instead use the `equals()` method described earlier:

```
if ( oneString.equals(anotherString) ) {
    // Do something if the two String values are equal
}
```

Finally, you can combine comparative expressions using the Boolean operators `&&` (and) and `||` (or):

```
if ( (i >= 4) && (i <= 10) ) {
  // Do something if i is between 4 and 10
}
```

That's it for our brief introduction to programming in the Java language. You should now know enough Java programming to follow the remaining examples in this part of the book.

Implicit JSP Objects

When you use scripting elements in a JSP page, you always have access to a number of objects (listed in Table 6-1) that the JSP container makes available. These are called *implicit objects*. These objects are instances of classes defined by the servlet and JSP specifications. Appendix B, *JSP API Reference*, contains complete descriptions of all methods for each class, and we will cover them in more detail as we move through the book. However, I want to briefly introduce them here, as they are used in a number of examples throughout this book.

Table 6-1. Implicit JSP Objects

Variable Name	Java Type
request	`javax.servlet.http.HttpServletRequest`
response	`javax.servlet.http.HttpServletResponse`
pageContext	`javax.servlet.jsp.PageContext`
session	`javax.servlet.http.HttpSession`
application	`javax.servlet.ServletContext`
out	`javax.servlet.jsp.JspWriter`
config	`javax.servlet.ServletConfig`
page	`java.lang.Object`
exception	`java.lang.Throwable`

Here is some more information about each of these implicit objects:

request

> The `request` object is an instance of the class named `javax.servlet.http.HttpServletRequest`. This object provides methods that let you access all the information that's available about the current request, such as request parameters, attributes, headers, and cookies. We use the `request` object in a couple of examples later in this chapter.

response

> The `response` object represents the current response message. It's an instance of the `javax.servlet.http.HttpServletResponse` class, with

methods for setting headers and the status code and for adding cookies. It also provides methods related to session tracking. These methods are the response methods you're most likely to use. We'll look at them in detail in Chapter 8, *Sharing Data Between JSP Pages, Requests, and Users.*

session

The session object allows you to access the client's session data, managed by the server. It's an instance of the javax.servlet.http.HttpSession class. Typically you do not need to directly access this object, since JSP also lets you access the session data through action elements, as you will see in Chapter 8. One method you may use, however, is invalidate(), which explicitly terminates a session. An example of this is shown in Chapter 10, *Authentication and Personalization.*

application

The application object is another object that you typically access indirectly through action elements. It's an instance of the javax.servlet.Servlet-Context class. This object is used to hold references to other objects that more than one user may require access to, such as a database connection shared by all application users. It also contains log() methods that you can use to write messages to the container's log file, as you will see in an example later in this chapter.

out

The out object is an instance of javax.servlet.jsp.JspWriter. You can use the print() and println() methods provided by this object to add text to the response message body. We look at an example of this later in this chapter. In most cases, however, you will just use template text and JSP action elements instead of explicitly printing to the out object.

exception

The exception object is available only in error pages and contains information about a runtime error. Chapter 7, *Error Handling and Debugging,* describes in more detail how you can use this object.

The remaining three implicit objects (pageContext, config, and page) are so rarely used in scripting elements that we will not discuss them here. If you're interested, you can read about them in Appendix B.

All variable names listed in Table 6-1 are reserved for the implicit objects. If you declare your own variables in a JSP page, as you will soon see how to do, you must not use these reserved names for other variables.

Conditional Processing

In most web applications, you produce different output based on runtime conditions, such as the state of a bean or the value of a request header such as UserAgent (containing information about the type of client that is accessing the page).

If the differences are not too great, you can use JSP scripting elements to control which parts of the JSP page are sent to the browser, generating alternative outputs from the same JSP page. However, if the outputs are completely different, I recommend using a separate JSP page for each alternative and passing control from one page to another. This chapter contains a number of examples in which one page is used. In the remainder of this book you'll see plenty of examples where multiple pages are used instead.

Using JavaBeans Properties

In Chapter 5, *Generating Dynamic Content*, you saw how to use the <jsp:get-Property> and the <jsp:setProperty> actions to access a bean's properties. However, a bean is just a Java class that follows certain coding conventions, so you can also call its methods directly.

Briefly, a bean is a class with a constructor that doesn't take an argument. This makes it possible for a tool, such as the JSP container, to create an instance of the bean class simply by knowing the class name. The other condition of a bean that we are concerned with is the naming of the methods used to access its properties. The method names for reading and writing a property value, collectively known as the bean's *accessor* methods, must be composed of the keywords get and set, respectively, plus the name of the property. For instance, you can retrieve the value of a property named month in a bean with the method getMonth() and set it with the method setMonth(). Individually, the accessor method for reading a property value is known as the *getter* method, and the accessor method for writing a property value is the *setter* method. A property can be read-only, write-only, or read/write depending on whether a getter method, a setter method, or both methods are provided in the class. The Java type for a property, finally, is the type returned by the getter method and the type of the setter methods argument.

To use a bean's property value in a scripting element, call the accessor method directly. To illustrate this, let's use one of the properties of the java.util.Date class introduced in Chapter 5. Table 6-2 shows a bean property sheet for the hours property. (These tables should be getting clearer now, by the way.) It's a read-only property of the type int.

Table 6-2. java.util.Date hours Property

Property Name	Java Type	Access	Description
hours	int	read	The hour as a number between 0 (midnight) and 23

Example 6-2 revisits an example from the first chapter: this page uses the value of this property to greet the user with an appropriate message depending on the time of day.

Example 6-2. Conditional Greeting Page (greeting.jsp)

```
<%@ page language="java" contentType="text/html" %>
<html>
<body bgcolor="white">
<jsp:useBean id="clock" class="java.util.Date" />

<% if (clock.getHours() < 12) { %>
  Good morning!
<% } else if (clock.getHours() < 17) { %>
  Good day!
<% } else { %>
  Good evening!
<% } %>

</body>
</html>
```

As we discussed before, this page will show a different message depending on when you request it. What we didn't elaborate on in the first chapter, however, is that this magic is accomplished using a set of JSP *scriptlet* elements. A scriptlet is a block of code enclosed between a scriptlet-start identifier, <%, and an end identifier, %>.

Let's look in detail at Example 6-2. The <jsp:useBean> action is first used to create a bean. Besides making the bean available to other actions, such as <jsp:getProperty> and <jsp:setProperty>, the <jsp:useBean> action also creates a Java variable that holds a reference to the bean. The name of the variable is the name specified by the id attribute, in this case clock.

The clock bean is then used in four scriptlets, together forming a complete Java if statement with template text in the if and else blocks:

```
<% if (clock.getHours() < 12) { %>
```
    An if statement, testing if it's before noon, with a block start brace.

```
<% } else if (clock.getHours() < 17) { %>
```
The if block end brace and an else-if statement, testing if it's before 5:00 P.M., with its block start brace.

```
<% } else { %>
```
The else-if block end brace, and a final else block start brace, handling the case when it's after 5:00 P.M.

```
<% } %>
```
The final else block end brace.

The JSP container combines the code segment in the four scriptlets with code for writing the template text to the response body. The end result is that when the first if statement is true, "Good morning!" is displayed; when the second if statement is true, "Good day!" is displayed; and if none of the if statements is true, the final else block is used, displaying, "Good evening!"

The tricky part when using scriptlets like this is making sure that all the start and end braces are in place. If you miss even one brace, the code that the JSP container generates is not syntactically correct. And unfortunately, the error message you get is not always easy to interpret.

Using Request Information

Let's look at another example, in which the implicit object request is used to display different messages depending on whether the Internet Explorer or Netscape Navigator browser is used. Example 6-3 shows the complete page.

Example 6-3. Browser-Dependent Page (browser.jsp)

```
<%@ page language="java" contentType="text/html" %>
<html>
<body bgcolor="white">

<% if (request.getHeader("User-Agent").indexOf("MSIE") != -1) { %>
  You're using Internet Explorer.
<%
    } else
      if (request.getHeader("User-Agent").indexOf("Mozilla") != 1) {
%>
  You're using Netscape.
<% } else { %>
  You're using a browser I don't know about.
<% } %>

</body>
</html>
```

As in Example 6-2, four scriptlets are used to provide the code for the conditional message. The difference is the actual `if` statements used to figure out which type of browser is requesting the page. Let's look at all the objects and methods used here.

The `request` object is not a bean, since it doesn't follow all the JavaBeans conventions described above, but it does provide a number of methods you can use to get information about the request. For instance, the `request` object's `getHeader()` method is used to get the value of a specific request header. Recall that each request contains a number of headers that provide detailed information the server may use to process the request. In this case, the `User-Agent` header retrieved in Example 6-2 contains a description of the browser making the request.

The `getHeader()` method returns a `String` object, so we can then use the `indexOf()` method of the `String` class to look for the piece of a string that identifies the browser. This method returns an integer offset from the beginning of the string if the text is found, or -1 if the text is not found. Note that both Internet Explorer and Netscape send a description that contains the text "Mozilla", but Internet Explorer also includes the text "MSIE", so we must look for "MSIE" first. If we find it, we know it's an Internet Explorer browser. If we don't find "MSIE" but find "Mozilla", it's most likely a Netscape browser. The final `else` block takes care of other browsers, such as Lynx and Opera.

Working with Arrays

Another common use of scriptlets is to loop over an array. In Example 6-4, we let the user pick a number of items from a group of checkboxes, and then use scriptlets to display all the choices.

Example 6-4. Looping Over Parameter Array (loop.jsp)

```
<%@ page language="java" contentType="text/html" %>
<html>
<body bgcolor="white">

  <form action="loop.jsp">
    <input type="checkbox" name="fruits" value="Apple">Apple<br>
    <input type="checkbox" name="fruits" value="Banana">Banana<br>
    <input type="checkbox" name="fruits" value="Orange">Orange<br>
    <input type="submit" value="Enter">
  </form>

  <%
    String[] picked = request.getParameterValues("fruits");
    if (picked != null && picked.length != 0) {
  %>
```

Example 6-4. Looping Over Parameter Array (loop.jsp) (continued)

```
    You picked the following fruits:
    <ul>
    <%
      for (int i = 0; i < picked.length; i++) {
        out.println("<li>" + picked[i]);
      }
    %>
    </ul>
  <% } %>

</body>
</html>
```

Figure 6-2 shows an example of the resulting page.

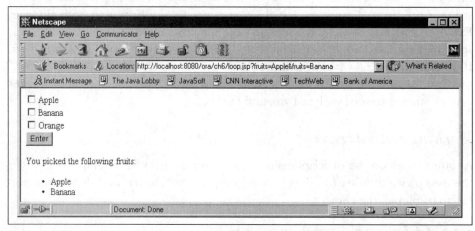

Figure 6-2. Page showing values of multivalue parameter

The first part of the page in Example 6-4 is a regular HTML form, with three checkboxes and a Submit button. Again, note that the action of the form is to return to the same page, *loop.jsp*, but this time with parameter values. Then follows three scriptlets. In the first, we use another request method, `getParameter-Values()`:

```
  <%
    String[] picked = request.getParameterValues("fruits");
    if (picked != null && picked.length != 0) {
  %>
```

This method returns a `String[]` containing all values for the parameter specified as the argument. Here, it's the name used for all checkboxes in the form. If no checkbox is selected, this parameter has no value; `getParameterValues()`

returns `null`. So before we try to loop through the array, an `if` statement is used to verify that we in fact received at least one value.

The next scriptlet contains the actual loop:

```
<%
    for (int i = 0; i < picked.length; i++) {
       out.println("<li>" + picked[i]);
    }
  }
%>
```

A `for` statement is used to process each array component. Here you can also see how the implicit `out` object is used to add content to the response body.

Again, make sure the braces in the three scriptlets form complete code blocks when they are combined with the template text by the JSP container. Note how the start brace for the `if` block is included in the first scriptlet, and the end brace is in the third scriptlet. These braces must balance, or the JSP server will return an error.

Displaying Values

Besides using scriptlets for conditional output, one more way to employ scripting elements is by using a JSP *expression element* to insert values into the response. A JSP expression element can be used instead of the `<jsp:getProperty>` action in some places, but it is also useful to insert the value of any Java expression that can be treated as a `String`.

An expression starts with `<%=` and ends with `%>`. Note that the only syntax difference compared to a scriptlet is the equals sign (=) in the start identifier. An example is:

```
<%= userInfo.getUserName() %>
```

The result of the expression is written to the response body. One thing is important to note: as opposed to statements in a scriptlet, the code in an expression must not end with a semicolon. This is because the JSP container combines the expression code with code for writing the result to the response body. If the expression ends with a semicolon, the combined code will not be syntactically correct.

In the final example of Chapter 5, we used `<jsp:getProperty>` actions to fill out the form fields with `UserInfoBean` values. To recap, it looked like this:

```
<tr>
  <td>Name:</td>
  <td><input type="text" name="userName"
```

```
        value="<jsp:getProperty
               name="userInfo"
               property="userNameFormatted"
            />">
    </td>
  </tr>
```

In this case, the `<jsp:getProperty>` syntax is distracting, since it's used as the value of an HTML element. You can use expressions to make the user input form page easier to read. The following example shows the same part of the page with the `<jsp:getProperty>` action replaced with an expression:

```
<tr>
  <td>Name:</td>
  <td><input type="text" name="userName"
    value="<%= userInfo.getUserNameFormatted() %>" >
  </td>
</tr>
```

The result is exactly the same, but this is more compact.

Expressions help you write more compact code, but they can also help you with something even more important. The `UserInfoBean` provides a set of properties with values formatted for HTML output; that's what we used in Chapter 5 to avoid confusing the browser with special characters in the bean property values. However, it's much easier to reuse a bean if it doesn't need to format its property values for a certain type of output. With expressions, we can let the bean be ignorant of how its property values are used, and use a utility class to do the formatting instead, as in Example 6-5.

Example 6-5. Formatting HTML Output (userinfo4.jsp)

```
<%@ page import="com.ora.jsp.util.*" %>
    ...
<tr>
  <td>Name:</td>
  <td><input type="text" name="userName"
    value="<%= StringFormat.toHTMLString(userInfo.getUserName()) %>" >
  </td>
</tr>
```

This example shows yet another version of the form we first used in Chapter 5. Here a utility class called com.ora.jsp.util.StringFormat is used to handle special characters in the property values. I use the term *utility class* for a class that doesn't represent an entity such as a customer, order, or product. Instead, it's just a collection of useful methods. In this case, the StringFormat class simply contains methods for formatting strings. All of its methods are described in Appendix C, *Book Example Custom Actions and Classes Reference*.

The `StringFormat` class has a method called `toHTMLString()`. It formats its argument for HTML output the same way as the `UserInfoBean` does, converting all HTML special characters to the corresponding HTML character entities. Here we pass it the unformatted property value by calling the bean's regular property getter method. Using this utility class, the ties between the `UserInfoBean` and HTML can be removed and the formatting can be done where it belongs.

Packages

You may have noticed that the full name of the class in Example 6-5 is `com.ora.jsp.util.StringFormat`, but in the expression it's simply referred to as `StringFormat`. This requires an explanation.

A large application may use many different classes, some of them part of the standard Java libraries, and others developed in-house or by third parties. To organize all these classes, Java provides the notion of a *package*. A package is a group of related classes. The fully qualified name of a class is the combination of the package name and the class name. For instance, the fully qualified name of the class used in Example 6-5 is `com.ora.jsp.util.StringFormat`. You can always use the fully qualified name in your Java code, but to save you some typing, you can also *import* a package and then refer to the class with just the short class name. If you look at the top of Example 6-5, you see a `page` directive with the `import` attribute set to the name of the package the `StringFormat` class belongs to:

```
<%@ page import="com.ora.jsp.util.*" %>
```

Importing a package doesn't mean that it's physically included in the page. It only tells Java to look for classes with short names in the named package. You can use multiple `page` directives with `import` attributes in the same page, or use one with a comma-separated list of import declarations, if you need to import more than one package. In other words, this directive:

```
<%@ page import="java.util.*, com.ora.jsp.util.*" %>
```

has the same effect as these two directives:

```
<%@ page import="java.util.* " %>
<%@ page import="com.ora.jsp.util.*" %>
```

Checking Off Checkboxes Dynamically

In Example 6-4, a `for` statement is used to loop through an array, but arrays can also be used in many other ways. If the array represents choices the user can make at one time and change at a later time, a form for changing the information can contain a set of checkboxes with the current choices checked off. An application like this typically gets the current choices from a database, and you will see an

example of this in Chapter 10. To demonstrate a technique for dynamically checking off checkboxes in a form, however, we keep it simple and use the `String[]`
with fruit choices from Example 6-4.

Example 6-6 is a modified version of the loop example.

Example 6-6. Setting Checkbox Values Dynamically (checkbox.jsp)

```
<%@ page language="java" contentType="text/html" %>
<%@ page import="com.ora.jsp.util.*" %>
<html>
<body bgcolor="white">

  <form action="checkbox.jsp">
    <input type="checkbox" name="fruits" value="Apple">Apple<br>
    <input type="checkbox" name="fruits" value="Banana">Banana<br>
    <input type="checkbox" name="fruits" value="Orange">Orange<br>
    <input type="submit" value="Enter">
  </form>

  <%
    String[] picked = request.getParameterValues("fruits");
    if (picked != null && picked.length != 0) {
  %>
      You picked the following fruits:
      <form>
        <input type="checkbox" name="fruits" value="Apple"
          <%= ArraySupport.contains(picked, "Apple") ?
          "checked" : "" %> >Apple<br>
        <input type="checkbox" name="fruits" value="Banana"
          <%= ArraySupport.contains(picked, "Banana") ?
              "checked" : "" %> >Banana<br>
        <input type="checkbox" name="fruits" value="Orange"
          <%= ArraySupport.contains(picked, "Orange") ?
              "checked" : "" %> >Orange<br>
      </form>
  <% } %>
</body>
</html>
```

Here, the loop is replaced with a second form with the same checkboxes as in the
form at the top of the page. A browser shows a checkbox as checked off if the
HTML `<input>` element includes the `checked` keyword. The trick, then, is to add
that keyword for all checkboxes in the second form that the user had checked off
in the first form.

The result of this example is shown in Figure 6-3.

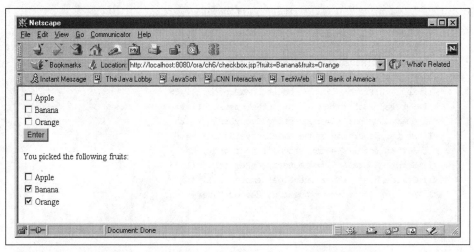

Figure 6-3. Setting checkboxes dynamically

Another utility class from the com.ora.jsp.util package, ArraySupport, has the method contains(). This method takes two arguments: a String[] (string array) and the String that you want to test to see if it's a component in that array. If the second argument is a component in the array, the method returns true.

The contains() method is used in JSP expressions in Example 6-6, inserted in the middle of each HTML <input> element. The expressions use the conditional operator (?) described in the Java primer earlier in this chapter. As you may recall, the expression before the operator is first evaluated. If the result is true, the expression returns the value after the ?. If it's false, the value after the colon is returned. Here the result is that if the array contains the choice represented by the checkbox, the checked attribute is inserted to render the checkbox as checked. Otherwise, an empty string is inserted, leaving the checkbox unchecked.

Using More Request Methods

We have already used one of the methods of the implicit request object, but this object provides a wealth of information you may be interested in. So let's use some more request methods.

Example 6-7 shows a page with a number of JSP expressions, each one displaying a piece of information about the current request.

Example 6-7. Displaying Request Info (reqinfo.jsp)

```
<%@ page language="java" contentType="text/html" %>
<html>
  <body bgcolor="white">
```

Example 6-7. Displaying Request Info (reqinfo.jsp) (continued)

```
The following information was received:
<ul>
  <li>Request Method: <%= request.getMethod() %>
  <li>Request URI: <%= request.getRequestURI() %>
  <li>Request Protocol: <%= request.getProtocol() %>
  <li>Servlet Path: <%= request.getServletPath() %>
  <li>Query String: <%= request.getQueryString() %>
  <li>Server Name: <%= request.getServerName() %>
  <li>Server Port: <%= request.getServerPort() %>
  <li>Remote Address: <%= request.getRemoteAddr() %>
  <li>Remote Host: <%= request.getRemoteHost() %>
  <li>Browser Type: <%= request.getHeader("User-Agent") %>
</ul>
</body>
</html>
```

If you don't remember what some of these things mean, look back at Chapter 2, *HTTP and Servlet Basics.* (The methods are also described in Appendix B.) Figure 6-4 shows an example of the output from this page.

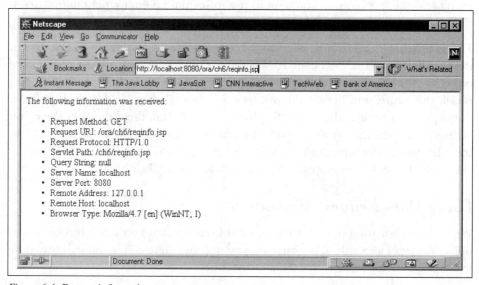

Figure 6-4. Request information page

Using an Expression to Set an Attribute

In all our JSP action element examples so far, the attributes are set to literal string values. But in many cases, the value of an attribute is not known when you write the JSP page; instead, the value must be calculated when the JSP page is requested. For situations like this, you can use a JSP expression as an attribute value. This is called a *request-time attribute value*. Here is an example of how this can be used to set an attribute of a fictitious log entry bean:

```
<jsp:useBean id="logEntry" class="com.foo.LogEntryBean" />
<jsp:setProperty name="logEntry" property="entryTime"
  value="<%= new java.util.Date() %>" />
...
```

This bean has a property named `entryTime` that holds a timestamp for a log entry, while other properties hold the information to be logged. To set the time-stamp to the time when the JSP page is requested, a `<jsp:setProperty>` action with a request-time attribute value is used.

The attribute value is represented by the same type of JSP expression as in the previous snippet, here an expression that creates a new `java.util.Date` object (representing the current date and time). The request-time attribute is evaluated when the page is requested, and the corresponding attribute is set to the result of the expression. As you might have guessed, any property you set this way must have a Java type matching the result of the expression. In this case, the `entryDate` property must be of type `java.util.Date`.

Not all attributes support request-time values. One reason is that some attribute values must be known when the page is converted into a servlet. For instance, the `class` attribute value in the `<jsp:useBean>` action must be known in the translation phase so that the JSP container can generate valid Java code for the servlet. Request-time attributes also require a bit more processing than static string values, so it's up to the custom action developer to decide if request-time attribute values are supported or not. Appendix A, *JSP Elements Syntax Reference*, shows which attributes for the standard actions accept request-time attributes, and Appendix C provides the same information for the custom actions used in this book. If you're a programmer, you may also want to skip ahead to Chapter 16, *Developing JSP Custom Actions*, to see how to declare that an attribute in a custom action accepts request-time attributes.

Declaring Variables and Methods

We have used two of the three JSP scripting elements in this chapter: scriptlets and expressions. There's one more, called a *declaration element*, which is used to declare Java variables and methods in a JSP page. My advice is this: don't use it. Let me explain why.

Java variables can be declared either within a method or outside the body of all methods, like this:

```
public class SomeClass {
    // Instance variable
```

```
    private String anInstanceVariable;

    // Method
    public void doSomething() {
      String aLocalVariable;
    }
  }
```

A variable declared outside the body of all methods is called an *instance variable*. Its value can be accessed from any method in the class, and it keeps its value even when the method that sets it returns. A variable declared within the body of a method is called a *local variable*. A local variable can be accessed only from the method where it's declared. When the method returns, the local variable disappears.

Recall from Chapter 3 that a JSP page is turned into a servlet class when it's first requested, and the JSP container creates one instance of this class. If the same page is requested by more than one user at a time, the same instance is used for each request. Each user is assigned what is called a *thread* in the server, and each thread executes the main method in the JSP object. When more than one thread executes the same code, you have to make sure the code is *thread-safe*. This means that the code must behave the same when many threads are executing as when just one thread executes the code.

Multithreading and thread-safe code strategies are best left to programmers. However, you should know that using a JSP declaration element to declare variables exposes your page to multithreading problems. That's because a variable declared using a JSP declaration element ends up as an instance variable in the generated servlet, not as a local variable in a method. Since an instance variable keeps its value when the method executed by a thread returns, it is visible to all threads executing code in the same instance. If one thread changes the value of the instance variable, the value is changed for all threads. To put this in JSP terms, if the instance variable is changed because one user accesses the page, all users accessing the same page will use the new value.

When you declare a variable within a scriptlet element instead of in a JSP declaration block, the variable ends up as a local variable in the generated servlet's request processing method. Each thread has its own copy of a local variable, so local variables can't cause any problems if more than one thread executes the same code. If the value of a local variable is changed, it will not affect the other threads.

That being said, let's look at a simple example. We use two `int` variables: one declared as an instance variable using a JSP expression, and the other declared as a local variable. We increment them both by one and display the new values. Example 6-8 shows the test page.

Example 6-8. Using a Declaration Element (counter.jsp)

```
<%@ page language="java" contentType="text/html" %>
<%!
  int globalCounter = 0;
%>
<html>
  <head>
    <title>A page with a counter</title>
  </head>
  <body bgcolor="white">
    This page has been visited: <%= ++globalCounter %> times.
    <p>
    <%
      int localCounter = 0;
    %>
    This counter never increases its value: <%= ++localCounter %>
  </body>
</html>
```

The JSP declaration element is right at the beginning of the page, starting with <%! and ending with %>. Note the exclamation point (!) in the start identifier; that's what makes it a declaration as opposed to a scriptlet. The declaration element declares an instance variable named globalCounter, shared by all requests for the page. In the body section of the page, a JSP expression increments the variable's value. Next comes a scriptlet, enclosed by <% and %>, that declares a local variable named localCounter. The last scriptlet increments the value of the local variable.

When you run this example, the globalCounter value increases every time you load the page, but localCounter stays the same. Again, this is because globalCounter is an instance variable (its value is available to all requests and remains between requests) while localCounter is a local variable (its value is available only to the current request and is dropped when the request ends).

In this example, nothing terribly bad happens if more than one user hits the page at the same time. The worst that could happen is that you skip a number or show the same globalCounter value twice. This can happen if two requests come in at the same time, and both requests increment the value before it's inserted in the response. You can imagine the consequences, however, if you use an instance variable to save something more important, such as a customer's credit card number or other sensitive information. So even though it may be tempting to create an instance variable (using a JSP expression) to keep a value such as a counter between requests, I recommend that you stay away from this technique. We'll look at better ways to share information between requests in Chapter 8.

A JSP declaration element can also be used to declare a method that can then be used in scriptlets in the same page. The only harm this could cause is that your JSP pages end up containing too much code, making it hard to maintain the application. A far better approach is to use JavaBeans and custom actions. But to be complete, Example 6-9 shows an example of how it can be done.

Example 6-9. Method Declaration and Use (color.jsp)

```
<%@ page language="java" contentType="text/html" %>
<html>
<body bgcolor="white">

  <%!
    String randomColor() {
      java.util.Random random = new java.util.Random();
      int red = (int) (random.nextFloat() * 255);
      int green = (int) (random.nextFloat() * 255);
      int blue = (int) (random.nextFloat() * 255);
      return "#" +
        Integer.toString(red, 16) +
        Integer.toString(green, 16) +
        Integer.toString(blue, 16);
    }
  %>

  <h1>Random Color</h1>

    <table bgcolor="<%= randomColor() %>" >
      <tr><td width="100" height="100"> </td></tr>
    </table>

</body>
</html>
```

The method named randomColor(), declared between <%! and %>, returns a randomly generated String in a format that can be used as an HTML color value. This method is then called from an expression element to set the background color for a table. Every time you reload this page, you see a single table cell with a randomly selected color.

jspInit( ) and jspDestroy( )

You may remember from Chapter 2 that a servlet has two methods that the container calls when the servlet is loaded and shut down. These methods are called init() and destroy(), and they allow the servlet to initialize instance variables when it's loaded and clean up when it's shut down, respectively. As you already know, a JSP page is turned into a servlet, so it has the same capability. However, with JSP, the methods are called `jspInit()` and `jspDestroy()` instead.

Again, I recommend that you do not declare any instance variables for your JSP pages. If you follow this advice, there's also no reason to declare the `jspInit()` and `jspDestroy()` methods. But I know you're curious, so here's an example of how they can be used.

Expanding on Example 6-8, the `jspInit()` method can be used to set an instance variable to a `java.util.Date()` object, which represents the date and time when the page is loaded. This variable can then be used in the page to show when the counter was started:

```
<%@ page language="java" contentType="text/html" %>
<%@ page import="java.util.Date" %>
<%!
  int globalCounter = 0;
  Date startDate;

  public void jspInit() {
    startDate = new Date();
  }

  public void jspDestroy() {
    ServletContext context = getServletConfig().getServletContext();
    context.log("test.jsp was visited " + globalCounter +
      " times between " + startDate + " and " + (new Date()));
  }
%>
<html>
  <head>
    <title>A page with a counter</title>
  </head>
  <body bgcolor="white">
    This page has been visited: <%= ++globalCounter %> times
    since <%= startDate %>.
  </body>
</html>
```

The `jspDestroy()` method retrieves a reference to the `ServletContext` for the page and writes a message to the container's log file. If you recall that the implicit `application` variable contains a reference to the `ServletContext`, you may be wondering why it's not used here. The reason is that the implicit variables are available only in the method that the JSP container generates to process the page requests, not in the methods that you declare yourself.

Why Two Notations?

You may have noticed that two different notations are used for the different JSP elements: XML-style notation, like `<jsp:useBean>`, for action elements, and `<% %>` notation for directives and scripting elements. If you're a purist, you may be wondering why the authors of the JSP specification mixed styles like this. Given that XML seems to be the future for all markup languages, why not use XML notation for all JSP elements?

There are two good reasons for not using the XML notation for directives and scripting elements:

- Scripting elements contain scripting code, and many characters used in code are not valid in an XML document. If XML notation were used for the scripting elements, you would have to manually encode characters like < and > so they wouldn't be mistaken for XML control characters. That would be messy and a source of pernicious errors.

- The `<%@ directive %>`, `<% code %>`, `<%= expression %>`, and `<%! declaration %>` notations are familiar for many developers since they are also used in Microsoft's Active Server Pages (ASP).

JSP actually defines XML-style equivalents for directives and scripting elements. But the XML notation for these elements is intended to be used only by tools that generate complete JSP pages. The tools can handle encoding of special characters automatically, as well as a number of other details needed to make a JSP page a well-formed XML document. The XML style is also not completely defined in JSP 1.1; therefore, a JSP 1.1 container is not required to support it.

7

Error Handling and Debugging

When you develop any application that's more than a trivial example, errors are inevitable. A JSP-based application is no exception. There are many types of errors you will deal with. Simple syntax errors in the JSP pages are almost a given during the development phase. And even after you have fixed all the syntax errors, you may still have to figure out why the application doesn't work as you intended due to design mistakes. The application must also be designed to deal with problems that can occur when it's deployed for production use. Users can enter invalid values and try to use the application in ways you never imagined. External systems, such as databases, can fail or become unavailable due to network problems.

Since a web application is the face of a company, making sure it behaves well, even when the users misbehave and the world around it falls apart, is extremely important for a positive customer perception. Proper design and testing is the only way to accomplish this goal. Unfortunately, many developers seem to forget the hard-learned lessons from traditional application development when designing web applications. For instance, a survey of 100 e-commerce managers, conducted by *InternetWeek* magazine (April 3, 2000 issue), shows that 50% of all web site problems were caused by application coding errors. That's the highest ranking reason in the survey, ahead of poor server performance (38%), poor service provider performance (35%), and poor network performance (22%).

In this chapter, we look at the types of problems you can expect during development, as well as those common in a production system. We see how you can track down JSP syntax and design errors, and how to deal with runtime problems in a graceful manner.

Dealing with Syntax Errors

The first type of error you will encounter is the one you, or your co-workers, create by simple typos: in other words, syntax error. The JSP container needs every JSP element to be written exactly as it's defined in the specification in order to turn the JSP page into a valid servlet class. When it finds something that's not right, it will tell you. But how easy it is to understand what it tells you depends on the type of error, the JSP container implementation, and sometimes, on how fluent you are in computer gibberish.

Element Syntax Errors

Let's first look at how Tomcat reports some typical syntax errors in JSP directives and action elements. Example 7-1 shows a version of the *date.jsp* page from Chapter 5, *Generating Dynamic Content*, with a syntax error.

Example 7-1. Improperly Terminated Directive (error1.jsp)

```
<%@ page language="java" contentType="text/html" >
<html>
<body bgcolor="white">
<jsp:useBean id="clock" class="java.util.Date" />

The current time at the server is:
<ul>
<li>Date: <jsp:getProperty name="clock" property="date" />
<li>Month: <jsp:getProperty name="clock" property="month" />
<li>Year: <jsp:getProperty name="clock" property="year" />
<li>Hours: <jsp:getProperty name="clock" property="hours" />
<li>Minutes: <jsp:getProperty name="clock" property="minutes" />
</ul>

</body>
</html>
```

The syntax error here is that the page directive on the first line is not closed properly with %>; the percent sign is missing. Figure 7-1 shows what Tomcat has to say about it.

Tomcat reports the error by sending an error message to the browser. This is the default behavior for Tomcat, but it's not mandated by the JSP specification. The specification requires only that a response with the HTTP status code for a severe error (500) is returned, but how a JSP container reports the details is vendor-specific. For instance, the error message can be written to a file instead of to the browser. If you use a container other than Tomcat, check the container documentation to see how it reports these types of errors.

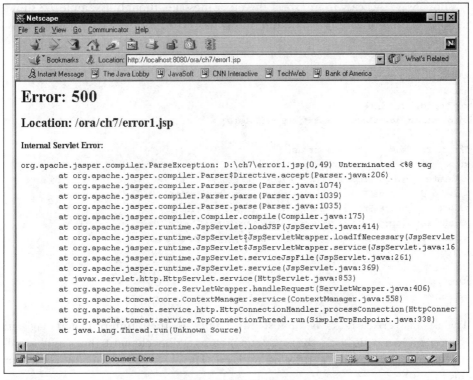

Figure 7-1. Error message about an unterminated JSP directive

The actual error message in Figure 7-1 is what is called an exception stack trace. When something goes really wrong in a Java method, it typically *throws an exception.* An exception is a special Java object, and throwing an exception is the method's way of saying it doesn't know how to handle a problem. Sometimes another part of the program can take care of the problem in a graceful manner, but in many cases the best that can be done is to tell the user about it and move on. That's what the Tomcat container does when it finds a problem with a JSP page during the translation phase: it sends the exception stack trace to the browser. The stack trace contains a message about what went wrong and where the problem occurred. The message is intended to be informative enough for a user to understand, but the actual trace information is of value only to a programmer. As you can see in Figure 7-1, the message is:

```
D:\ch7\error1.jsp(0,49) Unterminated <%@ tag
```

The first part of the message is the name of the JSP page. The numbers within parentheses indicate on which line and character position in the file the error was found (both the line and the position are numbered from 0), and then the message states what the problem is. So this message tells us that a directive on the first line (a tag starting with <@) is not terminated as expected at position 49. And in this case it's both the correct diagnosis and the right location.

It's not always this easy to interpret the error message, though. Example 7-2 shows another version of *date.jsp* with a different syntax error.

Example 7-2. Improperly Terminated Action (error2.jsp)

```
<%@ page language="java" contentType="text/html" %>
<html>
<body bgcolor="white">
<jsp:useBean id="clock" class="java.util.Date" >

The current time at the server is:
<ul>
<li>Date: <jsp:getProperty name="clock" property="date" />
<li>Month: <jsp:getProperty name="clock" property="month" />
<li>Year: <jsp:getProperty name="clock" property="year" />
<li>Hours: <jsp:getProperty name="clock" property="hours" />
<li>Minutes: <jsp:getProperty name="clock" property="minutes" />
</ul>

</body>
</html>
```

The syntax error here is almost the same as the "unterminated tag" in Example 7-1, but now it's the `<jsp:useBean>` action element that's not terminated properly (it's missing the closing slash). The message reported by Tomcat in this case is:

```
D:\ch7\error2.jsp(16,0) useBean tag must begin and end in the same
physical file
```

This is not as easy to relate to the actual location of the error. The line and position information points to the last character in the file. The reason for this is that since the action element doesn't have a body, the opening tag must end with `/>`, as you may remember from Chapter 5. But in Example 7-2, it's terminated with just `>`. Since that's valid syntax for a JSP action that contains a body, the JSP container can't tell that it's a syntax error at this point. Instead it treats it as the opening tag for an element with a body, and complains that it can't find the closing tag before the file ends. In this case, it's still not too hard to figure out what the real problem is, but if you have multiple `<jsp:useBean>` elements in the same file, it can be more complicated.

Another common error is a typo in an attribute name, as shown in Example 7-3. In the first `<jsp:getProperty>` action, the name attribute is missing the e.

Example 7-3. Mistyped Attribute Name (error3.jsp)

```
<%@ page language="java" contentType="text/html" %>
<html>
<body bgcolor="white">
<jsp:useBean id="clock" class="java.util.Date" />
```

Example 7-3. Mistyped Attribute Name (error3.jsp) (continued)

```
The current time at the server is:
<ul>
<li>Date: <jsp:getProperty nam="clock" property="date" />
<li>Month: <jsp:getProperty name="clock" property="month" />
<li>Year: <jsp:getProperty name="clock" property="year" />
<li>Hours: <jsp:getProperty name="clock" property="hours" />
<li>Minutes: <jsp:getProperty name="clock" property="minutes" />
</ul>

</body>
</html>
```

Tomcat reports the problem like this:

```
D:\ch7\error3.jsp(7,10) getProperty: Mandatory attribute name missing
```

In this case, the typo is in the name of a mandatory attribute, so Tomcat reports it as missing. If the typo is in the name of an optional attribute, Tomcat reports it as an invalid attribute name.

The examples here are the most common ones for JSP actions, and as you can see, Tomcat can give you pretty good information about what's wrong in these cases. But this is still an area where I expect many improvements to be implemented in later versions of Tomcat as well as other JSP containers. The JSP authoring tools that are emerging now also help. By providing GUI-based interfaces that generate the action elements automatically, they can eliminate this type of syntax problem.

Scripting Syntax Errors

So far, so good, right? Not quite. Unfortunately, syntax errors in scripting elements result in error messages that are much harder to interpret. This is because of the way the JSP container deals with scripting code when it converts a JSP page into a servlet. The container reads the JSP page and generates servlet code by replacing all JSP directives and actions with code that produces the appropriate result. To do this, it needs to analyze these types of elements in detail. If there's a syntax error in a directive or action element, it can easily tell which element is incorrect (as you saw in the previous section).

Scripting elements, on the other hand, are more or less used as-is in the generated servlet code. A syntax error in scripting code is not discovered when the JSP page is read, but instead when the generated servlet is compiled. The compiler reports an error in terms of its location in the generated servlet code (as opposed to the location in the JSP page), with messages that don't always make sense to a JSP page author. Let's look at some examples to illustrate this.

Example 7-4 shows a modified version of the *greeting.jsp* page from Chapter 6, *Using Scripting Elements.* The last scriptlet, with a brace closing the last `else` block, is missing.

Example 7-4. Missing End Brace (error4.jsp)

```
<%@ page language="java" contentType="text/html" %>
<html>
<body bgcolor="white">
<jsp:useBean id="clock" class="java.util.Date" />

<% if (clock.getHours() < 12) { %>
  Good morning!
<% } else if (clock.getHours() < 17) { %>
  Good day!
<% } else { %>
  Good evening!

</body>
</html>
```

This is the error description Tomcat sends to the browser (with some line breaks added to make it fit the page):

```
org.apache.jasper.JasperException: Unable to compile class for JSP
D:\tmp\Tomcat\jakarta-tomcat\work\localhost_8080%2Fora\
_0002fch_00037_0002ferror_00034_0002ejsperror4_jsp_0.java:105:
'catch' without 'try'.
        } catch (Exception ex) {
          ^
D:\tmp\Tomcat\jakarta-tomcat\work\localhost_8080%2Fora\
_0002fch_00037_0002ferror_00034_0002ejsperror4_jsp_0.java:114:
'try' without 'catch' or 'finally'.
}
^
D:\tmp\Tomcat\jakarta-tomcat\work\localhost_8080%2Fora\
_0002fch_00037_0002ferror_00034_0002ejsperror4_jsp_0.java:114:
'}' expected.
}
  ^
3 errors
```

This message probably doesn't make much sense to you. First of all, the filename is not the name of the JSP page, it's the name of the generated servlet, which contains sequence numbers and special encodings to make it a unique filename. Part of the name corresponds to the JSP page name, but a different JSP container than Tomcat may not use the same kind of naming convention, so there's no guarantee that this is true for all containers. Secondly, the line numbers listed are line numbers in the generated servlet source code file, not the line numbers in the JSP file. And lastly, the error message refers to 'catch' without 'try', which doesn't seem to match any code in the JSP page scriptlets. That's because the code with the missing brace is inserted into the block of code that outputs template text, invokes actions, and so forth—so the compiler gets confused about what the real problem is.

How can you find the real problem when you get this type of message? If you know how to program Java, you can look at the generated servlet source file and try to figure out what's really wrong. Most JSP containers can be configured to save the generated source code for you to look at. For Tomcat, it's the default behavior, and the complete name of the file is shown in the error message.

But if you're not a programmer, the only thing you can do is to study all scriptlets in your JSP page carefully and try to figure out what's wrong. That's not always easy, and it's yet another reason to avoid scripting in your JSP pages in the first place. When you have to use scripting, use only extremely simple code and be very careful with the syntax.

Let's look at couple of other common syntax errors so you at least know the types of messages to expect. Example 7-5 shows a version of the *browser.jsp* file from Chapter 6 in which a closing parenthesis for the first if statement is missing.

Example 7-5. Missing Closing Parenthesis (error5.jsp)

```
<%@ page language="java" contentType="text/html" %>
<html>
<body bgcolor="white">

<% if (request.getHeader("User-Agent").indexOf("MSIE") != -1 { %>
  You're using Internet Explorer.
<%
    } else
      if (request.getHeader("User-Agent").indexOf("Mozilla") != 1) {
%>
  You're using Netscape.
<% } else { %>
  You're using a browser I don't know about.
<% } %>

</body>
</html>
```

The error message for this type of error is a bit easier to understand:

```
org.apache.jasper.JasperException: Unable to compile class for JSP
D:\tmp\Tomcat\jakarta-tomcat\work\localhost_8080%2Fora\
_0002fch_00037_0002ferror_00035_0002ejsperror5_jsp_0.java:61:
')' expected.
    if (request.getHeader("User-Agent").indexOf("MSIE") != -1 {
                                                              ^
```

```
D:\tmp\Tomcat\jakarta-tomcat\work\localhost_8080%2Fora\
_0002fch_00037_0002ferror_00035_0002ejsperror5_jsp_0.java:68:
'else' without 'if'.
    } else
      ^
2 errors
```

Here the syntax error doesn't cause any strange side effect errors when the scripting code is combined with other generated code, as the error in Example 7-4 did. Instead, the message shows the code fragment where the real error is located.

Another typical mistake is shown in Example 7-6. It's a part of the *reqinfo.jsp* page from Chapter 6.

Example 7-6. Scriptlet Instead of Expression (error6.jsp)

```
<%@ page language="java" contentType="text/html" %>
<html>
<body bgcolor="white">

  The following information was received:
  <ul>
    <li>Request Method: <%= request.getMethod() %>
    <li>Request URI: <% request.getRequestURI() %>
    <li>Request Protocol: <%= request.getProtocol() %>
  </ul>
</body>
</html>
```

This is simply a case where the opening tag for a JSP expression (<%=) has been mistakenly written as the opening tag for a JSP scriptlet (<%). It looks like an innocent error, but the error message does not give you much help to find it:

```
org.apache.jasper.JasperException: Unable to compile class for JSP
D:\tmp\Tomcat\jakarta-tomcat\work\localhost_8080%2Fora\
_0002fch_00037_0002ferror_00036_0002ejsperror6_jsp_0.java:67:
Invalid type expression.
                   request.getRequestURI()
                            ^
D:\tmp\Tomcat\jakarta-tomcat\work\localhost_8080%2Fora\
_0002fch_00037_0002ferror_00036_0002ejsperror6_jsp_0.java:70:
Invalid declaration.
              out.write("\r\n
  Request Protocol: ");
                 ^
2 errors
```

Again, the scripting code and the generated code clash, resulting in a message that's hard to understand; but at least you can recognize the code from the JSP page and try to see what's really wrong.

The misleading and confusing error messages reported for scripting syntax errors are, in my opinion, a big problem, and one that's hard to solve completely, even with better JSP container implementations and tools. It can be minimized, for instance by providing information about where in the JSP page the error is introduced, but it's always hard for a container to pinpoint the real problem when scripting code is mixed with other generated code. My only advice at this point is (again) to avoid scripting code as much as possible.

Debugging a JSP-Based Application

After you have fixed all syntax errors, pat yourself on the back and enjoy the moment. If the application is more than a trivial example, however, this moment will probably be short-lived: you will likely find that one or more things still don't work as you expected. Logic errors, such as not taking care of all possible input combinations, can easily slip into an application during development. Finding and correcting this type of problem is called debugging.

For applications developed in compiled languages such as Java, C, or C++, a tool called a debugger is often used in this phase. A debugger steps through the program line by line or runs until it reaches a break point that you have defined, and lets you inspect the values of all variables in the program. With careful analysis of the program flow in runtime, you can discover why it works the way it does, and not the way you want it to. There are debuggers for JSP as well, such as IBM's Visual Age for Java. This product lets you debug a JSP page exactly the same way as you would a program written in a more traditional programming language.

But a real debugger is often overkill for JSP pages. If your pages are so complex that you feel you need a debugger, you may want to move code from the pages into JavaBeans or custom actions instead. These components can then be debugged with a standard Java debugger, which can be found in most Java Interactive Development Environments (IDEs). To debug JSP pages, another time-tested debugging approach is usually sufficient: simply add code to print variable values to the screen.

Example 7-7 shows how you can use this approach to find an error in a modified version of the *browser.jsp* page from Chapter 6.

Example 7-7. Testing Header Values in the Wrong Order (browser.jsp)

```
<%@ page language="java" contentType="text/html" %>
<html>
<body bgcolor="white">

<% if (request.getHeader("User-Agent").indexOf("Mozilla") != -1) { %>
  You're using Netscape.
```

Example 7-7. Testing Header Values in the Wrong Order (browser.jsp) (continued)

```
<%
  } else
    if (request.getHeader("User-Agent").indexOf("MSIE") != 1) {
%>
  You're using Internet Explorer.
<% } else { %>
  You're using a browser I don't know about.
<% } %>


</body>
</html>
```

If you run this example in a Netscape browser, it responds with "You're using Netscape," as expected. The problem is that if you run it with Internet Explorer, you get the same response. Clearly there's something wrong with the way the User-Agent header value is tested.

To find out why it doesn't work with Internet Explorer, you can add a one-line JSP expression that includes the value of the User-Agent header in the response:

```
<%@ page language="java" contentType="text/html" %>
<html>
<body bgcolor="white">

User-Agent header value: <%= request.getHeader("User-Agent") %>
<p>
...
```

The result is shown in Figure 7-2.

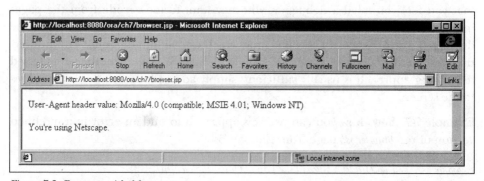

Figure 7-2. Response with debug output

Now it's clear why it doesn't work: the User-Agent header value set by Internet Explorer also contains the string "Mozilla". So the test in the JSP page must be reversed, first looking for the string "MSIE" (to identify Internet Explorer) and looking for "Mozilla" only if it's not found.

Adding a couple of JSP expressions to see variable values as part of the response in the browser is the easiest way to debug a JSP page. But sometimes multiple pages are involved in the processing of a single request, as you will see in Chapter 8, *Sharing Data Between JSP Pages, Requests, and Users*. In this case, it may be better to write the debug output to a file or the command window where you started the server instead. To write to the standard log file for the server, replace the JSP expression with this scriptlet:

```
<% application.log("User-Agent header value: " +
        request.getHeader("User-Agent")); %>
```

The `application` variable is one of the implicit JSP objects described in Chapter 6, containing a reference to the `javax.servlet.ServletContext` object for the application. It provides a `log()` method that writes messages to the application log file. The name and location of the file are server-dependent. With a default configuration of Tomcat, it's named *logs/servlet.log*.

Most servers, including Tomcat, also let you write messages to the window where the server was started, represented by the `System.out` object:

```
<% System.out.println("User-Agent header value: " +
        request.getHeader("User-Agent")); %>
```

This approach works fine during development, when you run your own web server started in a command window, but you need to remember to remove these lines in your production code. Writing to the log file is useful when you debug an application that is running in a web server you don't have control over, or if you need to record the debug messages in a file for further analysis later.

To make it easier to generate the most common types of debug output, you can use the `DebugBean` class that I developed for this book. Its properties represent information that's available in a JSP page, as shown in Table 7-1.

Table 7-1. Properties of com.ora.jsp.util.DebugBean

Property Name	Java Type	Access	Description
pageContext	javax.servlet. jsp.PageContext	write	Must be set in order for the bean to find the value of its other properties
elapsedTime	String	read	A string with the number of milliseconds elapsed since the bean was created or this property was last read
requestInfo	String	read	A string, formatted as a table, with information about the request, such as authentication type, content length and encoding, path information, remote host and user, etc.

Table 7-1. Properties of com.ora.jsp.util.DebugBean (continued)

Property Name	Java Type	Access	Description
headers	String	read	A string, formatted as a table, with the names and values of all headers received with the request
cookies	String	read	A string, formatted as a table, with the names and values of all cookies received with the request
parameters	String	read	A string, formatted as a table, with the names and values of all parameters received with the request
pageScope	String	read	A string, formatted as a table, with the names and values of all page scope variables
requestScope	String	read	A string, formatted as a table, with the names and values of all request scope variables
sessionScope	String	read	A string, formatted as a table, with the names and values of all session scope variables
applicationScope	String	read	A string, formatted as a table, with the names and values of all application scope variables

The DebugBean has one write-only property, pageContext, that must be set to the corresponding implicit object to provide the bean access to all the information it can report on. All the other properties are read-only, providing access to different subsets of information of interest when debugging a JSP application.

To control where the information is written, pass a debug parameter with the request for the page with the bean. This parameter must have one or more of the following values (separated by plus signs):

resp
    Include the debug information in the response as an HTML table

stdout
    Write the debug information to System.out

log
    Write the debug information to the application log file

Let's look at an example. The JSP page shown in Example 7-8 creates an instance of the DebugBean using a <jsp:useBean> action. It also sets the mandatory pageContext property using a nested <jsp:setProperty> action. The <jsp:setProperty> uses a request-time attribute value to assign the pageContext property a reference to the implicit pageContext variable.

Example 7-8. Page with the DebugBean (debug.jsp)

```
<%@ page language="java" contentType="text/html" %>
<%@ page import="java.util.*" %>
<html>
<body bgcolor="white">

  <jsp:useBean id="debug" class="com.ora.jsp.util.DebugBean" >
    <jsp:setProperty name="debug" property="pageContext"
      value="<%= pageContext %>"
    />
  </jsp:useBean>
  <p>

  <%-- Add test variables to the request scope --%>
  <%
    String[] arr = {"a", "b", "c"};
    request.setAttribute("arr", arr);
    java.util.Date date = new Date();
    request.setAttribute("now", date);
  %>

  <jsp:getProperty name="debug" property="headers" />
  <jsp:getProperty name="debug" property="cookies" />
  <jsp:getProperty name="debug" property="parameters" />
  <jsp:getProperty name="debug" property="requestScope" />
  <jsp:getProperty name="debug" property="elapsedTime" />

</body>
</html>
```

A scriptlet is used to set two request attributes, referred to in JSP as placing objects in the *request scope*. Objects placed in the request scope can be accessed by all JSP pages used to process the same request. Don't worry about how this works now; you'll learn more about all the JSP scopes in Chapter 8. Here, it's only used to show you how the DebugBean displays scope information. Next, five <jsp:getProperty> actions are used to display the headers, cookies, parameters, requestScope, and elapsedTime properties.

The DebugBean returns its property values only if the request contains a debug parameter with a valid value. Therefore, you can keep the bean in your pages all the time and activate it only when you need the debug info. If you request the page with the URL:

http://localhost:8080/ora/ch7/debug.jsp?debug=resp+stdout&a=b

you get the response shown in Figure 7-3.

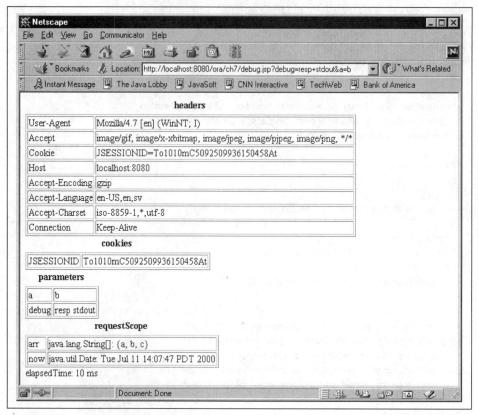

Figure 7-3. Debug output

Since the debug parameter specifies both `resp` and `stdout`, you also get all the debug information in the window where you started Tomcat.

Dealing with Runtime Errors

Eventually, your application will work as you like. But things can still go wrong due to problems with external systems that your application depends on, such as a database. And even though you have tested and debugged your application, there may be runtime conditions that you didn't anticipate.

Well-behaved components such as JavaBeans or JSP actions (standard and custom) deal with expected error conditions in a graceful manner. For instance, the `UserInfo` bean used in Chapter 5 has a `valid` attribute that is `false` unless all properties are set to valid values. Your JSP page can then test the property value and present the user with an appropriate message.

But if something happens that makes it impossible for the component to do its job, it needs to tell the user about the problem. The standard way Java does this is to throw an exception. That's what the JSP container does when it finds a problem with a JSP page during the translation phase, as I described in the first section of this chapter. Components, such as JavaBeans and JSP actions, and the code in JSP scripting elements, can also throw exceptions when something goes really wrong. By default, the JSP container catches the exception and displays its message and stack trace in the browser, similar to what's shown in Figure 7-1. But that's hardly the type of error message you want the application users to see. It's better to tell the JSP container to use a customized error page instead.

Example 7-9 shows a JSP page with a page directive that defines an error page.

Example 7-9. Page with an Error Page Definition (calc.jsp)

```
<%@ page language="java" contentType="text/html" %>
<%@ page errorPage="errorpage.jsp?debug=log" %>
<% request.setAttribute("sourcePage", request.getRequestURI()); %>
<html>
<body bgcolor="white">

  <jsp:useBean id="calc" class="com.ora.jsp.beans.calc.CalcBean">
    <jsp:setProperty name="calc" property="*" />
  </jsp:useBean>

  <%-- Calculate the new numbers and state info --%>
  <% String currentNumber = calc.getCurrentNumber(); %>
  <form action="calc.jsp" method="post">
    <table border=1>
      <tr>
        <td colspan="4" align="right">
          <%= currentNumber.equals("") ? " " :
            currentNumber %>
          <input type="hidden" name="currentNumber"
            value="<%= currentNumber %>">
          <input type="hidden" name="previousNumber"
            value="<%= calc.getPreviousNumber() %>">
          <input type="hidden" name="currentOperation"
            value="<%= calc.getCurrentOperation() %>">
          <input type="hidden" name="previousOperation"
            value="<%= calc.getPreviousOperation() %>">
          <input type="hidden" name="reset"
            value="<%= calc.getReset() %>">
        </td>
      </tr>
      <tr>
        <td><input type="submit" name="digit" value=" 7 "></td>
        <td><input type="submit" name="digit" value=" 8 "></td>
        <td><input type="submit" name="digit" value=" 9 "></td>
        <td><input type="submit" name="oper" value=" / "></td>
      </tr>
```

Example 7-9. Page with an Error Page Definition (calc.jsp) (continued)

```
  <tr>
    <td><input type="submit" name="digit" value=" 4 "></td>
    <td><input type="submit" name="digit" value=" 5 "></td>
    <td><input type="submit" name="digit" value=" 6 "></td>
    <td><input type="submit" name="oper" value=" * "></td>
  </tr>
  <tr>
    <td><input type="submit" name="digit" value=" 1 "></td>
    <td><input type="submit" name="digit" value=" 2 "></td>
    <td><input type="submit" name="digit" value=" 3 "></td>
    <td><input type="submit" name="oper" value=" - "></td>
  </tr>
  <tr>
    <td><input type="submit" name="digit" value=" 0 "></td>
    <td> </td>
    <td><input type="submit" name="dot" value=" . "></td>
    <td><input type="submit" name="oper" value=" + "></td>
  </tr>
  <tr>
    <td> </td>
    <td> </td>
    <td><input type="submit" name="clear" value=" C "></td>
    <td><input type="submit" name="oper" value=" = "></td>
  </table>
  </form>

</body>
</html>
```

The `errorPage` attribute in the page directive specifies the URL path for the page displayed if an exception is thrown by any component or scripting code. In JSP 1.1, you cannot specify a regular HTML page as the error page; it must be another JSP page. When the path is specified as in Example 7-9, the error page must be located in the same directory as the page that references it. However, if it starts with a slash (/), it's interpreted as relative to the application's *context path*. The context path is simply the root for all HTML, image, and JSP pages in an application, such as *C:\Jakarta\jakarta-tomcat\webapps\ora* for the application containing all book examples (if you installed it in the directory specified in Chapter 4, *Setting Up the JSP Environment*). This means you can define a common error page for all the JSP pages in an application, even if you place them in multiple subdirectories, by using a path like `/errorpage.jsp`.

Also note that the error page URL in Example 7-9 includes the `debug` request parameter, and that a scriptlet is used to set a request attribute:

```
<%@ page errorPage="errorpage.jsp?debug=log" %>
<% request.setAttribute("sourcePage", request.getRequestURI()); %>
```

The `debug` parameter lets you use the `DebugBean` to log information about what went wrong in the error page. The `sourcePage` attribute, set to the URL for the current page, is also used in the error page, as you will see shortly.

The rest of the page in Example 7-9 implements a simple calculator, shown in Figure 7-4. It's intended only to illustrate how the error page handling works, so I will not describe it in detail. When you're done reading this book, it might be a good exercise to figure it out yourself by looking at the source code.

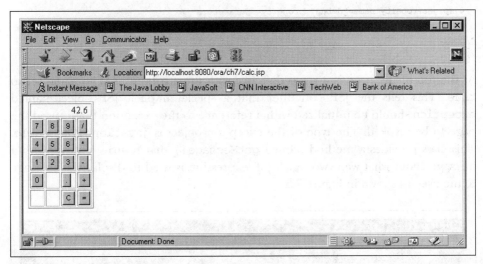

Figure 7-4. Calculator page

If a user tries to divide a number by zero, the `CalcBean` used in this page to implement the calculator throws an exception. This triggers the error page shown in Example 7-10 to be invoked.

Example 7-10. Error Page (errorpage.jsp)

```
<%@ page language="java" contentType="text/html" %>
<%@ page isErrorPage="true" %>
<html>
<body bgcolor="white">
  We're sorry but the request could not be processed. The processing
  error message is:
  <blockquote>
  <%= exception.getMessage() %>
  </blockquote>
  The message has been logged together with more detailed information
  about the error so we can analyze it further. Please try again, and
  <a href="mailto:webmaster@mycompany.com">let us know</a> if the
  problem persists.
```

Example 7-10. Error Page (errorpage.jsp) (continued)

```
<%
  application.log((String) request.getAttribute("sourcePage"),
    exception);
%>
<jsp:useBean id="debug" class="com.ora.jsp.util.DebugBean">
  <jsp:setProperty name="debug" property="pageContext"
    value="<%= pageContext %>" />
</jsp:useBean>
<jsp:getProperty name="debug" property="parameters" />


</body>
</html>
```

At the top of the page is a `page` directive with the attribute `isErrorPage` set to `true`. This tells the JSP container that a special implicit JSP object named `exception` should be initialized with a reference to the exception that caused the page to be invoked. The type of the exception object is `java.lang.Throwable`. This class provides a method named `getMessage()` that returns a string with a message about what went wrong. A JSP expression is used to display this message to the user, as shown in Figure 7-5.

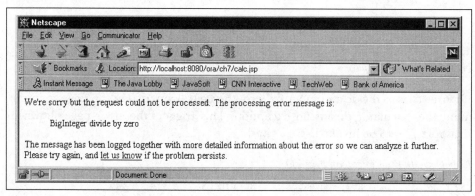

Figure 7-5. Customized error page

Next follows a scriptlet and a couple of actions to create and use the `DebugBean` introduced in the previous section. The scriptlet writes the value of the `sourcePage` request attribute plus the exception itself to the application log file, and the `DebugBean` writes all parameters received with the request to the same file. In this way, information about which page caused the problem, the exception that was thrown, and all parameter values that were received with the request causing the problem is logged in the application log file when something unexpected happens. You can therefore look at the log file from time to time and see what kinds of problems occur frequently, and hopefully fine-tune the application to avoid them or at least provide more specific error messages.

Dealing with syntax errors and bugs is part of the application development process. In this chapter, we have looked at some of the ways you can ease the pain. To minimize syntax errors, you can use the types of JSP development tools listed in Appendix E, *JSP Resource Reference*, that provide JSP syntax highlighting. You can also minimize the scripting code you put in your JSP pages by using beans and custom actions instead. The DebugBean presented in this chapter helps you to see what's going on at runtime, and you can use it in a customized error page to log information about unexpected errors.

8

Sharing Data Between JSP Pages, Requests, and Users

So far we've covered the JSP basics: how to generate dynamic content and capture user input using JSP standard action elements for working with beans, how to do conditional processing and embed Java code in pages using JSP scripting elements, and how to locate and fix different types of errors in a JSP page. With that out of the way, we can turn our attention to the JSP features and techniques needed to develop real applications.

Any real application consists of more than a single page, and multiple pages often need access to the same information and server-side resources. When multiple pages are used to process the same request, for instance one page that retrieves the data the user asked for and another that displays it, there must be a way to pass data from one page to another. In an application in which the user is asked to provide information in multiple steps, such as an online shopping application, there must be a way to collect the information received with each request and get access to the complete set when the user is ready. Other information and resources need to be shared among multiple pages, requests, and all users. Examples are information about currently logged-in users, database connection pool objects, and cache objects to avoid frequent database lookups.

In this chapter you will learn how scopes in JSP provide access to this type of shared data. You will also see how using multiple pages to process a request leads to an application that's easier to maintain and expand, and learn about a JSP action that lets you pass control between the different pages.

Passing Control and Data Between Pages

As discussed in Chapter 3, *JSP Overview*, one of the most fundamental features of JSP technology is that it allows for separation of request processing, business logic, and presentation, using what's known as the Model-View-Controller (MVC) model. As you may recall, the roles of Model, View, and Controller can be assigned to different types of server-side components. In this part of the book, JSP pages are used for both the Controller and View roles, and the Model role is played by either a bean or a JSP page. This is not necessarily the best approach, but it lets us focus on JSP features instead of getting into Java programming. If you're a programmer and interested in other role assignments, you may want to take a peek at Chapter 13, *Web Application Models*, and Chapter 14, *Combining Servlets and JSP*. These chapters describe other alternatives and focus on using a servlet as the Controller.

Using different JSP pages as Controller and View means that more than one page is used to process a request. To make this happen, you need to be able to do two things:

1. Pass control from one page to another.

2. Pass data from one page to another.

In this section, we look at a concrete example of how to separate the different aspects of an application and how JSP supports the two requirements above.

Let's revisit the User Info example developed in Chapter 5, *Generating Dynamic Content*, to describe how the different aspects of an application can be separated. In this example, the business logic piece is trivial. However, it sets the stage for more advanced application examples in the next section and the remaining chapters in this part of the book, all using the model introduced here.

We can categorize the different aspects of the User Info example like this:

- Display the form for user input (presentation).

- Validate the input (request processing and business logic).

- Display the result of the validation (presentation).

Let's use a separate JSP page for each aspect. The restructured application contains three JSP pages, as shown in Figure 8-1.

Here's how it works. The *userinfoinput.jsp* page displays an input form. The user submits this form to *userinputvalidate.jsp* to validate the input. This page processes the request using the UserInfoBean and passes control (forwards) to either the *userinfoinput.jsp* page (if the input is invalid) or the *userinfovalid.jsp* page (if the input is valid). If valid, the *userinfovalid.jsp* page displays a "thank you" message. In this example, the UserInfoBean represents the Model, the *userinputvalidate.jsp* page the Controller, and *userinfoinput.jsp* and *userinfovalid.jsp* represent the Views.

This gives you the flexibility and maintainability discussed in Chapter 3. If the validation rules change, a Java programmer can change the UserInfoBean implementation without touching any other part of the application. If the

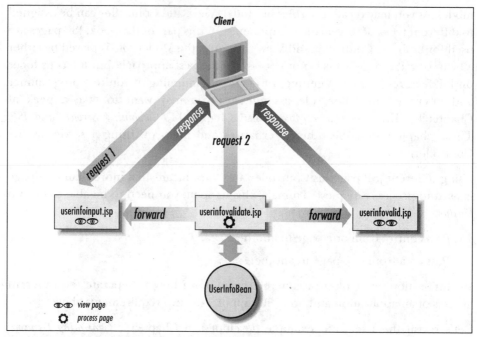

Figure 8-1. User Info application pages

customer wants a different look, a page author can modify the View JSP pages without touching the request processing or business logic code.

Passing Control from One Page to Another

Before digging into the modified example pages, let's go through the basic mechanisms. As shown in Figure 8-1, the *userinfovalidate.jsp* page passes control to one of two other pages based on the result of the input validation. JSP supports this through the <jsp:forward> action:

```
<jsp:forward page="userinfovalid.jsp" />
```

This action stops processing one page and starts processing the page specified by the page attribute instead, called the *target page*. The control never returns to the original page.

The target page has access to all information about the request, including all request parameters. You can also add additional request parameters when you pass control to another page by using one or more nested <jsp:param> action elements:

```
<jsp:forward page="userinfovalid.jsp" >
  <jsp:param name="msg" value="Invalid email address" />
</jsp:forward>
```

Parameters specified with `<jsp:param>` elements are added to the parameters received with the original request. The target page, therefore, has access to both the original parameters and the new ones, and can access both types in the same way. If a parameter is added to the request using the name of a parameter that already exists, the new value is added to the list of values for the existing parameter.

The `page` attribute is interpreted relative to the location of the current page if it doesn't start with /. This is called a *page-relative path*. If the source and target page are located in the same directory, just use the name of the target page as the `page` attribute value, as in the previous example. You can also refer to a file in a different directory using notation like *../foo/bar.jsp* or */foo/bar.jsp*. When the page reference starts with /, it's interpreted relative to the top directory for the application's web page files. This is called a *context-relative path*.

Let's look at some concrete examples to make this clear. If the application's top directory is *C:\Tomcat\webapps\myapp*, page references in a JSP page located in *C:\Tomcat\webapps\myapp\registration\userinfo* are interpreted like this:

`page="bar.jsp"`
> *C:\Tomcat\webapps\myapp\registration\userinfo\bar.jsp*

`page="../foo/bar.jsp"`
> *C:\Tomcat\webapps\myapp\registration\foo\bar.jsp*

`page="/foo/bar.jsp"`
> *C:\Tomcat\webapps\myapp\foo\bar.jsp*

Passing Data from One Page to Another

JSP provides different *scopes* for sharing data objects between pages, requests, and users. The scope defines for how long the object is available and whether it's available only to one user or to all application users. The following scopes are defined:

- Page
- Request
- Session
- Application

Objects placed in the default scope, the *page scope*, are available only to actions and scriptlets within one page. That's the scope used in all examples you have seen so far. The *request scope* is for objects that need to be available to all pages processing the same request. The *session scope* is for objects shared by multiple requests by the same user, and the *application scope* is for objects shared by all users of the application. See Figure 8-2.

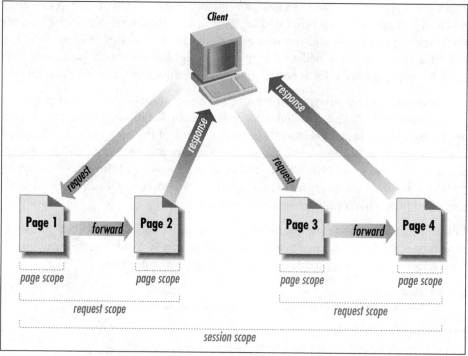

Figure 8-2. Lifetime of objects in different scopes

The `<jsp:useBean>` action has a `scope` attribute that you use to specify in what scope the bean should be placed. Here is an example:

```
<jsp:useBean id="userInfo" scope="request"
    class="com.ora.jsp.beans.userinfo.UserInfoBean" />
```

The `<jsp:useBean>` action looks for a bean with the name specified by the `id` attribute in the specified scope. If one already exists, it uses that one. If it cannot find one, it creates a new instance of the class specified by the `class` attribute and makes it available with the specified name within the specified scope. If you would like to perform an action only when the bean is created, place the elements in the body of the `<jsp:useBean>` action:

```
<jsp:useBean id="userInfo" scope="request"
    class="com.ora.jsp.beans.userinfo.UserInfoBean" >
    <jsp:setProperty name="userInfo" property="*" />
</jsp:useBean>
```

In this example, the nested `<jsp:setProperty>` action sets all properties when the bean is created. If the bean already exists, the `<jsp:useBean>` action associates it with the name specified by the `id` attribute so it can be accessed by other actions and scripting code. In this case, the `<jsp:setProperty>` action is not executed.

All Together Now

At this point, you have seen the two mechanisms needed to let multiple pages process the same request: passing control and passing data. These mechanisms allow you to employ the MVC design, using one page for request processing and business logic, and another for presentation. The <jsp:forward> action can be used to pass control between the pages, and information placed in the request scope is available to all pages processing the same request.

Let's apply this to the User Info example. In Chapter 5, different output was produced depending on whether or not the user input was valid. This was done by using a UserInfoBean property called propertyStatusMsg to display either a success or failure message. Yet the input form was always shown, even when the input was valid.

No more of that. When we split up the different aspects of the application into separate JSP pages as shown in Figure 8-1, we will also change the example so that the form is shown only when something needs to be corrected. When all input is valid a confirmation page is shown instead.

Example 8-1 shows the top part of the *userinfoinput.jsp* page.

Example 8-1. Page for Displaying Entry Form (userinfoinput.jsp)

```
<%@ page language="java" contentType="text/html" %>
<html>
  <head>
    <title>User Info Entry Form</title>
  </head>
  <body bgcolor="white">

    <jsp:useBean
      id="userInfo"
      scope="request"
      class="com.ora.jsp.beans.userinfo.UserInfoBean" />

    <%-- Output list of values with invalid format, if any --%>
    <font color="red">
      <jsp:getProperty name="userInfo" property="propertyStatusMsg" />
    </font>

    <%-- Output form with submitted valid values --%>
    <form action="userinfovalidate.jsp" method="post">
      <table>
        <tr>
          <td>Name:</td>
          <td><input type="text" name="userName"
```

Example 8-1. Page for Displaying Entry Form (userinfoinput.jsp) (continued)

```
    value="<%= StringFormat.toHTMLString(userInfo.getUserName()) %>" >
        </td>
      </tr>
      ...
```

The rest of the example is the same as before. If you compare Example 8-1 with the JSP page used in Chapter 5, the only differences are that the `userInfo` bean is placed in the request scope (the `scope` attribute is set to `request`) and the form's `action` attribute is set to the URL for the validation page instead of pointing back to the same page.

The validation page, *userinfovalidate.jsp*, is given in Example 8-2.

Example 8-2. Input Validation Page (userinfovalidate.jsp)

```
<%@ page language="java" %>
<jsp:useBean
  id="userInfo"
  scope="request"
  class="com.ora.jsp.beans.userinfo.UserInfoBean" >
  <jsp:setProperty name="userInfo" property="*" />
</jsp:useBean>

<% if (userInfo.isValid()) { %>

  <jsp:forward page="userinfovalid.jsp" />

<% } else { %>

  <jsp:forward page="userinfoinput.jsp" />

<% } %>
```

This is the request processing page, using the bean to perform the business logic. Note that there's no HTML at all in this page, only a page directive specifying the scripting language, action elements, and scriptlets. This is typical of a request processing page: it doesn't produce a visible response message, it simply takes care of business and passes control to the appropriate presentation page.

This example is relatively simple. We first create a new `userInfo Bean` named `userInfo` in the request scope and set its properties from the request parameters of the previous form. (Note that we don't obtain the data from an already existing `userInfo Bean` in that scope; we'll see why shortly.) A scriptlet calls the bean's `isValid()` method to validate the properties and uses the `<jsp:forward>` action to pass control to the appropriate View page.

If the input is invalid, the *userinfoinput.jsp* page is used again. This time the <jsp: useBean> action finds the existing userInfo bean in the request scope, and its properties are used to show an error message and fill out the fields that were entered correctly, if any. If all input is valid, the control is passed to the *userinfovalid.jsp* page shown in Example 8-3 to present the "thank you" message.

Example 8-3. Valid Input Message Page (userinfovalid.jsp)

```
<html>
  <head>
    <title>User Info Validated</title>
  </head>
  <body bgcolor="white">
    <font color=green size=+3>
      Thanks for entering valid information!
    </font>
  </body>
</html>
```

This page tells the user all input was correct. It consists only of template text, so this could have been a regular HTML file. Making it a JSP page allows you to add dynamic content later without changing the referring page, however. The results are shown in Figure 8-3.

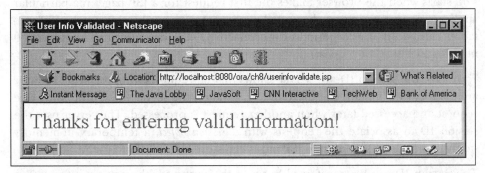

Figure 8-3. The valid input message page

Let's review how placing the bean in the request scope lets you access the same bean in all pages. The user first requests the *userinfoinput.jsp* page (Example 8-1). A new instance of the userInfo bean is created in the request scope and used to generate the "enter all fields" status message. The user fills out the form and submits it as a new request to the *userinfovalidate.jsp* page (Example 8-2). The previous bean is then out of scope, so this page creates a new userInfo bean in the request scope and sets all bean properties based on the form field values. If the input is invalid, the <jsp:forward> action passes the control back to the *userinfoinput.jsp* page. Note that we're still processing the same request that initially created the bean and set all the property values. Since the bean is saved in the request scope, the `<jsp:useBean>` action finds it and uses it to generate an appropriate error message and fill out the form with any valid values already entered.

Sharing Session and Application Data

As described in Chapter 2, *HTTP and Servlet Basics*, HTTP is a stateless, request-response protocol. This means that the browser sends a request for a web resource, and the web server processes the request and returns a response. The server then forgets this transaction ever happened. So when the same browser sends a new request, the web server has no idea that this request is related to the previous one. This is fine if you're dealing with static files, but it's a problem in an interactive web application. In a travel agency application, for instance, it's important to remember the dates and destination entered to book the flight so the customer doesn't have to enter the same information again when it's time to make hotel and rental car reservations.

The way to solve this problem is to let the server send a piece of information to the browser that the browser then includes in all subsequent requests. This piece of information, called a *session ID*, is used by the server to recognize a set of requests from the same browser as related: in other words, as part of the same *session*. A session starts when the browser makes the first request for a JSP page in a particular application. The session can be ended explicitly by the application, or the JSP container can end it after a period of user inactivity (the default value is typically 30 minutes after the last request).

Thanks to the session ID, the server knows that all requests from the same browser are related. Information can therefore be saved on the server while processing one request and accessed later when another request is processed. The server uses the session ID to associate the requests with a *session object*, a temporary in-memory storage area where servlets and JSP pages can store information.

The session ID can be transferred between the server and browser in a few different ways. The Servlet 2.2 API, which is the foundation for the JSP 1.1 specification, identifies three methods: using cookies, using encoded URLs, and using the session mechanism built into the Secure Socket Layer (SSL), the encryption technology used by HTTPS. SSL-based session tracking is currently not supported by any of the major servlet containers, but all of them support the cookie and URL rewriting techniques. JSP hides most of the details about how the session ID is transferred and how the session object is created and accessed, providing you with the session scope to handle session data at a convenient level of abstraction. Information saved in the session scope is available to all pages requested by the same browser during the lifetime of the session.

However, some information is needed by multiple pages independent of who the current user is. JSP supports access to this type of shared information through another scope, the application scope. Information saved in the application scope by one page can later be accessed by another page, even if the two pages were requested by different users. Examples of information typically shared through the application scope are database connection pool objects, information about currently logged-in users, and cache objects to avoid frequent database lookups.

Figure 8-4 shows how the server provides access to the two scopes for different clients.

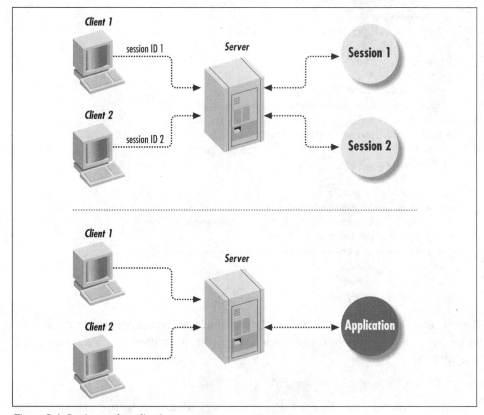

Figure 8-4. Session and application scopes

The upcoming examples in this chapter will help you see how the session and application scopes can be used.

Counting Page Hits

A simple page counter bean can be used to illustrate how the scope affects the lifetime and reach of shared information. The difference between the two scopes becomes apparent when you place the bean in both the session and application scopes. Consider the page shown in Example 8-4.

Example 8-4. Page with Counter Beans (counter1.jsp)

```
<%@ page language="java" contentType="text/html" %>
<html>
  <head>
    <title>Counter page</title>
  </head>
  <body bgcolor="white">
    <jsp:useBean
      id="sessionCounter"
      scope="session"
      class="com.ora.jsp.beans.counter.CounterBean"
    />
    <jsp:useBean
      id="applCounter"
      scope="application"
      class="com.ora.jsp.beans.counter.CounterBean"
    />
    <% String uri = request.getRequestURI(); %>

    <h1>Counter page</h1>

    This page has been visited <b>
    <%= sessionCounter.getNextValue(uri) %>
    </b> times by the current user in the current session, and <b>
    <%= applCounter.getNextValue(uri) %>
    </b> times by all users since the application was started.

  </body>
</html>
```

The bean used in this example, the `com.ora.jsp.beans.counter.Counter-Bean`, keeps a separate counter for each page where it's used. It's a class with just one method:

```
public int getNextValue(String uri);
```

The method increments the counter for the page identified by the `uri` argument and returns the new value.

In Example 8-4, two `<jsp:useBean>` actions are used to create one bean each for the session and application scopes. The bean placed in the session scope is found every time the same browser requests this page, and therefore counts hits per browser. The bean in the application scope, on the other hand, is shared by all users, so it counts the total number of hits for this page.

A scriptlet is used to ask the `request` object for the URI of the current page. The URI is then passed as an argument to the bean's `getNextValue()` method. A page is uniquely identified by its URI, so the bean uses the URI as a unique identifier to represent the counter it manages for each page. If you run this example, you should see a page similar to Figure 8-5.

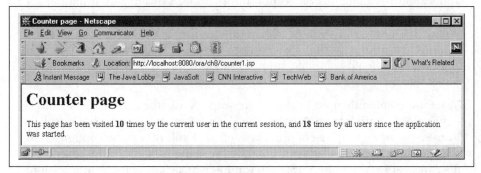

Figure 8-5. A page with session and application page hit counters

As long as you use the same browser, the session and application counters stay in sync. But if you exit your browser and restart it, a new session is created when you access the first page. The session counter starts from 1 again but the application counter takes off from where it was at the end of the first session.

Note that the bean described here keeps the counter values in memory only, so if you restart the server, both will start from 0 again.

Thread-safe beans

You probably noticed that the `CounterBean` doesn't have the type of property getter method used in the examples in previous chapters. Instead, it has a method named `getNextValue()` that takes the URI for the page as an argument. The `<jsp:getProperty>` action can be used only to display properties when the bean implements the standard no-arguments getter methods, so in Example 8-4, JSP expressions are used to display the counter values instead.

The use of a method with an argument instead of a typical no-argument Java-Beans getter method is by design, and highlights a very important consideration for beans used in the session and application scopes. In Chapter 6, *Using Scripting Elements*, we discussed how multiple requests are handled by the server in parallel by separate threads. The server assigns one execution thread to each request, and all threads have access to the same variable values for variables declared with JSP declaration elements. The result is that if such a variable is changed while processing one page request, the new values are used by all other requests as well. Beans in the session and application scopes are open to the same kind of problem, since they are also shared by multiple threads.

Sessions and Multiple Windows

Even though session tracking lets an application recognize related requests, there's still one problem. This problem is related to the server's lack of knowledge of the client, and does not become obvious until you start testing an application that depends on session information. Consider what happens if you open two browser windows and start accessing the same web application. Will each window be associated with its own session, or will they share the same session? Unfortunately, the answer is not well-defined. And it doesn't matter if the server-side logic is implemented as servlets, JSP, ASP, CGI, or any other server-side technology.

The most commonly used browsers, Netscape Navigator and Microsoft Internet Explorer, both let you open multiple windows that are actually controlled by the same operating system process. Internet Explorer can be configured so that each window is instead controlled by a separate process. In the latter case, it's easy to answer the question: each window is associated with its own session. It's only when one process controls multiple windows that it gets a bit tricky; in this case, the answer depends on whether URL rewriting or cookies are used for session tracking.

When URL rewriting is used, the first request to the application from one window doesn't include a session ID, since no response with the session ID has been received yet. The server sends back the new session ID encoded in all URLs in the page. If a request is then submitted from the other window, the same thing happens: the server sends back a response with a new session ID. Hence, in this scenario each window is associated with a separate session.

If cookies are used to pass the session ID, the reverse is true. The first request submitted from one window doesn't contain a session ID, so the server generates a new ID and sends it back as a cookie. Cookies are shared by all windows controlled by the same process. When a request is then made from the other window, it contains the session ID cookie received as a result of the first request. The server recognizes the session ID and therefore assumes that the request belongs to the same session as the first request; both windows share the same session.

There's not much you can do about this. If you want each window to have its own session, most servers can be configured to always use the URL rewriting method for session tracking. But this is not foolproof. The user can open a new window by using the mouse pop-up menu for a link (with the session ID encoded in the URI) and ask to see the linked page in a new window. Now there are two windows with the same session ID anyway. The only way to handle this, unfortunately, is to educate your users.

To illustrate this, let's look at what could happen if we used a bean with the traditional setter and getter methods to implement the counter instead. Such a bean could have the properties shown in Table 8-1.

Table 8-1. Traditional Counter Bean Properties

Property Name	Java Type	Access	Description
uri	String	write	The unique URI used to identify the page counter
nextValue	int	read	The counter's value incremented by one read-only property

Part of the JSP page would then look like this:

```
<jsp:useBean
    id="applCounter"
    scope="application"
    class="com.ora.jsp.beans.counter.CounterBean"
/>
<jsp:setProperty
    name="applCounter"
    property="uri"
    value="<%= request.getRequestURI() %>"
/>

<h1>Counter page</h1>

This page has been visited <b>
<jsp:getProperty
    name="applCounter"
    property="nextValue"
/>
</b> times by all users since the application was started.
```

The first time you access this page, the `<jsp:useBean>` action creates the bean and saves it in the `application` scope. The `<jsp:setProperty>` action sets the uri property to the unique URI for this page. Then the `<jsp:getProperty>` action calls the nextValue property getter method. This method uses the uri property value to locate the counter for the page and increments it.

As long as you use this bean in only one page, this works fine. But if you want to keep track of all hits for two pages, each with its unique URI, and the two pages are requested at almost the same time, you're in trouble. Say one user requests the first page, called */ora/pageOne*. This page sets the uri property to */ora/pageOne*. But before it gets to the `<jsp:getProperty>` action, another user requests the second page, say */ora/pageTwo*. Now the second page finds the same bean (`applCounter`) and sets the uri property to its URI (*/ora/pageTwo*). So when the first page eventually executes the `<jsp:getProperty>` action, it increments and displays the counter for the second page instead of its own counter.

Here I used a bean in the application scope as an example, because it's easy to understand that beans shared by all users can be accessed by more than one request at a time. But session scope beans can also be accessed at roughly the same time, by the same user. A good example of when two requests are made at nearly the same time by the same user is when an HTML frame set is used and each frame contains a JSP page.

You can solve this problem by using a bean with a regular method that takes the URI as an argument, instead of setting the URI with one setter method and incrementing the corresponding counter value with another method that depends on the URI value set by the first. This way, the method gets all the information it needs in one shot, and there's no risk of interference by other threads.

URL Rewriting

As I mentioned earlier, the session ID needed to keep track of requests within the same session can be transferred between the server and the browser in a number of different ways. One way is to encode it in the URLs created by the JSP pages, called *URL rewriting*. This approach works even if the browser doesn't support cookies (perhaps because the user has disabled them). A URL with a session ID looks like this:

```
counter3.jsp;jsessionid=be8d691ddb4128be093fdbde4d5be54e00
```

When the user clicks on a link with an encoded URL, the server extracts the session ID from the request URI and associates the request with the correct session. The JSP page can then access the session data in the same fashion as when cookies are used to keep track of the session ID, so you don't have to worry about how it's handled. What you do need to do, however, is to call a method that lets the JSP container encode the URL when needed. To see how it's done, let's create two pages that reference each other using a regular HTML link. A `CounterBean` in the session scope is used to increment a counter for each page. Example 8-5 shows one of the pages. The other page is identical, except for the title and the link at the bottom.

Example 8-5. Page with an Encoded Reference to Another Page (counter2.jsp)

```
<%@ page language="java" contentType="text/html" %>
<html>
  <head>
    <title>Counter page 1</title>
  </head>
  <body bgcolor="white">
    <jsp:useBean
      id="sessionCounter"
```

Example 8-5. Page with an Encoded Reference to Another Page (counter2.jsp) (continued)

```
    scope="session"
    class="com.ora.jsp.beans.counter.CounterBean"
/>
<% String uri = request.getRequestURI(); %>

<h1>Counter page 1</h1>

This page has been visited <b>
<%= sessionCounter.getNextValue(uri) %>
</b> times by the current user in the current session.
<p>
Click here to get to
<a href="<%= response.encodeURL("counter3.jsp") %>">
    Counter page 2</a>.

  </body>
</html>
```

The only differences compared to Example 8-4 are that only the session counter is used, and the link to the other page has been added.

The `<a>` element's `href` attribute value is converted using the `encodeURL()` method of the implicit JSP `response` object, described in Chapter 6. If a cookie is used to transfer the session ID between the browser and server, the `encodeURL()` method just returns the URL untouched. But if the browser doesn't support cookies, or cookie support is disabled, this method returns the URL with the session ID encoded as a part of the URL, as shown earlier.

If you want to provide session tracking for browsers that don't support cookies, you must use the `encodeURL()` method to rewrite *all* URL references in your application: in `<a>` tags, `<form>` tags, and `<frameset>` tags. This means all pages in your application (or at least all pages with references to other pages) must be JSP pages, so that all references can be dynamically encoded. If you miss one single URL, the server will lose track of the session.

I recommend that you take the time to add `encodeURL()` calls for all references up front, even if you know that all your current users have browsers that support cookies. One day you may want to extend the user base and lose control over the browsers they use. It's also common that users disable cookies in fear of Big Brother watching. Yet another reason to prepare for URL rewriting from the beginning is to support new types of clients that are becoming more and more common, such as PDAs and cell phones. Cookie support in these small devices is not a given.

Using Custom Actions

You might be wondering if we are stretching the bean model too far in the previous example. Perhaps. The CounterBean does more than hold information; it also has a non-conforming method for incrementing the counter. If we stray away from the purely bean model and use methods with arguments, this may force us to use scriptlets instead of the standard actions. That's not necessarily bad, but in this case we can do better using a *custom action* instead of a bean and the standard actions.

A custom action is just like the standard actions we've used so far. It has a start tag, which may contain attributes, and an end tag. It can also have a body. Here's what a custom action looks like:

```
<ora:incrementCounter scope="session"/>
```

The JSP specification defines how the standard set of actions can be extended with custom actions developed by Java programmers in the team or by a third party. A custom action is used in a JSP page in exactly the same way as the standard JSP actions you have seen in previous examples, such as <jsp:getProperty>. This makes them easier to use than beans with methods that must be invoked with scripting code, since you don't have to worry about missing braces and semicolons and other syntax details. A custom action can do pretty much anything: it has access to all information about the request and can add content to the response body as well as set response headers.

If you're a programmer, you should know that a custom action is basically a Java-Beans class, with property setter methods corresponding to the action's attributes, plus a few extra methods used by the JSP container to invoke the action. You can read all about how to develop your own custom actions in Chapter 16, *Developing JSP Custom Actions.*

As is often the case in software development, it's hard to say exactly whether a bean or a custom action is the preferred component type. My rule of thumb is that a bean is a great carrier of information, and a custom action is great for processing information. Custom actions can use beans as input and output. For instance, an action can be used to save the properties of a bean in a database, or to get information from a database and make it available to the page as a bean.

If you're a page author, you don't have to worry about the implementation details. All you need to know right now is how to use the custom actions you have available. You'll find many custom actions in this book that you can use, and more are available from open source projects and commercial companies listed in Appendix E, *JSP Resource Reference.*

Custom actions are grouped together in a *tag library.* Consequently, you often see custom actions referred to as *custom tags,* even though that is not strictly correct. A tag library consists of a Tag Library Descriptor (TLD) and the Java classes used to implement the custom actions. The TLD contains information about the action names and attributes. It's used by the JSP container during the translation phase to verify that all actions are used correctly in the page, for instance that all mandatory attributes are specified. Typically, the TLD and all classes are packaged in a Java Archive (JAR) file. You install such a library by placing the JAR file in the *WEB-INF/lib* subdirectory for the application in which it's used. If you look at the files in your Tomcat installation for the *ora* application (containing all the book examples), you see the JAR file in *WEB-INF/lib/orataglib_1_0.jar* and the TLD in *WEB-INF/tlds/orataglib_1_0.tld.*

When you use custom actions in a JSP page, you must identify the library using the `taglib` directive:

```
<%@ taglib uri="/orataglib" prefix="ora" %>
```

The `uri` attribute value identifies the library. Depending on how the library is installed, different types of values are used: a symbolic name, the path to the JAR file, or the path to the TLD file. My recommendation is to use a symbolic name, as shown in the example. The symbolic name must then be mapped to the location of the library in the *WEB-INF/web.xml* file for the application:

```
<web-app>
  ...
  <taglib>
    <taglib-uri>
      /orataglib
    </taglib-uri>
    <taglib-location>
      /WEB-INF/tlds/orataglib_1_0.tld
    </taglib-location>
  </taglib>
  ...
</web-app>
```

The `<taglib-uri>` element contains the symbolic name, and the `<taglib-location>` element contains the path to either the JAR file or the TLD file. The path typically starts with a slash (/) and is then interpreted as a context-relative path, in other words, relative to the top directory for the application. This indirection—using a symbolic name that's mapped to the real location—is especially helpful as it allows you to change the name of the tag library file for all JSP pages in one place, for instance when you upgrade to a later version of the library.

For a simple application, you may feel that the indirection is overkill. If so, you can use the path to the JAR file explicitly as the `uri` attribute value:

```
<%@ taglib uri="/WEB-INF/lib/orataglib_1_0.jar" prefix="ora" %>
```

All JSP 1.1–compliant containers should be able to find the TLD file in the JAR file, but this is a recent clarification of the specification. If the container you use doesn't support this yet (such as Tomcat 3.1), you must use the path to the TLD file instead of the path to the JAR file:

```
<%@ taglib uri="/WEB-INF/tlds/orataglib_1_0.tld" prefix="ora" %>
```

In both cases, the path may start with a slash and is then interpreted as a context-relative path. Without a starting slash, the path is interpreted as relative to the JSP page.

The prefix attribute defines a prefix used for the actions in this library. This prefix is used as part of the custom action names, as you will soon see. If you use more than one library in a page, each must have a unique prefix. You can use any prefix you like except jsp, jspx, java, javax, servlet, sun, and sunw, which are reserved. The ora prefix is used for all custom actions in the examples in this book.

As I mentioned earlier, a custom action is used in a JSP page just like the standard actions we've used so far. In other words, it has a start tag, which may contain attributes, and an end tag. It can also have a body. Let's revisit our example from earlier:

```
<ora:incrementCounter scope="session"/>
```

The name consists of the prefix you specified with the taglib directive, and a unique name within the library, separated by a colon (:). As with standard actions, all attribute names are case-sensitive, and the value must be enclosed in single or double quotes.

Now let's see how we can use two custom tags to improve the counter example. The attributes for the custom actions are described in Tables 8-2 and 8-3.

Table 8-2. Attributes for <ora:incrementCounter>

Attribute Name	Java Type	Request-Time Value Accepted	Description
scope	String	No	Specifies the scope for the counter. Valid values are page, request, session, and application. Default is page.

The <ora:incrementCounter> action increments a unique counter for the page where it's used. The counter can be placed in any of the standard JSP scopes. For instance, it can be placed in the session scope to count hits by different clients, or the application scope to count hits by all clients. The first time the action is used for a specific scope, the counter is created and set to 1.

Table 8-3. Attributes for <ora:showCounter>

Attribute Name	Java Type	Request-Time Value Accepted	Description
scope	String	No	Specifies the scope for the counter. Valid values are page, request, session, and application. Default is page.

The <ora:showCounter> action inserts the value of the page counter for the specified scope in the response. If a counter has not been created using the <ora: incrementCounter> action, the value –1 is displayed.

These two actions are generic, so you can use them in your own pages if you want to keep track of the number of hits. The type of information shown in Tables 8-2 and 8-3 is what you should expect (or even demand!) from the custom action developer, whether it's developed in-house or by a third party.

Example 8-6 shows how our custom actions are used.

Example 8-6. Page with Counter Custom Actions (counter4.jsp)

```
<%@ page language="java" contentType="text/html" %>
<%@ taglib uri="/orataglib" prefix="ora" %>
<html>
  <head>
    <title>Counter page 1</title>
  </head>
  <body bgcolor="white">
    <ora:incrementCounter scope="session"/>
    <ora:incrementCounter scope="application"/>

    <h1>Counter page 1</h1>

    This page has been visited <b>
    <ora:showCounter scope="session"/>
    </b> times by the current user in the current session, and <b>
    <ora:showCounter scope="application"/>
    </b> times by all users since the counter was reset.
    <p>
    To see that a unique counter is maintained per page,
    take a look at
    <a href="<ora:encodeURL url="counter5.jsp" />">Counter page 2</a>.

  </body>
</html>
```

As described in Tables 8-2 and 8-3, both actions have a scope attribute, supporting the same scopes as the JSP standard actions: page, request, session, and application. The <ora:incrementCounter> action finds or creates a counter for the current page in the specified scope and increments it by one, while <ora: showCounter> displays the current value of the counter. Notice that you don't have to tell the actions about the URI as you did with the beans in Example 8-5. That's because the JSP container makes all the implicit objects, such as the request object, available to a custom action automatically. The action can therefore figure out the current URI all by itself.

Another custom action, `<ora:encodeURL>`, is used to take care of the URL encoding of the link to the next page. It's described in Table 8-4.

Table 8-4. Attributes for <ora:encodeURL>

Attribute Name	Java Type	Request-Time Value Accepted	Description
url	String	Yes	Mandatory. Specifies the URL to encode.

You can use this action element as an alternative to the scripting code used for URL encoding in Example 8-5. This action performs the same session ID encoding as the scripting code. Also, it encodes the parameters defined by nested `<ora:param>` actions (see Table 8-5) according to the syntax rules for HTTP parameters:

```
<ora:encodeURL url="product.jsp">
  <ora:param name="id" value="<%= product.getId()%>" />
  <ora:param name="customer" value="Hans Bergsten" />
</ora:encodeURL>
```

Recall that all special characters, such as whitespace, quotes, etc., in a parameter value must be encoded. For instance, all spaces in a parameter value must be replaced with plus signs. When you use the `<ora:encodeURL>` action, it takes care of all this encoding. The encoded URL created by the action for this example looks something like this:

```
product.jsp;jsessionid=be8d691ddb4128be0?id=3&customer=Hans+Bergsten
```

Here, the session ID and the request parameters are added, and encoded if needed (the space between "Hans" and "Bergsten" is replaced with a plus sign).

Table 8-5. Attributes for <ora:param>

Attribute Name	Java Type	Request-Time Value Accepted	Description
name	String	Yes	Mandatory. The parameter name.
value	String	Yes	Mandatory. The parameter value.

As illustrated by the counter example, custom actions allow you to write cleaner pages, avoiding most (if not all) scripting code. Since pages without code are easier to develop and maintain, plenty of custom actions are used in the remainder of the examples in this book. Many are generic, so you can use them in your own applications as well. How to implement most of them is described in Chapters 16 and 17, and you'll find the source code for all actions included in the example code package for this book.

You may be wondering why it's necessary to develop custom actions for generic things such as looping and URL encoding, as well as for common functions such as accessing a database. The reason is that the specification writers only defined a small set of standard actions in JSP 1.1. This was primarily motivated by time constraints; it was important to get the JSP 1.1 specification released as soon as possible. But perhaps more importantly, before specifying a larger set of actions, the specification group wanted feedback on the type of actions users needed. At the time this book is being written, a specification of more standard actions is being prepared. It will likely contain many actions similar to the custom actions you find in this book to be rolled into a future version of the JSP specification.

Online Shopping

Now let's look at a more useful example: an online shopping site. Besides showing you how the session and application scopes can be used effectively in a larger application, this example also introduces many other useful tools. You'll see a number of generic custom actions you can use in your own applications, and learn how to use the `java.text.NumberFormat` class to format numbers.

The application consists of three pages. The main page lists all available products. Each product is linked to a product description page, where the product can be added to the shopping cart. A product is added to the shopping cart by a request processing page. The main page with the product list is then displayed again, but now with the current contents of the shopping cart as well, as shown in Figure 8-6.

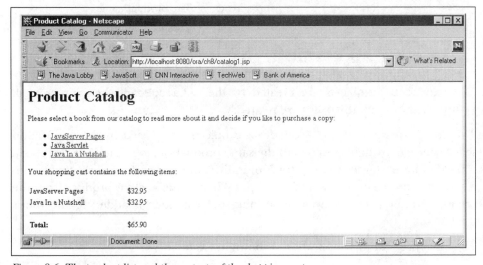

Figure 8-6. The product list and the contents of the shopping cart

Two beans are used to keep track of the products: the `com.ora.jsp.beans.shopping.CatalogBean` contains all available products, and the `com.ora.jsp.beans.shopping.CartBean` represents one user's shopping cart. Each product in the catalog is represented by a `ProductBean`.

Tables 8-6, 8-7, and 8-8 show all the properties for the beans.

Table 8-6. Properties for com.ora.jsp.beans.shopping.CatalogBean

Property Name	Java Type	Access	Description
productList	com.ora.jsp.beans. shopping.ProductBean[]	read	A list of all products in the catalog

Table 8-7. Properties for com.ora.jsp.beans.shopping.CartBean

Property Name	Java Type	Access	Description
empty	boolean	read	true if the cart is empty, false otherwise
productList	com.ora.jsp.beans. shopping.ProductBean[]	read	A list of all products in the cart
product	com.ora.jsp.beans. shopping.ProductBean	write	Adds a product to the cart
total	float	read	The total price for all products in the cart

Table 8-8. Properties for com.ora.jsp.beans.shopping.ProductBean

Property Name	Java Type	Access	Description
name	String	read	The product name
price	float	read	The product price
id	String	read	The unique product ID
descr	String	read	A description of the product

The `ProductBean` objects are created by the `CatalogBean` when it's created. Figure 8-7 shows how the beans are related.

The `CatalogBean` and the `ProductBean` objects are placed in the application scope, since all users have access to the same product catalog. A unique `CartBean` is needed for each user to keep track of individual purchases, so each user has an instance of this bean in the session scope. When a user picks a product from the catalog, a reference to the corresponding `ProductBean` is added to the user's `CartBean`.

The main page for this application is shown in Example 8-7.

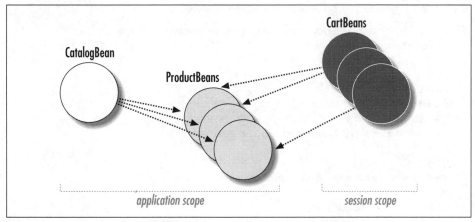

Figure 8-7. Application and session scope beans

Example 8-7. Page with a List of Products (catalog.jsp)

```
<%@ page language="java" contentType="text/html" %>
<%@ page import="java.text.*" %>
<%@ taglib uri="/orataglib" prefix="ora" %>
<html>
  <head>
    <title>Product Catalog</title>
  </head>
  <body bgcolor="white">
    <h1>Product Catalog</h1>

    Please select a book from our catalog to read more about it and
    decide if you would like to purchase a copy:

    <jsp:useBean
      id="catalog"
      scope="application"
      class="com.ora.jsp.beans.shopping.CatalogBean"
    />

    <%--
      Generate a list of all products with links to the product page.
    --%>
    <ul>
      <ora:loop name="catalog"
        property="productList"
        loopId="product"
        className="com.ora.jsp.beans.shopping.ProductBean">
        <li>
          <a href="<ora:encodeURL url="product.jsp">
                    <ora:param name="id"
                      value="<%= product.getId()%>"/>
```

Example 8-7. Page with a List of Products (catalog.jsp) (continued)

```
                        </ora:encodeURL>"><%= product.getName() %></a>
      </ora:loop>
  </ul>

  <jsp:useBean
    id="cart"
    scope="session"
    class="com.ora.jsp.beans.shopping.CartBean"
  />

  <%-- Show the contents of the shopping cart, if any --%>
  <%
      if (!cart.isEmpty()) {
          NumberFormat numFormat = NumberFormat.getCurrencyInstance();
  %>
      Your shopping cart contains the following items:
      <p>
      <table border=0>
        <ora:loop name="cart"
          property="productList"
          loopId="product"
          className="com.ora.jsp.beans.shopping.ProductBean">
          <tr>
            <td><%= product.getName() %></td>
            <td><%= numFormat.format(product.getPrice()) %></td>
          </tr>
        </ora:loop>

        <tr><td colspan=2><hr></td></tr>
        <tr>
          <td><b>Total:</b></td>
          <td><%= numFormat.format(cart.getTotal()) %></td></tr>
      </table>
    <% } %>

  </body>
</html>
```

The `<jsp:useBean>` action near the top of Example 8-7 creates an instance of the CatalogBean the first time a user requests the page. Since the bean is placed in the application scope, all users will then share this single instance.

The CatalogBean has a property that contains a list of all the products in the catalog, named productList. Its value is an array of ProductBean objects. A custom action called `<ora:loop>`, described in Table 8-9, is used to loop through the list and generate an HTML list item element for each product.

Table 8-9. Attributes for <ora:loop>

Attribute Name	Java Type	Request-Time Value Accepted	Description
name	String	No	Mandatory. The name of a data structure object or bean. The object must be of type `Object[]`, `Vector`, `Dictionary`, or `Enumeration`, or be a bean with a property of one of these types. The object or bean can be located in any JSP scope.
property	String	No	Optional. The name of a bean property. The property must be of type `Object[]`, `Vector`, `Dictionary`, or `Enumeration`.
loopId	String	No	Mandatory. The name of the variable that holds a reference to the current element when the action's body is evaluated.
className	String	No	Mandatory. The class name for the elements of the bean or property.

The `<ora:loop>` action iterates through the elements of an object, or the elements represented by a property, and evaluates the body once for each element, making the element available to other actions and scripting elements in the body through the variable name specified by `loopId`. The implementation of the loop action is described in Chapter 16.

In Example 8-7, the `name` attribute specifies the `catalog` bean. The `catalog` bean has an indexed (multivalue) property named `productList`. That's the one we ask the `<ora:loop>` action to loop over, by naming it in the `property` attribute. Finally, we set the `loopId` attribute to `product`, so we can use `product` as a variable name in the action element body, and specify the class name for the `ProductBean` with the `className` attribute.

The body of the `<ora:loop>` action is evaluated once per element. The action body can contain a mixture of template text, scripting elements, and other actions. Here the body contains the HTML for a list item with a reference to another page, using the product name as the link text. Let's look at how the link is generated:

```
<a href="<ora:encodeURL url="product1.jsp">
  <ora:param name="id"
    value="<%= product.getId()%>"/>
  </ora:encodeURL>"><%= product.getName() %></a>
```

Within the body, the `<ora:encodeURL>` custom action described earlier is used to generate the `<a>` element's `href` attribute value. A nested `<ora:param>` action adds a parameter named `id` with the value set to the product ID for the current product. It's done by using a JSP expression (a request-time attribute value, described in Chapter 6) that calls the `ProductBean` property getter method `getID()`. A similar expression is used to set the link text to the name of the current product.

After the code for generating the product list in Example 8-7, you see almost identical code for generating a list of the current contents of the shopping cart. First, the <jsp:useBean> action places the cart bean in the session scope, as opposed to the catalog bean, which is placed in the application scope. This means that each user gets a unique shopping cart that remains on the server for the duration of the session, while all users share the same catalog.

Number Formatting

Unless the shopping cart is empty, the second <ora:loop> action generates a list of the contents as an HTML table with the name and price of each product. Note the java.text.NumberFormat object created in the same scriptlet as the if statement:

```
<%
  if (!cart.isEmpty()) {
    NumberFormat numFormat = NumberFormat.getCurrencyInstance();
%>
```

The NumberFormat class is a Java standard class used to format numbers. You can set up rules for the number of decimals to show, where to put number grouping characters, prefix and suffix, etc. Even more important, the number is formatted according to the number format rules for the specific geographical, political, or cultural region where the server is located (by default). A collection of rules for a region is called a *locale*. It defines things such as which characters to use as a decimal separator, thousand grouping, and currency symbol. You can read more about the NumberFormat class in the standard Java API documentation. We will discuss locales in detail in Chapter 11, *Internationalization*, but to give you an idea of how formatting varies between regions, here's an example of the number 10,000.00 formatted as currency for USA, Sweden, and Italy:

USA: $10,000.00
Sweden: 10 000,00 kr
Italy: L. 10 000

We get a reference to the default formatter for currency information, using the getCurrencyInstance() method, and assign it to a variable named numFormat It's then used in the <ora:loop> body to format the price information for each product and for everything in the cart.

Using Request Parameters

As discussed earlier, a link to a description page for each product is generated using the <ora:loop> action in the main page, shown in Example 8-7. The link includes the request parameter id, specifying the product to display information

about. When the user clicks on one of the links, the page shown in Example 8-8 is
invoked.

Example 8-8. Product Description Page (product.jsp)

```
<%@ page language="java" contentType="text/html" %>
<%@ taglib uri="/orataglib" prefix="ora" %>
<html>
  <head>
    <title>Product Description</title>
  </head>
  <body bgcolor="white">

    <jsp:useBean
      id="catalog"
      scope="application"
      class="com.ora.jsp.beans.shopping.CatalogBean"
    />

    <%-- Get the ProductBean from the catalog --%>
    <ora:useProperty id="product" name="catalog" property="product"
      arg="<%= request.getParameter(\"id\") %>"
      className="com.ora.jsp.beans.shopping.ProductBean" />

    <h1>
      <jsp:getProperty name="product" property="name" />
    </h1>

    <jsp:getProperty name="product" property="descr" />

    <p>
    <a href="<ora:encodeURL url="addtocart.jsp">
              <ora:param name="id" value="<%= product.getId() %>"/>
            </ora:encodeURL>">Add this book to the shopping cart</a>

  </body>
</html>
```

The value of a request parameter can be retrieved from the implicit request
object using the getParameter() method. As described in Chapter 6, the
request object is an instance of the class HttpServletRequest, and provides
methods to find out everything the server knows about the request. The results are
shown in Figure 8-8.

In Example 8-8, the getParameter() method is used as a request-time attribute
value to set the arg attribute for the <ora:useProperty> custom action,
described in Table 8-10.

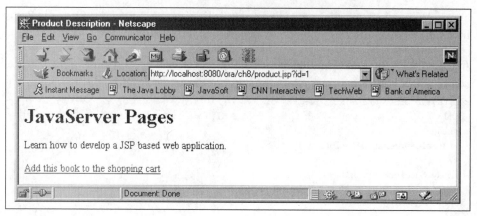

Figure 8-8. The product description page

Table 8-10. Attributes for <ora:useProperty>

Attribute Name	Java Type	Request-Time Value Accepted	Description
id	String	No	Mandatory. The name of the variable to hold the retrieved bean. The bean is placed in the page scope.
name	String	No	Mandatory. The name of the object with the bean to retrieve. The object must be available in one of the standard scopes.
property	String	No	Mandatory. The name of the property holding the bean.
arg	String	Yes	Optional. The argument value used to identify one specific bean.
className	String	No	Mandatory. The class name for the retrieved bean.

The <ora:useProperty> action is similar to the <jsp:useBean> action in that it associates a bean with a variable name. But instead of trying to locate the bean in a specified scope and create it if it isn't found, the <ora:useProperty> action gets the bean from another object (available in any of the standard scopes). It does this by calling the getter method for the specified property with the argument specified by the arg attribute if present. In Example 8-8, the <ora:useProperty> action is used to get the ProductBean that matches the ID passed as a parameter to the page from the catalog.

Note how the double quotes in the getParameter() method argument are preceded with a backslash (\):

```
arg="<%= request.getParameter(\"id\") %>"
```

Whenever you use the same type of quote within an attribute value as you use to enclose the attribute value, you must escape it with a backslash. If you forget this, the JSP container is unable to figure out where the attribute value ends, and the page will not be converted to a valid servlet. Instead you will get a syntax error message when you access the page the first time. An alternative is to use one type of quote within the value and another to enclose the value. For instance, here you could use single quotes to enclose the value instead:

```
arg='<%= request.getParameter("id") %>'
```

The remainder of Example 8-8 uses actions we have already discussed to generate the product information and the link to the business logic page that adds the product to the shopping cart. The request processing page is shown in Example 8-9.

Example 8-9. Adding a Product to the Shopping Cart (addtocart.jsp)

```
<%@ page language="java" contentType="text/html" %>
<%@ taglib uri="/orataglib " prefix="ora" %>  .

<jsp:useBean
  id="catalog"
  scope="application"
  class="com.ora.jsp.beans.shopping.CatalogBean"
/>

<jsp:useBean
  id="cart"
  scope="session"
  class="com.ora.jsp.beans.shopping.CartBean"
/>

<%-- Get the ProductBean from the catalog and save it in the cart --%>
<ora:useProperty id="product" name="catalog" property="product"
  arg='<%= request.getParameter("id") %>'
  className="com.ora.jsp.beans.shopping.ProductBean" />

<jsp:setProperty name="cart" property="product"
  value="<%= product %>" />

<%-- Redirect back to the catalog page --%>
<ora:redirect page="catalog.jsp" />
```

Since this is a request processing page, it doesn't contain any HTML. The <jsp: useBean> actions locate the CatalogBean and CartBean and associate them with the variables catalog and cart, respectively. Next, the <ora:useProperty> action gets the ProductBean corresponding to the id request parameter value and associates it with the variable named `product`. A standard `<jsp:setProperty>` action adds a reference to the product in the `cart` bean. Once all this is done, the application needs to redisplay the catalog page.

Redirect Versus Forward

There are two ways you can invoke another page: redirecting or forwarding. Forwarding is used in Example 8-2 to display an appropriate page depending on the result of the user input validation. In Example 8-9, redirection is used to display the main page for the application after adding a new product to the cart, using the `<ora:redirect>` custom action described in Table 8-11.

Table 8-11. Attributes for <ora:redirect>

Attribute Name	Java Type	Request-Time Value Accepted	Description
page	String	Yes	Mandatory. The URL of the page to redirect to, relative to the current page or, if it starts with a /, relative to the context path.

The `<ora:redirect>` action sends a redirect response to the client with the new location defined by the `page` attribute. If URL rewriting is used for session tracking, the URL is encoded with the session ID. If the body of this action contains `<ora:param>` actions, described in Table 8-5, each parameter is added to the URL as a query string parameter, encoded according to rules in the HTTP specification.

There's an important difference between a forward and a redirect. When you forward, the target page is invoked through an internal method call by the JSP container; the new page continues to process the same request and the browser is not aware that more than one page is involved. A redirect, on the other hand, means that the first page tells the browser to make a new request to the target page. The URL shown in the browser therefore changes to the URL of the new page when you redirect, but stays unchanged when you use forward. A redirect is slower than a forward, since the browser has to make a new request. Also, because it results in a new request, request scope objects are no longer available after a redirect.

So how do you decide if you should use forward or redirect? To a large extent it's a matter of preference. I look at it like this: forwarding is always faster, so that's the first choice. But since the URL in the browser refers to the start page even after the forward, I ask myself what happens if the user decides to reload the page (or even just resize the window; this often reloads the page automatically). In this example, the start page is the page that adds an item to the shopping cart. I don't want it to be invoked again on a reload, so I redirect to the page that displays the catalog and shopping cart content instead.

Memory Usage Considerations

You should be aware that all objects you save in the application and session scopes take up memory in the server process. It's easy to calculate how much memory is used for application objects since you have full control over the number of objects you place there. But the total number of objects in the session scope depends on the number of concurrent sessions, so in addition to the size of each object, you also need to know how many concurrent users you have and how long a session lasts. Let's look at an example.

The CartBean used in this chapter is small. It stores only references to ProductBean instances, not copies of the beans. An object reference in Java is 8 bytes, so with three products in the cart we need 24 bytes. The java.util. Vector object used to hold the references adds some overhead, say 32 bytes. All in all, we need 56 bytes per shopping cart bean with three products.

If this site has a modest number of customers, you may have 10 users shopping per hour. The default timeout for a session is 30 minutes, so let's say that at any given moment, you have 10 active users and another 10 sessions that are not active but have not timed out yet. This gives a total of 20 sessions times 56 bytes per session, a total of 1,120 bytes. In other words, a bit more than 1 KB. That's nothing to worry about.

Now let's say your site becomes extremely popular, with 2,000 customers per hour. Using the same method to calculate the number of concurrent sessions, you now have 4,000 sessions at 56 bytes, a total of roughly 220 KB—still nothing to worry about. However, if you store larger objects in each session, for instance the results of a database search, with an average of 10 KB per active session, that corresponds to roughly 40 MB for 4,000 sessions. A lot more, but still not extreme, at least not for a site intended to handle this amount of traffic. However, it should become apparent that with that many users, you have to be a bit more careful with how you use the session scope.

Here are some things you can do to keep the memory requirements under control:

- Place only those objects that really need to be unique for each session in the session scope. In the shopping cart example, for instance, each cart contains references only to the shared product beans, and the catalog bean is shared by all users.

- Set the timeout period for sessions to a lower value than the default. If you know it's rare that your users leave the site for 30 minutes and then return, use a shorter period. You can change the timeout for all sessions in an application through the application's Deployment Descriptor (see Appendix D, *Web-Application Structure and Deployment Descriptor Reference*), or call session.setMax-InactiveInterval() (see Appendix B, *JSP API Reference*) to change it for an individual session.

- Provide a way to end the session explicitly. A good example is a logout function. Another possibility is to invalidate the session when something is completed (such as submitting the order form). You can use the `session.invalidate()` method to invalidate a session and make all objects available for garbage collection (the term used when the Java runtime is allowed to remove unused objects to conserve memory). You will see an example of this in Chapter 10, *Authentication and Personalization.*

We have covered a lot of ground in this chapter, so let's recap the key points.

The scope concept gives you full control over the lifetime and reach of shared information at a convenient abstraction level. However, be careful about designing your beans for thread safety if they are to be used in the session and application scope, and resist the temptation to keep too much information around in the session scope.

Action elements for passing control between pages, such as the standard `<jsp:forward>` action and the custom `<ora:redirect>` action, allow you to allocate different roles to different pages. Other actions, such as the `<ora:loop>` and `<ora:encodeURL>` custom actions, can be used to minimize the amount of scripting code needed in the JSP pages. The scope abstraction and the actions together make it possible to develop JSP-based applications that are easy to maintain and extend.

9

Database Access

Almost any web application you see on the Internet accesses a database. Databases are used to store customer information, order information, product information, even discussion forum messages—in short, all information that needs to survive a server restart and is too complex to handle in plain text files.

There are many types of databases used in the industry today. However, relational databases are by far the most common. A relational database uses tables to represent the information it handles. A table consists of rows of columns, with each column holding a single value of a predefined datatype. Examples of these data types are text data, numeric data, dates, and binary data such as images and sound. A specialized language called Structured Query Language (SQL) is used to access the data. SQL is an ANSI standard and is supported by all major database vendors.

Relational database engines come in all shapes and sizes, from simple one-person databases with limited features to sophisticated databases capable of handling large numbers of concurrent users, with support for transactions distributed over multiple servers and extremely optimized search algorithms. Even though they all use SQL as the data access language, the API used to execute SQL statements is different for each database engine. To help programmers write code that's portable between database engines, the standard Java libraries include an API called the Java Database Connectivity (JDBC) API. JDBC defines a set of classes that can be used to execute SQL statements the same way in any relational database.

The complexity of databases varies extensively. A database for an online discussion forum, for instance, requires only one or two tables, while a database for a human resources system may contain hundreds of related tables. In this chapter, we look at a set of generic database custom actions you can use to build any type of database-driven web application. But if the database is complex, you may want to use another approach: hiding the database behind application-specific beans and custom actions, or moving all the database processing to a servlet and using JSP only to show the result. Both these approaches are discussed briefly at the end of this chapter, and in more detail in Chapter 13, *Web Application Models*, Chapter 14, *Combining Servlets and JSP*, and Chapter 17, *Developing Database Access Components*.

Accessing a Database from a JSP Page

First, the bad news: JSP 1.1 doesn't specify a standard way to access databases from a JSP page. As I mentioned in Chapter 8, *Sharing Data Between JSP Pages, Requests, and Users*, work is underway to define a larger set of standard JSP action elements, and actions for database access are high on the priority list.

The good news is that the JDBC API allows Java applications to access databases in a vendor-independent way. You could use JDBC directly in your JSP pages, embedding code in scriptlet elements. But this quickly gets out of hand, leading to too much code in the pages, minimal amount of reuse, and, in general, a web application that's hard to maintain. A better approach is to develop a set of custom action elements based on JDBC. That's what I have done here, and in this chapter we look at how to use them in an employee register application. If you're a programmer and interested in how they are implemented, skip ahead and glance at Chapters 16 and 17. Chapter 16, *Developing JSP Custom Actions*, describes how to develop custom actions in general, and Chapter 17, *Developing Database Access Components*, describes the actual database access custom actions.

The database access custom actions developed for this book provide the following features:

- Using a connection pool for better performance and scalability
- Supporting queries, updates, and inserts
- Handling the most common datatype conversions
- Supporting a combination of database operations in one transaction

These custom actions are generic, so you can use them to develop your own database-driven web application. Each action is introduced as it is used in the examples in this chapter. In addition, you can find a complete description of all the actions in Appendix C, *Book Example Custom Actions and Classes Reference*.

Example Application Architecture

In this chapter, we build an employee register application. This application contains functions for adding and changing employee information, as well as for searching for employees. The employee information is stored in a relational database and accessed through the database access custom actions.

The employee registration part of the application contains the pages shown in Figure 9-1.

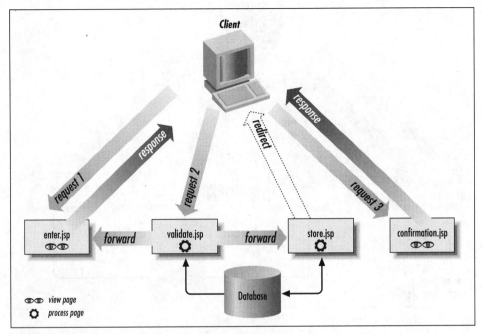

Figure 9-1. Employee registration pages

This example looks similar (but not identical) to our example from the previous chapter. The *enter.jsp* page presents a form where the user enters information about an employee. When the form is submitted, it invokes the *validate.jsp* page, where all input is validated. If the input is invalid, the request is forwarded back to the *enter.jsp* page to display an error message and the form with all the values the user previously entered. The user can then correct the invalid values and submit the form again. When all input is valid, the *validate.jsp* page forwards the request to the *store.jsp* page, where the information is stored in the database. Finally, the *store.jsp* page redirects to the *confirmation.jsp* page, which displays the information actually stored in the database as a confirmation to the user.

Figure 9-2 shows the pages used to implement the employee search function.

The *search.html* page is a regular HTML page with a form for entering the search criteria. The user can enter a partial first name, last name, and department name. Submitting the form invokes the *find.jsp* page. Here the database is searched for employees matching the criteria specified by the user, and the result is kept in the request scope. The *find.jsp* page forwards to the *list.jsp* page, where the result is displayed. For each employee listed, the *list.jsp* page adds a Delete button. Clicking

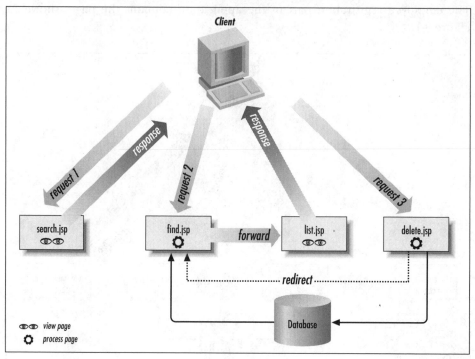

Figure 9-2. Employee search pages

on the Delete button invokes the *delete.jsp* page, removing the employee information from the database. The *delete.jsp* then redirects to the *find.jsp* page to get an
updated collection of employees matching the search criteria, and the *find.jsp* forwards to *list.jsp* as before, to show the result after deleting the employee.

Example Tables

If you develop a database-driven web application from scratch, you must first
develop a database schema. The database schema shows how all persistent information in the application is modeled as a set of related tables. For a large application this is a great deal of work, and it's extremely important to find the right
balance between flexibility and performance of frequent queries. How database
schemas are developed is beyond the scope of this book, but there are plenty of
other books available on this subject. Examples are C. J. Date's classic, very aca-
demic *An Introduction to Database Systems* (Addison Wesley), and a book that's easier to read, *Database Design for Mere Mortals: A Hands-On Guide to Relational Database
Design* by Michael J. Hernandez (Addison Wesley). In the event that you're developing a web interface to an existing database, you're probably relieved of the
schema development, but you should study the schema anyway to make sure you
understand how all the tables fit together.

The schema for the examples in this chapter is simple. To store the employee information, we need only the information described in Table 9-1.

Table 9-1. Employee Database Table

Column Name	SQL Datatype	Primary Key
UserName	CHAR (Text)	Yes
Password	CHAR (Text)	No
FirstName	CHAR (Text)	No
LastName	CHAR (Text)	No
Dept	CHAR (Text)	No
EmpDate	DATE (Date/Time)	No
EmailAddr	CHAR (Text)	No
ModDate	TIMESTAMP (Date/Time)	No

In a relational database, one column (or a combination of columns) can be marked as a *primary key*. The primary key uniquely identifies one specific row in the table; no two rows can have the same primary key. Here we use a column called UserName as the unique primary key for the table. Each employee must therefore be assigned a unique username, just like the username used to log into an operating system. As you will see in Chapter 10, *Authentication and Personalization*, the username, combined with the password you also find in the Employee table, can be used for application-controlled authentication. Assigning unique usernames can, however, be a problem in a web application available to anyone on the Internet. Therefore, some applications use a numeric code as the unique identifier instead, such as social security number or a generated sequence number. The tables above are only intended as an example of how to work with databases in JSP, so we allow ourselves to keep it simple.

The SQL datatype name within parentheses in Table 9-1 is the name used in the Microsoft Access product, to help you create the tables in this commonly used database. This is by no means an endorsement of the Access database for a database-driven web site. (In fact, I recommend that you *don't* use Access for a real application. It's a product that's intended as a single-user database, and it doesn't work well with the number of accesses typical for a web application.) For a real site, you should use a more robust multiuser database such as Oracle, Sybase, DB2, or Microsoft SQL Server. The only reason I use Access in this book when I refer to a specific product is that it's a database that you may already have installed. It's also easy to use during development of an application. If you don't have a database installed and you're not ready to spend big bucks for one of the products just listed, there are plenty of free or inexpensive databases you can use. Two examples are Lutris Technologies' InstantDB, a pure Java database available at *http://www. lutris.com/products/instantDBNews.html,* and T.c.X's mySQL, a popular database that you can use free of charge for most purposes, available at *http://www.mysql.com.*

To run the examples described in this chapter, you must first create the table outlined in Table 9-1 in your database. How to do this varies between database engines, so consult the documentation for the database engine you use.

Reading and Storing Information in a Database

The first page the user loads to register an employee in the example application is *enter.jsp*. This page contains a form for entering all information about an employee, shown in Figure 9-3.

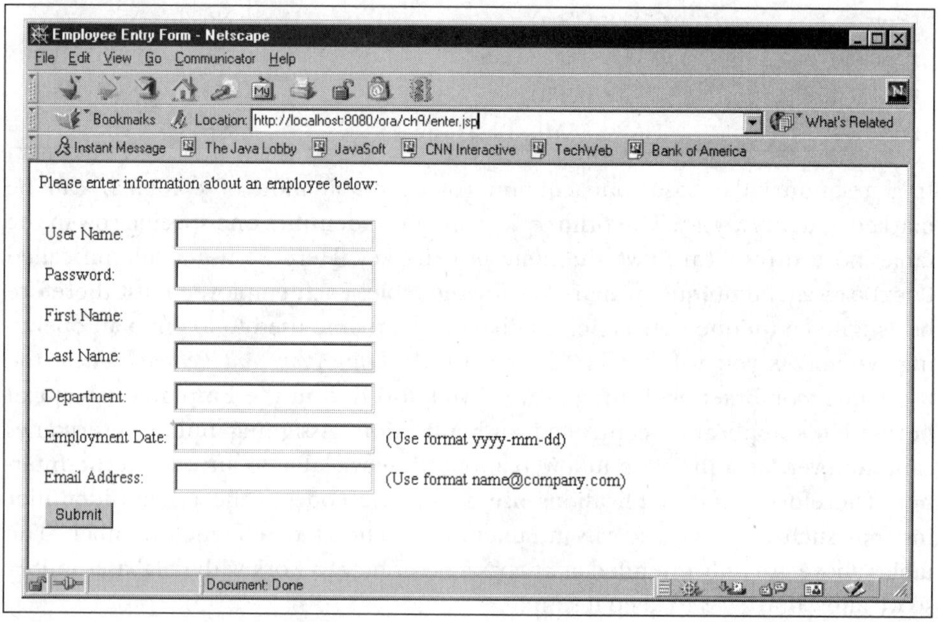

Figure 9-3. Employee information entry form

The input is validated by the *validate.jsp* page when the form is submitted. The *enter.jsp* and *validate.jsp* pages are similar to the pages discussed in detail in Chapter 8 and don't access the database. Instead of going through these pages now, let's jump directly to the *store.jsp* page, where the database access takes place. We'll return to the *enter.jsp* and *validate.jsp* pages at the end of this chapter, as they contain some interesting things not related to database access.

Example 9-1 shows the complete *store.jsp* page. This page first searches the database for information about an employee with the specified username. If one is found, the database is updated with all the other information about the employee the user entered. Otherwise, a new employee entry is stored in the database. Then all database information about the employee is collected and the request is forwarded to the *confirmation.jsp* page. Let's look at the complete page first and then discuss the different pieces in detail.

Example 9-1. Database Access Page (store.jsp)

```
<%@ page language="java" contentType="text/html" %>
<%@ taglib uri="/orataglib" prefix="ora" %>

<ora:useDataSource id="example"
  className="sun.jdbc.odbc.JdbcOdbcDriver"
  url="jdbc:odbc:example" />

<%--
  See if the employee is already defined. If not, insert the
  info, else update it.
--%>
<ora:sqlQuery id="empDbInfo" dataSource="example">
  SELECT * FROM Employee
    WHERE UserName = ?
  <ora:sqlStringValue param="userName" />
</ora:sqlQuery>

<% if (empDbInfo.size() == 0) { %>

    <ora:sqlUpdate dataSource="example">
      INSERT INTO Employee
        (UserName, Password, FirstName, LastName, Dept,
          EmpDate, EmailAddr, ModDate)
        VALUES(?, ?, ?, ?, ?, ?, ?, ?)
      <ora:sqlStringValue param="userName" />
      <ora:sqlStringValue param="password" />
      <ora:sqlStringValue param="firstName" />
      <ora:sqlStringValue param="lastName" />
      <ora:sqlStringValue param="dept" />
      <ora:sqlDateValue param="empDate" pattern="yyyy-MM-dd" />
      <ora:sqlStringValue param="emailAddr" />
      <ora:sqlTimestampValue value="<%= new java.util.Date() %>" />
    </ora:sqlUpdate>

<% } else { %>

    <ora:sqlUpdate dataSource="example">
      UPDATE Employee
        SET Password = ?,
            FirstName = ?,
            LastName = ?,
            Dept = ?,
            EmpDate = ?,
            EmailAddr = ?,
            ModDate = ?
        WHERE UserName = ?
      <ora:sqlStringValue param="password" />
      <ora:sqlStringValue param="firstName" />
```

Example 9-1. Database Access Page (store.jsp) (continued)

```
        <ora:sqlStringValue param="lastName" />
        <ora:sqlStringValue param="dept" />
        <ora:sqlDateValue param="empDate" pattern="yyyy-MM-dd" />
        <ora:sqlStringValue param="emailAddr" />
        <ora:sqlTimestampValue value="<%= new java.util.Date() %>" />
        <ora:sqlStringValue param="userName" />
    </ora:sqlUpdate>

<% } %>

<%-- Get the new or updated data from the database --%>
<ora:sqlQuery id="newEmpDbInfo" dataSource="example" scope="session">
  SELECT * FROM Employee
    WHERE UserName = ?
  <ora:sqlStringValue param="userName" />
</ora:sqlQuery>

<%-- Redirect to the confirmation page --%>
<ora:redirect page="confirmation.jsp" />
```

At the top of the page in Example 9-1 you find the `taglib` directive for the custom action library, as in the previous examples. Then follows a number of database custom actions.

JDBC drivers and the DataSource class

The first database custom action you see in Example 9-1 is the `<ora:useDataSource>` action (described in Table 9-2):

```
    <ora:useDataSource id="example"
      className="sun.jdbc.odbc.JdbcOdbcDriver" url="jdbc:odbc:example" />
```

Table 9-2. Attributes for <ora:useDataSource>

Attribute Name	Java Type	Request-Time Value Accepted	Description
id	String	No	Mandatory. The name used to reference the data source from other actions.
className	String	No	Mandatory. The name of the JDBC driver class used to access the database.
url	String	No	Mandatory. The JDBC URL for the database.
user	String	No	Optional. The database user account name.
pw	String	No	Optional. The password for the database user account name.

This action looks for a `javax.sql.DataSource` object with the name specified by the `id` attribute in the application scope. If it doesn't find it, it creates one for the

JDBC driver specified by the class attribute, associates it with the JDBC URL specified by the url attribute, then saves it in the application scope where it will be found the next time around. Before we continue with the rest of the page and the other database custom actions, let's review the DataSource, JDBC driver, and JDBC URL in more detail.

The DataSource class is defined by the JDBC 2.0 Standard Extension. It represents a data source that can be accessed through the JDBC API. The JDBC API is a set of classes and interfaces that allows a Java application to send SQL statements to a database in a vendor-independent way. For each type of database, an implementation of the interfaces defined by the JDBC API is needed. This is called a JDBC driver. Using different drivers that all provide the same interface allows you to develop your application on one platform (for instance, a PC with an Access database), and then deploy the application on another platform (for instance, a Solaris server with an Oracle database).

At least in theory it does. SQL is unfortunately one of these standards that leave a few things open, eagerly filled by different vendors' proprietary solutions. Examples are how to handle embedded quotes in a string value, how to deal with the input and output of date and time values, semantics for certain datatypes, and creation of unique numbers. The custom actions used in this book take care of some of this, such as string quoting and date/time string format, so if you use these actions and stick to ANSI SQL you should be able to migrate from one database to another without too much tweaking. However, you should always read your database documentation carefully and try to stay away from proprietary features. And be prepared to spend at least some time in transition when you need to move the application to another database.

All other database custom actions in the example tag library use the DataSource to get a database connection for executing the SQL statement. One nice thing with a DataSource is that it can represent something called a *connection pool*. This is described in more detail in Chapter 17, but a connection pool is exactly what it sounds like: a pool of database connections that can be shared by multiple clients. Opening a database connection is very time-consuming. With a connection pool, a connection to the database is opened once and stays open until the application is shut down. When a database custom action needs a connection, it gets it from the pool, through the DataSource object, and uses it to execute one or more SQL statements. When the action closes the connection, the connection is returned to the pool where it can be picked up by the next action that needs it. The DataSource created by the <ora:useDataSource> action implements a basic connection pool.

Back to our custom action. The <ora:useDataSource> action has three mandatory attributes: id, className, and url. Optionally you can also specify user and pw attributes, required to connect to some databases. The id attribute defines the name used for the DataSource object in the application scope. The className and url attributes require a bit more explanation.

As I mentioned earlier, what makes it possible to access databases from different vendors through the standard JDBC API is that JDBC relies on drivers, written for each specific database engine. A driver converts the JDBC API methods to the proprietary equivalents for a specific database engine. You can find JDBC drivers for most database engines on the market, both commercial and open source. If you can't get one from your vendor, Sun has a list of JDBC drivers from third parties at *http://industry.java.sun.com/products/jdbc/drivers/*.

The class attribute is used to specify the JDBC driver classname, for instance sun.jdbc.odbc.JdbcOdbcDriver. It must be specified as a fully qualified classname, i.e., it must include the package name. In this example we use the JDBC-ODBC bridge driver included in the Java SDK. This driver can be used to access databases that provide an ODBC interface but have no direct JDBC driver interface, as is the case for Microsoft Access. Sun doesn't recommend that you use the JDBC-ODBC driver for a production application, but for development it works fine. When you deploy your application, you should use production-quality drivers, available from the database vendor or a third party.

A database is identified by a JDBC URL. Different JDBC drivers use different URL syntax. All JDBC URLs start with jdbc:, followed by a JDBC driver identifier, such as odbc:, for the JDBC-ODBC bridge driver. The rest of the URL is used to identify the database instance. For the JDBC-ODBC bridge driver, it's an ODBC Data Source Name (DSN). If you use an Access database, you need to create a System DSN using the ODBC control in the Windows Control Panel to run this example, as shown in Figure 9-4. Note that you must create a System DSN as opposed to a User DSN. The reason for this is that the web server where your JSP pages are executed usually runs as a different user account than the account you use for development. If you specify a User DSN with your development account, the web server's servlet container will not be able to find it.

If you use a different JDBC driver than the JDBC-ODBC bridge driver or use a different ODBC DSN, modify the <ora:useDataSource> attributes in *store.jsp* accordingly before you try to run the example.

The <ora:useDataSource> action is intended only for simple examples or during the prototyping phase in a real project. From a maintenance standpoint, it's not a good idea to have the JDBC URL and driver classname in multiple pages. Also, if you need to specify a username and password, a JSP page is not a secure place to put this information. Another reason is that in JSP 1.1, there's no way for a custom action to know when an application is being shut down. This means a

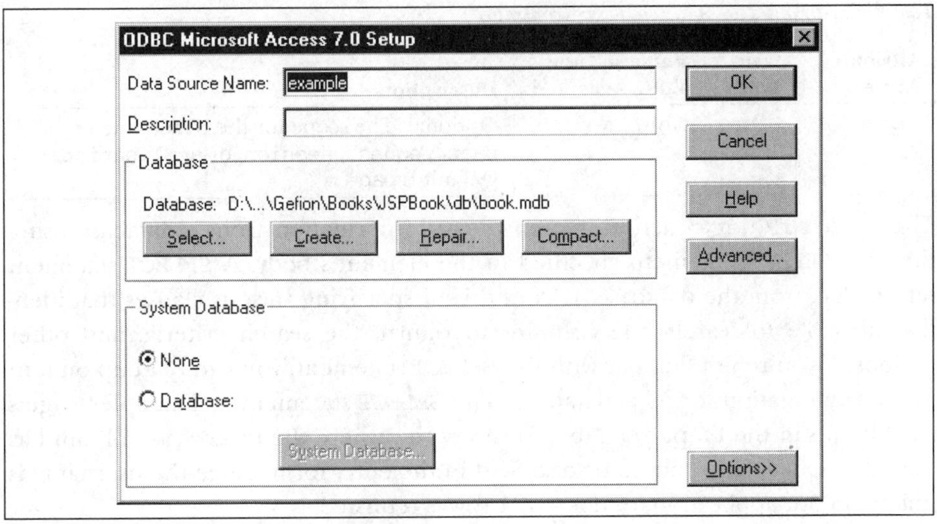

Figure 9-4. System DSN definition window

custom tag can't gracefully shut down the connections in the pool, potentially leading to problems with database resources not being released as they should.

Instead of using the `<ora:useDataSource>` action, you should use a servlet that's loaded when the application is started and notified when it's being shut down. This solves all of these problems, and we'll look at such a servlet in Chapter 17. As more and more database and JDBC driver vendors add support for JDBC 2.0 SE and implement their own connection pools, the servlet approach also lets you use a connection pool that's potentially more efficient than the one created by the custom action. No matter how the data source is created, other database custom actions described in this chapter work the same, since they just need the name the `DataSource` is saved under in the application scope.

Reading database information

Now that we've connected to a data source, we can begin to send queries to it. The first SQL custom action that accesses the database in Example 9-1 is the `<ora:sqlQuery>` action, described in Table 9-3.

Table 9-3. Attributes for <ora:sqlQuery>

Attribute Name	Java Type	Request-Time Value Accepted	Description
id	String	No	Mandatory. The name of the bean to hold the result.
dataSource	String	No	Mandatory, unless used with `<ora:sqlTransaction>`. The name of the data source.

Table 9-3. Attributes for <ora:sqlQuery> (continued)

Attribute Name	Java Type	Request-Time Value Accepted	Description
scope	String	No	Optional. The scope for the result, one of page, request, session, or application. Default is page.

The `<ora:sqlQuery>` action is used to read information from a database using the SQL `SELECT` statement specified in the element's body. A `SELECT` statement selects data from the database. It does this by specifying various clauses that identify the table to search, the columns to return, the search criteria, and other options. If you're not familiar with the `SELECT` statement, you can read up on it in the documentation for your database. The `SELECT` statement in Example 9-1 gets all columns in the Employee table for every row where the `UserName` column has the value specified in the `userName` field in the entry form. Since the username is unique in our application, either 0 or 1 row is returned.

The `<ora:sqlQuery>` action gets a connection from the data source identified by the `dataSource` attribute. It then executes the SQL `SELECT` statement in the action's body, and saves the result as a `java.util.Vector` with `com.ora.jsp.sql.Row` objects in the scope specified by the `scope` attribute, using the name specified by the `id` attribute. If no scope is specified, as in this example, the result is saved in the `page` scope. The `dataSource` attribute value must be the name of a `DataSource` available in the application scope. Note how it matches the `id` attribute of the `<ora:useDataSource>` action in Example 9-1.

Besides the SQL statement, the action element body also contains a `<ora:sqlStringValue>` action, described in Table 9-4.

Table 9-4. Attributes for <ora:sqlStringValue>

Attribute Name	Java Type	Request-Time Value Accepted	Description
value	String	Yes	Optional. The value to use for a placeholder in the enclosing database action.
param	String	Yes	Optional. The name of the request parameter holding the value.
name	String	No	Optional. The name of the bean with a property holding the value.
property	String	No	Mandatory if name is specified. The name of the bean property holding the value.
prefix	String	Yes	Optional. A string that should be concatenated to the beginning of the value.
suffix	String	Yes	Optional. A string that should be concatenated to the end of the value.

The <ora:sqlStringValue> action replaces a placeholder, marked with a question mark (?), in the SQL statement with a value. The value can be specified in one of three ways:

- Using the value attribute to specify the value as a literal string or as a request-time attribute that returns a String:

  ```
  <ora:sqlStringValue value='<%= anObject.getString("Arg") %>' />
  ```

- Using the param attribute to specify the name of a request parameter that holds the String value:

  ```
  <ora:sqlStringValue param="aParameterName" />
  ```

- Using the name and property attributes to specify a bean property that holds the String value:

  ```
  <ora:sqlStringValue name="aBeanName" property="aPropertyName" />
  ```

In Example 9-1, the param attribute is used to get the userName request parameter value, corresponding to the form field with the same name in the *enter.jsp* page:

```
<ora:sqlQuery id="empDbInfo" dataSource="example">
  SELECT * FROM Employee
    WHERE UserName = ?
  <ora:sqlStringValue param="userName" />
</ora:sqlQuery>
```

You *could* use a JSP expression in the body instead to insert the username directly into the SQL statement, like this:

```
<ora:sqlQuery id=" empDbInfo " dataSource="example">
  SELECT * FROM Employee
    WHERE UserName = '<%= request.getParameter("userName") %>'
</ora:sqlQuery>
```

But then you run into the problem of string quoting in SQL. Most database engines require a string literal to be enclosed in single quotes in a SQL statement. That's easy to handle by just putting single quotes around the JSP expression, like I've done in this example. What's not so easy is how to handle quotes within the string value. Different database engines employ different rules for how to encode embedded quotes. Most require a single quote in a string literal to be duplicated, while others use a backslash as an escape character or let you enclose the string literal with double quotes if the value includes single quotes. When you use the <ora:sqlStringValue> action, you don't have to worry about this type of formatting at all; the value is encoded according to the rules for the database you're currently accessing.

The <ora:sqlQuery> element body can contain multiple placeholders and <ora:sqlStringValue> actions. The first <ora:sqlStringValue> action replaces the first question mark in the SQL statement with its value, formatted correctly for the database engine you are currently using, the second replaces the second question mark, and so on. Only one dynamic value is needed in the query in Example 9-1. If you need more, just add question marks in the SQL statements and <ora: sqlStringValue> actions in the <ora:sqlQuery> body in the same order.

Back to the result generated by the <ora:sqlQuery> action. As I mentioned earlier, it's a java.util.Vector with com.ora.jsp.sql.Row objects. A Vector is like a dynamic array that provides methods for accessing its elements: one by one with the elementAt(), firstElement(), and lastElement() methods, or as a java.util.Enumeration of all elements with the elements() method. The Java API documents contain a complete list of the Vector methods. We look at the Row class later in this chapter.

The Vector class also provides a method used in Example 9-1 to see if the query returned any rows at all: the size() method. The SELECT statement searches the database for information about the employee entered in the form. If the employee is already registered, the query will return one row. To figure out whether or not the database already contains information about the employee, you can use the size() method to test on the number of rows using a simple scriptlet with an if statement:

```
<% if (empDbInfo.size() == 0) { %>
  insert
<% } else {
  update
<% } %>
```

Inserting database information

Now that you know how to retrieve data from the database, we can move on to inserting information. You can insert information into a database with a SQL INSERT statement. To execute an INSERT statement, use the <ora:sqlUpdate> custom action, described in Table 9-5.

Table 9-5. Attributes for <ora:sqlUpdate>

Attribute Name	Java Type	Request-Time Value Accepted	Description
id	String	No	Optional. The name of an Integer object to hold the number of rows affected by the statement.
dataSource	String	No	Mandatory, unless used with <ora: sqlTransaction>. The name of the data source.
scope	String	No	Optional. The scope for the result, one of page, request, session, or application. Default is page.

The <ora:sqlUpdate> action executes any SQL statement that doesn't return rows: INSERT, UPDATE, DELETE, and even so-called Data Definition Language (DDL) statements such as CREATE TABLE. These statements do exactly what they sound like they do: insert, update, and delete information, and create a new table, respectively. (Refer to your database documentation for details about the syntax.) For INSERT, UPDATE, and DELETE, the <ora:sqlUpdate> action can optionally save an Integer object, telling how many rows were affected by the statement. The Integer is saved in the scope specified by the scope attribute using the name specified by the id attribute. This feature is not used in Example 9-1, but in some applications it can be used as feedback to the user or to decide what to do next.

The only mandatory attribute for <ora:sqlUpdate> is dataSource. It must be the name of a DataSource available in the application scope, in the same way as for the <ora:sqlQuery> action. The <ora:sqlStringValue> action can be used in the body of an <ora:sqlUpdate> element as well. Multiple <ora:sql-StringValue> actions are used in Example 9-1, each one setting the value for a placeholder to the value of a request parameter:

```
<ora:sqlUpdate dataSource="example">
   INSERT INTO Employee
      (UserName, Password, FirstName, LastName, Dept,
         EmpDate, EmailAddr, ModDate)
      VALUES(?, ?, ?, ?, ?, ?, ?, ?)
   <ora:sqlStringValue param="userName" />
   <ora:sqlStringValue param="password" />
   <ora:sqlStringValue param="firstName" />
   <ora:sqlStringValue param="lastName" />
   <ora:sqlStringValue param="dept" />
   <ora:sqlDateValue param="empDate" pattern="yyyy-MM-dd" />
   <ora:sqlStringValue param="emailAddr" />
   <ora:sqlTimestampValue value="<%= new java.util.Date() %>" />
</ora:sqlUpdate>
```

Besides <ora:sqlStringValue> actions, an <ora:sqlDateValue> action is used to set the EmpDate column value. This action is described in Table 9-6.

Table 9-6. Attributes for <ora:sqlDateValue>

Attribute Name	Java Type	Request-Time Value Accepted	Description
value	java.util.Date	Yes	Optional. The value to use for a placeholder in the enclosing database action.
stringValue	String	Yes	Optional. The String to use as the value.
param	String	Yes	Optional. The name of the request parameter holding the value.

Table 9-6. Attributes for <ora:sqlDateValue> (continued)

Attribute Name	Java Type	Request-Time Value Accepted	Description
name	String	No	Optional. The name of the bean with a property holding the value.
property	String	No	Mandatory if name is specified. The name of the bean property holding the value.
pattern	String	Yes	The pattern used to interpret a String specified by the stringValue, param, or name/ property attributes.

Databases are picky about the format for date and time datatypes. In Example 9-1 we get the date from the form as a string in the format yyyy-MM-dd (e.g., 2000-03-31), but the EmpDate column is declared as a DATE column, as you can see in Table 9-1. Some databases accept a string in the format used here as a value for a DATE column, but others do not. To be on the safe side, it's best to convert the string into its native date format, a java.sql.Date object, before sending it to the database. The <ora:sqlDateValue> action does this for you when you specify the value using the stringValue, param, or name and property attributes (if the property is of type String).

The pattern attribute contains a pattern that describes the order and format of the year, month, and day parts in the string representation of the date. Appendix C shows all the types of patterns you can use—it's very flexible. Say, for instance, that you want the user to enter dates in a format like "Friday July 14, 2000." You then use the pattern EEEE MMMM dd, yyyy instead of the yyyy-MM-dd pattern used in this example to tell the <ora:sqlDateValue> action how to interpret the date string.

The Employee table also has a column named ModDate, to hold the date and time the information was last modified. It is declared as a TIMESTAMP column. To set its value, an instance of the java.util.Date class is used as the value attribute of a <ora:sqlTimestampValue> action in Example 9-1:

```
<ora:sqlTimestampValue value="<%= new java.util.Date() %>" />
```

Besides the SQL value actions for dates and timestamps described here, the custom library contains similar value actions for columns declared as TIME as well as all numeric datatypes. They all support the same attributes as the <ora: sqlDateValue> action and perform the conversion from a string value to the appropriate native type. Appendix C contains information about all of these actions.

Updating database information

Once you know how to insert information in a database, updating it is a piece of cake. You just use the `<ora:sqlUpdate>` action with a SQL `UPDATE` statement instead of an `INSERT` statement:

```
<ora:sqlUpdate dataSource="example">
  UPDATE Employee
    SET Password = ?,
        FirstName = ?,
        LastName = ?,
        Dept = ?,
        EmpDate = ?,
        EmailAddr = ?,
        ModDate = ?
    WHERE UserName = ?
  <ora:sqlStringValue param="password" />
  <ora:sqlStringValue param="firstName" />
  <ora:sqlStringValue param="lastName" />
  <ora:sqlStringValue param="dept" />
  <ora:sqlDateValue param="empDate" pattern="yyyy-MM-dd" />
  <ora:sqlStringValue param="emailAddr" />
  <ora:sqlTimestampValue value="<%= new java.util.Date() %>" />
  <ora:sqlStringValue param="userName" />
</ora:sqlUpdate>
```

No surprises here. The only difference from how you insert information is the SQL statement. The `UPDATE` statement sets all the specified values for rows matching the `WHERE` clause, in this case the single row for the specified employee.

Generating HTML from a Query Result

Just before the page in Example 9-1 redirects to the confirmation page, there's one more `<ora:sqlQuery>` action that retrieves the employee information that was just stored in the database:

```
<ora:sqlQuery id="newEmpDbInfo" dataSource="example" scope="session">
  SELECT * FROM Employee
    WHERE UserName = ?
  <ora:sqlStringValue param="userName" />
</ora:sqlQuery>
```

The intention here is to present the information actually stored in the database to the user on the final page in this application, shown in Figure 9-5, as a confirmation that the operation was successful.

Since we redirect to the confirmation page, ending the processing of the current request, the result is placed in the session scope. The redirect response tells the browser to automatically make a new request for the confirmation page. Because

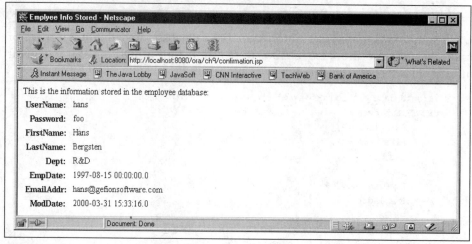

Figure 9-5. Employee registration confirmation page

the new request is part of the same session, it finds the result saved away by the previous page. Example 9-2 shows the code for the *confirmation.jsp* page.

Example 9-2. Page Displaying Query Result (confirmation.jsp)

```
<%@ page language="java" contentType="text/html" %>
<%@ page import="com.ora.jsp.sql.*" %>
<%@ taglib uri="/orataglib" prefix="ora" %>
<html>
  <head>
    <title>Employee Info Stored</title>
  </head>
  <body bgcolor="white">
    This is the information stored in the employee database:

    <table>
      <ora:loop name="newEmpDbInfo" loopId="row" className="Row" >
        <ora:loop name="row" property="columns" loopId="col"
          className="Column" >
          <tr>
            <td align=right>
              <b><jsp:getProperty name="col" property="name" />:</b>
            </td>
            <td>
              <jsp:getProperty name="col" property="string" />
            </td>
          </tr>
        </ora:loop>
      </ora:loop>
```

Example 9-2. Page Displaying Query Result (confirmation.jsp) (continued)

```
    </table>

  </body>
</html>
```

At the top of the page is the same JSP directive for using the custom action tag library as in Example 9-1, plus a page directive that imports the com.ora.jsp.sql package. This package contains two classes used to represent rows and columns in the query result, named Row and Column, respectively. You'll see how they are used in a moment.

Then comes a loop to create an HTML table with cells for all columns in the single row retrieved from the Employee table. The newEmpDbInfo variable contains the Vector of Row objects returned by the <ora:sqlQuery> action in Example 9-1. So far, we have used the <ora:loop> action only to loop through arrays, but it can also be used to loop through multiple values contained by a java.util.Vector, a java.util.Enumeration, or a java.util.Dictionary. Arrays and these three classes are all commonly used in Java to represent a set of values. You can read more about them in the Java API specification (*http://java. sun.com/docs/index.html*).

Inside the <ora:loop> action used to loop through the Vector of Row objects, another nested <ora:loop> action is used to loop through the columns of each Row. In the outer loop, the loopId attribute is set to row, which means that for each pass through the loop, a variable named row contains the current Row element of the Vector. In the inner loop, the row variable is used as the name attribute, and the property attribute is set to columns. The columns property of a Row object is an Enumeration of Column objects. A Column object, in turn, has properties name and string. The name property is a String containing the column's name, and the string property is a String representation of the value independent of its real datatype. The Column has other properties that let you access the value in its native form as well; see Appendix C for a complete list. In the body of the inner loop, the standard <jsp:getProperty> action is used to create cells with the column name and value.

Searching for Rows Based on Partial Information

Let's move on to the other part of the application, where a user can search for an employee based on a partial first name, last name, and department name. The first page, *search.html*, contains a form for entering the search criteria, shown in Figure 9-6.

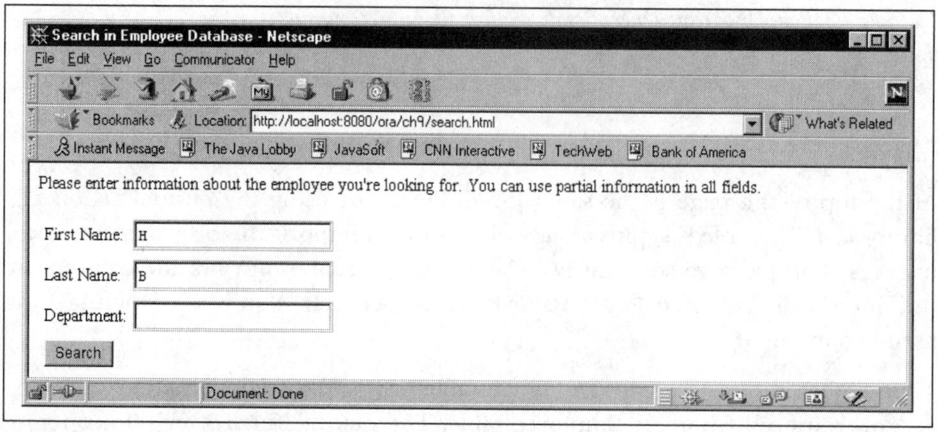

Figure 9-6. Search criteria form

The three fields in the *search.html* page are firstName, lastName, and dept, and when the user clicks the Search button, the *find.jsp* page is invoked with the information the user entered in the corresponding request parameters. Example 9-3 shows the complete *find.jsp* page.

Example 9-3. Search Based on Partial Information (find.jsp)

```
<%@ page language="java" contentType="text/html" %>
<%@ taglib uri="/orataglib" prefix="ora" %>

<ora:useDataSource id="example"
  className="sun.jdbc.odbc.JdbcOdbcDriver"
  url="jdbc:odbc:example" />

<ora:sqlQuery id="empList" dataSource="example" scope="request">
  SELECT * FROM Employee
    WHERE FirstName LIKE ?
      AND LastName LIKE ?
      AND Dept LIKE ?
    ORDER BY LastName
  <ora:sqlStringValue param="firstName" prefix="%" suffix="%" />
  <ora:sqlStringValue param="lastName" prefix="%" suffix="%" />
  <ora:sqlStringValue param="dept" prefix="%" suffix="%" />
</ora:sqlQuery>

<jsp:forward page="list.jsp" />
```

As you probably expected, the <ora:sqlQuery> action is used to search for the matching employees. But here, the SELECT statement uses the LIKE operator to find rows matching a pattern instead of an exact match condition. LIKE is a standard SQL operator. It must be followed by a string consisting of fixed text plus wildcard characters. There are two standard wildcard characters you can use: an underscore (_), which matches exactly one character, and a percent sign (%), which matches zero or more characters. In this example, we want to search for all rows that contain the values specified in the form somewhere in the corresponding column values. The form field values must therefore be enclosed with percent signs. This can be accomplished by using the <ora:sqlStringValue> action's prefix and suffix attributes, described in Table 9-4. The values of these attributes—in this case, percent signs—are added at the beginning and the end of the value, respectively. If you want to find values that start with any sequence of characters but end with the string entered by the user, use only the prefix attribute. If you use only the suffix attribute, you get the reverse result: values that start with the specified string but end with any characters.

The three LIKE conditions are combined with AND operators in Example 9-3. This means that the SELECT statement finds only rows where all three columns contain the corresponding values entered by the user.

Deleting Database Information

The *find.jsp* page forwards the request to the *list.jsp* page to display the result of the search. It generates an HTML table with one row per employee, as shown in Example 9-4.

Example 9-4. Displaying the Search Result (list.jsp)

```
...
<table border=1>
  <th>Last Name</th>
  <th>First Name</th>
  <th>Department</th>
  <th>Email Address</th>
  <th>Modified</th>
  <ora:loop name="empList" loopId="row"
    className="com.ora.jsp.sql.Row" >
    <tr>
      <td><%= row.getString("LastName") %></td>
      <td><%= row.getString("FirstName") %></td>
      <td><%= row.getString("Dept") %></td>
      <td><%= row.getString("EmailAddr") %></td>
      <td><%= row.getString("ModDate") %></td>
      <td>
        <form action="delete.jsp" method="post">
          <input type="hidden" name="userName"
            value='<%= StringFormat.toHTMLString(
              row.getString("UserName")) %>'>
          <input type="hidden" name="firstName"
            value='<%= StringFormat.toHTMLString(
              request.getParameter("firstName")) %>'>
```

Example 9-4. Displaying the Search Result (list.jsp) (continued)

```
            <input type="hidden" name="lastName"
             value='<%= StringFormat.toHTMLString(
                request.getParameter("lastName")) %>'>
            <input type="hidden" name="dept"
             value='<%= StringFormat.toHTMLString(
                request.getParameter("dept")) %>'>
            <input type="submit" value="Delete">
          </form>
        </td>
      </tr>
    </ora:loop>
  </table>
...
```

The result is shown in Figure 9-7.

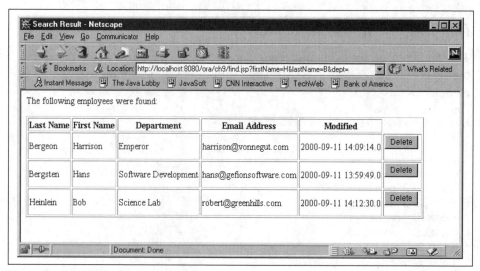

Figure 9-7. Displaying the search result

An `<ora:loop>` action is used to loop over all rows returned by the query in Example 9-3. The `loopId` attribute is set to `row`, so for each pass through the action body, a variable named `row` holds a reference to the current Row object. For each row, a number of table cells are generated. The value of the cell is retrieved from the Row using the `getString()` method:

```
public String getString(String columnName)
```

The argument to the method is the name of a column. The method returns the column's value as a `String`. Another version of this method takes an index number instead of a column name. The first column has index 1:

```
public String getString(int columnIndex)
```

The Row class also provides methods to get the column value in its native form, for instance as a Date:

```
public java.sql.Date getDate(String columnName)
public java.sql.Date getDate(int columnIndex)
```

You may want to use these methods if you use one query result as input to another query. Again, see Appendix C for a description of all the methods.

The last generated cell contains a simple HTML form with a Delete button and a number of hidden fields. The action for the form is set to invoke the *delete.jsp* page. The hidden fields hold the value of UserName for the current row, plus all the parameters used to perform the search. All hidden field values are encoded using the same StringFormat toHTMLString() method we used in Chapter 6, *Using Scripting Elements*, to make sure that quotes in the value don't cause syntax errors in the generated HTML. Example 9-5 shows how all these parameters are used in the *delete.jsp* page.

Example 9-5. Deleting a Row (delete.jsp)

```
<%@ page language="java" contentType="text/html" %>
<%@ taglib uri="/orataglib" prefix="ora" %>

<ora:useDataSource id="example"
  className="sun.jdbc.odbc.JdbcOdbcDriver"
  url="jdbc:odbc:example" />

<ora:sqlUpdate dataSource="example">
  DELETE FROM Employee
    WHERE UserName = ?
  <ora:sqlStringValue param="userName" />
</ora:sqlUpdate>

<ora:redirect page="find.jsp">
  <ora:param name="firstName"
    value='<%= request.getParameter("firstName") %>' />
  <ora:param name="lastName"
    value='<%= request.getParameter("lastName") %>' />
  <ora:param name="dept"
    value='<%= request.getParameter("dept") %>' />
</ora:redirect>
```

The userName request parameter value is used to uniquely identify the row to remove. The SQL DELETE statement supports the same type of WHERE clause condition you have seen used in SELECT and UPDATE statements previously. Here, the condition is used to make sure only the row for the right employee is deleted. And like the INSERT and UPDATE statements, a DELETE statement is executed with the help of the <ora:sqlUpdate> action.

The other parameters passed from the *list.jsp* page are used in the redirect call to the *find.jsp* page. This way, the *find.jsp* page uses the same search criteria as when it was called directly from the *search.html* file, so the new result is consistent with the first. The only difference is that the employee who was just deleted doesn't show up in the list.

Input Validation Without a Bean

Before we look at the two remaining database sections, let's go back and take a look at the two application pages we skipped earlier, namely the *enter.jsp* and *validate.jsp* pages used for input to the employee registration.

In Chapter 5, *Generating Dynamic Content,* I introduced you to validation of user input using an application-specific bean. The bean contains all validation code and provides an `isValid()` method that can be used in a JSP page to decide how to proceed. This is the approach I recommend, but if you're developing a JSP-based application and there isn't a Java programmer around, there's another way to do the validation. I'll describe this alternative here.

The *validate.jsp* page uses the `StringFormat` utility class to validate the input format without a bean. If an input parameter is not valid, an error message is saved in a `Vector` object and the request is forwarded back to the *enter.jsp* page. The *enter.jsp* page loops through all error messages in the `Vector` and adds them to the response, so to the user, the result is identical to that of the bean-based validation approach you saw in Chapter 5.

Let's look at *validate.jsp* first, shown in Example 9-6.

Example 9-6. Validation Without Application Beans (validate.jsp)

```
<%@ page language="java" %>
<%@ page import="com.ora.jsp.util.*" %>

<jsp:useBean id="errorMessages" scope="request"
  class="java.util.Vector" />

<%
  if (request.getParameter("userName").length() == 0) {
    errorMessages.addElement("User Name missing");
  }
  if (request.getParameter("password").length() == 0) {
    errorMessages.addElement("Password missing");
  }
  if (request.getParameter("firstName").length() == 0) {
    errorMessages.addElement("First Name missing");
  }
  if (request.getParameter("lastName").length() == 0) {
```

Example 9-6. Validation Without Application Beans (validate.jsp) (continued)

```
      errorMessages.addElement("Last Name missing");
   }
   if (request.getParameter("dept").length() == 0) {
      errorMessages.addElement("Department missing");
   }
   if (!StringFormat.isValidDate(request.getParameter("empDate"),
      "yyyy-MM-dd")) {
      errorMessages.addElement("Invalid Employment Date");
   }
   if (!StringFormat.isValidEmailAddr(
      request.getParameter("emailAddr"))) {
      errorMessages.addElement("Invalid Email Address");
   }

   if (errorMessages.size() > 0) {
%>
   <jsp:forward page="enter.jsp" />

<% } else { %>

   <jsp:forward page="store.jsp" />

<% } %>
```

At the top of Example 9-6, a `<jsp:useBean>` action creates a `Vector` instance in the request scope to hold possible error messages. Even though the `Vector` class doesn't provide bean getter and setter methods, an instance of this class can be created by the `<jsp:useBean>` action (because it has a no-argument constructor).

Next comes a scriptlet with an `if` statement for each input parameter that needs to be validated. For most of them, it's enough to verify that the parameter has a value. This is done by using the `length()` method. If the result is 0, the parameter doesn't have a value, and the body of the `if` block adds an appropriate error message to the `errorMessages` `Vector`.

Two parameters require a more careful validation: the `empDate` parameter must contain a valid date string, and the `emailAddr` a valid email address:

```
   if (!StringFormat.isValidDate(request.getParameter("empDate"),
      "yyyy-MM-dd")) {
      errorMessages.addElement("Invalid Employment Date");
   }
   if (!StringFormat.isValidEmailAddr(
      request.getParameter("emailAddr"))) {
      errorMessages.addElement("Invalid Email Address");
   }
```

The `empDate` parameter is validated with the `StringFormat isValidDate()` method. This method takes a string representation of a date, here retrieved from the `empDate` request parameter, and a date format pattern. The date format pattern is the same as for the `<ora:sqlDateValue>` action discussed earlier. If the date string forms a valid date when interpreted according to the pattern, this method returns `true`.

The `emailAddr` parameter is validated with another `StringFormat` method, called `isValidEmailAddr()`. This method returns `true` if the string looks like a valid email address, that is, if it has the form *name@company.topdomain*, for instance, *hans@gefionsoftware.com*.

After the validation scriptlets, there's another set of scriptlets. The `if` statement tests the size of the `errorMessages Vector`. If it's greater than 0, at least one parameter value is invalid, so the request is forwarded to the *enter.jsp* page again. Otherwise, the processing continues on the *store.jsp* page, as discussed in the first section of this chapter.

If the request is forwarded to the *enter.jsp* page, the error messages are displayed and all the values the user entered are used as the default values for all form fields. Example 9-7 shows how the error messages are handled.

Example 9-7. Displaying Error Messages (enter.jsp)

```
...
<jsp:useBean id="errorMessages" scope="request"
  class="java.util.Vector" />

<%-- Output list of values with invalid format, if any --%>
<ul>
  <font color="red">
    <ora:loop name="errorMessages" loopId="msg" class="String" >
      <li> <%= msg %>
    </ora:loop>
  </font>
</ul>
...
```

The `<jsp:useBean>` action finds the `Vector` created by the *validate.jsp* page and makes it available through the `errorMessages` variable. The `<ora:loop>` action is then used to loop through the `Vector` and display each message as a list item. The results are shown in Figure 9-8.

Example 9-8 shows how the form field values are filled out with the values submitted by the user.

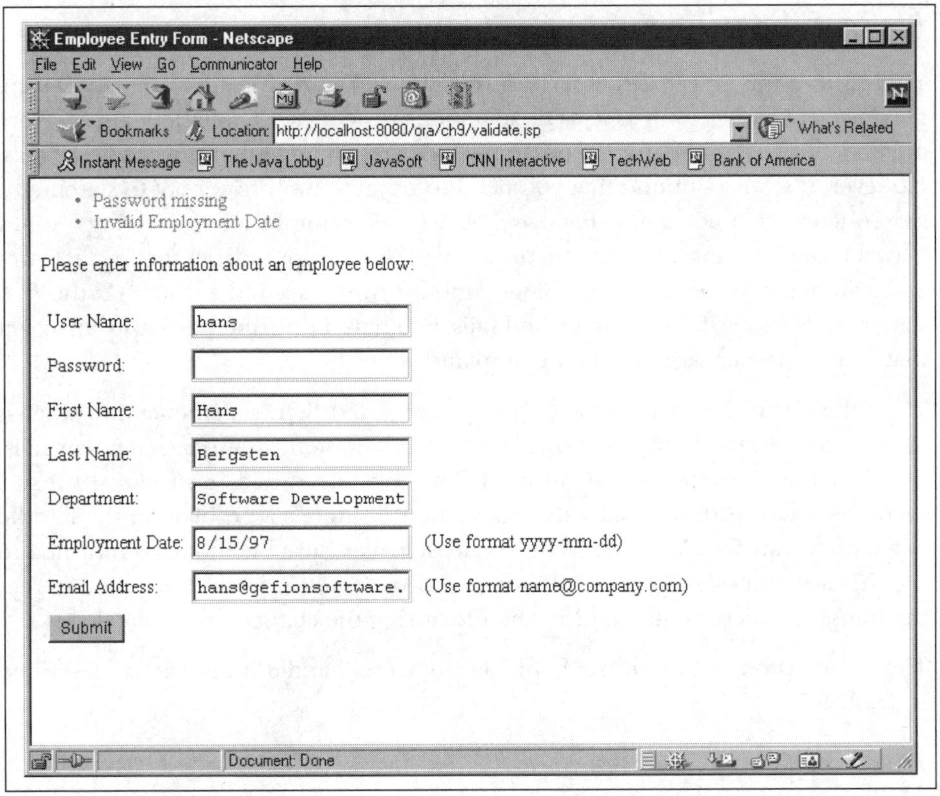

Figure 9-8. The enter.jsp page

Example 9-8. Filling Form Field Values with Request Data

```
...
<form action="validate.jsp" method="post">
  <table>
    <tr>
      <td>User Name:</td>
      <td><input type="text" name="userName"
        value='<%= StringFormat.toHTMLString(
          request.getParameter("userName")) %>' >
      </td>
    </tr>
...
```

This is very similar to how it was done with a bean in Chapter 5. The difference is that the value is retrieved from the implicit request object instead of a bean. Remember that since the *validate.jsp* page forwards to the *enter.jsp* page, the *enter.jsp* page is processing the same request as *validate.jsp;* therefore, all request parameters are still available. The request parameter value is formatted with the toHTMLString() method as before, to make sure possible quotes in the value don't confuse the browser.

Using Transactions

There's one important database feature we have not discussed yet. In the examples in this chapter, only one SQL statement is needed to complete all database modifications required for a function. This statement either succeeds or fails. However, it's very common that you need to execute two or more SQL statements in sequence to update the database. A typical example is transferring money between two accounts: one statement removes some amount from the first account and another statement adds the same amount to the second account. If the first statement is successful but the second fails, you have performed a disappearing act that your customers are not likely to applaud.

The solution to this problem is to group all related SQL statements into what is called a *transaction*. A transaction is an atomic operation, so if one statement fails, they all fail. Otherwise, they all succeed. This is referred to as *committing* (if it succeeds) or *rolling back* (if it fails) the transaction. If there's a problem in the middle of a money transfer, for instance, the database makes sure the money is returned to the first account by rolling back the transaction. If no problems are encountered, the transaction is committed, permanently storing the changes in the database.

There's a custom action in the book tag library to handle transactions, described in Table 9-7.

Table 9-7. Attributes for <ora:sqlTransaction>

Attribute Name	Java Type	Request-Time Value Accepted	Description
dataSource	String	No	Mandatory. The name of the data source to use for all nested database access actions.

We will use it for real in Chapter 10, but let's now take a quick look at how it could be used in this fictitious example:

```
<ora:sqlTransaction dataSource="example">

  <ora:sqlUpdate>
    UPDATE Account SET Balance = Balance - 1000
      WHERE AccountNumber = 1234
  </ora:sqlUpdate>
  <ora:sqlUpdate>
    UPDATE Account SET Balance = Balance + 1000
      WHERE AccountNumber = 5678
  </ora:sqlUpdate>

</ora:sqlTransaction>
```

All SQL actions that make up a transaction are placed in the body of an <ora: sqlTransaction> action. Note that instead of specifying the dataSource attribute for all database actions, it's specified only in the enclosing <ora: sqlTransaction> action.

The <ora:sqlTransaction> action gets a connection from the data source and makes it available to all database actions within its body. If one of the actions fails, the transaction is rolled back. Otherwise the transaction is committed at the end of the <ora:sqlTransaction> body.

Application-Specific Database Actions

You can use the database actions described in this chapter to develop many types of interesting web applications, such as product catalog interfaces, employee directories, or online billboards, without being a Java programmer. These types of applications account for a high percentage of the web applications developed today. But at some level of complexity, putting SQL statements directly in the web pages can become a maintenance problem. The SQL statements represent business logic, and for more complex applications, business logic is better developed as separate Java classes.

Therefore, for a complex application, it may be better to use application-specific custom actions instead of the generic database actions described in this chapter. For example, all of the generic database actions in Example 9-1, which SELECT and then INSERT or UPDATE the database, can be replaced with one application-specific action, like this:

```
<myLib:saveEmployeeInfo dataSource="example" />
```

Chapters 16 and 17 describe how you can develop this type of custom action. Besides making it easier for the page designer to deal with, the beauty of using an application-specific custom action is that it lets you evolve the application behind the scene. Initially, this action can be implemented so it uses JDBC to access the database directly, similar to how the generic actions work. But at some point it may make sense to migrate the application to an Enterprise JavaBeans architecture, perhaps to support types of clients other than web browsers. The action can then be modified to interact with an Enterprise JavaBeans component instead of directly accessing the database. From the JSP page developer's point of view, it doesn't matter; the custom action is still used in exactly the same way.

Another approach is to use a servlet for all database processing, and use JSP pages only to show the result. You will find an example of this approach in Chapter 14.

10

Authentication and Personalization

Authentication means establishing that a user really is who he or she claims to be. Today, it's typically done by asking the user for a username and a matching password, but other options are becoming more and more common. For example, most web servers support client certificates for authentication. Biometrics, which is the use of unique biological patterns like fingerprints for identification, will likely be another option in the near future. What's important is that an application should not be concerned with the way a user has been authenticated (since the method may change), but only that he or she has passed the test.

Access control, or *authorization*, is another security mechanism that's strongly related to authentication. Different users may be allowed different types of access to the content and services a web site offers. When you have established who the user is through an authentication process, access control mechanisms let you ensure that the user can access only what he or she is allowed to access.

In the end, authentication provides information about who the user is, and that's what is needed to provide personalized content and services. For some types of personalization, the procedures we might think of as authentication may be overkill. If the background colors and type of news listed on the front page are the extent of the personalization, a simple cookie can be used to track the user instead. But if personalization means getting access to information about taxes, medical records, or other confidential personal information, true authentication is definitely needed.

In this chapter we look at different approaches to authentication and access control with JSP, and we use the information about who the user is to provide modest personalization of the application pages. Security, however, is about more than authentication and access control. So the last section of this chapter presents a brief summary of other areas that need to be covered for applications dealing with sensitive data.

Container-Provided Authentication

A JSP page is always executing in a runtime environment provided by a container. Consequently, all authentication and access control can be handled by the container, relieving the application developer from the important task of implementing an appropriate security level. Security is hard to get right, so your first choice should always be to use the time-tested mechanisms provided by the container.

Authenticating Users

The Servlet 2.2 specification, which is the base for JSP 1.1, describes three authentication mechanisms supported by most web clients and web servers that a container can utilize:

- HTTP basic authentication
- HTTP digest authentication
- HTTPS client authentication

In addition, it specifies one additional mechanism that should be implemented by a compliant servlet container:

- Form-based authentication

HTTP basic authentication has been part of the HTTP protocol since the beginning. It's a very simple and not very secure authentication scheme. When a client requests access to a protected resource, the server sends back a response asking for the user's credentials (username and password). The web client prompts the user for this information and sends the same request again, but this time with the user credentials in one of the request headers so the server can authenticate the user. But the username and password are not encrypted, only slightly obfuscated by the well-known Base64 encoding. This means it can easily be reversed by anyone who grabs it as it's passed over the network. This problem can be resolved by using an encrypted connection between the client and the server, such as the Secure Sockets Layer (SSL) protocol. We talk more about this in the last section of this chapter.

HTTP 1.1 introduced HTTP digest authentication. As with basic authentication, the server sends a response back to the client when it receives a request for a protected resource. But with the response, it also sends a string called a *nonce*. The nonce is a unique string generated by the server, typically composed of a timestamp, information about the requested resource, and a server identifier. The client creates an MD5 checksum, also known as a *message digest*, of the username, the password, the given nonce value, the HTTP method, and the requested URI, and sends it back to the server in a new request. The use of an MD5 message digest means the password cannot easily be extracted from information recorded from the network. Additionally, using information such as timestamps and resource information in the nonce minimizes the risk of "replay" attacks. The digest authentication is a great improvement over basic authentication. The only problem is that it's not broadly supported in today's web clients and servers.

HTTPS client authentication is the most secure authentication method supported today. This mechanism requires the user to possess a Public Key Certificate (PKC). The certificate is passed to the server when the connection between the client and server is established, using a very secure challenge-response handshake process, and is used by the server to uniquely identify the user. As opposed to the mechanisms described above, the server keeps the information about the client's identity as long as the connection remains open. When the client requests a protected resource, the server uses this information to grant or refuse access.

The three mechanisms described here are defined by Internet standards. They are used for all sorts of web applications, servlet-based or not, and are usually implemented by the web server itself as opposed to the servlet container. The servlet specification only defines how an application can gain access to information about a user authenticated with one of them, as you will see soon.

The final mechanism, form-based authentication, is unique to the servlet specification and is implemented by the servlet container itself. Form-based authentication is about as insecure as basic authentication for the same reason: the user's credentials are sent as clear text over the network. To protect access to sensitive resources, it should be combined with encryption such as SSL.

Unlike basic and digest authentication, form-based authentication lets you control the appearance of the login screen. The login itself is a form containing two mandatory input fields named j_username and j_password, and the action attribute is set to the string j_security_check:

```
<form method="POST" action="j_security_check">
  <input type="text" name="j_username">
  <input type="password" name="j_password">
</form>
```

From the user's point of view, it works just like basic and digest authentication. When the user requests a protected resource, the login form is shown, prompting the user to enter a username and password. The j_security_check action attribute value is a special URI that is recognized by the container. When the user submits the form, the container authenticates the user using the j_username and j_password parameter values. If the authentication is successful, it redirects the client to the requested resource. Otherwise an error page is returned. We'll get to how you specify the login page and error page shortly.

Controlling Access to Web Resources

All of the authentication mechanisms described so far rely on two pieces of information: user definitions and information about the type of access control needed for the web application resources.

How users and groups of users are defined depends on the server you're using. Some web servers, such as Microsoft's Internet Information Server (IIS), can use the operating system's user and group definitions. Others, such as the iPlanet Web Server (formerly Netscape Enterprise Server), let you use its own user directory or an external LDAP server. The security mechanism defined by the servlet specification describes how to specify the access control constraints for a web application, but access is granted to a *role* instead of directly to a user or a group. A role is an abstract grouping of users that needs to be mapped to real user and group names for a particular server. How the mapping is done also depends on the server, so you need to consult your web server and servlet container documentation if you use a different server than Tomcat.

The Tomcat server uses a simple XML file to define users and assign them roles at the same time. The file is named *tomcat-users.xml* and is located in the *conf* directory. To run the examples in this chapter you need to define at least two users and assign one of them the role admin and the other the role user, like this:

```
<tomcat-users>
    <user name="paula" password="boss" roles="admin" />
    <user name="hans" password="secret" roles="user" />
</tomcat-users>
```

Here the user paula is assigned the admin role and hans is assigned the user role.

The type of access control that should be enforced for a web application resource, such as a JSP page or all files in a directory, is defined in the web application deployment descriptor. The deployment descriptor format is defined by the servlet specification, so all compliant servlet containers support this type of configuration file. It's an XML file named *web.xml*, located in the *WEB-INF* directory for the application. Details about how to package and deploy web applications, as well the complete syntax of the *web.xml* file, are described in Appendix D, *Web-Application Structure and Deployment Descriptor Reference*.

Let's look at how you can define the security constraints for the example we developed in Chapter 9, *Database Access*. To restrict access to all pages dealing with employee registration, it's best to place them in a separate directory. The directory with all examples for Chapter 10, *Authentication and Personalization*, has a subdirectory named *admin* where all these pages are stored. The part of the *web.xml* page that protects this resulting directory looks like this:

```
<security-constraint>
  <web-resource-collection>
```

```
    <web-resource-name>admin</web-resource-name>
    <url-pattern>/ch10/admin/*</url-pattern>
  </web-resource-collection>

  <auth-constraint>
    <role-name>admin</role-name>
  </auth-constraint>
</security-constraint>

<login-config>
  <auth-method>BASIC</auth-method>
  <realm-name>ORA Examples</realm-name>
</login-config>

<security-role>
  <role-name>admin</role-name>
</security-role>
```

The `<security-constraint>` element contains a `<web-resource-collection>` element that defines the resources to be protected, and an `<auth-constraint>` element that defines who has access to the protected resources. Within the `<web-resource-collection>` element, the URL pattern for the protected resource is specified with the `<url-pattern>` element; here it is set to the directory with all the registration pages: `/ch10/admin/*`. The `<role-name>` element within the `<auth-constraint>` element says that only users with the role admin can access the protected resources.

You define the type of authentication to use and a name associated with the protected parts of the application, known as the *realm*, with the `<login-config>` element. The `<auth-method>` element accepts the values BASIC, DIGEST, FORM, and CLIENT-CERT, corresponding to the authentication methods described earlier. Any text can be used as the value of the `<realm-name>` element. The text is shown as part of the message in the dialog the browser displays when it prompts the user for the credentials.

If you use form-based authentication, you must specify the names of your login form and error page in the `<login-config>` element as well:

```
<login-config>
  <auth-method>FORM</auth-method>
  <form-login-config>
    <form-login-page>/login/login.html</form-login-page>
    <form-error-page>/login/error.html</form-error-page>
  </form-login-config>
</login-config>
```

`<security-role>` elements are used to declare all role names that must be mapped to users and groups in the container's security domain. This information can be used by an application deployment tool to help the deployer with this task.

Some containers, like Tomcat, work fine without this element, but to make sure your application can be deployed in any compliant container, you should still declare all roles with `<security-role>` elements.

With these security requirement declarations in the *WEB-INF/web.xml* file, the web server and servlet container take care of all authentication and access control for you. But you may still need to know who the current user is, for instance to personalize the content. Or, if you configure your server to let different types of users access the same pages, you may need to know what type of user is actually accessing a page right now. The Servlet 2.2 API contains methods you can use to get access to this information in your JSP pages, using the implicit `request` object. Let's add another security constraint in the *WEB-INF/web.xml* file for the search pages from Chapter 9:

```
<security-constraint>
  <web-resource-collection>
   <web-resource-name>search</web-resource-name>
    <url-pattern>/ch10/search/*</url-pattern>
  </web-resource-collection>

  <auth-constraint>
    <role-name>admin</role-name>
    <role-name>user</role-name>
  </auth-constraint>
</security-constraint>
```

With this constraint, the server will allow only authenticated users with the roles `admin` and `user` to access the pages in the */ch10/search* directory. You can then use information about who the user is to provide different responses. Example 10-1 shows a fragment of a modified version of the *list.jsp* page from Chapter 9.

Example 10-1. Generating the Response Based on the Current User (list.jsp)

```
...
<ora:loop name="empList" loopId="row" class="Row" >
  <tr>
    <td><%= row.getString("LastName") %></td>
    <td><%= row.getString("FirstName") %></td>
    <td><%= row.getString("Dept") %></td>
    <td><%= row.getString("EmailAddr") %></td>
    <td><%= row.getString("ModDate") %></td>
    <% if (request.isUserInRole("admin") ||
      row.getString("UserName").equals(request.getRemoteUser())) { %>
    <td><%= row.getString("UserName") %></td>
    <td><%= row.getString("Password") %></td>
    <% } else { %>
    <td>****</td>
    <td>****</td>
    <% } %>
```

Example 10-1. Generating the Response Based on the Current User (list.jsp) (continued)

```
<% if (request.isUserInRole("admin")) { %>
  <td>
    <form action="delete.jsp" method="post">
      <input type="hidden" name="userName"
        value='<%= StringFormat.toHTMLString(
          row.getString("UserName")) %>'>
      <input type="hidden" name="firstName"
        value='<%= StringFormat.toHTMLString(
          request.getParameter("firstName")) %>'>
      <input type="hidden" name="lastName"
        value='<%= StringFormat.toHTMLString(
          request.getParameter("lastName")) %>'>
      <input type="hidden" name="dept"
        value='<%= StringFormat.toHTMLString(
          request.getParameter("dept")) %>'>
      <input type="submit" value="Delete">
    </form>
  </td>
  <% } %>
</tr>
</ora:loop>
...
```

The first scriptlet uses the `isUserInRole()` method to see if the authenticated user is an `admin`, and the `getRemoteUser()` method to see if the employee information to be displayed is information about the authenticated user or someone else. If it turns out that the authenticated user is either an `admin` or is displaying information about him- or herself, the username and password information is displayed. Otherwise, the username and password fields are filled with dummy values.

The second scriptlet uses the `isUserInRole()` method again. Here, it is used to add the form with the Delete button only if the user is an `admin`.

Application-Controlled Authentication

Using one of the container-provided mechanisms described in the previous section should be your first choice for authentication. But by definition, being container-provided means the application cannot dynamically add new users and roles to control who is granted access, at least not through a standard API defined by the servlet and JSP specifications.

For some types of applications, it's critical to have a very dynamic authentication model, one that doesn't require an administrator to define access rules before a new user can join the party. I'm sure you have seen countless sites where you can sign up for access to restricted content simply by filling out a form. One example is project management sites, where registered users can access document archives, discussion groups, calendars, and other tools for distributed cooperation. Another example is personalized news sites that you can customize to show news only about things you care about.

Unless you can define new users programmatically in the database used by an external authentication mechanism, you need to roll your own authentication and access control system for these types of applications. In this section, we'll look at the principles for how to do this. Note that this approach sends the user's password as clear text, so it has the same security issues as the container-provided basic and form-based authentication methods.

Application-controlled authentication and access control require the following:

1. User registration

2. A login page

3. The authentication mechanism, invoked by the login page

4. User information saved in the session scope to serve as proof of successful authentication

5. Validation of the session information in all JSP pages requiring restricted access

We'll reuse the example from Chapter 9 for user registration: this allows us to focus on the parts of the application that require access control. The application is a simple billboard service, where employees can post messages related to different projects they are involved with. An employee can customize the application to show messages only about the projects he or she is interested in. Figure 10-1 shows all the pages and how they are related.

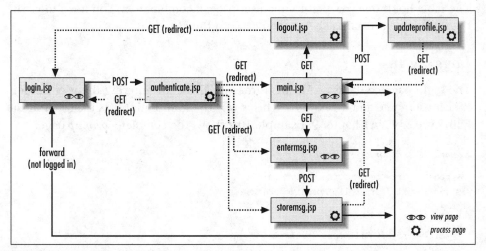

Figure 10-1. Application with authentication and access control

Let's go over it step by step. The *login.jsp* page is our login page. It contains a form that invokes the *authenticate.jsp* page, where the username and password are compared to the information in the employee information database created in Chapter 9. If a matching user is found, the *autheticate.jsp* page creates an EmployeeBean object and saves it in the session scope. This bean serves as proof of authentication. It then redirects the client to a true application page. The page the client is redirected to depends on if the user loaded the *login.jsp* page or tried to directly access an application page without first logging in. All application pages, that is *main.jsp*, *entermsg.jsp*, *storemsg.jsp*, and *updateprofile.jsp*, contain a custom action that looks for the EmployeeBean object and forwards to the *login.jsp* page if it's not found, so the user is forced to log in. When the *login.jsp* page is loaded this way, we keep track of the page that the user tried to access so we can automatically display it after successful authentication. Finally, there's the *logout.jsp* page; this page can be loaded from a link in the *main.jsp* page. It simply terminates the session and redirects to the *login.jsp* page again.

A Table for Personalization Information

Since the sample application in this chapter lets the user personalize the content of the billboard, we need a database table to store information about each employee's choices. The new table is shown in Table 10-1.

Table 10-1. EmployeeProjects Database Table

Column Name	SQL Datatype	Primary Key?
UserName	CHAR (Text)	Yes
ProjectName	CHAR (Text)	Yes

The table holds one row per unique user-project combination. You need to create this table in your database before you can run the example.

Logging In

The login page contains an HTML form with fields for entering the user credentials: a username and a password. This is why the information was included in the Employee table in Chapter 9. Example 10-2 shows the complete *login.jsp* page.

Example 10-2. Login Page (login.jsp)

```
<%@ page import="com.ora.jsp.util.*" %>
<%@ taglib uri="/orataglib" prefix="ora" %>
<html>
  <head>
    <title>Project Billboard</title>
  </head>
```

Example 10-2. Login Page (login.jsp) (continued)

```
<body bgcolor="white">
  <h1>Welcome to the Project Billboard</h1>
  Your personalized project news web site.
  <p>
  <font color="red">
    <% String errorMsg = request.getParameter("errorMsg"); %>
    <%= errorMsg == null ? "" : errorMsg %>
  </font>

  <form action="authenticate.jsp" method="post">

    <% String origURL = request.getParameter("origURL"); %>
    <input type="hidden" name="origURL"
      value="<%= origURL == null ? "" : origURL %>">

    Please enter your User Name and Password, and click Enter.
    <p>
    Name:
    <input name="userName"
      value="<ora:getCookieValue name="userName" />" size="10">
    Password:
    <input type="password" name="password"
      value="<ora:getCookieValue name="password" />" size="10">
    <input type="submit" value="Enter">
    <p>
    Remember my name and password:
    <input type="checkbox" name="remember"
      <%= CookieUtils.isCookieSet("userName", request) ?
        "checked" : "" %> >
    <br>
    (This feature requires cookies to be enabled in your browser.)
  </form>
</body>
</html>
```

The form contains the fields for the username and password, and the action attribute is set to the *authenticate.jsp* page as expected. However, it also contains scripting elements that need an explanation.

The following fragment is used to display a message that gives the user a hint about why the login page is shown after an error:

```
<font color="red">
  <% String errorMsg = request.getParameter("errorMsg"); %>
  <%= errorMsg == null ? "" : errorMsg %>
</font>
```

First, the `errorMsg` variable is set to the value of the `errorMsg` request parameter, using the implicit `request` object and accessed using the `getParameter()` method. This method returns the value of a parameter sent with the request, or `null` if the specified parameter isn't present. The `errMsg` parameter is set by the other pages when they forward to the login page, as you will soon see. When the user loads the *login.jsp* directly, the parameter is not available in the request, so the value of the `errorMsg` variable is set to `null`. The message, or an empty string if it's `null`, is displayed by a JSP expression using the conditional operator described in Chapter 6, *Using Scripting Elements*. Figure 10-2 shows an example of the login page with an error message.

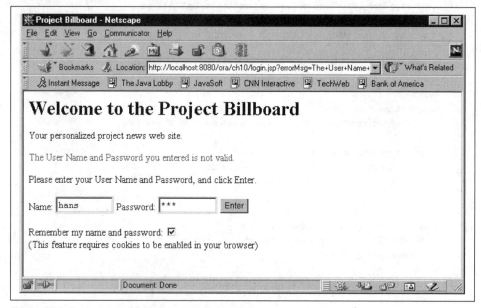

Figure 10-2. Login page with error message

Within the form, you find similar scripting elements:

```
<% String origURL = request.getParameter("origURL"); %>
<input type="hidden" name="origURL"
  value="<%= origURL == null ? "" : origURL %>">
```

Here, a hidden field is set to the value of the originally requested URL. The field is passed as a parameter to the login page when another page forwards to it. This is how we keep track of which page the user wasn't allowed access to because he or she wasn't authenticated yet. Later you'll see how this information is used to load the originally requested page after authentication.

Using cookies to remember the username and password

The more web applications with restricted access a web surfer uses, the more user-names and passwords he or she needs to remember. After a while, it may be tempting to resort to the greatest security sin of all: writing down all usernames and passwords in a file such as *mypasswords.txt*. This invites anyone with access to the user's computer to roam around in all the secret data.

It can be a big problem keeping track of all accounts. Some sites therefore offer to keep track of the username and password using cookies. Cookies are small pieces of text that a server sends to the browser. A cookie with an expiration date is saved on the hard disk and returned to the server every time the user visits the same site until the cookie expires. So is this feature a good thing? Not really, as it amounts to the same security risk as writing down the username and password in a file. Even greater, since anyone with access to the user's computer doesn't even have to find the *mypasswords.txt* file; the browser takes care of sending the credentials automatically. But for sites that use authentication mainly to provide personalization and that don't contain sensitive data, using cookies can be an appreciated tool.

This example shows you how it can be done. If you decide to use it, be sure to make it optional so the user can opt out. We use a custom action called <ora: getCookieValue> to set the value of the input fields for the username and password:

```
Name:
<input name="userName"
   value="<ora:getCookieValue name="userName" />" size="10">
Password:
<input type="password" name="password"
   value="<ora:getCookieValue name="password" />" size="10">
```

The action has just one attribute: name. It's set to the name of the cookie that you're looking for. The action writes the value of the cookie to the response. If the specified cookie is not available, an empty string is returned. Here, the <ora: getCookieValue> action is used to set the default values for the username and password fields if the corresponding cookies are received with the request. You'll see how to send a cookie to the browser later.

The last part of the form creates a checkbox where the user can tell if this feature should be used or not:

```
Remember my name and password:
<input type="checkbox" name="remember"
   <%= CookieUtils.isCookieSet("userName", request) ?
      "checked" : "" %> >
```

To set the checked attribute, a utility method called isCookieSet() in the com.
ora.jsp.util.CookieUtils class is used. It takes two arguments: the cookie
name and the implicit request object. If the cookie is found, the method returns
true; otherwise, it returns false. Here, the method is used with a conditional
operator to set the checked attribute only if the userName cookie is received from
the browser.

Authentication Using a Database

To authenticate a user, you need access to information about the registered users.
For this chapter's examples, we keep all user information in a database. There are
other options, including flat files and LDAP directories. When a user fills out the
login page form and clicks Enter, the authentication page shown in Example 10-3
is processed. This is a large page, so each part is discussed in detail after the complete page.

Example 10-3. Authentication Page (authenticate.jsp)

```
<%@ page language="java" %>
<%@ page import="com.ora.jsp.sql.*" %>
<%@ taglib uri="/orataglib" prefix="ora" %>

<%-- Remove the validUser session bean, if any --%>
<%   session.removeValue("validUser"); %>

<%
  if (request.getParameter("userName").length() == 0 ||
      request.getParameter("password").length() == 0) {
%>

      <ora:redirect page="login.jsp" >
        <ora:param name="errorMsg"
          value="You must enter a User Name and Password." />
      </ora:redirect>

<% } %>

<%--
  See if the user name and password combination is valid. If not,
  redirect back to the login page with a message.
--%>
<ora:useDataSource id="example"
  className="sun.jdbc.odbc.JdbcOdbcDriver"
  url="jdbc:odbc:example" />

<ora:sqlQuery id="empInfo" dataSource="example">
  SELECT * FROM Employee
```

Example 10-3. Authentication Page (authenticate.jsp) (continued)

```
    WHERE UserName = ? AND Password = ?
  <ora:sqlStringValue param="userName" />
  <ora:sqlStringValue param="password" />
</ora:sqlQuery>

<% if (empInfo.size() != 1) { %>

    <ora:redirect page="login.jsp" >
      <ora:param name="errorMsg"
      value="The User Name and Password you entered are not valid." />
    </ora:redirect>

<% } else { %>

    <%--
      Create an EmployeeBean and save it in
      the session scope and redirect to the appropriate page.
    --%>
    <% Row oneRow = (Row) empInfo.firstElement();  %>

    <jsp:useBean id="validUser" scope="session"
      class="com.ora.jsp.beans.emp.EmployeeBean" >
      <jsp:setProperty name="validUser" property="userName"
        value='<%= oneRow.getString("UserName") %>' />
      <jsp:setProperty name="validUser" property="firstName"
        value='<%= oneRow.getString("FirstName") %>' />
      <jsp:setProperty name="validUser" property="lastName"
        value='<%= oneRow.getString("LastName") %>' />
      <jsp:setProperty name="validUser" property="dept"
        value='<%= oneRow.getString("Dept") %>' />
      <jsp:setProperty name="validUser" property="empDate"
        value='<%= oneRow.getString("EmpDate") %>' />
      <jsp:setProperty name="validUser" property="emailAddr"
        value='<%= oneRow.getString("EmailAddr") %>' />
    </jsp:useBean>

    <%-- Add the projects --%>
    <ora:sqlQuery id="empProjects" dataSource="example">
      SELECT * FROM EmployeeProjects
        WHERE UserName = ?
      <ora:sqlStringValue param="userName" />
    </ora:sqlQuery>

    <%
      String[] projects = new String[empProjects.size()];
      int i = 0;
    %>
    <ora:loop name="empProjects" loopId="row"
```

Example 10-3. Authentication Page (authenticate.jsp) (continued)

```
      className="com.ora.jsp.sql.Row" >
      <% projects[i++] = row.getString("ProjectName"); %>
    </ora:loop>

    <jsp:setProperty name="validUser" property="projects"
     value="<%= projects %>" />

    <% if (request.getParameter("remember") != null) { %>

        <ora:addCookie name="userName"
          value='<%= request.getParameter("userName") %>'
          maxAge="2592000" />
        <ora:addCookie name="password"
          value='<%= request.getParameter("password") %>'
         maxAge="2592000" />

    <% } else { %>

        <ora:addCookie name="userName"
          value='<%= request.getParameter("userName") %>'
          maxAge="0" />
        <ora:addCookie name="password"
          value='<%= request.getParameter("password") %>'
          maxAge="0" />
    <% } %>

    <%--
      Redirect to the main page or to the original URL, if
      invoked as a result of an access attempt to a protected
      page.
    --%>
    <% if (request.getParameter("origURL").length() != 0) { %>
        <ora:redirect
          page='<%= request.getParameter("origURL") %>' />
    <% } else { %>
        <ora:redirect page="main.jsp" />
    <% } %>


<% } %>
```

The first thing that happens in Example 10-3 is that a session scope object named validUser is removed if it exists. As you will see later, validUser is the name we use for the EmployeeBean object, and its presence in the session scope indicates that the corresponding user has successfully logged in. If an EmployeeBean object is already saved in the session scope, it may represent a user that forgot to log out, so we must make sure it's removed when a new login attempt is made.

Next, a scriptlet is used to ensure that both the username and the password are passed as parameters. The same getParameter() method used in Example 10-2 is used here to retrieve the parameter values. If one or both parameters are missing, the <ora:redirect> action redirects back to the login page again. Here you see how the errorMsg parameter used in the *login.page* gets its value.

If the request contains both parameters, one of the database actions introduced in Chapter 9 is used to see if there's a user with the specified name and password in the database:

```
<ora:sqlQuery id="empInfo" dataSource="example">
  SELECT * FROM Employee
    WHERE UserName = ? AND Password = ?
  <ora:sqlStringValue param="userName" />
  <ora:sqlStringValue param="password" />
</ora:sqlQuery>

<% if (empInfo.size() == 0) { %>

    <ora:redirect page="login.jsp" >
      <ora:param name="errorMsg"
        value="The User Name and Password you entered are not valid." />
    </ora:redirect>
```

If the query doesn't match a registered user (i.e., empInfo.size() returns 0), an <ora:redirect> action redirects back to the login page with an appropriate error message. Otherwise, the processing continues.

Creating the validation object

If a user is found, the single row from the query result is extracted and the column values are used to populate the single value properties of an EmployeeBean object. An EmployeeBean has the properties shown in Table 10-2.

Table 10-2. Properties for com.ora.jsp.beans.emp.EmployeeBean

Property Name	Java Type	Access	Description
userName	String	read/write	The employee's unique username
firstName	String	read/write	The employee's first name
lastName	String	read/write	The employee's last name
dept	String	read/write	The employee's department name
empDate	String	read/write	The employee's employment date in the format yyyy-MM-dd
emailAddr	String	read/write	The employee's email address
projects	String[]	read/write	A list of all projects the employee is involved in

The bean is named `validUser` and placed in the session scope using the standard `<jsp:useBean>` action. All properties are set to the values returned from the database using `<jsp:setProperty>` actions:

```
<% Row oneRow = (Row) empInfo.firstElement();  %>

<jsp:useBean id="validUser" scope="session"
  class="com.ora.jsp.beans.emp.EmployeeBean" >
  <jsp:setProperty name="validUser" property="userName"
    value='<%= oneRow.getString("UserName") %>' />
  <jsp:setProperty name="validUser" property="firstName"
    value='<%= oneRow.getString("FirstName") %>' />
  <jsp:setProperty name="validUser" property="lastName"
    value='<%= oneRow.getString("LastName") %>' />
  <jsp:setProperty name="validUser" property="dept"
    value='<%= oneRow.getString("Dept") %>' />
  <jsp:setProperty name="validUser" property="empDate"
    value='<%= oneRow.getString("EmpDate") %>' />
  <jsp:setProperty name="validUser" property="emailAddr"
    value='<%= oneRow.getString("EmailAddr") %>' />
</jsp:useBean>
```

As I mentioned earlier, this application lets the user select the projects he or she is interested in, so that only messages related to these projects are shown on the main page. The user's choices are stored in the `EmployeeProjects` database table described in Table 10-1. Next, we retrieve all projects from `Employee-Projects` for the current user and set the value of the corresponding property in the bean to the complete list:

```
<%-- Add the projects --%>
<ora:sqlQuery id="empProjects" dataSource="example">
  SELECT * FROM EmployeeProjects
    WHERE UserName = ?
  <ora:sqlStringValue param="userName" />
</ora:sqlQuery>

<%
  String[] projects = new String[empProjects.size()];
  int i = 0;
%>
<ora:loop name="empProjects" loopId="row" class="Row" >
  <% projects[i++] = row.getString("ProjectName"); %>
</ora:loop>

<jsp:setProperty name="validUser" property="projects"
  value="<%= projects %>" />
```

The value of the `EmployeeBean` projects property must be set as a `String` array. A scriptlet combined with an `<ora:loop>` action is used to first create a `String` array with the result from the database. A `<jsp:setProperty>` action is then used to set it as the `projects` property value of the `validUser` bean.

Setting and deleting cookies

If the user asked for the user credentials to be remembered, we need to send the corresponding cookies to the browser. The checkbox value is sent to the authentication page as a parameter named `remember`:

```
<% if (request.getParameter("remember") != null) { %>

    <ora:addCookie name="userName"
      value='<%= request.getParameter("userName") %>'
      maxAge="2592000" />
    <ora:addCookie name="password"
      value='<%= request.getParameter("password") %>'
     maxAge="2592000" />

<% } else { %>

    <ora:addCookie name="userName"
      value='<%= request.getParameter("userName") %>'
      maxAge="0" />
    <ora:addCookie name="password"
      value='<%= request.getParameter("password") %>'
      maxAge="0" />
<% } %>
```

The `<ora:addCookie>` custom action is used to send cookies to the browser. If the parameter is set, the cookies are sent with a maximum age value representing 30 days, expressed in seconds (2592000). As long as the user returns to this site within this time frame, the cookies are sent with the request and the login page uses the values to automatically fill out the form fields. If the user decides not to use this feature and unchecks the box, we still send the cookies, but with a maximum age of 0. This means the cookies expire immediately and will never be sent to this server again. If you want to send a cookie to a browser that should be valid only until the user closes the browser, set the maximum age to a negative number (i.e., –1).

Redirect to the application page

The only thing left is to redirect the browser to the appropriate page. If the authentication process was started as a result of the user requesting a protected page without being logged in, the original URL is sent by the login page as the value of the `origURL` parameter:

```
<% if (request.getParameter("origURL").length() != 0) { %>
    <ora:redirect
```

```
              page='<%= request.getParameter("origURL") %>' />
      <% } else { %>
          <ora:redirect page="main.jsp" />
      <% } %>
```

If this parameter has a value, the browser is redirected to the originally requested page; otherwise, it is redirected to the main entry page for the application.

Checking for a Valid Session

Authentication is only half of the solution. We must also add access control to each page in the application. Example 10-4 shows the *main.jsp* page as an example of a protected page. This page shows all messages for the projects of the user's choice. It also has a form where the user can change the list of projects, and links to a page for posting new messages and to log out.

Example 10-4. Protected JSP Page (main.jsp)

```
<%@ page language="java" contentType="text/html" %>
<%@ page import="com.ora.jsp.beans.news.*" %>
<%@ page import="com.ora.jsp.util.*" %>
<%@ taglib uri="/orataglib" prefix="ora" %>
<html>
  <head>
    <title>Project Billboard</title>
  </head>
  <body bgcolor="white">

    <%-- Verify that the user is logged in --%>
    <ora:validateSession name="validUser"
      loginPage="login.jsp" errorMsg="Please log in first." />

    <jsp:useBean id="validUser" scope="session"
        class="com.ora.jsp.beans.emp.EmployeeBean" />

    <h1>Welcome <%= validUser.getFirstName() %></h1>
    Your profile currently shows you like information about the
    following checked-off projects. If you would like to update your
    profile, make the appropriate changes below and click
    Update Profile.
    <form action="updateprofile.jsp" method="post">
      <input type="checkbox" name="projects" value="JSP"
        <%= ArraySupport.contains(validUser.getProjects(), "JSP") ?
             "checked" : "" %> >JSP<br>
      <input type="checkbox" name="projects" value="Servlet"
        <%= ArraySupport.contains(validUser.getProjects(), "Servlet") ?
             "checked" : "" %> >Servlet<br>
      <input type="checkbox" name="projects" value="EJB"
        <%= ArraySupport.contains(validUser.getProjects(), "EJB") ?
```

Example 10-4. Protected JSP Page (main.jsp) (continued)

```
            "checked" : "" %> >EJB<br>
  <input type="submit" value="Update Profile">
</form>
<hr>

When you're done reading the news, please <a href="logout.jsp">
log out</a>.

<hr>
<a href=entermsg.jsp>Post a new message</a>
<p>

<jsp:useBean id="news" scope="application"
  class="com.ora.jsp.beans.news.NewsBean" />

<%
  NewsItemBean[] newsItems =
    news.getNewsItems(validUser.getProjects());
  pageContext.setAttribute("newsItems", newsItems);
%>

<table>
  <ora:loop name="newsItems" loopId="newsItem"
    className=" com.ora.jsp.beans.news.NewsItemBean" >
    <tr>
      <td colspan="2">
        Project:
          <jsp:getProperty name="newsItem" property="category" />
      </td>
    </tr>
    <tr>
      <td>
        <jsp:getProperty name="newsItem" property="postedBy" />
      </td>
      <td>
        <jsp:getProperty name="newsItem" property="postedDate" />
      </td>
    </tr>
    <tr>
      <td colspan="2">
        <jsp:getProperty name="newsItem" property="msg" />
      </td>
    </tr>
    <tr>
      <td colspan="2"><hr></td>
    </tr>
```

Example 10-4. Protected JSP Page (main.jsp) (continued)

```
      </ora:loop>
    </table>
  </body>
</html>
```

The most interesting piece of the example, from an access control point of view, is this:

```
<%-- Verify that the user is logged in --%>
    <ora:validateSession name="validUser"
      loginPage="login.jsp" errorMsg="Please log in first." />
```

The `<ora:validateSession>` custom action must be placed at the beginning of all protected pages in the application. It has three mandatory attributes. The `name` attribute specifies the name of the session scope object used to indicate that the session belongs to an authenticated user. Here we specify a name for the `EmployeeBean` object created by the authentication page. If the specified object is not found in the session, it means the page is being requested by a user that has not been authenticated. The custom action then forwards to the URL specified by the `loginPage` attribute, adding an `errorMsg` parameter with the value specified by the `errorMsg` attribute. As in Example 10-2, the `errorMsg` parameter is used to add a message on the login page to let the user know why a different page than the requested one is displayed. As with a regular forward, the conditional forward function implemented by the `<ora:validateSession>` action aborts the processing of the rest of the page.

Providing personalized content

The rest of the page shown in Example 10-4 produces a personalized page for the authenticated user. Figure 10-3 shows what it might look like.

First, the `validUser` bean properties are used to welcome the user to the site by name. Next comes a form with checkboxes for all projects. The same technique used in Chapter 6 is also used here to set the checked attribute for the projects listed in the user's profile. The user can modify the list of projects and click Update Profile to invoke the *updateprofile.jsp* page. This page modifies the profile information in the database. We'll take a look at how it's done later.

A `NewsBean` containing `NewsItemBean` objects is then used to display news items for all projects matching the user's profile. The implementations of these beans are intended only as examples. Initially, the `NewsBean` contains one hard-coded message for each news category, and the news items are kept in memory only. A real implementation would likely store all news items permanently in a database.

Example 10-4 also contains a link to a page where a news item can be posted. If you look at the source for the *entermsg.jsp* file, you can see that it's just a JSP page

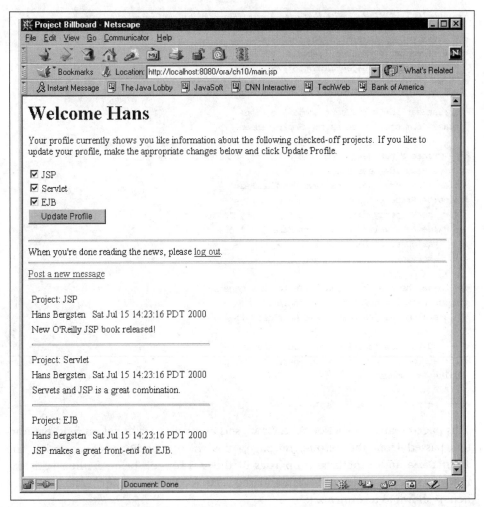

Figure 10-3. Personalized application page

with the `<ora:validateSession>` action at the top and a regular HTML form
that invokes the *storemsg.jsp* file with a POST request. The POST method is appropriate here, since the form fields are used to update information on the server (the
in-memory NewsBean database).

The complete *storemsg.jsp* page is shown in Example 10-5.

Example 10-5. POST Page with Restricted Access (storemsg.jsp)

```
<%@ page language="java" %>
<%@ taglib uri="/orataglib" prefix="ora" %>

<%-- Verify that the user is logged in --%>
<ora:validateSession name="validUser"
  loginPage="login.jsp" errorMsg="Please log in first." />
```

Example 10-5. POST Page with Restricted Access (storemsg.jsp) (continued)

```
<%-- Verify that it's a POST method --%>
<% if (!request.getMethod().equals("POST")) { %>
    <ora:redirect page="main.jsp" />
<% } %>

<jsp:useBean id="validUser" scope="session"
  class="com.ora.jsp.beans.emp.EmployeeBean" />

<%-- Create a new news item bean with the submitted info --%>
<jsp:useBean id="newsItem"
  class="com.ora.jsp.beans.news.NewsItemBean" >
  <jsp:setProperty name="newsItem" property="*" />
  <jsp:setProperty name="newsItem" property="postedBy"
    value='<%= validUser.getFirstName() + " " +
      validUser.getLastName() %>' />
</jsp:useBean>

<%-- Make the news bean available to this page --%>
<jsp:useBean id="news" scope="application"
  class="com.ora.jsp.beans.news.NewsBean" />

<%-- Add the new news item bean to the list --%>
<jsp:setProperty name="news" property="newsItem"
  value="<%= newsItem %>" />

<ora:redirect page="main.jsp" />
```

This page creates a new `NewsItemBean`, sets all properties based on field parameters passed from the *entermsg.jsp* page, plus the `postedBy` property using the `firstName` and `lastName` properties of the `validUser` bean. It then adds the new news item to the `NewsBean` and redirects to the main page, where the new item is shown as a confirmation.

Let's focus on the access control aspects. At the top of the page, you find the same `<ora:validateSession>` action as with all other protected application pages. If a user fills out the form in *entermsg.jsp* and walks away from the computer without submitting the form, the user's session may time out. When the user then returns and clicks Submit, the `<ora:validateSession>` action doesn't find the `validUser` bean in the session and therefore forwards to the login page, setting the `origURL` parameter to the URL of the *storemsg.jsp*. After successful authentication, the authentication page redirects to the original URL, the *storemsg.jsp*. However, a redirect is always a GET request.* All the parameters sent with the original POST request for *storemsg.jsp* are lost; a POST request carries the parameter values

---

* The HTTP specification (RFC 2616) states that a browser is not allowed to change the method for the request when it receives a redirect response (status code 302). But, as acknowledged by the HTTP specification, all major browsers available today change a POST request into a GET anyway.

in the message body, instead of in the URL (as a query string) as a GET request does, so the original URL we saved doesn't include the parameters. If we don't take care of this special case, an empty NewsItemBean will be added to the list.

There are at least two ways to deal with this. In Example 10-5, the <ora: validateSession> action is followed by a scriptlet checking that the request for this page is a POST request. If not, it redirects to the main page without processing the request. This is the easiest way to deal with the problem, but it also means that the user will have to retype the message again. The chance that a session times out before a form is submitted is small, so in most cases this is not a big deal. It's therefore the solution I recommend.

If you absolutely must find a way to not lose the POST parameters when a session times out, here is a brief outline of a solution:

1. Modify the <ora:validateSession> action to send a URL in the origURL parameter suitable for use as a forward URL, as opposed to a redirect URL, if the page is invoked with a POST request. A forward URL must be relative to the servlet context path, while a redirect URL should be absolute.

2. Use a scriptlet in the login page to save all POST parameter values as hidden fields in the form, along with a hidden field that tells if the original request was a GET or a POST request.

3. In the authentication page, *forward* to the originally requested URL if the method was a POST and *redirect* only if it was a GET. The authentication page is always invoked as a POST request. A forward is just a way to let another page continue to process the same request, so the originally requested page is invoked with a POST request as expected, along with all the originally submitted parameters saved as hidden fields in the login page.

Depending on your application, you may also need to save session data as hidden fields in the page that submits the POST request, so that the requested page doesn't have to rely on session information. But this leads to another problem. What if someone other than the user who filled out the form comes along and submits it? Information will then be updated on the server with information submitted by a user that's no longer logged in. One way out of this is to save information about the current user as a hidden field in the form that sends the POST request, and let the authentication page compare this information with the new user's information. If they don't match, the client can be redirected to the main application page instead of forwarded to the originally requested URL.

As you can see, there are a number of things to think about. Whether or not it makes sense to address all the issues depends on the application. My general advice is to keep it simple and stick to the first solution unless your application warrants a more complex approach.

Updating the User Profile

The *updateprofile.jsp* page, used if the user makes new project selections in the main page and clicks Update Profile, is also invoked through the POST method. It follows the same approach as the *storemsg.jsp* page, and is shown in Example 10-6. But what's interesting about the *updateprofile.jsp* page is that it shows how to replace multirow data for a user, and is an instance of when you need to care about transactions.

Example 10-6. Updating Multiple Database Rows (updateprofile.jsp)

```
<%@ page language="java" %>
<%@ taglib uri="/orataglib" prefix="ora" %>

<%-- Verify that the user is logged in --%>
<ora:validateSession name="validUser"
  loginPage="login.jsp" errorMsg="Please log in first." />

<%-- Verify that it's a POST method --%>
<% if (!request.getMethod().equals("POST")) { %>
    <ora:redirect page="main.jsp" />
<% } %>

<%-- Make the bean available for scripting elements --%>
<jsp:useBean id="validUser" scope="session"
  class="com.ora.jsp.beans.emp.EmployeeBean" />

<%-- Update the project list in the bean --%>
<jsp:setProperty name="validUser" property="projects"
  value='<%= request.getParameterValues("projects") %>' />

<ora:useDataSource id="example"
  className="sun.jdbc.odbc.JdbcOdbcDriver"
  url="jdbc:odbc:example" />

<ora:sqlTransaction dataSource="example">

  <%-- Delete the old project (if any) and insert the new ones --%>
  <ora:sqlUpdate>
    DELETE FROM EmployeeProjects
      WHERE UserName = ?
    <ora:sqlStringValue name="validUser" property="userName" />
  </ora:sqlUpdate>

  <ora:loop name="validUser" property="projects" loopId="project"
    className="String" >
    <ora:sqlUpdate>
      INSERT INTO EmployeeProjects
        (UserName, ProjectName) VALUES(?, ?)
```

Example 10-6. Updating Multiple Database Rows (updateprofile.jsp) (continued)

```
      <ora:sqlStringValue name="validUser" property="userName" />
      <ora:sqlStringValue value="<%= project %>" />
    </ora:sqlUpdate>
  </ora:loop>

</ora:sqlTransaction>

<%-- Redirect to main page --%>
<ora:redirect page="main.jsp" />
```

The list of new projects selected by the user is sent to the *updateprofile.jsp* page in the projects request parameter. The projects bean property can therefore be updated using a <jsp:setProperty> action, setting the value to the result of the getParameterValues() method. As you may remember from Chapter 6, this method returns a String[] with all values for a parameter, and that's also the data type defined for the projects property in the bean.

One important item to note here. If the user deselects all checkboxes in the *main. jsp* page (Example 10-4), all projects should be removed from the bean as well. The problem here is that if no checkbox is selected, the projects request parameter is not sent at all. You must therefore use the type of request-time attribute value shown in Example 10-6, as opposed to using the param property, for the <jsp:setProperty> action. The <jsp:setProperty> action calls a property setter method only if it can find a corresponding parameter in the request. With no checkbox selected, the project's property setter is not called and the previous value is not cleared. When you use the getParameterValues() method as a request-time attribute value, however, it works as it should: if no checkbox is selected the method returns null, clearing the property value; otherwise, it returns a String[] with the currently selected values, setting the property to the current list.

The EmployeeProjects table (Table 10-1) contains one row per project for a user, with the username in the UserName column and the project name in the ProjectName column. The easiest way to update the database information is to first delete all existing rows, if any, and then insert rows for the new projects selected by the user. Since this requires execution of multiple SQL statements and all must either succeed or fail, the <ora:sqlUpdate> actions are placed within the body of an <ora:sqlTransaction> action. If the first <ora:sqlUpdate> action is successful but one of the others fails, the database information deleted by the first is restored so the database correctly reflects the state before the change.

To delete the rows in the database, use the <ora:sqlUpdate> action with a SQL DELETE statement. A WHERE clause is used so that only the rows for the current user are deleted. Then the <ora:loop> action is used to loop through all projects for the `validUser` bean. The body of the `<ora:loop>` action contains an `<ora:sqlUpdate>` action that executes an `INSERT` statement for each project:

```
<ora:loop name="validUser" property="projects" loopId="project"
   className="String" >
   <ora:sqlUpdate>
     INSERT INTO EmployeeProjects
        (UserName, ProjectName) VALUES(?, ?)
        <ora:sqlStringValue name="validUser" property="userName" />
        <ora:sqlStringValue value="<%= project %>" />
   </ora:sqlUpdate>
</ora:loop>
```

The variable name to use for the component within the loop body is specified by the `loopId` attribute. Here it's set to `project`. Within the body, the loop variable is then used with the `<ora:sqlStringValue>` action to set the value for the `ProjectName` column, so a new value is used for each pass through the `projects` property array. The `UserName` column has the same value in each row, so the `validUser` bean's `userName` property is used as the value for the corresponding `<ora:sqlStringValue>` action.

Logging Out

Since the proof of authentication is kept in the session scope, the user will be automatically logged out when the session times out. But even so, an application that requires authentication should always provide a way for the user to explicitly log out. This way a user can be sure that if he or she leaves the desk, no one else can come by and use the application.

The main page in the example application contains a link to the logout page, shown in Example 10-7.

Example 10-7. Logout Page (logout.jsp)

```
<%@ page language="java" %>
<%@ taglib uri="/orataglib" prefix="ora" %>


<%--
   Terminate the session and redirect to the login page.
--%>
<% session.invalidate(); %>


<ora:redirect page="login.jsp" />
```

This page explicitly terminates the session by calling the `invalidate()` method of the `session` object in a scriptlet, and then redirects back to the login page. All objects kept in the session are removed and the session is marked as invalid. The next time someone logs in, a new session is created.

If you want to test the examples described in this chapter, you first must create at least one user with the application we developed in Chapter 9. To see how the automatic redirect to the originally requested page works, you can open two browser windows and log in from both. They both share the same session, so if you log out using one window and then try to load the "post a new message" page with the other, you will first be redirected to the login page. After you've entered your username and password, you're redirected to the page for posting a message.

Other Security Concerns

In this chapter we have discussed only authentication and access control, but there's a lot more to web application security. You also need to ensure that no one listening on the network can read the data. In addition, you need to consider ways to verify that the data has not been modified. The common terms for these concepts (also used in the Servlet 2.2 specification) are *confidentiality* and *data privacy* for the first, and *integrity checking* for the second.

On an intranet, users can usually be trusted not to use network listeners to get to data they shouldn't see. But on the Internet, you can make no assumptions. If you provide access to sensitive data, you have to make sure it's protected appropriately. Network security is a huge subject area, and clearly not within the scope of this book. Therefore I will touch on only the most common way to take care of both confidentiality and integrity checking: the Secure Socket Layer (SSL) protocol.

SSL is a protocol based on public key cryptography: it relies on a public key and a private key pair. Messages sent by someone, or something (such as a server), are encoded using the private key, and can be decoded by the receiver only by using the corresponding public key. Besides confidentiality and integrity checking, public key cryptography also provides the means for very secure authentication: if a message can be decoded with a certain public key, you know it was encoded with the corresponding private key. The keys are issued, in the form of certificates together with user identity information, by a trusted organization such as VeriSign (*http://www.verisign.com*).

Both the client and the server can have certificates. However, the most common scenario today is that only the server has a certificate, and can thereby positively identify itself to the client. The SSL protocol takes care of this server authentication during the handshaking phase of setting up the connection. If the server certificate doesn't match the server's hostname, the user is warned or the connection is refused. If the client also has a certificate, it can be used to authenticate the client to the server in a more secure fashion than basic and digest authentication.

Even if only a server certificate is used, however, the communication between the client and the server is still encrypted. This means that the issue of sending passwords as clear text for basic authentication and form-based authentication, as well as the application-controlled authentication we developed in this chapter, is nullfied.

Most web servers today support server certificates and SSL. When you use HTTP over SSL (HTTPS), the URLs start with `https` instead of `http`. Not all applications need the kind of tight security offered by HTTPS, but you should be aware of all security threats, and carefully evaluate if the risks of not using it are acceptable for your application.

11

Internationalization

Taking the term World Wide Web literally means that your web site needs to respect the languages and customs of all visitors, no matter where they come from. More and more, large web sites provide content in several different languages. Just look at a site like Yahoo!, which provides directory services in the local languages of more than 20 countries in Europe, Asia, and North America. Other good examples are CNN, with local news for 8 different countries, and Vitaminic (*http://www. vitaminic.com*), a site with MP3 music and artist information customized for different countries. If the site contains only static content, it's fairly easy to support multiple languages: just make a static version of the site for each language. But this approach is not practical for a site with dynamic content. If you develop a separate site for each language, you will have to duplicate the code that generates the dynamic content as well, leading to maintenance problems when errors are discovered or when it's time to add new features. Luckily, Java and JSP provide a number of tools to make it easier to develop one version of a site that can handle multiple languages.

The process of developing an application that caters to the needs of users from different parts of the world includes two phases: *internationalization* and *localization*.

Internationalization means preparing the application by identifying everything that will be different for different geographical regions, and providing means to use different versions of all these items instead of hardcoded values. Examples of this are labels and messages, online help texts, graphics, format of dates, times, and numbers, currencies, measurements, and sometimes even the page layouts and colors. You should note that instead of spelling out the word internationalization, the abbreviation I18N is often used. It stands for "an I followed by 18 characters and an N."

When an application has been internationalized, it can also be localized for different regions. This means providing the messages, the help texts, the graphics and so forth, as well as the rules for formatting dates, times, and numbers, for one or more regions that the internationalized application can use. Localization is sometimes abbreviated L10N, following the same logic as the I18N abbreviation. The set of localized information for one region is called a *locale*. Support for new locales can be added without changing the application itself.

In this chapter, we first look at the basic Java classes used for internationalization. If you're not a programmer, you can skim through this section without worrying about the details. (However, you should understand the terminology, and knowing a bit about the inner workings of these classes also makes it easier to understand the rest of the chapter.) We then develop a web application in which visitors can answer a poll question and see statistics over how other visitors have answered, using a set of custom actions that hide the Java classes to make internationalization a lot easier. You can reuse these custom actions in your own application to handle most internationalization needs. The poll site is localized for three languages. The initial language is based on the user's browser configuration. The user can also explicitly select one of the supported languages.

How Java Supports Internationalization and Localization

Java was designed with internationalization in mind and includes a number of classes to make the effort as painless as possible. The primary class used for internationalization represents a specific geographical region. Instances of this class are used by other classes to format dates and numbers, as well as including localized strings and other objects in an application. There are also classes for dealing with different character encodings, which we will see later in the chapter.

The Locale Class

All Java classes that provide localization support use a class named `java.util.Locale`. An instance of this class represents a particular geographical, political, or cultural region, as specified by a combination of a language code and a country code. Java classes that perform tasks that differ depending on a user's language and local customs, called locale-sensitive operations, use a `Locale` instance to decide how to operate. Examples of locale-sensitive operations are the interpretation of date strings and formatting numeric values.

You create a `Locale` instance using a constructor that takes the country code and language code as arguments:

```
java.util.Locale usLocale = new Locale("en", "US");
```

Here, a `Locale` for U.S. English is created. George Bernard Shaw (a famous Irish playwright) once observed, "England and America are two countries divided by a common language," so it's no surprise that both a language code and a country code are needed to describe some locales completely. The language code, a lower-case two-letter combination, is defined by the ISO 639 standard, available at *http:// www.ics.uci.edu/pub/ietf/http/related/iso639.txt*. The country code, an uppercase two-letter combination, is defined by the ISO 3166 standard, available at *http://www. chemie.fu-berlin.de/diverse/doc/ISO_3166.html*. Tables 11-1 and 11-2 show some of these codes.

Table 11-1. ISO-639 Language Codes

Language Code	Language
af	Afrikaans
da	Danish
de	German
el	Greek
en	English
es	Spanish
fr	French
ja	Japanese
pl	Polish
ru	Russian
sv	Swedish
zh	Chinese

Table 11-2. ISO-3166 Country Codes

Country Code	Country
DK	Denmark
DE	Germany
GR	Greece
MX	Mexico
NZ	New Zealand
ZA	South Africa
GB	United Kingdom
US	United States

As luck would have it, these two standards are also used to define language and country codes in HTTP. As you may remember from Chapter 2, *HTTP and Servlet Basics*, a browser can send an `Accept-Language` header with a request for a web resource such as a JSP page. The value of this header contains one or more codes for languages that the user prefers, based on how the browser is configured. If you use a Netscape 4 browser, you can specify your preferred languages in the Edit-> Preferences dialog, under the Languages tab. In Internet Explorer 4, you find the same thing in View->Internet Options when you click the Language button under the General tab. If you specify more than one language, they are included in the header as a comma-separated list:

```
Accept-Language: en-US, en, sv
```

The languages are listed in order of preference, with each language represented either by just the language code or by the language code and country code separated by a dash (-). This example header specifies the first choice as U.S. English, followed by any type of English, and finally Swedish. The HTTP specification allows an alternative to listing the codes in order of preference, namely adding a so-called q-value to each code. The q-value is a value between 0.0 and 1.0 indicating the relative preference between the codes. Very few browsers, if any, use this alternative today, however.

The Accept-Language header helps you localize your application. You could write code that reads this header and creates the corresponding Locale instances. The good news is you don't have to do this yourself; the servlet container takes care of it for you and makes the locale information available through two methods on the implicit request object:

```
java.util.Locale preferredLocale = request.getLocale();
java.util.Enumeration allLocales = request.getLocales();
```

The getLocale() method returns the Locale with the highest preference ranking, and the getLocales() method returns an Enumeration of all locales in order of preference. All you have to do is match the preferred locales to the ones that your web application supports. The easiest way to do this is to loop through the preferred locales and stop when you find a match. As you will see later, the custom actions developed for this book relieve you of all of this, but now you know how it's done.

Formatting Numbers and Dates

Let's look at how a locale can be used. One thing that we who live on this planet have a hard time agreeing upon is how to write dates and numbers. The order of the month, the day, and the year; if the numeric value or the name should be used for the month; what character to use to separate the fractional part of a number: all of these details differ between countries, even between countries that speak the same language. And even though these details may seem picky, using the wrong format can cause a great deal of confusion. For instance, if you ask for something to be done by 5/2, an American thinks you mean May 2 while a Swede believes that it's due by February 5.

Java provides two main classes to deal with formatting of numbers and dates for a specific locale, appropriately named `java.text.NumberFormat` and `java.text.DateFormat`, respectively.

The `NumberFormat` class was used in Chapter 9, *Database Access*, to format the price information for items in a shopping cart according to the customs of the country where the server is located. By default, the `NumberFormat` class uses the locale of the underlying operating system. If used on a server configured to use a U.S. English locale, it formats numbers according to American customs; on a server configured with an Italian locale, it formats them according to Italian customs, and so forth. But you can also explicitly specify the locale to format numbers according to the rules for locales other than the one used by the operating system:

```
java.util.Locale locale = request.getLocale();
java.text.NumberFormat nf =
  java.text.NumberFormat.getNumberInstance(locale);
String localNumber = nf.format(10000.00);
```

This piece of code creates a `String` with the number 10000.00 formatted according to the locale that corresponds to the preferred language specified by the `Accept-Language` header in a request. Besides the `getNumberInstance()` method, you can use the `getPercentInstance()` and the `getCurrencyInstance()` to format a decimal number as a percentage string or any number as a currency string.

The `DateFormat` class works basically the same way, but how dates are written differs a lot more between locales than numbers do, since the day and month names are sometimes spelled out in the local language. Besides the locale, a formatting style is also specified as one of DEFAULT, SHORT, MEDIUM, LONG, or FULL:

```
java.util.Locale locale = request.getLocale();
java.text.DateFormat df =
  java.text.DateFormat.getDateInstance(df.SHORT, locale);
String localDate = df.format(new java.util.Date());
```

If the current date is May 2, 2000, this code formats the date as 5/2/00 with an American locale and as 2000-05-02 with a Swedish locale. If you use the FULL formatting style, the results are Tuesday, May 2, 2000 and den 2 maj 2000 instead.

As with the `NumberFormat` class, there are other specialized date formatters besides the one used here. You can use the `getDateTimeInstance()` and `getTimeInstance()` methods to produce strings including both the date and time or just the time.

Using Localized Text

Automatic translation of numbers and dates into the local language is a great help. But until automatic translation software is a lot smarter than it is today, you have to translate all the text used in the application yourself. A set of Java classes then helps you pick the right version for a specific locale.

The main class for dealing with localized resources (such as text, images, and sounds) is named `java.util.ResourceBundle`. This class is actually the abstract superclass for the two subclasses that do the real work, `ListResourceBundle` and `PropertyResourceBundle`, but it provides methods that let you get an appropriate subclass instance, hiding the details about which subclass actually provides the resources. Details about the difference between these two subclasses are beyond the scope of this book. It suffices to say, however, that the `ListResourceBundle` is overkill for our needs when developing web applications, so we will be using an instance of the `PropertyResourceBundle`. To learn more about these classes, I suggest glancing at the Java API documentation.

A `PropertyResourceBundle` instance is associated with a named set of localized text resources, where each resource is identified by a key. The keys and their corresponding text strings are stored in a regular text file as key-value pairs:

```
site_name=The Big Corporation Inc.
company_logo=/images/logo_en.gif
welcome_msg=Hello!
```

Here, three keys, `site_name`, `company_logo`, and `welcome_msg`, have been assigned string values. The key is a string, without spaces or other special characters, and the value is any text. If the value spans more than one line, the line break must be escaped with a backslash character (\):

```
multi_line_msg=This text value\
continues on the next line.
```

The file must use the extension *.properties*, for instance *sitetext.properties*, and be located in the class path used by the Java Virtual Machine. In the case of web applications, you should store the file in the application's *WEB-INF/classes* directory, since this directory is always included in the class path.

When you have created a properties file, you can obtain the text corresponding to a key like this:

```
java.util.Locale locale = request.getLocale();
java.util.ResourceBundle bundle =
  java.util.ResourceBundle.getBundle("sitetext", locale);
String msg = bundle.getString("welcome_msg");
```

Note that the getBundle() method takes two arguments: a Locale argument, the same as the methods for getting number and date formatters; and a bundle name. These arguments are used like this: the method gets the language and country codes from the Locale object and starts looking for a file with a name composed of both the bundle name and the language and country codes. If you pass it a locale for Mexican Spanish, for example, it first looks for a file named *sitetext_es_MX.properties*, where *es* is the language code for Spanish and *MX* is the country code for Mexico. If it can't find a file with this name, it looks for *sitetext_es.properties*, ignoring the country code. If there's still no such file, it uses the file with just the bundle name, *sitetext.properties*.

As you can see, this makes it possible for you to create multiple properties files, each with the text values translated into a specific language for a specific country. In other words, you can create one file for each supported locale. The Resource-Bundle ensures that when you ask for a bundle, you get the one that most closely matches the specified locale, or the default bundle if there is no match. We'll look at an example in detail in the next section.

Besides the ResourceBundle class, there's a class named java.text.Message-Format that you can use for messages composed of fixed text plus variable values, such as, "An earthquake measuring 6.7 on the Richter scale hit Northridge, CA, on January 17, 1994." Here, each underlined word represents a variable value. Another class related to localization is the java.text.Collator class, used for localized string comparison and sorting. These classes are less commonly used, so they are not covered in detail here. You can read more about them in the Java API documentation.

Generating Localized Output

Now that you have an understanding of the type of internationalization support Java provides, let's look at a concrete example. But instead of using the internationalization classes directly in the pages, let's use a set of custom actions based on these classes. Using custom actions minimizes the need for Java code in the JSP pages, making it easier for page authors to develop an internationalized site.

The example application, briefly described in the introduction to this chapter, lets visitors voice their opinions by selecting one of the answers to a question, as well as seeing how others have answered. The text, numbers, and dates are available in three different languages. Figure 11-1 shows all pages used in this application and how they are related.

The first page the user sees is the *poll.jsp* page, shown in Figure 11-2. The language used to display the contents the first time this page is displayed is based on the Accept-Language header value in the request. The top part of the page

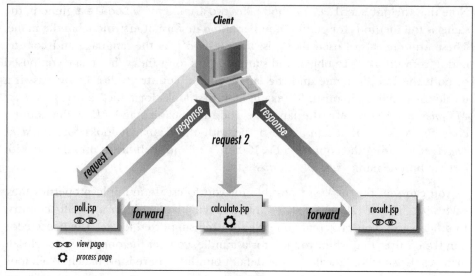

Figure 11-1. Localized poll application pages

contains radio buttons for the three supported languages and a Submit button. If the user wants the application to be presented in another language, he or she selects the corresponding radio button and clicks Submit, causing the page to be requested again, this time with a language parameter included in the request. The value of the language parameter is then used to display the page in the selected language. Information about the selected language is saved as session data, so it's available to all the other application pages.

The *poll.jsp* page also includes a question, linked to a page with background information for the question, and a group of radio buttons representing the different answers, as well as a Submit button. Clicking on the Submit button invokes the *calculate.jsp* page, where the vote is validated. If it's valid, it's added to the global poll result. The request is then forwarded to the *result.jsp* page, which displays the poll statistics with all numbers formatted according to the selected locale. If it's not valid, the request is forwarded back to the *poll.jsp* page.

Both the *poll.jsp* page and the *result.jsp* page are designed to show text, numbers, and dates according to the selected locale using custom actions based on the Java classes described in the previous section. This approach is perfect when the amount of text is small; only one page has to be maintained. But if a page needs to contain a great deal of text, typing it into a properties file and escaping all line breaks may not be the best approach. Some pages also need to use different layouts, colors, images, and general appearances based on the locale. In this case, it's easier to use a separate page per locale. This approach is illustrated by the pages providing more detailed information about the question in this example. The link

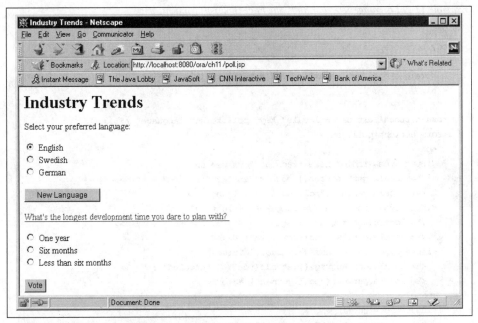

Figure 11-2. The language selection and question page

on the *poll.jsp* page leads to different JSP pages depending on the selected language, named according to the same naming convention as ResourceBundle properties files: *details.jsp*, *details_de.jsp*, and *details_sv.jsp* for English (the default), German, and Swedish pages, respectively. Let's look at the one-page and the multi-page approaches separately.

Using One Page for Multiple Locales

Example 11-1 shows the *poll.jsp* page. That's where the magic of locale selection happens, and the selection is then used to produce text in the corresponding language throughout the page.

Example 11-1. Language Selection and Vote Page (poll.jsp)

```
<%@ page language="java" contentType="text/html" %>
<%@ taglib uri="/orataglib" prefix="ora" %>

<ora:useLocaleBundle id="locale" bundleName="poll"
  supportedLangs="en, sv, de" />

<html>
  <head>
    <title>
      <ora:getLocalText name="locale" key="poll.title" />
    </title>
```

Example 11-1. Language Selection and Vote Page (poll.jsp) (continued)

```
  </head>
  <body bgcolor="white">
    <h1>
      <ora:getLocalText name="locale" key="poll.title" />
    </h1>


    <ora:getLocalText name="locale" key="poll.select_language" />:
    <form action="poll.jsp">
      <p>
      <input type="radio" name="language" value="en"
        <%= locale.getLanguage().equals("en") ? "checked" : "" %>>
        <%= locale.getText("poll.english") %><br>
      <input type="radio" name="language" value="sv"
        <%= locale.getLanguage().equals("sv") ? "checked" : "" %>>
        <%= locale.getText("poll.swedish") %><br>
      <input type="radio" name="language" value="de"
        <%= locale.getLanguage().equals("de") ? "checked" : "" %>>
        <%= locale.getText("poll.german") %><br>
      <p>
      <input type="submit"
        value="<ora:getLocalText name="locale"
          key="poll.new_language" />">
    </form>


    <a href="<ora:getLocalPageName
      name="locale" pageName="details.jsp" />">
      <ora:getLocalText name="locale" key="poll.question" />
    </a>
    <form action="calculate.jsp" method="post">
      <input type="radio" name="answerId" value="1">
      <ora:getLocalText name="locale" key="poll.answer1" />
      <br>
      <input type="radio" name="answerId" value="2">
      <ora:getLocalText name="locale" key="poll.answer2" />
      <br>
      <input type="radio" name="answerId" value="3">
      <ora:getLocalText name="locale" key="poll.answer3" />
      <p>
      <input type="submit"
        value="<ora:getLocalText name="locale"
          key="poll.submit" />">
    </form>
  </body>
</html>
```

At the top of the page, the `taglib` directive is used to identify the library containing all custom actions, as in previous chapters. Then follows the first custom action for localization: `<ora:useLocaleBundle>`. It's described in Table 11-3.

Table 11-3. Attributes for <ora:useLocaleBundle>

Attribute Name	Java Type	Request-Time Value Accepted	Description
id	String	No	Mandatory. The name used to reference the LocaleBean instance.
bundleName	String	Yes	Mandatory. The base name for text resource properties files.
supportedLangs	String	Yes	Mandatory. A comma-separated list of language/country codes. The first code is used as the default language.

This innocent-looking action does a number of things. First, it looks for a LocaleBean with the name specified by the id attribute in the session scope, and creates one if it doesn't exist. The LocaleBean, described in Table 11-4, handles all localization tasks. It can be used as-is, as you will soon see, but in most cases it's used indirectly by other custom actions in the set of localization actions. The action then asks the implicit request object for the list of locales specified by the Accept-Language header, and uses that list to set the bean's requestLocales property. It also looks for a request parameter named language, and if it's present, it uses the value to set the corresponding language property in the bean. Finally, it sets the bean's supportedLangs property to the value of the action attribute with the same name. Both the language property and the supportedLangs property take a value that's either just a language code, or a language code plus a country code separated by a dash (e.g., Es-MX). As shown in Example 11-1, you can specify a number of supported languages as a comma-separated list of codes. The final attribute is called bundleName; this attribute is the base name for a set of ResourceBundle properties files, as described in the first section of this chapter.

Table 11-4. Properties for com.ora.jsp.bean.locale.LocaleBean

Property Name	Java Type	Access	Description
bundleName	String	write	The base name for the properties files
charset	String	write	The charset used to decode parameters
language	String	read/write	The language code for the selected locale
locale	java.util.Locale	read	The locale, selected based on other properties
requestLocales	java.util.Locale[]	write	The locales received with the request
supportedLangs	String	write	A comma-separated list of language codes

With all these properties set, the bean can decide which locale to use for the user requesting the page. The first time the page is requested, the `language` property is not set, so it compares the language specified by each locale in the `requestLocales` property to the set of languages in the `supportedLangs` property, and selects the first locale that is supported. Since the request locales are ordered by preference, the locale with the highest ranking that represents a supported language is selected. As you will soon see, the user can also request this page with a specific language specified by the `language` parameter. In this case, the action sets the corresponding bean property and the bean uses this value to select the locale, assuming it's one of the supported languages. If neither the request locales nor the explicitly specified language is supported, the bean selects a locale that represents the first language listed in the `supportedLanguages` property.

The next action in Example 11-1 is `<ora:getLocalText>`. This is described in Table 11-5.

Table 11-5. Attributes for <ora:getLocalText>

Attribute Name	Java Type	Request-Time Value Accepted	Description
name	String	No	Mandatory. The name of the `LocaleBean` instance.
key	String	Yes	Mandatory. The name of a property in the text resource properties files.

The `<ora:getLocalText>` action is used to get the page title and header. The `name` attribute specifies the name of the `LocaleBean` created by the `<ora:useLocaleBundle>` action, and the `key` attribute specifies one of the properties in the files with localized strings. These files are named exactly like the files used by the `ResourceBundle` described in the previous section. In other words, you need one file with the same name as the base name (specified as the `bundleName` for the `<ora:useLocaleBundle>` action) for the default locale, and one file with a name that combines the base name and a language code for all other locales. In this example, then, you need the files *poll.properties, poll_de.properties*, and *poll_sv. properties*. If you want to add support for another language, say Italian, just create a *poll_it.properties* file and add `it` (the language code for Italian) to the list of supported languages for the `<ora:useLocaleBundle>` action. All properties files must be placed in the *WEB-INF/classes* directory for the web application so that the `ResourceBundle` can find them. Here's what the *poll.properties* file looks like:

```
poll.title=Industry Trends
poll.select_language=Select your preferred language
poll.new_language=New Language
poll.english=English
```

```
poll.swedish=Swedish
poll.german=German
poll.question=What's the longest development time you dare to plan with?
poll.answer1=One year
poll.answer2=Six months
poll.answer3=Less than six months
poll.submit=Vote
poll.number_of_votes=Total number of votes
poll.result=Poll result
```

The value of the `poll.title` key, used by the first two `<ora:getLocalText>` actions, is set to "Industry Trends"; that's what will appear as the title and header of the page when the default locale is selected. If a Swedish locale was selected instead, the text "Industri Trender" would be used, which is how it is listed in the *poll_sv.properties* file. The `<ora:getLocalText>` action is used with different keys for all text content in the page. Internally, it uses one of the bean's regular methods:

```
public String getText(String propertyName)
```

This method returns the specified property (the action element uses the `key` attribute value) from the properties file that most closely matches the selected locale. The bean provides similar methods for date and numeric values, as you can see in Appendix C, *Book Example Custom Actions and Classes Reference.*

To let the user pick another language than the one selected based on the `Accept-Language` header, the page contains a form with a set of radio buttons and a Submit button. Every time the page is displayed, the radio button group must reflect the currently selected language. This is done by calling the bean's `language` property access method and comparing the return value with the language code represented by each radio button:

```
...
<input type="radio" name="language" value="en"
  <%= locale.getLanguage().equals("en") ? "checked" : "" %>>
  <%= locale.getText("poll.english") %><br>
...
```

You probably recognize the type of JSP expression used to set the checked attribute for the radio button from previous chapters. The `getLanguage()` method returns the language code for the selected locale as a `String`. The `equals()` method compares the return value to its argument and returns `true` if they are the same. If they are, the first string after the question mark is returned as the value of the expression. If not, the second string is used. You also may have noticed that you can use the bean's `getText()` method directly, as an alternative to the `<ora:getLocalText>` action. Which alternative to use is largely a matter of preference. I used the method here because it's more compact and less intrusive when the text is used as part of an HTML element.

All radio button elements have the name `language`, which means that they form a group where only one of them can be selected. When the user clicks on the Submit button, the same page is requested with the value of the selected radio button included as a request parameter named `language`. As described above, this triggers the `<ora:useLocaleBundle>` action to switch to the selected language.

Next comes another form with radio buttons representing the three possible answers to the poll question. As you can see, both the question and the answers are displayed in the selected language. When the user selects an answer and clicks on the button to submit a vote, the *calculate.jsp* page shown in Example 11-2 is invoked.

Example 11-2. Validation and Calculation of Votes (calculate.jsp)

```
<jsp:useBean id="pollResult" scope="application"
  class="com.ora.jsp.beans.poll.PollBean" />


<jsp:useBean id="answer" class="com.ora.jsp.beans.poll.AnswerBean" >
  <jsp:setProperty name="answer" property="*" />
</jsp:useBean>


<% if (answer.isValid()) { %>
    <jsp:setProperty name="pollResult" property="answer"
      value="<%= answer %>" />
    <jsp:forward page="result.jsp" />
<% } else { %>
    <jsp:forward page="poll.jsp" />
<% } %>
```

As with all pure logic pages, this page contains only actions and a few simple scriptlets; no response text is generated. A `PollBean` in the application scope is used to keep track of the answers from all visitors, and an `AnswerBean` in the page scope captures and validates a single answer. The `AnswerBean` has one property named `answer`, which is set to the value of the corresponding request parameter using the `<jsp:setProperty>` action. It also has an `isValid()` method, used in a scriptlet to test if the answer is valid or not. In this example, it returns `true` if the answer ID is valid (1, 2, or 3). However, in a real application you may want to include other validation rules. For instance, if the poll information was stored in a database, you could use cookies or a username to make sure each user answers only once. If the answer is valid, a `<jsp:setProperty>` action is used to set the `answer` property of the `PollBean` to the valid answer, and the request is forwarded to the *result.jsp* page to display the poll statistics. Figure 11-3 shows a sample of the result page with the Swedish locale.

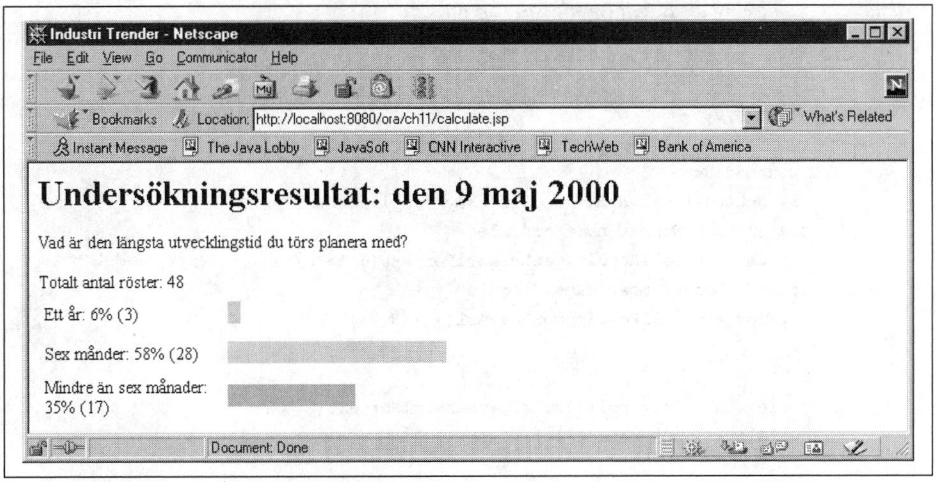

Figure 11-3. The result page using the Swedish locale

The *result.jsp* page, shown in Example 11-3, uses a couple of custom actions we haven't covered yet to display the localized date and numbers.

Example 11-3. Showing the Result (result.jsp)

```
<%@ page language="java" contentType="text/html" %>
<%@ page import="java.util.Date" %>
<%@ taglib uri="/orataglib" prefix="ora" %>

<ora:useLocaleBundle id="locale" bundleName="poll"
  supportedLangs="en, sv, de" />

<html>
  <head>
    <title>
      <ora:getLocalText name="locale" key="poll.title" />
    </title>
  </head>
  <body bgcolor="white">
    <jsp:useBean id="pollResult" scope="application"
        class="com.ora.jsp.beans.poll.PollBean" />

    <h1>
      <ora:getLocalText name="locale" key="poll.result" />:
      <ora:getLocalDate name="locale" date="<%= new Date() %>" />
    </h1>

    <ora:getLocalText name="locale" key="poll.question" />
    <p>
    <ora:getLocalText name="locale" key="poll.number_of_votes" />:
    <ora:getLocalNumber name="locale"
```

Example 11-3. Showing the Result (result.jsp) (continued)

```
      value="<%= pollResult.getTotal() %>" />

<table width="70%">
  <tr>
    <td width="30%">
      <ora:getLocalText name="locale" key="poll.answer1" />:
      <ora:getLocalNumber name="locale"
        value="<%= pollResult.getAnswer1Percent() %>" />%
      (<ora:getLocalNumber name="locale"
        value="<%= pollResult.getAnswer1() %>" />)
    </td>
    <td>
      <table width="<%= pollResult.getAnswer1Percent() %>%"
        bgcolor="lightgreen">
        <tr>
          <td> </td>
        </tr>
      </table>
    </td>
  </tr>
  <tr>
    <td width="30%">
      <ora:getLocalText name="locale" key="poll.answer2" />:
      <ora:getLocalNumber name="locale"
        value="<%= pollResult.getAnswer2Percent() %>" />%
      (<ora:getLocalNumber name="locale"
        value="<%= pollResult.getAnswer2() %>" />)
    </td>
    <td>
      <table width="<%= pollResult.getAnswer2Percent() %>%"
        bgcolor="lightblue">
        <tr>
          <td> </td>
        </tr>
      </table>
    </td>
  </tr>
  <tr>
    <td width="30%">
      <ora:getLocalText name="locale" key="poll.answer3" />:
      <ora:getLocalNumber name="locale"
        value="<%= pollResult.getAnswer3Percent() %>" />%
      (<ora:getLocalNumber name="locale"
        value="<%= pollResult.getAnswer3() %>" />)
    </td>
    <td>
      <table width="<%= pollResult.getAnswer3Percent() %>%"
        bgcolor="orange">
```

Example 11-3. Showing the Result (result.jsp) (continued)

```
            <tr>
              <td> </td>
            </tr>
          </table>
        </td>
      </tr>
    </table>
  </body>
</html>
```

This page starts with the `<ora:useLocaleBundle>` action, just like the *poll.jsp* page, to make the `LocaleBean` available to the other actions and scriptlets on the page. It also uses a number of `<ora:getLocalText>` actions to produce text in the selected language.

The first new action is the `<ora:getLocalDate>` action, described in Table 11-6.

Table 11-6. Attributes for <ora:getLocalDate>

Attribute Name	Java Type	Request-Time Value Accepted	Description
name	String	No	Mandatory. The name of the `LocaleBean` instance.
date	java.util.Date	Yes	Mandatory. The date to format according to the selected locale.

The `<ora:getLocalDate>` action is used to add today's date to the header. As with all other localization actions, it has a `name` attribute to specify the name of the bean. The date to format (as dictated by the selected locale) is specified by the `date` attribute. In Example 11-3, a JSP expression that creates a new `Date` object representing the current date is used as the attribute value. When you play around with this application, you see how the date format changes depending on the language you select.

The other new action is the `<ora:getLocalNumber>` action, used to generate numeric values formatted according to the selected locale. It's described in Table 11-7.

Table 11-7. Attributes for <ora:getLocalNumber>

Attribute Name	Java Type	Request-Time Value Accepted	Description
name	String	No	Mandatory. The name of the `LocaleBean` instance.
value	double	Yes	Mandatory. The number to format according to the selected locale.

The first occurrence of the `<ora:getLocalNumber>` action is used to display the total number of votes, just before the table that shows the distribution of the votes. Besides the `name` attribute, it has an attribute named `value` that specifies the number to be formatted. In Example 11-3, it calls the poll bean's `getTotal()` method to set the value.

The table with details about the distribution comes next. Here I have used a trick with nested tables to generate a simple bar chart:

```
...
<table width="70%">
  <tr>
    <td width="30%">
      <ora:getLocalText name="locale" key="poll.answer1" />:
      <ora:getLocalNumber name="locale"
        value="<%= pollResult.getAnswer1Percent() %>" />%
      (<ora:getLocalNumber name="locale"
         value="<%= pollResult.getAnswer1() %>" />)
    </td>
    <td>
      <table width="<%= pollResult.getAnswer1Percent() %>%"
        bgcolor="lightgreen">
        <tr>
          <td> </td>
        </tr>
      </table>
    </td>
  </tr>
...
```

The main table contains a row with two cells for each poll answer. The first cell is just a regular cell, containing the answer text, the percentage of votes with this answer, and the absolute number of votes with this answer. The values are generated by the `<ora:getLocalText>` and `<ora:getLocalNumber>` actions. The next cell, however, is more interesting. It contains a nested table, and the width of the table is set to the same percentage value as the percentage of votes with this answer. By specifying a required space (using the ` ` HTML code) as the value of the single cell and a unique background color, the result is a simple dynamic bar chart. As the percentage values of the answers change, the width of each nested table changes as well, as shown in Figure 11-3. Pretty neat!

Using a Separate Page for Each Locale

The `<ora:getLocalText>` action, as well as the other localization actions, makes it easy to use the same page for all locales. But as described earlier, sometimes it's better to use a separate page for each locale. The poll example uses this approach for the detailed description of the question.

As shown in Example 11-1, the *poll.jsp* page uses the `<ora:getLocalPageName>` action to insert the name of a localized page in an HTML link:

```
<a href="<ora:getLocalPageName
    name="locale" pageName="details.jsp" />">
    <ora:getLocalText name="locale" key="poll.question" />
  </a>
```

This action, described in Table 11-8, generates filenames based on the same naming convention as for localized property files.

Table 11-8. Attributes for <ora:getLocalPageName>

Attribute Name	Java Type	Request-Time Value Accepted	Description
name	String	No	Mandatory. The name of the `LocaleBean` instance.
pageName	String	Yes	Mandatory. The page base name.

The `pageName` attribute value represents the page base name. From this base name, the action inserts the language code and the country code (if any) of the selected locale, unless the selected locale represents the default language. The default language is the first language listed in the `supportedLang` attribute for the `<ora:useLocaleBundle>` action. For the languages supported in this example, you therefore need the *details.jsp* file for the English locale (default), the *details_de.jsp* file for the German locale, and the *details_sv.jsp* file for the Swedish locale. Note that the `<ora:getLocalPageName>` action doesn't verify that the localized page exists; it just generates the name of the localized page, based on the currently selected locale. Example 11-4 shows the Swedish page.

Example 11-4. Swedish Details Page (details_sv.jsp)

```
<%@ page language="java" contentType="text/html" %>
<%@ taglib uri="/orataglib" prefix="ora" %>

<ora:useLocaleBundle id="locale" bundleName="poll"
  supportedLangs="en, sv, de" />

<html>
  <head>
    <title>
      <ora:getLocalText name="locale" key="poll.title" />
    </title>
  </head>
  <body bgcolor="yellow">
    <h1>
      <font color="blue">
        <ora:getLocalText name="locale" key="poll.question" />
```

Example 11-4. Swedish Details Page (details_sv.jsp) (continued)

```
      </font>
    </h1>
    <font color="blue">
      Idag introduceras nya teknologier och affärsideer mycket
      snabbt. Produkter som såg ut som givna vinstbringare
      igår är idag så vanliga att det inte går att tjäna
      pengar på dem, med flera versioner tillgängliga gratis
      som Open Source. En affärsplan baserad på inkomst från
      annonser på en populär web site, eller att lägga till
      ".com" till företagsnamnet, väcker inte samma intresse
      hos investerare idag som det gjorde för bara några månader
      sedan.
      <p>
      I en industri som rör sig så här snabbt, hur lång tid
      törs du allokera till utveckling av en ny produkt eller
      tjänst, utan att riskera att den är ointressant när den
      väl är färdig?
    </font>
  </body>
</html>
```

As you can see, most of this page consists of Swedish text. The colors of the Swedish flag (yellow and blue) are also used as the background, header, and text colors. The detail pages for the other locales follow the same pattern. When the amount of text is large and other details of the page differ, like the colors in this example, it's often convenient to use a separate page for each locale instead of the one-page approach described earlier.

A Brief History of Bits

Before we discuss the different charsets, let's shift gears a little. Once upon a time, not so long ago, bits were very expensive. Hard disks for storing bits, memory for loading bits, communication equipment for sending bits over the wire; all the resources needed to handle bits were costly. To save on these expensive resources, characters were initially represented by only seven bits. This was enough to represent all letters in the English alphabet, the numbers 0 through 9, punctuation characters, and some control characters. And that was all that was really needed in the early days of computing, since most computers were kept busy doing number crunching.

But as computers were given new tasks, often dealing with human-readable text, seven bits didn't cut it. Adding one bit made it possible to represent all letters used in the western European languages. But there are other languages besides the western European languages, even though companies based in English-speaking countries often seem to ignore them. And eight bits is not enough to represent all characters used around the world. At first, this problem was partially solved by defining a number of standards for how eight bits should be used to represent different character subsets. Each of the ten ISO-8859 standards defines what is called a *charset:* a mapping between eight bits (a byte) and a character. For instance, ISO-8859-1, also known as Latin-1, defines the subset used for western European languages, such as English, French, Italian, Spanish, German, and Swedish. This is the default charset for HTTP. Other standards in the same series are ISO-8859-2, covering central and eastern European languages such as Hungarian, Polish, and Romanian; and ISO-8859-5, with Cyrillic letters used in Russian, Bulgarian, and Macedonian. You can find information about all ten charsets in the ISO-8859 series at *http://czyborra.com/charsets/iso8859.html.*

Some languages such as Chinese and Japanese contain thousands of characters, but with eight bits you can only represent 256. A set of multibyte charsets have therefore been defined to handle these languages, such as Big5 for Chinese, Shift_JIS for Japanese, and EUC-KR for Korean.

As you can imagine, all these different standards make it hard to exchange information encoded in different ways. To simplify life, the Unicode standard was defined by the Unicode Consortium, which was founded in 1991 by large companies such as Apple, IBM, Microsoft, Novell, Sun, and Xerox. Unicode uses two bytes (16 bits) to define unique codes for 49,194 characters in Version 3.0. Java uses Unicode for its internal representation of characters, and Unicode is also supported by many new technologies such as XML and LDAP. Support for Unicode is included in all modern browsers, such as Netscape and Internet Explorer since Version 4. If you would like to learn more about Unicode, visit *http://www.unicode.org.*

What does all of this mean to you as a web application developer? Well, since Latin-1 is the default charset for HTTP, you don't have to worry about this at all when you work with western European languages. But if you provide content in another language, such as Japanese or Russian, you need to tell the browser which charset you're using so it can interpret and render the characters correctly. In addition, the browser must be configured with a font that can display the characters. You find information about fonts for Netscape at *http://home.netscape.com/eng/intl/,* and for Internet Explorer at *http://www.microsoft.com/ie/intlhome.htm.*

You can specify a charset in a JSP page using the `page` directive and the `contentType` attribute, as shown in Example 11-5. The charset you specify is used for multiple purposes. First, it tells the JSP container the charset used to encode the bytes in the JSP page file itself, so the container can translate the bytes correctly to Unicode for internal processing. It's also used to convert the Unicode characters used internally to the specified charset encoding when the response is

sent to the browser, and to set the charset attribute in the `Content-Type` header
to let the browser know how to interpret the response. You may think it's a waste
of time to first convert from one charset to Unicode, and then from Unicode back
to the same charset. But using Unicode as an intermediary format makes it possible to store the page in one charset, say Shift_JIS, and send it to the browser as
another, for instance UTF-8 (an efficient charset that encodes Unicode characters
as one, two, or three bytes, as needed). This is not possible in JSP 1.1, but it's
being discussed for a future version.

Enough theory. Figure 11-4 shows a simple JSP page that sends the text "Hello
World" in Japanese to the browser. The Japanese characters are copied with permission from Jason Hunter's *Java Servlet Programming* (O'Reilly).

```
<%@ page language="java" contentType="text/html;charset=Shift_JIS" %>
<html>
  <body>
    Hello World in Japanese: 今日は世界
  </body>
</html>
```

Figure 11-4. Japanese JSP page (japanese.jsp)

To create a file in Japanese or another non-western language, you obviously need
a text editor that can handle multibyte characters. The JSP page in Figure 11-4 was
created with WordPad on a Windows NT system, using a Japanese font called MS
Gothic and saved as a file encoded with the Shift_JIS charset. Shift_JIS is therefore the charset specified by the `contentType` attribute, using the `charset`
attribute. Note that the page directive that defines the charset must appear as early
as possible in the JSP page, before any characters that can be interpreted only
when the charset is known. I recommend that you insert it as the first line in the
file to avoid problems.

Handling Localized Input

So far we have discussed only how to generate pages in different languages, but
most applications also need to deal with localized input. As long as you're supporting only western European languages, the only thing you typically need to worry
about is how to interpret dates and numbers. The `LocaleBean` introduced in the
previous section can help with this.

Example 11-5 shows a JSP page with the same form for selecting a language as you
saw in Example 11-1, plus a form with one field for a date and another for a
number.

Example 11-5. Date and Number Input Form (input.jsp)

```jsp
<%@ page language="java" contentType="text/html" %>
<%@ page import="java.util.*" %>
<%@ taglib uri="/orataglib" prefix="ora" %>

<ora:useLocaleBundle id="locale" bundleName="input"
  supportedLangs="en, sv, de" />

<html>
  <head>
    <title>
      <ora:getLocalText name="locale" key="input.title" />
    </title>
  </head>
  <body bgcolor="white">
    <h1>
      <ora:getLocalText name="locale" key="input.title" />
    </h1>

    <ora:getLocalText name="locale" key="input.select_language" />:
    <form action="input.jsp">
      <p>
      <input type="radio" name="language" value="en"
        <%= locale.getLanguage().equals("en") ? "checked" : "" %>>
        <%= locale.getText("input.english") %><br>
      <input type="radio" name="language" value="sv"
        <%= locale.getLanguage().equals("sv") ? "checked" : "" %>>
        <%= locale.getText("input.swedish") %><br>
      <input type="radio" name="language" value="de"
        <%= locale.getLanguage().equals("de") ? "checked" : "" %>>
        <%= locale.getText("input.german") %><br>
      <p>
      <input type="submit"
        value="<ora:getLocalText name="locale"
          key="input.new_language" />">
    </form>

    <form action="store.jsp" method="post">
      <ora:getLocalText name="locale" key="input.date" />
      <br>
      <input type="text" name="date">
      (<ora:getLocalDate name="locale" date="<%= new Date() %>" />)
      <p>
      <ora:getLocalText name="locale" key="input.number" />
      <br>
      <input type="text" name="number">
      (<ora:getLocalNumber name="locale" value="<%= 10000.11 %>" />)
      <p>
      <input type="submit"
```

Example 11-5. Date and Number Input Form (input.jsp) (continued)

```
        value="<ora:getLocalText name="locale"
          key="input.submit" />">
    </form>
  </body>
</html>
```

As in Example 11-1, custom actions are used to display various text labels in the selected language. In the date and number entry form, the `<ora:getLocalDate>` and `<ora:getLocalNumber>` actions are used as before to generate samples for the date and number format, respectively.

Now the interesting part. Example 11-6 shows the JSP page that is requested when the form is submitted.

Example 11-6. Processing Localized Input (store.jsp)

```
<%@ taglib uri="/orataglib" prefix="ora" %>

<ora:useLocaleBundle id="locale" bundleName="input"
  supportedLangs="en, sv, de" />

<ora:useDataSource id="example"
  class="sun.jdbc.odbc.JdbcOdbcDriver"
  url="jdbc:odbc:example" />

<ora:sqlUpdate dataSource="example">
  INSERT INTO InputTest VALUES(?, ?)
    <ora:sqlDateValue
      value='<%= locale.getDate(request.getParameter("date")) %>' />
    <ora:sqlDoubleValue
      value='<%= locale.getDouble(request.getParameter("number")) %>'/>
</ora:sqlUpdate>

<jsp:forward page="input.jsp" />
```

This page stores the values in a database. However, in order to do that, the date and number strings must be interpreted and turned into the corresponding Java object. The `LocaleBean` provides methods to handle the conversion, with a little bit of help from the `DateFormat` and `NumberFormat` classes described earlier:

```
public Date getDate(String date)
    throws ParseException
public double getDouble(String number)
    throws ParseException
```

These two methods use the format classes, initialized with the currently selected locale, to convert the `String` argument to the appropriate return type. With the strings converted to the corresponding Java type, the custom actions introduced in

Chapter 9 are used to store the values in a database. To run this example, you must first create a table named `InputTest` with a DATE and a NUMBER column in your database.

Dealing with Non–Western European Input

An HTML form can be used for input in languages other than western European languages, but the charset discussed in the previous section comes into play here as well. When you create a page with a form for entering non-western characters, you must define the charset with the `contentType` attribute of the page directive, the same as for any page with non-western content, as shown in Example 11-5. The user can then enter values with the characters of the corresponding language (e.g., Japanese characters).

There's something else to be aware of here. Parameter values sent from a form are encoded according to a special format. Characters other than a-z, A-Z, and 0-9 are converted to byte values in a hexadecimal format, preceded by a percent sign (`%`). For instance, the characters for "Hello World" in Japanese (shown in Figure 11-4) are sent like this:

```
%8D%A1%93%FA%82%CD%90%A2%8AE
```

This code represents the byte codes for the five Japanese characters. In order to process this information, the target JSP page must know which charset was used by the browser to encode it. The problem is that today's browser versions don't provide this information. You must therefore provide this information yourself, and convert the bytes in the parameter values accordingly. Let's see how that can be done.

Example 11-7 shows a JSP page with a form for entering a date and a text value in Japanese.

Example 11-7. Japanese Input Page (input_ja.jsp)

```
<%@ page language="java" contentType="text/html;charset=Shift_JIS" %>
<%@ page import="java.util.*" %>
<%@ taglib uri="/orataglib" prefix="ora" %>

<ora:useLocaleBundle id="locale" bundleName="input"
  supportedLangs="ja" />

<html>
  <head>
    <title>
      Japanese Input Test
    </title>
  </head>
```

Example 11-7. Japanese Input Page (input_ja.jsp) (continued)

```
<body bgcolor="white">
  <h1>
    Japanese Input Test
  </h1>

  <form action="process_ja.jsp" method="post">
    Enter a date:
    <br>
    <input type="text" name="date">
    (<ora:getLocalDate name="locale" date="<%= new Date() %>" />)
    <p>
    Enter some text:
    <br>
    <input type="text" name="text">
    <p>
    <input type="submit" value="Send" >
    <input type="hidden" name="charset" value="Shift_JIS">
  </form>
</body>
</html>
```

This page sets the charset to Shift_JIS and creates a `LocaleBean` for the Japanese locale through the `<ora:useLocaleBundle>` action with just one supported language: `ja`, the language code for Japanese. In the form, the `<ora:getLocalDate>` action is used to generate an example of how the date must be entered. The most important part of this page, however, is the hidden `charset` field, set to the same encoding value as is used for the page. This field value is sent to the target JSP page, *process_ja.jsp*, together with the other field values when the form is submitted. Example 11-8 shows the *process_ja.jsp* page.

Example 11-8. Processing Japanese Input (process_ja.jsp)

```
<%@ page language="java" contentType="text/html;charset=Shift_JIS" %>
<%@ taglib uri="/orataglib" prefix="ora" %>
<html>
  <head>
    <title>Processing Japanese Input</title>
  </head>
  <body>
    <h1>Processing Japanese Input</h1>

    <ora:useLocaleBundle id="locale" bundleName="input"
      supportedLangs="ja" />

    Text string converted to a Java Unicode string:
    <%= locale.getParameter("text") %>
    <p>
```

Example 11-8. Processing Japanese Input (process_ja.jsp) (continued)

```
Date string converted to the internal Java Date type:
<%= locale.getDate(locale.getParameter("date")) %>


</body>
</html>
```

The `LocaleBean`, initialized by the `<ora:useLocaleBundle>` action, takes care of all conversion for you. The action element reads the value of the `charset` parameter from the hidden field and sets the corresponding bean property. You can then use the following bean method to get the decoded values of all the other request parameters:

```
public String getParameter(String parameter)
    throws UnsupportedEncodingException
```

This method uses the specified charset value to decode the value for the parameter you ask for and returns it as a regular Java Unicode string. The string can then be used with all the other bean methods introduced in Example 11-6. For instance, the value of the `date` parameter can be converted to a Java `Date` object with the `getDate()` method, as shown in Example 11-8.

Note that if you use the `getParameter()` method provided by the implicit `request` object instead of the bean's method, you get a corrupt string. The reason for this is that the request object doesn't know how the parameter values were encoded, so it tries to interpret the values as if they were encoded based on the Latin-1 charset.

The result of the processing by the page in Example 11-8 is shown in Figure 11-5.

Figure 11-5. Processed Japanese input

In this example, we simply display the processed values. In a real-world application you can do anything you like with the values, such as storing them in a database.

12

Bits and Pieces

In the previous chapters, I have demonstrated the standard JSP features as well as a number of custom actions through practical, complete examples. But some features are hard to fit nicely into these examples without losing focus, so they are described separately in this chapter instead. Things covered here include buffering of the response body, ways to include shared page fragments, using XML and XSL with JSP, using client-side code to provide a more interactive interface, preventing JSP pages from being cached, and a discussion about the different types of URIs used in JSP pages.

Buffering

There's one important thing about how a JSP page is processed that has not been covered in any example so far: buffering of the response body. As you may recall from Chapter 2, *HTTP and Servlet Basics*, an HTTP response message contains both headers and a body. The headers tell the browser things like what type of data the body contains (HTML text, an image), the size of the body, if the body can be cached, and so forth. Headers are also used to set cookies and to tell the browser to automatically get another page (a redirect). All response headers must be sent to the browser before the body is sent.

As soon as a JSP page writes something to the body of the message, the JSP container may start sending the response to the browser. It is then too late to set headers, since they have to be sent first. In a servlet, you have full control over when something is written to the response body, so you can make sure that you set all the headers you need before you generate the body. In a JSP page, however, it's not that easy. Everything you put in a JSP page that is not a JSP element is written to the response body automatically by the JSP container. Here's the top part of the *autheticate.jsp* page from Chapter 10, *Authentication and Personalization*:

```
<%@ page language="java" %>
<%@ page import="com.ora.jsp.sql.*" %>
<%@ taglib uri="/orataglib" prefix="ora" %>

<%-- Remove the validUser session bean, if any --%>
<%   session.removeValue("validUser"); %>
...
```

It doesn't contain any HTML, so you may think that this does not add anything to the response body. But actually it does. This fragment contains six lines: five lines with JSP elements and one blank line. The JSP elements themselves are evaluated by the JSP container and never show up in the response, but the linefeed character at the end of each line is not a JSP element, so it's added to the response body.

Later in the same page, custom actions are used to set cookies, or in other words, set response headers:

```
<% if (request.getParameter("remember") != null) { %>

    <ora:addCookie name="userName"
      value='<%= request.getParameter("userName") %>'
      maxAge="2592000" />
    <ora:addCookie name="password"
      value='<%= request.getParameter("password") %>'
      maxAge="2592000" />

<% } else { %>

    <ora:addCookie name="userName"
      value='<%= request.getParameter("userName") %>'
      maxAge="0" />
    <ora:addCookie name="password"
      value='<%= request.getParameter("password") %>'
      maxAge="0" />
<% } %>
```

This does not work if the linefeed characters added to the body have caused the response to be sent to the browser (if the response has been *committed*, as it's called in the servlet specification). Besides not being able to set headers after the response has been committed, the servlet specification also prohibits a request to be forwarded when data has already been written to the response body. This is because when you forward to another JSP page or servlet, the target servlet should have full control over the request. If the originating page has already started to generate the response body, the target is no longer in charge.

Buffering solves this problem. Instead of sending the response to the browser as soon as something is written to the response body, the JSP container writes everything that's not a JSP element and all dynamic content generated by JSP elements to a buffer. At some point, such as when the buffer is full or the end of the page is reached, the container sends all headers that have been set, followed by the buffered body content. So in this example, all linefeed characters end up in the buffer, and the cookie headers are set. When the whole page has been processed, the JSP container sends all headers first and then the contents of the buffer. Works like a charm.

You can control the size of the buffer and what to do when the buffer is full with two page directive attributes:

```
<%@ page buffer="12kb" autoFlush="false" %>
```

Note that the buffer attribute accepts a value that specifies the minimum size of the buffer; the container may choose to use a bigger buffer than specified. The value must be the number of kilobytes followed by kb. A buffer that holds at least 8 KB is used by default. The keyword none is also accepted. If you use this keyword, the JSP container will not perform any buffering of the response body.

The autoFlush attribute can be set to true or false, with true being the default. It specifies what to do when the buffer is full. If the value is true, the headers currently set and the buffered content is sent (flushed) to the browser when the buffer is full, and the rest of the page gets buffered until the buffer is full again. If you specify the value false, the JSP container throws an exception when the buffer is full, ending the processing of the page.

In most cases, you want to use the default values. If you have an extremely large page where you set headers at the end of the page, you may need to increase the buffer size. 8 KB, however, is enough for most pages. Disabling buffering may make sense if you have a page that generates the result slowly and you want to send what's ready to the browser as soon as possible. But even if you disable the JSP buffering, the servlet container may still do some buffering of the result, so there's no guarantee that it will be sent immediately. No matter what value you use for the buffer attribute, however, you can force the buffer to be flushed with a scriptlet like this:

```
<% out.flush(); %>
```

Setting the autoFlush attribute to false is rare. A possible use for this is if you have no control over the size of the dynamic content you generate and you want to ensure that the processing is aborted if you reach a certain limit.

Including Page Fragments

You can use a JSP directive and an action to include page fragments in a JSP page. This is a useful technique when parts of all pages in an application are the same, such as headers, footers, and navigation bars.

The JSP `include` directive reads the content of the specified page in the translation phase (when the JSP page is converted into a servlet) and merges it with the original page:

```
<%@ include file="header.html" %>
```

The `file` attribute is a relative URL. If it starts with a slash, it's a context-relative path, interpreted relative to the URI prefix assigned for the application. If it doesn't start with a slash, it's a page-relative path, interpreted relative to the path for the page that includes the file.

The included file can contain only static content (such as HTML) or it can be a regular JSP page. Its contents are merged with the page that includes it, and the resulting page is converted into a servlet, as described in Chapter 3, *JSP Overview*. This means that all scripting variables declared in JSP declarations, scriptlets, or actions, such as `<jsp:useBean>` or custom actions that introduce scripting variables, are shared by the main page and all included pages. If the main page declares a variable and the same name is used to declare another variable in an included page, it will result in a translation phase error, since the combined page cannot be compiled.

What happens when the file you include using the `include` directive is changed actually isn't specified by the JSP specification. With Tomcat, you must change the modification date for the main page, for example using the *touch* command on a Unix system, before the changes take effect. An alternative is to delete the class file (the compiled version of the page) for the page. Other JSP containers may detect changes in included files automatically and go through the translation phase just like when you modify the main JSP page.

The `<jsp:include>` action is an alternative to the `include` directive, used to include another resource at runtime:

```
<jsp:include page="navigation.jsp" flush="true" />
```

The action is executed in the request processing phase instead of in the translation phase. The `page` attribute value is interpreted as a relative URI, the same way as the `include` directive's `file` attribute. The `<jsp:include>` action does not include the actual contents of the specified page: it includes the response produced by executing the page. This means you can specify any type of web resource (e.g., a servlet or a JSP page) that produces a response of the same content type as the JSP page. The JSP container executes the specified resource by an internal function call. Hence, the included resource helps to process the original request, and therefore has access to all objects in the request scope as well as all original request parameters.

Since the page is not included until the main page is requested, you can use a request-time attribute value for the page attribute to decide which page to include depending on a runtime condition, and add request parameters that can be read by the included page:

```
<jsp:include page="<%= pageSelectedAtRuntime %>" flush="true">
  <jsp:param name="aNewParamer" value="aStaticValue" />
  <jsp:param name="anotherParameter" value="<%= aDynamicValue %>" />
</jsp:include>
```

If you change the included JSP page, the new version is used immediately. This is because the included page is treated in the same way as a JSP page invoked directly by a browser: the container detects the modification and goes through the translation phase for the new version of the page.

The flush attribute requires an explanation. It specifies whether the response body should be flushed (sent to the browser) before the page is included or not. Due to limitations in the Servlet 2.2 API, this value must be set to true in JSP 1.1, meaning that the response body is always flushed before the page is included. The consequence is that the included page cannot set headers, such as cookies or redirect headers, or forward to another page. It also means that the main page cannot set headers or forward to another page after the <jsp:include> action element is executed. Work is in progress to remove the flushing requirement for a future version of the JSP specification.

Table 12-1 outlines the differences between the include directive and the <jsp:include> action.

Table 12-1. Differences Between the include Directive and the <jsp:include> Action

Syntax	When	What
`<%@ include file="relativeURI" %>`	Translation phase	Static text (HTML, JSP) merged with the JSP page before it's converted to a servlet
`<jsp:include page="relativeURI" flush="true" />`	Request processing phase	The response text generated by executing the page or servlet

Let's look at a concrete example of how you can use the two methods for including pages. Example 12-1 shows a page that includes three other pages.

Example 12-1. Including Pages (page1.jsp)

```
<%@ page language="java" contentType="text/html" %>
<%@ include file="header.html" %>
<table width="90%">
  <tr>
    <td valign="top" align="center" bgcolor="lightblue">
      <jsp:include page="navigation.jsp" flush="true" />
    </td>
    <td valign="middle" align="center" width="80%">
      This is page 1
    </td>
  </tr>
</table>
<%@ include file="footer.html" %>
```

The application here contains two more main pages, *page2.jsp* and *page3.jsp*, that differ from *page1.jsp* only in the HTML they contain (i.e., "This is page 2", "This is page 3"). The common header and footer for all pages in the example application consist of static HTML, shown in Examples 12-2 and 12-3. The include directive is used to include the header and footer files in each main page.

Example 12-2. Header (header.html)

```
<html>
  <head>
    <title>Welcome to My Site</title>
  </head>
  <body bgcolor="white">
    <h1>My Site</h1>
```

Note that the *header.html* file is not a complete HTML page. It contains only the start tags for the <html> and <body> elements.

Example 12-3. Footer (footer.html)

```
<hr>
  Copyright &copy; 2000 My Company
  </body>
</html>
```

The end tags for the <body> and <html> tags are included in the *footer.html* file. Merging *header.html*, one of the main pages, and *footer.html* results in a complete HTML page.

Each page in the application also has a navigation bar, with links to all pages in the application. The page names in the navigation bar are links to the corresponding pages, except for the current page, which is just written as plain text as shown in Figure 12-1.

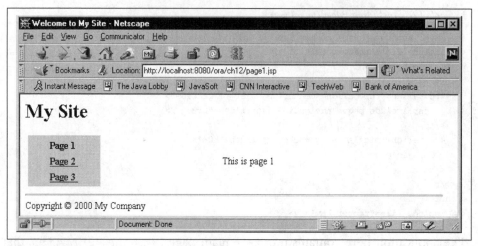

Figure 12-1. A page composed by including other pages

The JSP code for the navigation bar is separated out into its own file, shown in Example 12-4, and included in each page with the `<jsp:include>` action as shown in Example 12-1.

Example 12-4. Navigation Bar with Scriptlets (navigation_script.jsp)

```jsp
<%@ page language="java" %>
<% String uri = request.getServletPath(); %>
<table bgcolor="lightblue">
  <tr>
    <td>
    <% if (uri.equals("/ch12/page1.jsp")) { %>
      <b>Page 1</b>
    <% } else { %>
      <a href="page1.jsp">Page 1</a>
    <% } %>
    </td>
  </tr>
  <tr>
    <td>
    <% if (uri.equals("/ch12/page2.jsp")) { %>
      <b>Page 2</b>
    <% } else { %>
      <a href="page2.jsp">Page 2</a>
    <% } %>
    </td>
  </tr>
  <tr>
    <td>
    <% if (uri.equals("/ch12/page3.jsp")) { %>
      <b>Page 3</b>
```

Example 12-4. Navigation Bar with Scriptlets (navigation_script.jsp) (continued)

```
    <% } else { %>
        <a href="page3.jsp">Page 3</a>
    <% } %>
    </td>
  </tr>
</table>
```

The navigation bar page first gets the context-relative path for the current page by calling the getServletPath() method on the implicit request object. This works because the request object reflects the information about the page that includes the navigation bar page, not about the included page. An HTML table is then built with one cell for each main page in the application. In each cell, a scriptlet is used to test if the cell represents the current page or not. If it does, the page name is written as bold text; otherwise, it's written as an HTML link.

To be honest, Example 12-4 contains too much scripting code for my taste. An alternative is to use a custom action that does all the testing and generates the appropriate HTML, as shown in Example 12-5.

Example 12-5. Navigation Bar with Custom Action (navigation.jsp)

```
<%@ page language="java" %>
<%@ taglib uri="/orataglib" prefix="ora" %>
<table bgcolor="lightblue">
  <tr>
    <td>
      <ora:menuItem page="page1.jsp">
        <b>Page 1</b>
      </ora:menuItem>
    </td>
  </tr>
  <tr>
    <td>
      <ora:menuItem page="page2.jsp">
        <b>Page 2</b>
      </ora:menuItem>
    </td>
  </tr>
  <tr>
    <td>
      <ora:menuItem page="page3.jsp">
        <b>Page 3</b>
      </ora:menuItem>
    </td>
  </tr>
</table>
```

The <ora:menuItem> action inserts the HTML found in its body into the page. If the page specified by the page attribute is not the current page, the HTML is inserted as is. Otherwise, it's embedded as an HTML link element, the same way as with the scriptlets in Example 12-4. But unlike the scriptlet version of this page, the <ora:menuItem> action also performs URL rewriting on the HTML link URI if needed (this includes the session ID in the URI).

You may wonder why I use the include directive for the header and footer and the <jsp:include> action for the navigation bar. Either one will do for all files in this example, but I chose the action for the navigation bar because this page needs to be updated as new pages are added to the application. Using the action guarantees that the new version of the file is used immediately. I picked the directive for the header and footer pages because there's a slight performance penalty when using the action (the container must make a function call at request time). In this example, I assumed that both the header and footer contain stable information. In the rare event that they change, I'm willing to force the JSP container to go through the translation phase by deleting the class files corresponding to each main page or by changing the modification date for each page as described earlier.

If the included file sets headers or forwards to another page, you *must* use the include directive, since the <jsp:include> action flushes the buffer and commits the response before including the page. Same thing if you need to set headers or forward in the main page after including another page. On the other hand, if you can't decide which page to include until runtime, you must use the <jsp:include> action.

XML and JSP

If you're developing web sites for a living, you've surely encountered the Extensible Markup Language (XML). XML is a set of syntax rules for how to represent structured data using markup elements represented by a start tag (optionally with attributes), a body, and an end tag:

```
<employee id="123">
  <first-name>Hans</first-name>
  <last-name>Bergsten</last-name>
  <telephone>310-555-1212</telephone>
</employee>
```

This XML example contains four elements: <employee>, <first-name>, <last-name>, and <telephone>.

By selecting sensible element names, an XML file may be understandable to a human, but to make sense to a program it must use only a restricted set of elements in which each element has a well-defined meaning. This is known as an

XML application (the XML syntax applied to a certain application domain). A couple of examples are the Wireless Markup Language (WML), used for browsers in cellular phones and other small devices, and XHTML, which is HTML 4.0 reformulated as an XML application. Other examples are JSP action elements and the Web Application Deployment Descriptor elements introduced in Chapter 2.

Generating an XML Document

As we discussed in Chapters 3 and 5, everything in a JSP page that is not a JSP element is template text. In all the examples so far, we have used HTML as the template text. But we can use any text, such as XML elements. Example 12-6 shows a JSP page that sends a simple phone book to a wireless device, using the XML elements defined by the WML specification as the template text.

Example 12-6. WML Phone Book JSP Page (phone_wml.jsp)

```
<?xml version="1.0"?>
<!DOCTYPE wml PUBLIC "-//WAPFORUM//DTD WML 1.1//EN"
  "http://www.wapforum.org/DTD/wml_1.1.xml">
<%@ page contentType="text/vnd.wap.wml" %>
<wml>
  <card id="list" title="Phone List" newcontext="true">
    <p>
      <anchor>Bergsten, Hans
        <go href="#Bergsten_Hans"/>
      </anchor>
      <br/>
      <anchor>Eckstein, Robert
        <go href="#Eckstein_Robert"/>
      </anchor>
      <br/>
      <anchor>Ferguson, Paula
        <go href="#Ferguson_Paula"/>
      </anchor>
    </p>
  </card>

  <card id="Bergsten_Hans" title="Bergsten, Hans">
    <p>
      Phone: 310-555-1212
      <do type="prev" label="Back">
        <prev/>
      </do>
    </p>
  </card>
  <card id="Eckstein_Robert" title="Eckstein, Robert">
    <p>
      Phone: 512-555-5678
```

Example 12-6. WML Phone Book JSP Page (phone_wml.jsp) (continued)

```
        <do type="prev" label="Back">
          <prev/>
        </do>
      </p>
    </card>
    <card id="Ferguson_Paula" title="Ferguson, Paula">
      <p>
        Phone: 213-555-1234
        <do type="prev" label="Back">
          <prev/>
        </do>
      </p>
    </card>
</wml>
```

A discussion of the WML elements is outside the scope of this book, but let's look at some important details of the JSP page. The first line in Example 12-6 is an *XML declaration*, telling which version of XML the document conforms to. Some WML browsers are very picky that this is the very first thing in an XML document, and even whitespaces—regular spaces, linefeed characters, and tab characters—before the declaration can throw them off. In all examples you have seen so far, the JSP `page` directive has been on the first line. Here, I have moved it down, so that the linefeed character that ends the directive line doesn't cause any problems.

The second and third lines in Example 12-6 contain an XML *document type declaration*. This identifies the so-called Document Type Definition (DTD) for the document, basically the definition of all XML elements that a conforming document of this type can contain. Here, it's the DTD for the WML elements.

The JSP `page` directive on the fourth line is important. The content type for a JSP page is `html/text` by default. For a WML document, you must specify the content type `text/vnd.wap.wml` using the `contentType` attribute. Otherwise, the WML browser doesn't accept the document.

The rest of the page in Example 12-6 is just static WML code. To run this example, you need a WML browser. You can use the WML browser included in Nokia's WAP Toolkit, available at *http://www.forum.nokia.com*. Figure 12-2 shows what the phone list menu card and a details card look like in Nokia's WML browser. The toolkit also includes WML documentation, in case you want to learn more about how to serve content to devices like cellular phones and PDAs.

Transforming XML into HTML

You may also have heard about the Extensible Stylesheet Language (XSL). XSL defines one set of XML elements used to transform an XML document into some

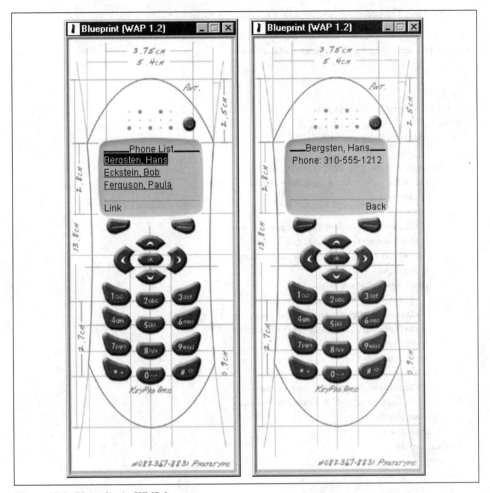

Figure 12-2. Phone list in WML browser

other type of document, and another set of elements used to produce a formatted version of an XML document suitable for display. The formatting part of XSL is used by browsers and other programs that need to render an XML document, using different styles for different elements, such as a bold large font for a header and a regular font for paragraph text. The transformation part of XSL is referred to as XSLT. XSLT can be used to turn a source XML document, such as a document representing an order, into different forms by using different stylesheets. This is useful in business-to-business (B2B) applications, where different partners often require the same information in slightly different formats. You can read more about XSL and XSLT at *http://www.w3.org/TR/xsl/*.

XSLT can also be used to transform structured XML data into HTML. Example 12-7 shows an example in which the same phone book information used in Example 12-6 is transformed into an HTML table.

Example 12-7. Transforming XML to HTML (phone_html.jsp)

```
<%@ page language="java" contentType="text/html" %>
<%@ taglib uri="/xsltaglib" prefix="xsl" %>

<html>
  <head>
    <title>Phone List</title>
  </head>
  <body bgcolor="white">

    <xsl:apply xsl="/ch12/htmltable.xsl">
      <?xml version="1.0" encoding="ISO-8859-1"?>
      <employees>
        <employee id="123">
          <first-name>Hans</first-name>
          <last-name>Bergsten</last-name>
          <telephone>310-555-1212</telephone>
        </employee>
        <employee id="456">
          <first-name>Robert</first-name>
          <last-name>Eckstein</last-name>
          <telephone>512-555-5678</telephone>
        </employee>
        <employee id="789">
          <first-name>Paula</first-name>
          <last-name>Ferguson</last-name>
          <telephone>213-555-1234</telephone>
        </employee>
      </employees>
    </xsl:apply>

  </body>
</html>
```

The transformation is performed by a custom action, named <xsl:apply>, from the Jakarta Taglibs project. The binary version of the Jakarta XSL tag library and the necessary JAR files with XML and XSL processing classes are bundled with the examples for this book, and can be downloaded from the book's catalog page (*http://www.oreilly.com/catalog/jserverpages/*). The body of the <xsl:apply> action contains an XML document with elements representing information about employees. The xsl attribute specifies an XSL stylesheet with XSLT elements that transform the XML document into an HTML table. The resulting table is inserted into the JSP page. Descriptions of all the XSLT elements would fill an entire book, but Example 12-8 shows the stylesheet used here to give you a glimpse of what XSLT looks like.

Example 12-8. XSL Stylesheet that Generates an HTML Table (htmltable.xsl)

```xml
<?xml version="1.0"?>
<xsl:stylesheet version="1.0"
  xmlns:xsl="http://www.w3.org/1999/XSL/Transform">

  <xsl:template match="employees">
    <html>
      <head>
        <title>Phone List</title>
      </head>
      <body bgcolor="white">
        <table border="1" width="100%">
          <tr>
            <th>ID</th>
            <th>Employee Name</th>
            <th>Phone Number</th>
          </tr>
          <xsl:for-each select="employee">
            <tr>
              <td>
                <xsl:value-of select="@id"/>
              </td>
              <td>
                <xsl:value-of select="last-name"/>,
                <xsl:value-of select="first-name"/>
              </td>
              <td>
                <xsl:value-of select="telephone"/>
              </td>
            </tr>
          </xsl:for-each>
        </table>
      </body>
    </html>
  </xsl:template>

</xsl:stylesheet>
```

The `<xsl:template>` uses the non-XSLT elements in its body as a template to generate a new document from the `<employees>` element in the source XML document. The `<xsl:for-each>` element loops over all `<employee>` elements in the source, and the `<xsl:value-of>` elements extracts the values of attributes and nested elements. You get the idea.

The `<xsl:apply>` action, together with other actions in the Jakarta Taglibs XSL library, can apply a stylesheet to XML documents from other sources than its body, such as an external file or a database column value saved as a `String` in one of the JSP scopes. You can read more about the Jakarta XSL tag library and download the source code from *http://jakarta.apache.org/taglibs/index.html*.

Transforming XML into a Request-Dependent Format

As a final example of using XML with JSP, let's look at a page that uses the `<xsl:apply>` action to apply different stylesheets depending on if the page is requested by a WML browser or an HTML browser. Example 12-9 shows such a page.

Example 12-9. XSL Stylesheet that Generates HTML or WML (phone.jsp)

```
<%@ taglib uri="/xsltaglib" prefix="xsl" %><%
  String xslURI = null;
  if (request.getHeader("User-Agent").indexOf("WAP") != -1) {
    xslURI = "/ch12/wml.xsl";
    response.setContentType("text/vnd.wap.wml");
  }
  else {
    xslURI = "/ch12/html.xsl";
    response.setContentType("text/html");
  }
%><xsl:apply
  xsl="<%= xslURI %>">
  <?xml version="1.0" encoding="ISO-8859-1"?>
  <employees>
    <employee id="123">
      <first-name>Hans</first-name>
      <last-name>Bergsten</last-name>
      <telephone>310-555-1212</telephone>
    </employee>
    <employee id="456">
      <first-name>Robert</first-name>
      <last-name>Eckstein</last-name>
      <telephone>512-555-5678</telephone>
    </employee>
    <employee id="789">
      <first-name>Paula</first-name>
      <last-name>Ferguson</last-name>
      <telephone>213-555-1234</telephone>
    </employee>
  </employees>
</xsl:apply>
```

There are a number of things to note here. First, this page uses the HTTP User-Agent header to figure out which type of browser is requesting the page, and selects an appropriate XSL stylesheet to transform the XML data for the current type of browser. Be aware that this test may not work for all WML browsers. The WML browser in Nokia's WAP Toolkit happens to include the WAP acronym in the User-Agent header, but that's not necessarily the case for other WML browsers. The two stylesheets used here, *wml.xsl* and *html.xsl*, generate complete WML and HTML pages, respectively.

Since the page can serve both HTML and WML content, the `page` directive's `contentType` attribute cannot be used to set the content type as we have done in all other examples. Instead, the content type is set to the appropriate type using the `setContentType()` method of the implicit `response` object, depending on the type of browser asking for the page.

Finally, note how the start tags for all JSP directives, scriptlets, and custom actions on this page are written on the same line as the end tag for the preceding element. This is to ensure that no extra linefeeds are added to the response. As described earlier, leading whitespace in a WML page can cause a WML browser to reject the page.

For a simple example like this, letting an XSLT stylesheet transform the XML source into a complete web page works fine. However, on most real web sites, the HTML version of the site differs significantly from the WML version. You want to provide a rich interface for HTML browsers with a nice layout, navigation bars, images, colors, nice fonts, and typically as much content as you can fit on each page. A WML browser, on the other hand, has a very small screen with limited layout, font, and graphics capabilities. Developing an efficient interface for this type of device is very different. A more practical approach for combining XML, XSL, and JSP to serve different types of browsers is to keep the actual content (articles, product information, phone lists, etc.) in a device-independent XML format, but use separate JSP pages for each device type. The JSP pages can then use a custom action like the `<xsl:apply>` action to transform the key content and merge it with the device dependent template text to form a complete page suitable for each specific device type, like in Example 12-9.

Mixing Client-Side and Server-Side Code

I touched on the differences between server-side code and client-side code in Chapter 3. JSP is a server-side technology, so all JSP elements such as actions and scriptlets execute on the server before the resulting page is sent to the browser. A page can also contain client-side code, such as JavaScript code or Java applets. This code is executed by the browser itself. There is no way that a JavaScript event handler such as `onClick` or `onSelect` can directly invoke a JSP element such as an action, a scriptlet, or a Java method declared with a JSP declaration.

However, a JSP page can generate JavaScript code dynamically the same way it generates HTML, WML, or any type of text content. Therefore, you can add client-side scripting code to your JSP pages to provide a more interactive user interface. You can also use applets on your pages to provide a more interesting and easier to use interface than what's possible with pure HTML.

Generating JavaScript Code

Example 12-10 shows a modified version of the User Info page used in the examples in Chapter 5.

Example 12-10. Input Form with Client-Side Validation Code (clientscript.jsp)

```
<%@ page language="java" contentType="text/html" %>
<%@ page import="com.ora.jsp.util.*" %>

<script language="JavaScript">
  <!-- Hide from browsers without JavaScript support

  function isValidForm(theForm) {
    if (isEmpty(theForm.userName.value)) {
      theForm.userName.focus();
      return false;
    }
    if (!isValidDate(theForm.birthDate.value)) {
      theForm.birthDate.focus();
      return false;
    }
    if (!isValidEmailAddr(theForm.emailAddr.value)) {
      theForm.emailAddr.focus();
      return false;
    }
    var choices = new Array("male", "female");
    if (!isValidChoice(theForm.sex.value, choices)) {
      theForm.sex.focus();
      return false;
    }
    if (!isValidNumber(theForm.luckyNumber.value, 1, 100)) {
      theForm.luckyNumber.focus();
      return false;
    }
    return true;
  }

  function isEmpty(aStr) {
    if (aStr.length == 0) {
      alert("Mandatory field is empty");
      return true;
    }
    return false;
  }

  function isValidDate(dateStr) {
    var matchArray = dateStr.match(/^[0-9]+-[0-1][0-9]-[0-3][0-9]$/)
    if (matchArray == null) {
```

Example 12-10. Input Form with Client-Side Validation Code (clientscript.jsp) (continued)

```
      alert("Invalid date: " + dateStr);
      return false;
    }
    return true;
  }


  function isValidEmailAddr(emailStr) {
    var matchArray = emailStr.match(/^(.+)@(.+)\.(.+)$/)
    if (matchArray == null) {
      alert("Invalid email address: " + emailStr);
      return false;
    }
    return true;
  }


  function isValidNumber(numbStr, start, stop) {
    var matchArray = numbStr.match(/^[0-9]+$/)
    if (matchArray == null) {
      alert("Invalid number: " + numbStr);
      return false;
    }
    if (numbStr < start || numbStr > stop) {
      alert("Number not within range (" + start + "-" +
        stop + "): " + numbStr);
      return false;
    }
    return true;
  }


  function isValidChoice(choiceStr, choices) {
    var isValid = false;
    for (var i = 0; i < choices.length; i++) {
      if (choices[i].toLowerCase() == choiceStr.toLowerCase()) {
        isValid = true;
        break;
      }
    }
    if (isValid == false) {
      alert("Invalid choice: " + choiceStr);
    }
    return isValid;
  }

-->
</script>

<html>
  <head>
```

Example 12-10. Input Form with Client-Side Validation Code (clientscript.jsp) (continued)

```
    <title>User Info Entry Form</title>
  </head>
  <body bgcolor="white">
    <jsp:useBean id="userInfo"
      class="com.ora.jsp.beans.userinfo.UserInfoBean"
      scope="request" />

    <%-- Output list of values with invalid format, if any --%>
    <font color="red">
      <jsp:getProperty name="userInfo" property="propertyStatusMsg" />
    </font>

    <%-- Output form with submitted valid values --%>
    <form action="userinfovalidate.jsp" method="post"
      onSubmit="return isValidForm(this)">
      <table>
        <tr>
          <td>Name:</td>
          <td><input type="text" name="userName"
            value="<%= StringFormat.toHTMLString(
              userInfo.getUserName()) %>" >
          </td>
        </tr>
        ...
        <tr>
          <td colspan=2><input type="submit"></td>
        </tr>
      </table>
    </form>
  </body>
</html>
```

When the user submits the form, the JavaScript `isValidForm()` method is first executed by the browser to validate all input field values. Only if all values pass the test is the form actually submitted to the *userinfovalidate.jsp* page specified as the form's action URI. In this way, the user is alerted to mistakes much faster, and the server is relieved from processing invalid requests.

However, the validation is also performed by the server when the form is finally submitted, in exactly the same way as described in Chapter 5. This is important, because you don't know if the user's browser supports JavaScript or if scripting has been disabled in the browser.

Note that the JavaScript validation code shown in Example 12-10 is far from perfect. It's really intended only as an example. You can find much better validation code on sites such as the JavaScript Source (*http://javascript.internet.com*).

In Example 12-10, all JavaScript code is written as static template text. However, nothing prevents you from generating parts of the JavaScript code, for instance a JavaScript array, with values retrieved from a database by the JSP page. Just remember which code executes where and when. To the code in the JSP page executing on the server, the JavaScript code it generates is just plain text; it doesn't even try to understand it. It's only when the page that contains the dynamically generated JavaScript code reaches the browser that it becomes meaningful and can be executed by the browser. The browser, on the other hand, couldn't care less that the JavaScript code was created by a JSP page; it has no idea how the code was created. It should be clear, then, that JavaScript code cannot call Java code in the JSP page, and vice versa.

Using Java Applets

A Java applet is a Java class that is embedded in an HTML page and executed by the browser. It can be used to provide a nice user interface on a web page. The problem here is that the native Java support in the web browsers doesn't keep up with the Java release cycles. Many users still have browsers that support only JDK 1.0, and more current browsers have so many limitations and bugs in their implementations that you're still limited to JDK 1.0 features to make the applet work.

To address this issue, Sun provides a Java runtime environment that can be integrated in a browser using the browser's native plug-in API. The product is appropriately named the Java Plug-in, and as of this writing the JDK 1.3 version is available for Netscape Navigator and Internet Explorer on Windows 95, 98, and NT, Linux, and Solaris. For an up-to-date list of supported platforms, visit Sun's Java Plug-in page at *http://java.sun.com/products/plugin/index.html*.

With the Java Plug-in, you can use the latest Java features in your applets, such as the Swing GUI classes, collection classes, enhanced security, and more. But there's one more hurdle you have to jump. The HTML element you need in a page to get the Java Plug-in (or any plug-in component) installed and loaded by the browser differs between Internet Explorer and Netscape Navigator. For Netscape, you need to use the <embed> element, while Internet Explorer requires the <object> element. Fortunately, JSP provides an easy solution to this problem, namely the <jsp:plugin> action.

The <jsp:plugin> action looks at the User-Agent request header to figure out which type of browser is requesting the page, and inserts the appropriate HTML element for using the Java Plug-in to run the applet. Example 12-11 shows an example borrowed from the Tomcat JSP examples.

Example 12-11. Embedding an Applet in a JSP Page (applet.jsp)

```
<%@ page language="java" contentType="text/html" %>
<html>
  <head>
    <title>Embedding an applet</title>
  </head>
  <body bgcolor="white">
    <h1>Embedding an applet</h1>
    <jsp:plugin type="applet" code="Clock2.class"
      codebase="applet"
      jreversion="1.2" width="160" height="150" >
      <jsp:params>
        <jsp:param name="bgcolor" value="ccddff" />
      </jsp:params>
      <jsp:fallback>
        Plugin tag OBJECT or EMBED not supported by browser.
      </jsp:fallback>
    </jsp:plugin>
  </body>
</body>
```

The `<jsp:plugin>` action has three mandatory attributes: `type`, `code`, and `codebase`. The `type` attribute must be set to either `applet` or `bean` (to include a JavaBeans object), `code` is used to specify the class name, and `codebase` is the absolute or relative URL for the directory or archive file that contains the class. Note that the applet class must be stored in a directory that can be accessed by the web browser; that is, it must be part of the public web page structure for the application. As you may recall, class files for beans and custom actions are typically stored in the *WEB-INF lib* and *classes* subdirectories, accessible only to the container. The different locations make sense when you think about where the code is executed: the applet is loaded and executed by the browser, and beans and custom action classes are loaded and executed by the container.

The `<jsp:plugin>` action also has a number of optional attributes, such as the `width`, `height`, and `jreversion` attributes used here. Appendix A, *JSP Elements Syntax Reference*, contains a description of all attributes.

The body of the action element can contain nested elements. The `<jsp:params>` element, which in turn contains one or more `<jsp:param>` elements, is used to provide parameter values to the applet. In Example 12-11, the applet's `bgcolor` parameter is set to the hexadecimal RGB value for light blue. The `<jsp:fallback>` element can optionally be used to specify text that should be displayed instead of the applet in a browser that doesn't support the HTML `<object>` or `<embed>` element.

Figure 12-3 shows what the page in Example 12-11 looks like in a browser.

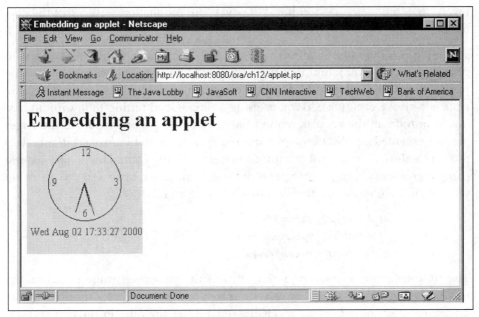

Figure 12-3. A page with an applet using the Java Plug-in

An applet can communicate with the server in many different ways, but how it's done is off-topic for this book. If you would like to learn how to develop applets that communicate with a servlet, I suggest you read Jason Hunter and William Crawford's *Java Servlet Programming* (O'Reilly).

Precompiling JSP Pages

To avoid hitting your site visitors with the delay caused by converting a JSP page into a servlet on the first access, you can *precompile* all pages in the application. Another use of precompilation is if you do not want anyone to change the pages in a JSP-based application after the application is deployed. In this case you can precompile all pages, define URI mappings for all JSP pages in the *WEB-INF/web.xml* file, and install the Java class files only for the compiled pages. We look at both these scenarios in this section.

One way of precompiling all pages in an application is to simply run through the application in a development environment and make sure you hit all pages. You can then copy the class files together with all the other application pages to the production server when you deploy the application. Where the class files are stored varies between containers. However, Tomcat stores all JSP page implementation classes in its *work* directory by default, in a subdirectory for the particular web application. As long as the modification dates of the class files are more recent than for the corresponding JSP pages, the production server uses the copied class files.

The JSP specification also defines a special request parameter that can be used to give the JSP container a hint that the page should be compiled without letting the page process the request. An advantage of using this method is that you can automatically invoke each page, perhaps using a simple load testing tool, without having to provide all the regular request parameters the pages use. Since the pages are not executed, application logic that requires pages to be invoked in a certain order or enforces similar rules cannot interfere with the compilation. The request parameter name is `jsp_precompile`, and valid values are `true` and `false`, or no value at all. In other words, the following URIs are all valid:

/ora/ch12/applet.jsp?jsp_precompile
/ora/ch12/applet.jsp?jsp_precompile=true
/ora/ch12/applet.jsp?jsp_precompile=false

The third example is not very useful, since if the parameter value is `false`, the request is treated exactly as any other request, and is therefore processed by the JSP page. A JSP container that receives a request like the ones in the first and second examples should compile the JSP page (go through the translation phase) but not allow the page to process the request. Most JSP containers support this feature, even though the specification doesn't require it. A compliant JSP container is allowed to ignore the compilation request, as long as it doesn't let a JSP page process a request that includes a `jsp_precompile` parameter with the value `true` or with no value at all.

When you have compiled the JSP pages, you can package your application without the JSP pages themselves by using only the generated servlet class files. You do this by adding URI mapping definitions in the *WEB-INF/web.xml* file for the applications, so that a request for a certain JSP page is served directly by the corresponding servlet instead. There are two reasons why you might want to do this. One is that using the servlet files directly is slightly faster, since the container doesn't have to go through the JSP container code to figure out which servlet class to use. The other is that if you do not include the JSP pages in the application packet, no one can change the application. This can be an advantage if you resell prepackaged JSP-based applications.

Unfortunately, it's much harder to do this than it should be if you use Tomcat as your web container. This is because Tomcat's JSP container uses a very creative naming convention for the class files it generates. Because Tomcat is such a widely used container, I describe this problem in detail here, even though other containers may handle this in a different way.

Tomcat stores all class files for an application's JSP pages in a subdirectory to its *work* directory, using filenames composed of the URI path for each JSP page plus a lot of extra characters to make sure the name doesn't contain any special characters that can cause problems. Here is an example:

```
_0002fch_00031_00032_0002fhello_0002ejsphello.class
```

This is the name Tomcat picks for a JSP file with the URI */ch12/hello.jsp*. The problem is that the filename does not match the Java class name, something the standard Java class loader expects. For instance, the class file here contains a class named:

```
ch_00031_00032._0002fch_00031_00032_0002fhello_0002ejsphello_jsp_0
```

When you let the JSP container handle the class, this name mismatch doesn't cause a problem because the container has its own class loader that's able to deal with this kind of class file. If, however, you want to use the generated class files as regular servlets, handled by a class loader that understands only the standard naming scheme, you have to rename the files. Here are the steps you need to go through to make the class files usable as regular servlets.

First, use the *javap* command (part of the Java runtime environment) to get the real class name for each class file.

```
javap _0002fch_00031_00032_0002fhello_0002ejsphello.class
```

This gives an error message that includes the real class name:

```
Error: Binary file '_0002fch_00031_00032_0002fhello_0002ejsphello'
contains ch_00031_00032._0002fch_00031_00032_0002fhello_0002ejsphello_jsp_0
```

Then move the class file to the *WEB-INF/classes* directory, using the real class name as the filename, in a subdirectory matching the package name, if any. In this example, the class file should be moved to a subdirectory named *ch_00031_00032*, like this:

```
WEB-INF/
  classes/
    ch_00031_00032/
      _0002fch_00031_00032_0002fhello_0002ejsphello_jsp_0.class
```

Finally, add a URI mapping rule for the JSP page in the *WEB-INF/web.xml* file. For this example, it should look like this:

```
<servlet-mapping>
  <servlet-name>
    ch_00031_00032._0002fch_00031_00032_0002fhello_0002ejsphello_jsp_0
  </servlet-name>
  <url-pattern>/ch12/hello.jsp</url-pattern>
</servlet-mapping>
```

You can then remove the JSP page file and the application will use the servlet class file directly instead.

Some containers, such as Allaire's JRun, provide proprietary programs you can use to convert JSP pages into servlets. Tomcat 3.2 includes an early version of a command-line tool for converting JSP pages into servlet Java files. The tool is named *jspc*, and it's invoked with the *jspc.bat* (Windows) or *jspc.sh* (Unix) script files in Tomcat's *bin* directory. It's not yet fully tested and currently doesn't compile the servlet source files it generates. These kinds of tools may eventually make the packaging and mapping of precompiled JSP pages easier.

There is one more thing to be aware of. The technique described in this section works fine as long as you compile and deploy the generated servlet classes using the same web container product, for instance generating the files in one Tomcat installation and deploying in another Tomcat installation. But a web container is allowed to use its own internal classes in the generated servlets, which means that you may not be able to generate the servlets with one web container (such as Tomcat) and deploy them in another (such as Unify's ServletExec).

Preventing Caching of JSP Pages

A browser can cache web pages so that it doesn't have to get them from the server every time the user asks for them. Proxy servers can also cache pages that are frequently requested by all users going through the proxy. Caching helps cut down the network traffic and server load, and provides the user with faster responses. But caching can also cause problems in a web application where you really want the user to see the latest version of a dynamically generated page.

Both browsers and proxy servers can be told not to cache a page by setting response headers. You can use a scriptlet like this in your JSP pages to set these headers:

```
<%
    response.addHeader("Pragma", "No-cache");
    response.addHeader("Cache-Control", "no-cache");
    response.addDateHeader("Expires", 1);
%>
```

An alternative is to use a custom action that's included with the book examples:

```
<%@ taglib uri="/orataglib" prefix="ora" %>
<ora:noCache/>
```

The `<ora:noCache>` action sets the exact same headers as the scriptlet example, but it's cleaner.

How URLs Are Interpreted

One thing that can be confusing in a JSP-based application is the different types of URIs used in the HTML and JSP elements. The confusion stems from a combination of conflicting terms used to describe URIs in the HTTP, servlet, and JSP specifications, as well as the fact that some types of URIs are interpreted differently in the HTML and the servlet world.

In HTML, URIs are used as attribute values in elements like <a>, <img>, and <form>. JSP elements that use URI attribute values are the page, include, and taglib directives and the <jsp:forward> and <jsp:include> actions. Custom actions can also define attributes that take URI values.

The HTTP/1.1 specification (RFC 2616, with more details in RFC 2396) defines a Uniform Resource Identifier (URI) as a string, following certain rules, that uniquely identifies a resource of some kind. A Uniform Resource Locator (URL) is just a special kind of URI that includes a location (such as the server name in an HTTP URL). An *absolute URI* is a URI that starts with the name of a so called scheme, such as http or https, followed by a colon (:) and the rest of the resource identifier. An example of an absolute URI for a resource accessed through the HTTP protocol is:

```
http://localhost:8080/ora/ch12/login.jsp
```

Here, http is the scheme, localhost:8080 is the location (a server name and a port number), and /ora/ch12/login.jsp is the path.

The URIs used in the HTML elements generated by a JSP page are interpreted by the browser. A browser needs the absolute URI to figure out how to send the requests for the resources referenced by the HTML elements. It uses the scheme to select the correct protocol, and the location to know where to send the request. The path is sent as part of the request to the server, so the server can figure out which resource is requested. But when you write a URI in an HTML document, such as the action attribute of a form element or the src attribute of an image element, you don't have to specify an absolute URI if the resource is located on the same server. Instead you can use just the URI path, like this:

```
<img src="/images/hello.gif">
```

This type of URI is called an *absolute path,* meaning it contains the complete path for the resource within a server; the only difference compared to an absolute URI is that the scheme and location are not specified. The browser interprets an absolute path URI as a reference to a resource on the same server, so it adds the scheme and location it used to make the request that returned the page to the absolute path URI it finds in the page. It then has the absolute URI it needs to make a request for the referenced resource.

Another type of URI is a *relative path*, interpreted relative to the path of the current page. A relative path is a path that does not start with a slash (/):

```
<form action="process.jsp">
<img src="../images/hello.gif"
```

Here the `action` attribute references a JSP file at the same level in the path structure as the page that contains the reference. The `src` attribute value uses the `../` notation to refer to a resource one level up in the structure. The browser interprets a relative path URI as relative to the URI path for the request that produced the page. If the two relative paths in this example are used in a page generated by a request for *http://localhost:8080/ora/ch12/login.jsp*, the browser interprets them as the following absolute URIs:

> *http://localhost:8080/ora/ch12/process.jsp*
> *http://localhost:8080/ora/images/hello.gif*

Relative URI paths offer a lot of flexibility. If all references between the web resources in an application are relative, you can move the application to a different part of the path structure without changing any URIs. For instance, if you move the pages from */ora/ch12* to */foo/bar*, the relative paths still reference the same resources.

So far, so good. Now let's see what happens in a Java web container when it receives a request. The first part of a URI for a servlet or JSP page has a special meaning. It's called the *context path*—one example is the */ora* path used for all examples in this book. As described in Chapter 2, a servlet container can contain multiple web applications, handled by a corresponding servlet context. Each web application is associated with a unique context path assigned when the web application is installed. When a request is received by the web container, it uses the context path to select the servlet context that's responsible for handling the request. The container hands over the request to the selected context, which then uses the URI path minus the context path to locate the requested resource (a servlet or a JSP page) within the context. For instance, an absolute URI like *http://localhost: 8080/ora/ch12/login.jsp* is interpreted by the container as a request for a JSP page named */ch12/login.jsp* within the context path */ora*.

Because a web application can be assigned any context path when the application is installed, the context path must not be part of the URIs used in JSP elements (and servlet methods) to refer to other parts of the same application. You can always use a relative-path URI, just as you do in HTML, for example to refer to another page in a `<jsp:include>` action:

```
<jsp:include page="navigation.jsp" flush="true" />
```

This type of URI is called a *page-relative path* in the JSP specification. It's interpreted by the container as relative to the page where it's used.

Sometimes it's nice to be able to refer to an internal application resource with a URI that is not interpreted relative to the containing page. An example is a reference to a customized error page that is used by all pages in the application independent of where in the path structure they are located:

```
<%@ page errorPage="/errorMsg.jsp" %>
```

A URI used as a JSP element attribute that starts with a slash is interpreted by the container as relative to the application's context path. The JSP specification calls this type of URI a *context-relative path*. This type of URI is useful for all sorts of common resources used in an application, such as error pages and images, that have fixed URIs within the application path structure.

In summary, a URI used in an HTML element can be:

- An absolute URI (including the scheme and server name)

- An absolute-path URI (a path starting with a slash), interpreted as the path to a resource on the same server

- A relative-path URI (a path not starting with a slash), interpreted as relative to the path for the page where it's used

A URI used in a JSP element (or a servlet method) can be:

- A context-relative path (a path starting with a slash), interpreted as relative to the application's context path

- A page-relative path (a path not starting with a slash), interpreted as relative to the path for the page where it's used

As long as you remember that URIs used in HTML elements are interpreted by the browser, and URIs used in JSP elements are interpreted by the web container, it's not so hard to figure out which type of URI to use in any given situation.

JSP IN J2EE AND JSP COMPONENT DEVELOPMENT

If you're a programmer, this is the part of the book where the real action is . Here you will learn how to develop your own custom actions and JavaBeans, and how to combine JSP with other Java server-side technologies, such as servlets and Enterprise JavaBeans (EJB).

13.

Web Application Models

Part II of this book described how you can create many different types of applications using only JSP pages with generic components, such as custom actions and beans, to access databases, present content in different languages, protect pages, and so forth—all without knowing much about Java programming. This approach works fine for many types of web applications, such as employee registers, product catalogs, and conference room reservation systems. But for applications with complicated schemas, intricate business rules, and tricky control flows, the generic components just don't cut it, and you suddenly find that you need a more powerful way to handle the request processing and the business logic.

As I mentioned in Chapter 3, *JSP Overview*, JSP pages can also be combined with other Java technologies such as servlets and EJB in more complex applications. In this chapter, we look at how JSP fits into this larger picture. After this brief description of the most common application models, Chapter 14, *Combining Servlets and JSP*, describes the combination of servlets and JSP pages in detail.

The material presented in this part of the book is geared towards Java programmers. If you're not a programmer, you may still want to browse through this part to get a feel for the possibilities, but don't expect to understand everything. To really appreciate the techniques described in this part of the book, you should have experience with Java programming in general and also be familiar with Java servlets.

The Java 2 Enterprise Edition Model

At the JavaOne conference in San Francisco in June 1999, Sun Microsystems announced a new architecture for Java, with separate editions for different types of applications: the Java 2 Platform, Standard Edition (J2SE) for desktop and workstation devices; the Java 2 Platform, Micro Edition (J2ME) for small devices like cell phones, pagers, and Personal Digital Assistants (PDAs); and the Java 2 Platform, Enterprise Edition (J2EE) for server-based applications.

J2EE is a compilation of various Java APIs that have previously been offered as separate packages, an Application Programming Model (APM), also known as the J2EE Blueprints, that describes how they can all be combined, and a test suite that J2EE vendors can use to test their products for compatibility. J2EE includes the following enterprise-specific APIs:

- JavaServer Pages (JSP)

- Java Servlets

- Enterprise JavaBeans (EJB)

- Java Database Connection (JDBC)

- Java Transaction API (JTA) and Java Transaction Service (JTS)

- Java Naming and Directory Interface (JNDI)

- Java Message Service (JMS)

- Java IDL and Remote Method Invocation (RMI)

- Java XML

In addition, all the J2SE APIs can be used when developing a J2EE application. These groups of APIs can be used in numerous combinations. The first three APIs—EJB, JSP, and servlets—represent different component technologies, managed by what the J2EE documents call *containers*. As you may remember from Chapters 2 and 3, servlets and JSP pages are managed by a container that provides the runtime environment for these components, translating requests and responses into standard Java objects. This container is called a *web container*. EJB components are similarly handled by an *EJB container*. Components in the two types of containers use the other APIs to access databases (JDBC and JTA/JTS), locate various resources (JNDI), and communicate with other server resources (JMS, Java IDL, RMI, and XML). Figure 13-1 shows a high-level view of all the pieces and their relationships.

Enterprise applications are often divided into a set of tiers, and J2EE identifies three: the client tier, the middle tier, and the Enterprise Information System (EIS) tier. The middle tier can be further divided into the web tier and the EJB tier. This logical separation, with well-defined interfaces, makes it possible to build scalable applications. Initially one or more tiers can be running on the same physical server. With increased demands, the tiers can be separated and distributed over multiple servers without modifying the code, just by changing the configuration.

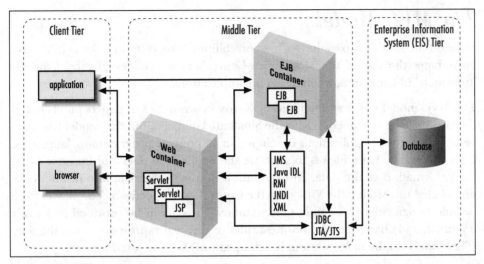

Figure 13-1. J2EE overview

The client tier contains browsers as well as regular GUI applications. A browser communicates with the web container using HTTP. A standalone application can also use HTTP or communicate directly with the EJB container using RMI or IIOP (a CORBA protocol). Another type of client that's becoming more and more popular is the extremely thin client, such as a cellular phone or PDA. This type of client typically uses the Wireless Access Protocol (WAP), often converted into HTTP via a gateway, to communicate with the web container.

The middle tier provides client services through the web container and the EJB container. A client that communicates through HTTP with the server uses components in the web container, such as servlets and JSP pages, as entry points to the application. Many applications can be implemented solely as web container components. In other applications, the web components just act as an interface to the application logic implemented by EJB components. A standalone application, written in Java or any other programming language, can also communicate directly with the EJB components. General guidelines for when to use the different approaches are discussed later in this chapter. Components in this tier can access databases and communicate with other server applications using all of the other J2EE APIs.

The Enterprise Information System (EIS) tier holds the application's business data. Typically, it consists of one or more relational database management servers, but other types of databases such as IMS databases, applications such as Enterprise Resource Planning (ERP), and mainframe transaction processing systems such as CICS, are also included in this tier. The middle tier uses J2EE APIs such as JDBC and JTA/JTS to interact with the EIS tier.

The MVC Model

In addition to the separation of responsibilities into different tiers, J2EE also encourages the use of the Model-View-Controller (MVC) design model, briefly introduced in Chapter 3, when designing applications.

The MVC model was first described by Xerox in a number of papers published in the late 1980s in conjunction with the Smalltalk language. But this model has since been used for GUI applications developed in all popular programming languages. Let's review: the basic idea is to separate the application data and business logic, the presentation of the data, and the interaction with the data into distinct entities labeled the Model, the View, and the Controller, respectively. This makes for a flexible design, where multiple presentations (Views) can be provided and easily modified, and changes in the business rules or physical representation of the data (the Model) can be made without touching any of the user interface code.

Even though the model was originally developed for standalone GUI applications, it translates fairly well into the multitier application domain of J2EE. The user interacts with the Controller to ask for things to be done, and the Controller relays these requests to the Model in a client-type independent way. Say, for instance, that you have two types of clients: an HTTP client such as a browser, and a GUI client application using IIOP to talk to the server. In this scenario you can have one Controller for each protocol that receives the requests and extracts the request information in a protocol-dependent manner. Both Controllers then call the Model the same way; the Model doesn't need to know what kind of client it was called by. The result of the request is then presented to the two types of clients using different Views. The HTTP client typically gets an HTTP response message, possibly created by a JSP page, while the GUI application may include a View component that communicates directly with the Model to get its new state and render it on the screen.

The assignment of roles to the different types of J2EE components varies depending on the scenario, the types of clients supported, and whether or not EJB is used. The following sections describe possible role assignments for the three most common scenarios where JSP pages play an important role.

Using Only JSP

The J2EE platform includes many APIs and component types, as I have just shown. However, there's no reason to use them all for a specific application. You can pick and choose the technology that makes most sense for your application scope and functionality, the longevity of the application, the skills in your development team, and so on.

As you saw in Part II of this book, there are all sorts of applications that can be developed using just JSP pages, a few JavaBeans components, and custom actions. If you're primarily a page author working alone, with limited or no Java knowledge, you can still develop fairly sophisticated applications using the custom actions in this book to access databases, serve localized content, perform authentication and access control, and so forth. And as JSP's popularity grows, I'm sure you'll see more and more generic tag libraries offered by both commercial companies and open source projects, making it possible to do even more with just the JSP part of the J2EE platform.

A pure JSP approach can be a good approach even for a team, if most of the team members are skilled in page design and layout and only a few are Java programmers. The programmers can then develop application-specific beans and custom actions to complement the generic components and minimize the amount of SQL and Java code in the JSP pages.

Using pure JSP is also a suitable model for testing out new ideas and prototyping. Using generic components, a bit of scripting code, and a few application-specific beans and actions is often the fastest way to reach a visible result. Once the ideas have been proven and the team has a better understanding of the problems, a decision can be made about the ultimate application architecture for the real thing. The danger here is that the last step—evaluating the prototype and deciding how it should be redesigned—never happens; I have seen prototypes being relabeled as production systems overnight too many times, and also experienced the inevitable maintenance nightmares that follow.

The MVC model makes sense even for a pure JSP play. I recommend that you use separate JSP pages for presentation (the View) and request processing (the Controller), and place all business logic in beans, (the Model), as shown in Figure 13-2. Let the Controller pages initialize the beans, and the View pages generate a response by reading its properties. That's the model used in most examples in Part II. If you follow this model, it's easy to move to a combination of servlets and JSP the day you find that the pure JSP application is becoming hard to maintain.

Using Servlets and JSP

The combination of servlets and JSP is a powerful tool for developing well-structured applications that are easy to maintain and extend as new requirements surface. Since a servlet is a regular Java class, you can use the full power of the Java language to implement the request processing, using standard Java development and debugging environments instead of debugging JSP pages filled with scripting code. JSP pages can then be used for what they are best at: rendering the response by including information collected or generated by the servlets.

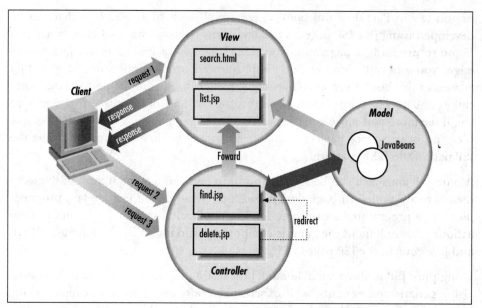

Figure 13-2. MVC roles in a pure JSP scenario

A common combination of servlets and JSP is to use a servlet as the Controller (or front component, as it's called in the J2EE documents) for an application, with a number of JSP pages acting as Views. The advantage of this model, compared to the pure JSP approach, becomes apparent as the application gets more complex. For instance, if you need to roll your own authentication and access control code, centralizing the security controls in a servlet instead of counting on everyone remembering to put custom actions in all protected pages is less error-prone. A servlet as the single entry point to the application also makes it easy to do application-specific logging (for instance, collecting statistics in a database), maintain a list of currently active users, and other things.

In this scenario, all requests are sent to the servlet acting as the Controller with an indication about what needs to be done. The indication can be in the form of a request parameter or as a part of the URI path. Figure 13-3 shows how the MVC roles are allocated in this scenario. The same way as in the pure JSP scenario, beans are used to represent the Model. The servlet locates the appropriate bean and asks it to perform the requested action. Depending on the result of the request, the Controller servlet picks an appropriate JSP page to generate a response to the user (a View). For instance, if a request to delete a document in a document archive is executed successfully, the servlet can pick a JSP page that shows the updated archive contents. If the request fails, it can pick a JSP page that describes exactly why it failed. We look at this approach in more detail later in Chapter 14.

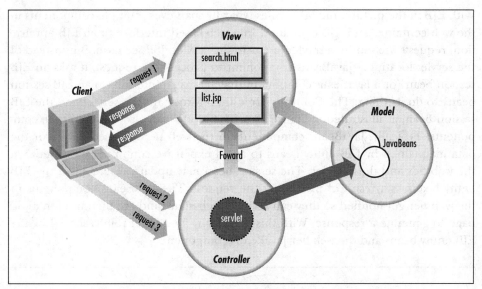

Figure 13-3. MVC roles in a servlet/JSP scenario

Using Servlets, JSP, and EJB

An application based on Enterprise JavaBeans (EJB) is commonly viewed as the Holy Grail today. However, this is the most complex model of the ones described in this chapter, and it therefore comes with overhead in the development, deployment, operation, and administration areas. Still, EJB may be the way to go for many types of applications.

What EJB brings to the table is primarily transaction management and a client type–independent component model. Even though it's impossible to say that a specific type of application should use EJB, if you develop an application with numerous database write-access operations accessed through different types of clients (such as browsers, standalone applications, PDAs, or another server in a B2B application), EJB is probably the way to go. An EJB-based application also enforces the separation between the Model, View, and Controller aspects, leading to an application that's easy to extend and maintain.

There are two primary types of EJB components: entity beans and session beans. An entity bean represents a specific piece of business data such as an employee or a customer. Each entity bean has a unique identity, and all clients that need access to the entity represented by the bean use the same bean instance. Session beans, on the other hand, are intended to handle business logic and are used only by the client that created them. Typically, a session bean operates on entity beans on behalf of its client.

With EJB in the picture, the MVC roles typically span over multiple components in the web container and EJB container. In a web-based interface to an EJB application, requests are sent to a servlet just as in the servlet/JSP scenario. But instead of the servlet locating a JavaBeans component to process the request, it asks an EJB session bean (or a JavaBeans component that acts as an interface to an EJB session bean) to do its thing. The Controller role therefore spans the servlet and the EJB session bean, as illustrated in Figure 13-4. The Model can also span multiple components. Typically, JavaBeans components in the web tier are used to mirror the data maintained by EJB entity beans to avoid expensive communication between the web tier and the EJB tier. The session bean may update a number of the EJB entity beans as a result of processing the request. The JavaBeans components in the web tier get notified so they can refresh their state, and are then used in a JSP page to generate a response. With this approach, the Model role is shared by the EJB entity beans and the web tier JavaBeans components.

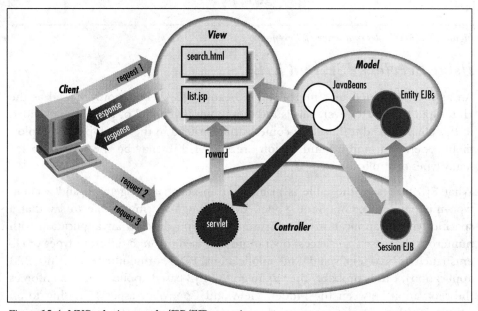

Figure 13-4. MVC roles in a servlet/JSP/EJB scenario

We have barely scratched the surface of how to use EJB in an application here. If you believe that this model fits your application, I recommend that you read the J2EE Blueprints (*http://java.sun.com/j2ee/blueprints/*) and a book dedicated to this subject, such as Richard Monson-Haefel's *Enterprise JavaBeans* (O'Reilly).

Scalability

For a large, complex application, there are many reasons to move to a model that includes Enterprise JavaBeans components. But, contrary to popular belief, scalability and great performance should not be the number one deciding factor. There are many ways to develop scalable applications using just JSP or the servlet/JSP combination, often with better performance than an EJB-based application, since the communication overhead between the web tier and EJB tier is avoided.

Scalability means that an application can deal with more and more users by changing the hardware configuration rather than the application itself. Typically this means, among other things, that it's partitioned into pieces that can run on separate servers. Most servlet- and JSP-based applications use a database to handle persistent data, so the database is one independent piece. They also use a mixture of static and dynamically generated content. Static content, such as images and regular HTML pages, is handled by a web server, while dynamic content is generated by the servlets and JSP pages running within a web container. So without even trying, we have three different pieces that can be deployed separately.

Initially, you can run all three pieces on the same server. However, both the web container and the database use a lot of memory. The web container needs memory to load all servlet and JSP classes, session data, and shared application information. The database server needs memory to work efficiently with prepared statements, cached indexes, statistics used for query optimization, etc. The server requirements for these two types of servers are also different; for instance, the web server must be able to cope with a large number of network connections, and the database server needs fast disk access. Therefore, the first step in scaling a web application is typically to use one server for the web server and servlet container, and another for the database.

If this is not enough, you can distribute the client requests over a set of servers processing HTTP requests. There are two common models: distributing requests only for dynamic content (servlet and JSP requests), or distributing requests for all kinds of content.

If the web server can keep up with the requests for static content, such as images, regular HTML, and audio and video files, but not with the servlet and JSP requests, you can spread the dynamic content processing over multiple web containers on separate servers, as shown in Figure 13-5. A number of load balancing web container modules are available for the major web servers (Apache, iPlanet Web Server, and Microsoft's Internet Information Server): for instance, Apache's Tomcat™ (*http://jakarta.apache.org*), BEA's WebLogic™ (*http://www.bea.com*), Caucho Technology's Resin™ (*http://www.caucho.com*), and Unify's ServletExec™ (*http://www.unify.com*).

The tricky part when distributing servlet loads over multiple servers is ensuring that session data is handled appropriately. Most containers keep session data in memory. The load balance module therefore picks the server with the lowest load to serve the first request from a client. If a session is created by this request, all sub-sequent requests within the same session are sent to the same server. But a container can also save session data on disk or in a database instead of in memory. It can then freely distribute each request over all servers in the cluster, and can also offer failure recovery in case a server crashes. A container is allowed to move a session from one server to another only for applications marked as *distributable*, as described in the next section.

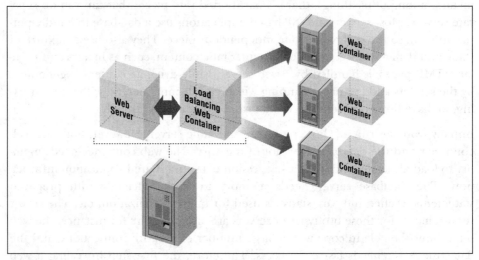

Figure 13-5. Web server distributing load over multiple web containers

For a high-traffic site, you may need to distribute requests for both static and dynamic content over multiple servers, as illustrated in Figure 13-6. You can then place a load balancing server in front of a set of servers, each running a web server and a servlet container. As with the previous configuration, session data must be considered when selecting a server for the request. The easiest way to deal with this is to use a load balancing product that sends all requests from the same client to the same server. This is not ideal, though, since all clients behind the same proxy or firewall appear as the same host. Some load balancing products try to solve this problem by using cookies or SSL sessions to identify individual clients behind prox-ies and firewalls. In this configuration, you get the best performance from a web server than runs a servlet container in the same process, eliminating the process-to-process communication between the web server and the servlet container. Most of the servlet containers mentioned above can also be used in-process with all the major web servers. Another alternate configuration is a pure Java server that acts both as a web server and a servlet container. Examples are Apache's Tomcat, Sun's Java Web Server (*http://www.sun.com/software/jwebserver/*), and Gefion software's LiteWebServer (*http://www.gefionsoftware.com/LiteWebServer/*). Compared to adding a servlet container to a standard web server, this all-in-one alternative is easier to configure and maintain. The traditional servers written in C or C++ may still be faster for serving static content, but with faster and faster Java runtimes, pure Java servers will soon be just as fast.

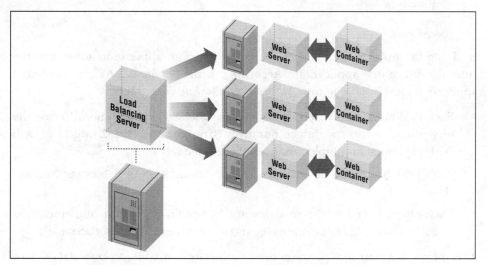

Figure 13-6. Load balancing server distributing requests over multiple servers

You should not rely on configuration strategies alone to handle the scalability needs of your application. The application must also be designed for scalability, using all the traditional tricks of the trade. Finally, you must load-test your application with the configuration you will deploy it on to make sure it can handle the expected load. There are many pure Java performance testing tools to choose from, from the simple but powerful Apache JMeter (*http://java.apache.org/jmeter/ index.html*) to sophisticated tools like Innovative IT Development's PureLoad (*http: //www.ideit.com/products/pureload/*), that support data-driven, session-aware tests to be executed on a cluster of test machines.

Preparing for Distributed Deployment

As described in the previous section, some web containers can distribute requests for a web application's resources over multiple servers, each server running its own Java Virtual Machines (JVM). Of course, this has implications for how you develop your application. So, by default, a web container must use only one JVM for an application.

If you want to take advantage of web container–controlled load balancing, you must do two things: mark the application as *distributable*, and follow the rules for a distributed application defined by the Servlet 2.2 API.

To mark an application as distributable means adding the following element to the *WEB-INF/web.xml* file for the application:

```
<web-app>
   ...
   <distributable/>
   ...
</web-app>
```

By doing so, you're telling the web container that your application adheres to the rules for distributed applications. According to the Servlet 2.2 API, a distributed application must be able to work within the following constraints:

- Each JVM has a unique servlet instance for each servlet definition. In case the servlet implements the `javax.servlet.SingleThreadModel` interface, each JVM may contain multiple instances of the same servlet.

- Each JVM has a unique instance of the `javax.servlet.ServletContext` class.

- Each object stored in the session must be serializable (must implement the `java.io.Serializable` interface, and all variables must be serializable).

This means that your servlets cannot rely on instance variables to keep data shared by all requests for a certain servlet. It also means that application scope objects (`ServletContext` attributes) are not shared between JVMs. In most cases, this is not a problem. For instance, if you use the application scope to provide shared access to cached read-only data, it just means that each JVM has its own copy. If you really need to share some resource between JVMs, you must share it through an external mechanism, such as a directory server accessed through JNDI, a database, or a file in a filesystem that is available to all servers.

The most interesting part about distributed applications is how sessions are handled. The web container allows only one server at a time to handle a request that's part of a session. But since all objects put into the session must be serializable, the container can save them on disk or in a database as well as in memory. If the server that handles a session gets overloaded or crashes, the container can therefore move the responsibility for the session to another server. The new server simply loads all serialized session data and picks up where the previous server left off.

14

Combining Servlets and JSP

As I described in the previous chapter, combining servlets and JSP pages lets you clearly separate the application logic from the presentation of the application; in other words, it lets you use the most appropriate component type for the roles of Model, View, and Controller. To illustrate how a servlet can act as the Controller for an application—using beans as the Model and JSP pages as Views—we redesign the Project Billboard application from Chapter 10, *Authentication and Personalization*, in this chapter. Along the way, we look at how servlets and JSP pages can share data, how to deal with URL references between servlets and JSP pages in a flexible manner, and how to handle runtime errors consistently in an application that mixes these two technologies.

Java servlets offer a powerful API that provides access to all the information about the request, the session, and the application data maintained as servlet context attributes. Chapter 2, *HTTP and Servlet Basics*, contains a very brief introduction to the servlet API, and Appendix B, *JSP API Reference*, contains reference material for the main classes and interfaces. To really make use of the techniques described in this chapter, however, you need to know more. If you haven't worked with servlets, I recommend that you read up on them (try Jason Hunter and William Crawford's *Java Servlet Programming* from O'Reilly) before you apply the ideas presented here in your own application.

Using a Servlet as the Controller

In an application in which all requests must be preprocessed or postprocessed in some way, using a servlet as the common entry point—the Controller—for all requests makes a lot of sense. Examples of this type of processing are application-controlled authentication and access control, application-specific logging, accessing a database, and so forth. Another common reason for using servlets instead of

JSP pages for parts of an application is that the request processing requires so much code that putting it in a JSP page makes the resulting application hard to develop, debug, and maintain. If you find yourself spending too much time trying to locate the source of code-based syntax errors or trying to figure out why the code in a page doesn't behave as it should, you may want to move the code to a servlet instead. Since a servlet is just a regular Java class, you can make use of a Java compiler and debugger to fix the problems.

The Project Billboard application introduced in Chapter 10 is a good candidate for using a servlet as the Controller; it uses application-controlled authentication and contains code for accessing a database. In this chapter, it's used as a concrete example of the servlet-based approach. The components of the new design are shown in Figure 14-1.

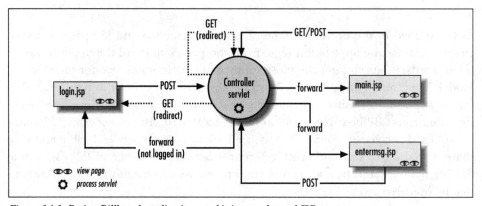

Figure 14-1. Project Billboard application combining servlet and JSP components

Compare this design with the one described in Chapter 10. Note that the pure presentation JSP pages remain the same, but the request processing pages are replaced by the servlet. So, as before, the user first requests the *login.jsp* page. This page still contains a form with fields for username and password, but with the new design it invokes the controller servlet instead of a request processing JSP page. The servlet is invoked with a request parameter named `action` with the value `authenticate`. The servlet performs the authentication, and if successful, it creates an `EmployeeBean` object and saves it in the session scope as proof of authentication. It then redirects the browser back to itself, this time with `action` set to `showPage` and a `page` parameter set to the URL of an application JSP page. When the servlet receives a request with a `showPage` action, it forwards the request to the specified page. (I will explain why it's done this way instead of just redirecting straight to the JSP page shortly.) As before, the selected page depends on whether the user loaded the *login.jsp* page or tried to access an application page directly, without first logging in.

The *main.jsp* page contains a form for updating the project subscription list, and links for posting a new message or logging out. The difference from the page in Chapter 10 is that the form and the links now invoke the servlet instead of request processing JSP pages. Different `action` parameter values are used to distinguish each type of request. For all types of requests, the servlet first verifies that the user is authenticated. If not, it forwards the request to the *login.jsp* page, where the URL for the requested page is saved as a hidden field in the same way as in Chapter 10. If the user is authenticated, the servlet performs the requested action and redirects to itself with the `showPage` action and the appropriate `page` parameter value, just as after a successful authentication. Redirecting to the servlet with a `showPage` action instead of directly invoking the JSP page lets the servlet perform access control for the JSP pages as well.

This example illustrates a number of interesting things: servlet-initialized application scope objects, centralized request processing, how to map a URL pattern to a servlet, and additional access-control requirements for protected JSP pages when using a servlet as the Controller.

Initializing Application Scope Objects

The Project Billboard application uses two business logic beans that must be available to all users; in other words, they must be available as application scope objects. You may remember the `NewsBean` from Chapter 10. This bean is the repository for all news items relating to projects, and it's used as the source for the personalized message list. The other business logic bean is called `Employee-RegistryBean`. It acts as an abstraction of the database with employee information, and contains methods for authenticating a user and retrieving and saving employee information. The `EmployeeRegistryBean` class is described in more detail in Chapter 15, *Developing JavaBeans for JSP*.

The controller servlet, named `PBControllerServlet`, needs access to these beans to do its work, so it's a good idea to let it create and initialize the beans. By placing references to the beans in `ServletContext` attributes, they are made available to all JSP pages in the application as application scope beans. That's because the application scope is just an abstraction of the `ServletContext` attributes. If a servlet places a reference to a bean in a context attribute, the bean can be accessed by any JSP page using the `<jsp:useBean>` action with the `scope` attribute set to `application`. Example 14-1 shows the `PBControllerServlet`'s `init()` method, where the two beans are initialized and saved as context attributes.

Example 14-1. Initialization of Application Scope Beans

```
package com.ora.jsp.servlets;

...
import javax.servlet.*;
```

Example 14-1. Initialization of Application Scope Beans (continued)

```
import javax.sql.*;
import com.ora.jsp.beans.emp.*;
import com.ora.jsp.beans.news.*;
import com.ora.jsp.sql.*;
public class PBControllerServlet extends HttpServlet {

    public void init() throws ServletException {
        DataSource ds = null;
        try {
            ds = new DataSourceWrapper("sun.jdbc.odbc.JdbcOdbcDriver",
                "jdbc:odbc:example", null, null);
        }
        catch (Exception e) {} // Ignore all in this example
        EmployeeRegistryBean empReg = new EmployeeRegistryBean();
        empReg.setDataSource(ds);
        getServletContext().setAttribute("empReg", empReg);

        NewsBean news = new NewsBean();
        getServletContext().setAttribute("news", news);
    }
...
```

First, a `javax.sql.DataSource` instance is created. The `DataSource`, an interface that's part of the JDBC 2.0 Standard Extension (SE) package, allows you to open JDBC database connections to retrieve and modify database data. It can represent a connection pool, letting connections be reused instead of opened and closed over and over again. Many JDBC driver vendors offer connection pool `DataSource` implementations, but here we use a simple wrapper class that implements its own connection pool based on standard JDBC 1.0 classes. The wrapper class is discussed in more detail in Chapter 17, *Developing Database Access Components*, where I also describe how to use a vendor-provided `DataSource` implementation. Also note that in Example 14-1, the `DataSource` instance is created with hardcoded values for the JDBC driver class and URL. Of course, that is not the best way. A better approach is to specify this information externally, for instance as servlet initialization parameters. Again, more about this in Chapter 17.

The `DataSource` is used by the `EmployeeRegistryBean`, which is the bean the Project Billboard application uses instead of accessing the database directly. An instance of the bean is created, initialized with the `DataSource`, and saved as a context attribute named `empReg`. Next, the `NewsBean` instance is created and saved as a context attribute named `news`. The implementation used in this book keeps all messages in memory as opposed to in a database. If a database were used, the `NewsBean` would also need to be initialized with the `DataSource`.

Servlets as well as JSP pages can now access these two beans by asking the context for the corresponding attribute. A servlet uses the `getAttribute()` method:

```
NewsBean newsBean =
    (NewsBean) getServletContext().getAttribute("news");
```

Note that the `getAttribute()` method has the return type `Object`, so you have to cast the attribute value to the correct type.

A JSP page uses the `<jsp:useBean>` action to make the bean available to other action elements and scriptlets in the page:

```
<jsp:useBean id="news" scope="application"
    class="com.ora.jsp.beans.news.NewsBean" />
```

Since the `id` attribute value matches the context attribute value, the `<jsp:useBean>` action retrieves the bean created by the servlet instead of creating a new one.

In the application described in this chapter, only one servlet is used. But that's not always the case. In a large application, it's sometimes better to use different controller servlets for different parts of the application, for instance, one controller for all functions used by an administrator, and another for end users. If that's the case, you can use a separate servlet with the sole purpose of taking care of all initialization of beans for the application. Whether you use the one-servlet approach described here or a separate application initialization servlet, the servlet that creates the beans used by the rest of the application must be loaded by the servlet container before any other parts of the application. You can tell a container to load a servlet when the web application is initialized by using elements in the application deployment descriptor, the *WEB-INF/web.xml* file:

```
<web-app>
  ...
  <servlet>
    <servlet-name>pbController</servlet-name>
    <servlet-class>
      com.ora.jsp.servlets.PBControllerServlet
    </servlet-class>
    <load-on-startup>1</load-on-startup>
  </servlet>
  ...
```

Within the `<servlet>` element, which is described in further detail later, the `<load-on-startup>` element specifies that this servlet must be loaded when the web application is started by the container. The value is a positive integer, indicating when this servlet should be loaded relative to other servlets. Servlets with low values are always loaded before servlets with higher values.

A servlet that creates and initializes shared beans should also make sure that the beans are being removed and shut down gracefully, if needed. This is done in the servlet's `destroy()` method, as shown in Example 14-2.

Example 14-2. Removing Application Scope Beans

```
public void destroy() {
    getServletContext().removeAttribute("empReg");
    getServletContext().removeAttribute("news");
}
```

Centralized Request Processing

When all requests for an application are first processed by one servlet, it's easy to handle common functions in one place. In this example, the controller servlet is used for authentication and access control. But there are other possibilities. Say you have a site where you charge the users based on what they do, or need to keep an audit log over all database modifications. A servlet serving as a common entry point for all application requests is a good place to put this logic.

The controller servlet needs to handle both GET and POST requests, so its doGet() method simply calls the doPost() method:

```
public void doGet(HttpServletRequest request,
    HttpServletResponse response)
    throws IOException, ServletException {
      doPost(request, response);
}
```

It's in the doPost() method, shown in Example 14-3, that all processing takes place.

Example 14-3. Centralized Request Processing

```
public void doPost(HttpServletRequest request,
    HttpServletResponse response)
    throws IOException, ServletException {

    String action = request.getParameter("action");

    // Check if the user is authenticated
    if (!isAuthenticated(request) &&
        !("authenticate".equals(action) ||
        "logout".equals(action))) {
        doForwardToLogin(request, response);
    }
    else {
        if ("authenticate".equals(action)) {
            doAuthenticate(request, response);
```

Example 14-3. Centralized Request Processing (continued)

```
    }
    else if ("logout".equals(action)) {
        doLogout(request, response);
    }
    else if ("storeMsg".equals(action)) {
        doStoreMsg(request, response);
    }
    else if ("updateProfile".equals(action)) {
        doUpdateProfile(request, response);
    }
    else if ("showPage".equals(action)) {
        doShowPage(request, response);
    }
    else {
        response.sendError(
            HttpServletResponse.SC_NOT_IMPLEMENTED);
    }
  }
}
```

In this example, a request parameter named action is used to decide what to do. An alternative to this is using part of the URI itself as the indication about which action to perform, as you will see in the next section when we look at the URI used to invoke the servlet. If the user isn't already authenticated, and the request is not to authenticate or log off, the request is forwarded to the login page.

The isAutheticated() method simply checks if an authentication token is available in the session:

```
private boolean isAuthenticated(HttpServletRequest request) {
    boolean isAuthenticated = false;
    HttpSession session = request.getSession();
    if (session.getAttribute("validUser") != null) {
        isAuthenticated = true;
    }
    return isAuthenticated;
}
```

In this example, a bean named validUser is used as an authentication token. This bean is placed in the session scope by the servlet's doAuthenticate() method if the user is successfully authenticated. The isAuthenticated() method looks for the bean. If it finds it, it knows that the user has already been authenticated.

If the user is not authenticated, the doForwardToLogin() method is called:

```
private void doForwardToLogin(HttpServletRequest request,
    HttpServletResponse response)
```

```
    throws IOException, ServletException {
    String origURL = HttpUtils.getRequestURL(request).toString();
    String queryString = request.getQueryString();
    if (queryString != null) {
        origURL += "?" + queryString;
    }
    String loginURL = "login.jsp" + "?origURL=" +
        URLEncoder.encode(origURL) +
        "&errorMsg=" + URLEncoder.encode("Please log in first");
    forward(loginURL, request, response);
}
```

In order for the login page to save the URL of the requested page so it can be
shown automatically after successful authentication, the URL must be passed to
the *login.jsp* page as a parameter. The URL is constructed from the
getRequestURL() method, which returns the URL of the current request minus
the query string; a call is made to getQueryString() to append the query string
if it's present. The complete URL is then used as the value of the origURL parameter. Another parameter, errorMsg, is added with a message to display on the
login page. Both parameter values are encoded using the java.net.URLEncoder
class. This is necessary to convert special characters, such as the space character,
into encoded values that are accepted in a URL.

The request is finally forwarded to the URL for the *login.jsp* page, including both
parameters, using the forward() method:

```
private void forward(String url, HttpServletRequest request,
    HttpServletResponse response)
    throws IOException, ServletException {
    RequestDispatcher rd = request.getRequestDispatcher(url);
    rd.forward(request, response);
}
```

The RequestDispatcher is a servlet API class used to programmatically invoke
another servlet or a JSP page to continue the processing of a request. The servlet's
forward() method gets an instance of the RequestDispatcher class that represents the *login.jsp* page and calls its forward() method. This is almost exactly what
the <jsp:forward> action element in a JSP page does. The difference is that the
action element also aborts processing of the rest of the page. When a request is
forwarded, the originating servlet delegates all processing of the request to the target servlet (or JSP page). The originating servlet is not allowed to modify the
response in any way, neither before calling forward() nor when the method
returns. In most cases, it should simply return after calling forward(), possibly
after doing some cleanup that does not involve modifying the response. As you
can see in Example 14-3, the PBControllerServlet doesn't do anything after
calling doForwardToLogin(), which in turn calls the forward() method.

If the user is authenticated, the requested action is performed by calling the corresponding method. Some of the methods are described in the next section. You can look at the source code for the `PBControllerServlet` class to see how the other actions are performed.

Mapping a URI Pattern to a Servlet

Using a URI starting with */servlet* to invoke a servlet is a convention introduced by Sun's Java Web Server (JWS), the first product to support servlets before the API was standardized. This convention is supported by most servlet containers today. But using this type of URI has a couple of problems. First, it makes it perfectly clear to a user (at least a user who knows about servlets) what technology is used to implement the application. Not that you shouldn't be proud of using servlets, but a hint like this can help a hacker explore possible security holes. Even though no servlet-related security issues are known at this time, it never hurts to be a bit paranoid when it comes to security. The other problem is of a more practical nature.

As I described in Chapter 12, *Bits and Pieces*, using relative URIs to refer to resources within an application makes life a lot easier. As you know, a relative URI is interpreted as relative to the URI of the current request. But if a servlet, like the controller servlet in this chapter, is invoked using a URI like */ora/servlet/PBController*, it can't easily use a relative URI to refer to a View JSP page, such as */ora/ch14/main.jsp*. This is because the two resources are identified by URIs at different levels in the application's URI path structure. If you invoke the servlet with this type of URI, it has to refer to the JSP page with a relative path like *../ch14/main.jsp*, or a context-relative path like */ch14/main.jsp*. This works, but if you later decide to change the path structure, for instance to use the path */billboard/main.jsp* instead, you have to modify all path references in the servlet.

A simple solution to this problem is to define a URI pattern mapping for the servlet, so it can be accessed using a URI with the same path structure as the JSP pages. This type of mapping has been supported by servlet containers in a proprietary way for a long time, but the Servlet 2.2 API standardizes the rules. The mapping is done with XML elements in the web application's deployment descriptor (the *WEB-INF/web.xml* file) like this:

```
<web-app>
  ...
  <servlet>
    <servlet-name>pbController</servlet-name>
    <servlet-class>
      com.ora.jsp.servlets.PBControllerServlet
    </servlet-class>
  </servlet>
  ...
```

```
<servlet-mapping>
  <servlet-name>pbController</servlet-name>
  <url-pattern>/ch14/process</url-pattern>
</servlet-mapping>
...
```

Two main elements are used here. The `<servlet>` element, with subelements `<servlet-name>` and `<servlet-class>`, are used to associate the servlet class with a symbolic name. The name must be unique within the application. The `<servlet-mapping>` element is then used to define the path pattern used to invoke the servlet. The `<servlet-name>` subelement value must match the symbolic name of the servlet, and the `<url-pattern>` subelement defines the pattern. The pattern can be a context-relative path, as in this example. This type of pattern tells the container to invoke the named servlet only if the request URI path matches the pattern exactly (a query string is of course allowed, but no other path parts).

This is the pattern used for the servlet in the Project Billboard application described in this chapter. To see how it works, let's first look at the action attribute in the *login.jsp* page:

```
<form action="process?action=authenticate" method="post">
```

The action attribute contains a relative path (i.e., it doesn't start with a slash). Since the *login.jsp* page is requested with the URI */ora/ch14/login.jsp*, the browser converts the relative path into the absolute path */ora/ch14/process?action=authenticate*. The */ora* part is the context path, and the rest of the path, */ch14/process*, matches the context-relative path pattern for the servlet in the *web.xml* file. If you decide to install this web application with a different context path, the action URI still invokes the correct servlet. If you then decide to change the internal application path structure, you only have to change the pattern in the *web.xml* file; no changes to paths in the JSP pages or the servlet are needed.

Other types of patterns let you use a part of the URI path to indicate what the servlet is asked to do instead of using an `action` parameter. A *path pattern* matches a URI starting with the specified path (as opposed to the exact path match required in the previous case):

```
  ...
<servlet-mapping>
  <servlet-name>pbController</servlet-name>
  <url-pattern>/ch14/process/*</url-pattern>
</servlet-mapping>
  ...
```

Note that the pattern ends with */**, which is a wildcard sequence matching any subpath. With a path pattern, the servlet can be invoked with a URI such as

/ch14/process/autheticate, and it can get the action name specified by the last part
of the URI with this code:

```
public void doPost(HttpServletRequest request,
    HttpServletResponse response)
    throws IOException, ServletException {

    String action = request.getPathInfo();
    ...
```

Another popular way to invoke the controller server is with a URI that ends with a
special extension, like */ch14/authenticate.do,* instead of a special URI prefix. To
have all requests with the selected extension processed by the controller servlet,
use an extension pattern:

```
    ...
  <servlet-mapping>
    <servlet-name>pbController</servlet-name>
    <url-pattern>*.do</url-pattern>
  </servlet-mapping>
    ...
```

The servlet then gets the action name by stripping off the extension:

```
public void doPost(HttpServletRequest request,
    HttpServletResponse response)
    throws IOException, ServletException {

    String action = request.getServletPath();
    int extension = action.lastIndexOf(".");
    if (extension != -1) {
        action = action.substring(0, extension);
    }
...
```

All pattern-mapping types described here allow you to use a relative path to invoke
the controller servlet, making it easier to refer to all the pieces of the application.

Relative paths are also supported by the servlet API methods used to forward and
redirect to another resource within the same application. To forward a request,
you first need to get a `RequestDispatcher`. There are two ways to obtain one. To
use a relative path URI, call the `ServletRequest`'s `getRequestDispatcher()`
method, like in the `forward()` method in the servlet described earlier:

```
private void forward(String url, HttpServletRequest request,
    HttpServletResponse response)
    throws IOException, ServletException {

    RequestDispatcher rd = request.getRequestDispatcher(url);
    rd.forward(request, response);
}
```

If you look at how this method is called in the previous section, you see that a relative path (*login.jsp*) is passed as the value of the url parameter. The request object knows the absolute path that was used to make the current request, so it can use a relative path to locate the target resource. The javax.servlet. ServletContext class also has a getRequestDispatcher() method, but it works only with context-relative paths, since the context has no knowledge about the absolute path for the current request.

In versions of the servlet API prior to 2.2, the sendRedirect() method, used to send a redirect response to the browser, required that an absolute URL was used to specify the target resource. However, in the 2.2 version, this requirement was relaxed, so both absolute and relative paths are now also supported (note that context-relative paths are not supported, for backward-compatibility reasons: there's no way to distinguish an absolute path from a context-relative path, since both start with a slash). The method that handles the logout action in the controller servlet uses a relative path to redirect to the login page:

```
private void doLogout(HttpServletRequest request,
    HttpServletResponse response) throws IOException {

    HttpSession session = request.getSession();
    session.invalidate();
    response.sendRedirect("login.jsp");
}
```

Access Control for JSP Pages

You may have noticed that the access control performed by the controller servlet in Example 14-3 doesn't prevent a user from invoking one of the protected JSP pages directly, for instance with a URL like */ch14/main.jsp* instead of */ch14/process?action=showPage&page=main.jsp*. In most applications, this is not as bad as it looks. When you use a servlet as the controller, it is responsible for retrieving all protected data, and the JSP page displays only the data it receives from the servlet. Invoking the JSP page directly, without going through the controller servlet, therefore yields a page with only static template text.

However, if some of your application contains JSP pages or HTML pages with static data that needs to be protected, you can configure the application with a security constraint in the *WEB-INF/web.xml* file that makes it impossible for anyone to load the pages directly:

```
<security-constraint>
    <web-resource-collection>
        <web-resource-name>no-access</web-resource-name>
        <url-pattern>/ch14/main.jsp</url-pattern>
        <url-pattern>/ch14/entermsg.jsp</url-pattern>
    </web-resource-collection>
```

```
<auth-constraint>
    <role-name>nobody</role-name>
</auth-constraint>
</security-constraint>
```

This protects the two JSP pages in the example application, identified by the `<url-pattern>` elements. The `<auth-constraint>` element defines a single role named `nobody`. If no user is assigned this role, nobody can access these pages directly. When the controller servlet is invoked with the `showPage` action, however, it uses a `RequestDispatcher` to forward control to the pages. Since forwarding is an internal affair, the security constraint doesn't have any effect.

A More Modular Design Using Action Objects

The approach in Example 14-3 is to implement each action as a separate method in the servlet, so every time you add a new action, you also have to update the servlet. In a large application, you may find yourself adding more and more code to the controller servlet, eventually ending up with a class that's hard to maintain.

A more modular approach is to treat each action as a separate class that implements a common interface, for instance called `Action`.[*] The `Action` interface may look like this:

```
import java.io.*;
import javax.servlet.*;
import javax.servlet.http.*;


public interface Action {
    public void perform(HttpServlet servlet,
        HttpServletRequest request,
        HttpServletResponse response)
        throws IOException, ServletException;
}
```

The single method, `perform()`, has arguments that give the action class access to all the same objects as a regular servlet: the `request` and `response` objects. In addition, the `servlet` argument lets the action class access the servlet context and servlet configuration objects if needed.

With this approach, each action ends up as a simple class. For instance, the logout action is handled by a nice little class like this:

```
import java.io.*;
import javax.servlet.*;
```

---

[*] There is an `Action` interface already defined in the Java Swing (JFC) classes. However, since you will probably not be using the Swing GUI classes in this context, the two should not conflict.

```
import javax.servlet.http.*;

public class LogoutAction implements Action {
    public void perform(HttpServlet servlet,
        HttpServletRequest request,
        HttpServletResponse response)
        throws IOException, ServletException {

        HttpSession session = request.getSession();
        session.invalidate();
        response.sendRedirect("login.jsp");
    }
}
```

In most cases, you can develop the action classes so that they do not keep any state information in instance variables. The controller servlet therefore only needs one instance of each class. They can be created when the first request is received for a certain action ("lazy instantiation") or in the controller servlet's `init()` method:

```
public void init() throws ServletException {
    ...
    initActions();
}

private void initActions() {
    actions = new Hashtable();
    actions.put("authenticate", new AuthenticateAction());
    actions.put("logout", new LogoutAction());
    actions.put("storeMsg", new StoreMsgAction());
    actions.put("updateProfile", new UpdateProfileAction());
    actions.put("showPage", new ShowPageAction());
    actions.put("login", new LoginAction());
}
```

In this example, all action class names are hardcoded. An alternative is to use servlet initialization parameters or a separate configuration file to specify the mapping between action names and action class names. If you do that, you can add new actions to the application without touching the controller servlet code at all.

With the action class approach, the controller servlet's `doPost()` method gets the action name from an action parameter (or a part of the URL, as discussed earlier), finds the corresponding action class, and calls its `perform()` method:

```
public void doPost(HttpServletRequest request,
    HttpServletResponse response)
    throws IOException, ServletException {

    String actionName = request.getParameter("action");
    if (actionName == null) {
        response.sendError(HttpServletResponse.SC_NOT_ACCEPTABLE);
```

```
            return;
        }

        Action action = (Action) actions.get(actionName);
        if (action == null) {
            response.sendError(HttpServletResponse.SC_NOT_IMPLEMENTED);
            return;
        }

        // Use the login action if the user is not authenticated
        if (!isAuthenticated(request) &&
            (!"authenticate".equals(actionName) ||
            "logout".equals(actionName))) {
            action = (Action) actions.get("login");
        }
        action.perform(this, request, response);
    }
```

The source code for a controller servlet and action classes using this approach is available in the code package for this book, so you can look at the details of all classes yourself. A framework for applications using a servlet with action classes and JSP pages is also available as part of the Apache Jakarta project, at *http:// jakarta.apache.org/struts/index.html*.

Sharing Data Between Servlets and JSP Pages

When you use servlets for request processing and JSP pages to render the user interface, you often need a way to let the different components access the same data. The model I recommend is having the servlet create beans and pass them to a JSP page for display.

As I described earlier, the application scope is just a JSP abstraction of `javax. servlet.ServletContext` attributes. Similarly, the request and session scopes are JSP abstractions for attributes associated with `javax.servlet.ServletRequest` and `javax.servlet.http.HttpSession`, respectively. All three classes provide `setAttribute()`, `getAttribute()`, and `removeAttribute()` methods. A servlet uses the `setAttribute()` method to make a bean available to a JSP page. For instance, a servlet can create a bean, save it as a request attribute, and then forward control to a JSP page like this:

```
public void doGet(HttpServletRequest request,
    HttpServletResponse response) throws ServletException,
    IOException {

    String userName = request.getParameter("userName");
    UserInfoBean userInfo = userReg.getUserInfo(userName);
```

```
        request.setAttribute("userInfo", userInfo);
        RequestDispatcher rd =
            request.getRequestDispatcher("welcome.jsp");
        rd.forward(request, response);
    }
```

To the JSP page, the bean appears as a request scope variable. It can therefore obtain the bean using the `<jsp:useBean>` action and then access the properties of the bean as usual, in this case using `<jsp:getProperty>`:

```
<h1>Welcome
  <jsp:useBean id="userInfo" scope="request"
    class="com.ora.jsp.beans.userinfo.UserInfoBean" />
  <jsp:getProperty name="userInfo" property="userName" />
</h1>
```

The `<jsp:useBean>` action, with an `id` attribute value matching the request attribute name set by the servlet, is needed to make the bean known to the JSP container before other actions or scripting code can access it.

If the bean needs to be available throughout the session, the servlet uses an `HttpSession` attribute instead:

```
HttpSession session = request.getSession();
session.setAttribute("userInfo", userInfo);
```

Using a `ServletContext` attribute, the bean becomes available in the application scope:

```
ServletContext context = getServletContext();
context.setAttribute("userInfo", userInfo);
```

The only difference in the JSP page is that the scope attribute for the `<jsp:useBean>` action must match the scope used by the servlet.

Passing beans in the other direction, from a JSP page to a servlet, is not so common, but it can be done. Here's how. The JSP page creates the bean using `<jsp:useBean>` and sets the properties using `<jsp:setProperty>`:

```
<jsp:useBean id="userInfo" scope="request"
  class="com.ora.jsp.beans.userinfo.UserInfoBean" >
  <jsp:setProperty name="userInfo" property="*" />
</jsp:useBean>

<jsp:forward page="/myServlet" />
```

It then forwards the request to the servlet (mapped to the URI `/myServlet`) using `<jsp:forward>`, and the servlet retrieves the bean using `getAttribute()`:

```
UserInfoBean userInfo =
    (UserInfoBean) request.getAttribute("userInfo");
```

Using a JSP Error Page for All Runtime Errors

Even if an application is developed with different types of components, it should deal with runtime errors in a consistent way. Recall from Chapter 7, *Error Handling and Debugging*, how the page directive can specify a JSP page to be used when code in the JSP page throws an exception. The error page gets access to the exception through an implicit variable named exception, and can display a user-friendly message as well as log details about the problem. The way the error page is invoked and how the implicit variable gets its value can easily be mimicked by a servlet. Example 14-4 shows how to do this in the controller servlet used in previous examples in this chapter.

Example 14-4. Invoking a JSP Error Page from a Servlet

```
public void doPost(HttpServletRequest request,
    HttpServletResponse response) {
    ...
    try {
        action.perform(this, request, response);
    }
    catch (Throwable t) {
        request.setAttribute("javax.servlet.jsp.jspException", t);

        RequestDispatcher rd =
            getServletContext().getRequestDispatcher("/error.jsp");
        rd.forward(request, response);
    }
}
```

The servlet calls the action's perform() method within a try block. If any type of exception occurs while executing an action, the servlet catches it, sets the javax.servlet.jsp.jspException request attribute to the exception object, and forwards the request to the error JSP page. The javax.servlet.jsp.jspException attribute name is reserved for the exception object in the JSP specification, so the JSP container picks up the exception object from the request attribute and makes it available to the JSP page through the exception variable.

15

Developing JavaBeans
for JSP

The JavaBeans specification* was primarily developed with graphical components in mind. But JavaBeans represents a design pattern for components that also makes sense for faceless components used to structure a server-side application. The JSP specification provides a number of standard actions to support the use of JavaBeans, as described in the previous chapters.

You can use JavaBeans components in a pure JSP application to structure the application and minimize the amount of code needed in the JSP pages. In an application that uses both servlets and JSP pages, beans can be used as a carrier of data between the two domains. By using beans with an eye towards the recommendations in the J2EE application programming model, you can also make it easier to migrate the business logic to Enterprise JavaBeans when warranted by new requirements.

In this chapter, we look at the JavaBeans model and how it applies to the type of faceless JavaBeans you can use in a server-side application, using some of the beans from previous chapters as examples.

JavaBeans as JSP Components

JavaBeans are simply regular Java classes designed according to a set of guidelines. By following these guidelines, development tools can figure out how the bean is intended to be used and how it can be linked to other beans. The JavaBeans specification characterizes beans as classes that:

- Support *introspection* so that a builder tool can analyze how a bean works

- Support *customization*, so that when using an application builder, a user can customize the appearance and behavior of a bean

---

* This specification is available at *http://java.sun.com/beans/docs/spec.html.*

- Support *events* as a simple communication metaphor that can be used to notify beans of interesting things

- Support *properties*, both for customization through a tool and for programmatic use

- Support *persistence*, so that a bean can be customized in an application builder and then have its state saved away and reloaded later

Introspection means that information about a class, such as details about its methods and their arguments and return type, can be discovered by another class. By following certain naming conventions for the methods, the external class can figure out how the bean class is intended to be used. Specifically, the bean's properties and the events it generates or observes can be found using introspection. For GUI beans, introspection is typically used by a builder tool to allow properties to be set by the user in a property window. In a JSP scenario, the JSP standard actions and custom actions use introspection to find the methods used for reading or writing property values, and to declare variables of appropriate types.

A property is an attribute of a bean that can be read or written by the bean's client through regular methods named according to the JavaBeans guidelines. Typically, the property value is represented by an instance variable in the bean, but a read-only property can also represent a value that's calculated at runtime. The property methods are intended to be used to customize the bean, for instance, setting the label text for a bean used as a button in a GUI application, or setting the name of the data source to be used for a faceless server-side bean. Besides property access methods, a bean class can have regular methods that perform actions such as saving the bean's properties in a database or sending a mail composed from its properties.

A bean can generate or observe events. In a GUI bean, typical events are "button clicked" and "item selected." A server-side bean can deal with events indicating that the source of the data it represents has been updated so it can refresh its copy.

Support for persistence means that a bean should implement the `java.io.Serializable` interface. This interface flags a class that can be saved in an external format, such as a file. When tools are used to customize a bean, it is possible to save the customized state during application development and then let the customized bean be instantiated in runtime. The `<jsp:useBean>` action allows you to take advantage of this feature, but it's not commonly used today since no JSP authoring tools provide a customization interface yet. There's another reason for supporting persistence in JSP beans, however. A servlet container can support session persistence, saving all session data when a servlet context is shut down and reloading it again when the context is restarted. This works only if the beans you save in the session scope implement `Serializable`. In addition, beans (or any other object) placed in the session scope of an application marked as being distributable must be serializable, so that the container can migrate the session from one server to another.

JavaBeans Naming Conventions

As we mentioned early in the book, a Java bean is a class that has a no-argument constructor and conforms to the JavaBeans naming conventions. The bean properties are accessed through *getter* and *setter* methods, collectively known as a bean's *accessor* methods. Getter and setter method names are composed of the word *get* or *set*, respectively, plus the property name, with the first character of each word capitalized. A regular getter method has no arguments, but returns a value of the property's type, while a setter method takes a single argument of the property's type and has a void return type. Here's an example:

```
public class CustomerBean implements java.io.Serializable {

    private String firstName;
    private String lastName;
    private int accountNumber;
    private int[] categories;
    private boolean preferred;

    public String getFirstName() {
      return firstName;
    }

    public void setFirstName(String firstName) {
      this.firstName = firstName;
    }
```

A readable property has getter methods, a writable property has setter methods. Depending on the combination of getter and setter methods, a property is read-only, write-only, or read/write.

A read-only property doesn't necessarily have to match an instance variable exactly. Instead, it can combine instance variable values, or any values, and return a computed value:

```
    public String getFullName() {
      return (new StringBuffer(firstName).append(" ")
        .append(lastName).toString());
    }
```

The type of a property can be a Java class, interface, or a primitive type such as int:

```
public int getAccountNumber() {
    return accountNumber;
}
```

Besides simple single-value properties, beans can also have multivalue properties represented by an array of any type. This is called an *indexed property* in the specification. Two types of access methods can be used for an indexed property: methods reading or writing the whole array, or methods working with just one element, specified by an index:

```
public int[] getCategories() {
    return categories;
}

public void setCategories(int[] categories) {
    this.categories = categories;
}

public int getCategories(int i) {
    return categories[i];
}

public void setCategories(int i, int category) {
    this.categories[i] = category;
}
```

The naming convention for a Boolean property getter method is different than for all other types. You could use the regular getter name patterns, but the recommendation is to use the word *is* combined with the property name, to form a question:

```
public boolean isPreferred() {
    return preferred;
}
```

This helps to make the source code more readable. The setter method for a Boolean property follows the regular pattern:

```
public void setPreferred(boolean preferred) {
    this.preferred = preferred;
    }
}
```

Event handling is based on observers implementing a listener interface, and generators providing methods for observers to register their interest in the events. A listener interface defines the methods a listener needs to implement to be notified when the corresponding event is triggered. A bean identifies itself as a listener by declaring that it's implementing a listener interface, and an event source is identified by its listener registration methods.

Let's look at an example. A listener interface for observing events related to the customer data handled by the example bean looks like this:

```
import java.util.EventListener;

public interface CustomerUpdatedListener extends EventListener {
    void customerUpdated(CustomerUpdatedEvent e);
}
```

The interface shown here defines only one event, but an interface may also group a number of related events. The CustomerBean identifies itself as an observer of the event by implementing the interface:

```
public class CustomerBean implements CustomerUpdatedListener {
    ...
    public void customerUpdated(CustomerUpdatedEvent e) {
        if (e.getAccountNumber() == accountNumber) {
            // Refresh local copy
        }
    }
}
```

Another bean, perhaps one acting as the gatekeeper to the customer database, identifies itself as a source for the event by defining methods for registration of listeners:

```
import java.util.Vector;

public class CustomerRegister {
    private Vector listeners = new Vector();

    public
    void addCustomerUpdatedListener(CustomerUpdatedListener cul) {
        listeners.addElement(cul);
    }

    public
    void removeCustomerUpdatedListener(CustomerUpdatedListener cul) {
        listeners.removeElement(cul);
    }

    public void updateCustomer(CustomerBean customer) {
        // Update persistent customer storage
        notifyUpdated(customer);
    }
```

It notifies all listeners when the customer data is modified, like this:

```
    protected void notifyUpdated(CustomerBean customer) {
        Vector l;
        CustomerUpdatedEvent e =
            new CustomerUpdatedEvent(this, customer.getAccountNumber());
        synchronized(listeners) {
```

```
            l = (Vector)listeners.clone();
        }
        for (int i = 0; i < l.size(); i++) {
            ((CustomerUpdatedListener)l.elementAt(i)).customerUpdated(e);
        }
    }
}
```

By following these simple naming conventions, the JSP standard actions <jsp:getProperty> and <jsp:setProperty>, as well as custom actions like <ora:loop>, can discover how to use your beans correctly. At this time, no JSP features rely on the event naming conventions, but future development tools may do so. So if your beans need to handle events, it's a good idea to follow the conventions. Besides, it's a well-known design pattern, so using it makes your code more readable to other developers familiar with this design.

Handling session events

A bean used in a JSP application can actually register itself to receive session-related events. The servlet API includes an interface called javax.servlet.http.HttpSessionBindingListener. An object that implements this interface is notified when the object is placed in or removed from a session, through these two methods:

```
public void valueBound(HttpSessionBindingEvent event);
public void valueUnbound(HttpSessionBindingEvent event);
```

The valueBound() method is called when the object is added to a session, and the valueUnbound() method when it's removed. The HttpSessionBinding-Event class contains these two methods:

```
public String getName();
public HttpSession getSession();
```

The getName() method returns the name used for the object in the session, and the getSession() method returns a reference to the session object itself.

One way to use a bean that implements the HttpSessionBindingListener interface is to keep track of currently logged-in users. A bean representing a user is added to the session after a successful authentication, and is given access to the servlet context for the application through a write-access property. In the valueBound() method, the bean adds a reference to itself to the list of users maintained by a context attribute object, such as a java.util.Vector. The valueUnbound() method removes the reference:

```
import java.io.*;
import java.util.*;
```

```
import javax.servlet.*;
import javax.servlet.http.*;

public class UserBean implements HttpSessionBindingListener,
  Serializable {

  private ServletContext context;
  private String name;
  ...

  public void setContext(ServletContext context) {
    this.context = context;
  }

  public void setName(String name) {
    this.name = name;
  }
  ...

  public void valueBound(HttpSessionBindingEvent e) {
    Vector currentUsers =
      (Vector) context.getAttribute("currentUsers");
    if (currentUsers == null) {
      currentUsers = new Vector();
    }
    currentUsers.addElement(this);
  }

  public void valueUnbound(HttpSessionBindingEvent e) {
    Vector currentUsers =
      (Vector) context.getAttribute("currentUsers");
    currentUsers.removeElement(this);
  }
  ...
}
```

A JSP page can then generate a list of all current users by looping through the Vector, available as an application scope object.

JSP Bean Examples

In a JSP-based application, two types of beans are primarily used: *value beans* and *utility beans.* A value bean encapsulates all information about some entity, such as a user or a product. A utility bean performs some action, such as saving information in a database or sending email. Utility beans can use value beans as input, or produce value beans as a result of an action.

If you develop JavaBeans for your application, you're also preparing for migration to a full-blown J2EE application. The utility beans can be changed into proxies for one or more EJB session beans, acting as controllers for the application.

Value beans may be used as-is, acting as what are called Value Objects in Sun's paper, "Developing Enterprise Applications With the Java 2 Platform, Enterprise Edition," also known as the J2EE blueprint. In EJB-based applications, the application's data is represented by EJB entity beans. Getting a property value from an EJB entity bean requires a remote call, consuming both system resources and bandwidth. Instead of making a remote call for each property value that is needed, the web component can make one remote call to an EJB session bean (possibly via a JSP utility bean) that returns all properties of interest packaged as a value bean. The web component can then get all the properties from the value bean with inexpensive local calls. The value bean can also act as cache in the web container to minimize remote calls even more, and can combine information from multiple EJB entity beans that is meaningful to the web interface. If you plan to eventually move to the EJB model, I recommend that you read the J2EE blueprint paper (*http://java.sun.com/j2ee/blueprints/*) before you design your application, so that you can make the migration as smooth as possible.

Value Beans

Value beans are useful even without EJB. They are handy for capturing form input, since the `<jsp:setProperty>` JSP action automatically sets all properties with names corresponding to request parameter names, as described in Chapter 5, *Generating Dynamic Content*. In addition, the `<jsp:getProperty>` action lets you include the property values in the response without using scriptlets.

Another benefit of value beans is that they can be used to minimize expensive database accesses for entities that rarely change their value. By placing a value bean in the application scope, all users of your application can use the cached value instead. Example 15-1 shows the source code for the `ProductBean` used in Chapter 8, *Sharing Data Between JSP Pages, Requests, and Users*, to represent products in an online shopping application. This is a pure value bean, with only property accessor methods, that could represent data stored in a database.

Example 15-1. ProductBean

```
package com.ora.jsp.beans.shopping;

import java.io.*;

public class ProductBean implements Serializable {
    private int id;
    private String name;
```

Example 15-1. ProductBean (continued)

```
    private String descr;
    private float price;

    public int getId() {
        return id;
    }

    public String getName() {
        return name;
    }

    public String getDescr() {
        return descr;
    }

    public float getPrice() {
        return price;
    }

    void setId(int id) {
        this.id = id;
    }

    void setName(String name) {
        this.name = name;
    }

    void setDescr(String descr) {
        this.descr = descr;
    }

    void setPrice(float price) {
        this.price = price;
    }
}
```

This bean is created and initialized by the single instance of the `CatalogBean`. All setter methods have package accessibility, while the getter methods are public. Using package accessibility for the setter methods ensures that only the `Catalog-Bean` can set the property values. For instance, a JSP page can read the product information, but not change the price.

Another example of a value bean is the `UserInfoBean` introduced in Chapter 5. Part of this bean is shown in Example 15-2. Besides encapsulating the property values of the entity it represents, it also provides methods for validating the data.

Example 15-2. Part of the UserInfoBean

```
package com.ora.jsp.beans.userinfo;

import java.io.*;
import java.util.*;
import com.ora.jsp.util.*;

public class UserInfoBean implements Serializable {
    // Validation constants
    private static String DATE_FORMAT_PATTERN = "yyyy-MM-dd";
    private static String[] SEX_LIST = {"male", "female"};
    private static int MIN_LUCKY_NUMBER = 0;
    private static int MAX_LUCKY_NUMBER = 100;

    // Properties
    private String birthDate;
    private String birthDateInput;
    private String emailAddr;
    private String emailAddrInput;
    private String[] interests;
    private String luckyNumber;
    private String luckyNumberInput;
    private String sex;
    private String sexInput;
    private String userName;
    private boolean isInitialized;

    public String getBirthDate() {
        return birthDate;
    }

    public void setBirthDate(String birthDate) {
        isInitialized = true;
        birthDateInput = birthDate;
        if (StringFormat.isValidDate(birthDate, DATE_FORMAT_PATTERN)) {
            this.birthDate = birthDate;
        }
    }
    ...
```

All setter methods save the value passed as the argument in an instance variable representing the input value. They then validate the value and, if it's valid, save it in another instance variable representing the property. The getter methods return the value of the property value variable. The effect is that only validated values can be accessed through the getter methods. The saved input values are, however, used for another purpose, as shown in Example 15-3.

Example 15-3. UserInfoBean Validation Methods

```
public String getPropertyStatusMsg() {
    StringBuffer msg = new StringBuffer();
    if (!isInitialized()) {
        msg.append("Please enter values in all fields");
    }
    else if (!isValid()) {
        msg.append("The following values are missing or invalid: ");
        msg.append("<ul>");
        if (birthDate == null) {
            if (birthDateInput == null) {
                msg.append("<li>Birth date is missing");
            }
            else {
                msg.append("<li>Birth date value is invalid: " +
                    birthDateInput);
            }
        }
        if (emailAddr == null) {
            if (emailAddrInput == null) {
                msg.append("<li>Email address is missing");
            }
            else {
                msg.append("<li>Email address value is invalid: " +
                    emailAddrInput);
            }
        }
        ...
    }
    else {
        msg.append("Thanks for telling us about yourself!");
    }
    return msg.toString();
}

public boolean isInitialized() {
    return isInitialized;
}

public boolean isValid() {
    return isInitialized() &&
        getBirthDate() != null &&
        getEmailAddr() != null &&
        getLuckyNumber() != null &&
        getSex() != null &&
        getUserName() != null;
}
```

The getPropertyStatusMsg() method returns a string with a message about the validation status of the properties. If one or more properties have invalid values, the message contains an HTML list with a list item element for each invalid value, showing the input value plus an explanation about why it was not accepted.

This behavior serves a purpose in the examples where the bean is used, as it allows me to introduce one JSP concept at a time. But it may not be ideal for a real application. First, it may be better to always save the input value as the property value, and let the isValid() method, instead of the setter method, handle all validation. This way, the getter methods return the input value whether it's valid or not. When the bean is used to fill out an input form, like in the last two examples in Chapter 5, the user will then be able to correct the invalid values instead of typing new values from scratch. Example 15-4 shows an outline of these changes.

Example 15-4. Centralized UserInfoBean Validation

```
package com.ora.jsp.beans.userinfo;

import java.io.*;
import java.util.*;
import com.ora.jsp.util.*;

public class UserInfoBean implements Serializable {
    // Validation constants
    private static String DATE_FORMAT_PATTERN = "yyyy-MM-dd";
    private static String[] SEX_LIST = {"male", "female"};
    private static int MIN_LUCKY_NUMBER = 0;
    private static int MAX_LUCKY_NUMBER = 100;

    // Properties
    private String birthDate;
    private String emailAddr;
    private String[] interests;
    private String luckyNumber;
    private String sex;
    private String userName;
    private boolean isInitialized;

    public String getBirthDate() {
        return birthDate;
    }

    public void setBirthDate(String birthDate) {
        isInitialized = true;
        this.birthDate = birthDate;
    }
    ...
    public boolean isValid() {
        return
```

Example 15-4. Centralized UserInfoBean Validation (continued)

```
             StringFormat.isValidDate(birthDate, DATE_FORMAT_PATTERN) &&
             StringFormat.isValidEmailAddr(emailAddr) &&
             StringFormat.isValidInteger(luckyNumber, MIN_LUCKY_NUMBER,
                 MAX_LUCKY_NUMBER) &&
             StringFormat.isValidString(sex, SEX_LIST, true) &&
             userName != null;
    }
```

Secondly, a bean is easier to reuse if it's not tied to one form of presentation. It's therefore a good idea to remove the HTML in the getPropertyStatusMsg() method. One way of doing this is by splitting the method into two methods, as outlined in Example 15-5.

Example 15-5. HTML Free Status Messages

```
    public String getPropertyStatusMsg() {
        String msg = "Thanks for telling us about yourself!";
        if (!isInitialized()) {
            msg ="Please enter values in all fields";
        }
        else if (!isValid()) {
            msg = "The following values are missing or invalid: ";
        }
        return msg;
    }


    public String[] getPropertyStatusDetails() {
        Vector details = new Vector();
        if (isInitialized() && !isValid()) {
            if (birthDate == null) {
                details.addElement("Birth date is missing");
            }
            else if (!StringFormat.isValidDate(birthDate,
                DATE_FORMAT_PATTERN)) {
                details.addElement("Birth date value is invalid: " +
                    birthDate);
            }
            ...
        }
        String[] arr = new String[details.size()];
        details.copyInto(arr);
        return arr;
    }
```

With this approach, a JSP page can render the messages in any format that fits the overall layout of the page. First it gets the main message, and then it loops through the indexed propertyStatusDetails values:

```
    <font color="red">
      <jsp:getProperty name="userInfo" property="propertyStatusMsg" />
```

```
<ul>
  <ora:loop name=userInfo" property="propertyStatusDetails"
    loopId="details" className="String" >
    <li><%= details %>
  </ora:loop>
</ul>
</font>
```

Utility Beans

A utility bean performs some action, such as processing information, as opposed to simply acting as a container for information.

The UserInfoBean contains processing code, namely code for encoding special characters such as HTML character entities and for validation of all property values. We can move this code to a separate bean so that the UserInfoBean becomes a pure property value container. Whether this change makes sense or not depends on the application that uses it.

One set of property getter methods used in Chapter 5 returns the UserInfoBean property values with all special characters that can cause problems in an HTML form converted to the corresponding HTML character entity codes. Here's one example:

```
public String getUserNameFormatted() {
    return StringFormat.toHTMLString(getUserName());
}
```

The actual conversion is performed by a method in the com.ora.jsp.util. StringFormat utility class:

```
public static String toHTMLString(String in) {
    StringBuffer out = new StringBuffer();
    for (int i = 0; in != null && i < in.length(); i++) {
        char c = in.charAt(i);
        if (c == '\'') {
            out.append("&#39;");
        }
        else if (c == '\"') {
            out.append("&#34;");
        }
        else if (c == '<') {
            out.append("&lt;");
        }
        else if (c == '>') {
            out.append("&gt;");
        }
        else if (c == '&') {
            out.append("&amp;");
```

```
            }
        else {
            out.append(c);
        }
    }
    return out.toString();
}
```

Moving this HTML-specific code out of the bean and instead using the utility class directly in the JSP page makes the bean easier to reuse in parts of the application that do not render the values as HTML.

The way the `UserInfoBean` bean is used in this book, it's perfectly okay to keep the validation code in the bean itself. However, let's say you would like to add a property referencing another bean, a `friends` property for instance, that holds an array of other `UserInfoBean` objects. It may then be better to let a utility bean that knows about all users in the application perform the validation, including verifying that the friends exist.

A bean used for validation is one example of a utility bean that makes the application easy to maintain. The `CatalogBean` used in Chapter 8 is another example. The version developed for this book simply creates a set of `ProductBean` objects with hardcoded values, and provides a method that returns all products in the catalog. In a real application, it would likely get the information from a database and have methods for updating catalog information, such as adding and removing products or changing the information about a product, as well as methods that return only products matching a search criterion. If all catalog update requests go through the `CatalogBean`, it can create, delete, and update the `ProductBean` objects so that they always match the information stored in the database. The number of database accesses can be greatly reduced this way.

Chapter 9, *Database Access*, and Chapter 10, *Authentication and Personalization*, offer another example of how you can use a utility bean. The purpose of these chapters is to show you how to use the generic database custom actions to access a database, but a Java programmer may want to encapsulate all database-access code in a bean instead. Example 15-6 shows part of a utility bean that handles all database interactions needed for these two chapters.

Example 15-6. EmployeeRegistryBean

```
package com.ora.jsp.beans.emp;

import java.io.*;
import java.sql.*;
import java.text.*;
import java.util.*;
import javax.sql.*;
```

Example 15-6. EmployeeRegistryBean (continued)

```java
import com.ora.jsp.sql.*;
import com.ora.jsp.sql.value.*;
import com.ora.jsp.util.*;

public class EmployeeRegistryBean implements Serializable {
    private DataSource dataSource;

    /**
     * Sets the dataSource property value.
     */
    public void setDataSource(DataSource dataSource) {
        this.dataSource = dataSource;
    }

    /**
     * Returns true if the specified user name and password
     * match an employee in the database.
     */
    public boolean authenticate(String userName, String password)
        throws SQLException {

        EmployeeBean empInfo = getEmployee(userName);
        if (empInfo != null &&
            empInfo.getPassword().equals(password)) {
            return true;
        }
        return false;
    }

    /**
     * Returns an EmployeeBean initialized with the information
     * found in the database for the specified employee, or null if
     * not found.
     */
    public EmployeeBean getEmployee(String userName)
        throws SQLException {

        // Get the user info from the database
        Connection conn = dataSource.getConnection();
        Row empRow = null;
        Vector projectRows = null;
        try {
            empRow = getSingleValueProps(userName, conn);
            projectRows = getProjects(userName, conn);
        }
        finally {
            try {
                conn.close();
```

Example 15-6. EmployeeRegistryBean (continued)

```
        }
        catch (SQLException e) {} // Ignore
    }


    // Create a EmployeeBean if the user was found
    if (empRow == null) {
        // Not found
        return null;
    }


    EmployeeBean empInfo = new EmployeeBean();
    try {
        empInfo.setDept(empRow.getString("Dept"));
        empInfo.setEmpDate(empRow.getString("EmpDate"));
        empInfo.setEmailAddr(empRow.getString("EmailAddr"));
        empInfo.setFirstName(empRow.getString("FirstName"));
        empInfo.setLastName(empRow.getString("LastName"));
        empInfo.setPassword(empRow.getString("Password"));
        empInfo.setUserName(empRow.getString("UserName"));
        empInfo.setProjects(toProjectsArray(projectRows));
    }
    catch (NoSuchColumnException nsce) {} // Cannot happen here
    catch (UnsupportedConversionException nsce) {}
    return empInfo;
}


/**
 * Inserts the information about the specified employee, or
 * updates the information if it's already defined.
 */
public void saveEmployee(EmployeeBean empInfo) throws SQLException {

    // Save the user info from the database
    Connection conn = dataSource.getConnection();
    conn.setAutoCommit(false);
    Row userRow = null;
    Vector interestRows = null;
    try {
        saveSingleValueProps(empInfo, conn);
        saveProjects(empInfo, conn);
        conn.commit();
    }
    finally {
        try {
            conn.setAutoCommit(true);
            conn.close();
        }
        catch (SQLException e) {} // Ignore
```

Example 15-6. EmployeeRegistryBean (continued)

```
    }
}

/**
 * Returns a Row with all information about the specified
 * employee except the project list, or null if not found.
 */
private Row getSingleValueProps(String userName, Connection conn)
    throws SQLException {

    if (userName == null) {
        return null;
    }

    SQLCommandBean sqlCommandBean = new SQLCommandBean();
    sqlCommandBean.setConnection(conn);
    StringBuffer sql = new StringBuffer();
    sql.append("SELECT * FROM Employee ")
       .append("WHERE UserName = ?");
    sqlCommandBean.setSqlValue(sql.toString());
    Vector values = new Vector();
    values.addElement(new StringValue(userName));
    sqlCommandBean.setValues(values);
    Vector rows = null;
    try {
        rows = sqlCommandBean.executeQuery();
    }
    catch (UnsupportedTypeException e) {} // Cannot happen here

    if (rows == null || rows.size() == 0) {
        // User not found
        return null;
    }
    return (Row) rows.firstElement();
}
...
```

The EmployeeRegistryBean has one property, dataSource, that needs to be set when the bean is created. Chapter 14, *Combining Servlets and JSP*, describes how a servlet can create the bean and initialize it with a DataSource when the application starts, and then save it in the application scope where all JSP pages can reach it. The other public methods in this bean perform the same functions as the generic database actions in Chapters 9 and 10. The getSingleValueProps() method, as well other private methods not shown in Example 15-6, use an SQLCommandBean to execute the SQL statement. This bean is included in the source code package for this book, so you can use it in your own beans as well. We will take a look at the implementation in Chapter 17, *Developing Database Access Components.*

Using the `EmployeeRegistryBean` instead of the generic database actions means you can greatly simplify the JSP pages. For instance, the authentication code in Example 10-3 can be reduced to this:

```
<jsp:useBean id="empReg" scope="application"
  class="com.ora.jsp.beans.emp.EmployeeRegistryBean" />

<%
  String userName = request.getParameter("userName");
  String password = request.getParameter("password");
  if (!userReg.authenticate(userName, password)) {
%>

    <ora:redirect page="index.jsp" >
      <ora:param name="errorMsg"
        value="The User Name and Password you entered are not valid." />
    </ora:redirect>

<%
  }
  else {
    com.ora.jsp.beans.emp.EmployeeBean validUser =
      empReg.getEmployee(userName);
    session.setAttribute("validUser", validUser);
%>
```

The `<jsp:useBean>` action finds the single instance in the application scope and associates it with a scripting variable named `empReg`, which is then used in the scriptlets to call the bean's methods.

Multithreading Considerations

As you have seen, putting business logic in beans leads to a more structured and maintainable application. But there's one thing you need to be aware of: beans shared between multiple pages must be thread-safe.

Multithreading is an issue only for beans in the session and application scopes. Beans in the page and request scopes are executed by only one thread at a time. A bean in the session scope can be executed by more than one thread, initiated by requests from the same client. This may happen if the user brings up multiple browsers, repeatedly clicks a Submit button in a form, or if the application uses frames to request multiple JSP pages at the same time. Application scope beans are shared by all application users, hence it's very likely that more than one thread is using an application scope bean.

Java provides mechanisms for dealing with concurrent access to resources, such as synchronized blocks and thread notification methods. But there are other ways to avoid multithreading issues in the type of beans used in JSP pages.

Value beans are typically placed in the request or session scope, as containers of related information used in multiple pages. In most cases, they are created and initialized in one place only, such as by a Controller servlet or by a `<jsp:useBean>` and `<jsp:setProperty>` combination in the request processing page invoked by a form, or by a custom action or utility bean. In all other places, the bean is used only with `<jsp:getProperty>` or scripting elements to read its property values. Since only one thread writes to the bean and all others just read it, you don't have to worry about different threads overwriting each other.

But if you have a value bean that can be updated, such as the NewsBean used in Chapter 10, you have to be careful. The NewsBean contains an instance variable that holds a list of NewsItemBean objects and has methods for retrieving new items matching a search criterion, as well as for adding and removing new items. If one thread calls removeNewsItem() while another is executing getNewsItems(), a runtime exception may occur. Example 15-7 shows how you can use synchronization to guard against this problem.

Example 15-7. Synchronized Access to Instance Variable

```
package com.ora.jsp.beans.news;

import java.io.*;
import java.util.*;
import com.ora.jsp.util.*;

public class NewsBean implements Serializable {
    private Vector newsItems = new Vector();
    private int[] idSequence = new int[1];

    ...
    public NewsItemBean[] getNewsItems(String[] categories) {
        Vector matches = new Vector();
        synchronized (newsItems) {
            for (int i = 0; i < newsItems.size(); i++) {
                NewsItemBean item =
                    (NewsItemBean) newsItems.elementAt(i);
                if (ArraySupport.contains(categories,
                    item.getCategory())) {
                    matches.addElement(item);
                }
            }
        }
        NewsItemBean[] matchingItems =
```

Example 15-7. Synchronized Access to Instance Variable (continued)

```
            new NewsItemBean[matches.size()];
        matches.copyInto(matchingItems);
        return matchingItems;
    }

    public void setNewsItem(NewsItemBean newsItem) {
        synchronized (idSequence) {
            newsItem.setId(idSequence[0]++);
        }
        newsItems.addElement(newsItem);
    }

    public void removeNewsItem(int id) {
        synchronized (newsItems) {
            for (int i = 0; i < newsItems.size(); i++) {
                NewsItemBean item =
                    (NewsItemBean) newsItems.elementAt(i);
                if (id == item.getId()) {
                    newsItems.removeElementAt(i);
                    break;
                }
            }
        }
    }
    ...
```

Both the getNewsItems() and the removeNewsItem() methods synchronize on the newsItems object, and the addElement() method used in setNewsItem() is a synchronized method. The effect is that while one thread is manipulating the list of news items through one of these methods, all other threads wait until the current thread leaves the synchronized block.

The setNewsItem() method also synchronizes on idSequence, a variable used to generate a unique ID for each item. idSequence is an int array with one component. It's a neat trick to be able to use synchronization for an integer value: Java doesn't allow synchronization on primitive types, only on objects, but an array is an object. You could use an Integer object instead, but you can't change the value of an Integer. To increment the value, a new Integer must be created. Using an array avoids these repeated object creations (and creating an object is a fairly expensive operation in Java).

Another approach that avoids multithreading problems is used in the utility beans in this book, such as the CounterBean used in Chapter 8 and the Employee-RegistryBean described in the previous section. These beans only define setter methods for customization that takes place when the bean is created, and define all data needed to perform a function as method arguments instead of properties.

Each thread has its own copies of argument values and local variables, so with this approach there's no risk of one thread stepping on another.

Unexpected <jsp:setProperty> Behavior

The <jsp:setProperty> action can be used to automatically set all properties in a bean with names matching the names of the parameters received with the request. This is a great feature that's used in many of the examples in this book. But unless you know how this works behind the scenes, you could be in for a surprise.

When the <jsp:setProperty> code is invoked, it gets a list of all request parameter names and uses bean introspection to find the corresponding property setter methods. It then calls all setter methods to set the properties to the values of the parameters. This means that if you have a property in your bean that doesn't match a parameter, the setter method for this property is not called. In most cases, this is not surprising. However, if the parameter is present in some requests but not in others, things may get a bit confusing. This is the case with parameters corresponding to checkbox, radio button, and selection list elements in an HTML form. If this type of element is selected, the browser sends a parameter with the element's name and the value of the selected item. But if the element is not selected, it doesn't send a parameter at all.

For example, let's say you have a bean with an indexed property, such as the projects property in the com.ora.jsp.beans.emp.EmployeeBean used in Chapter 10. This bean is kept in the session scope. The user can change the value of the property through a group of checkboxes in a form. To unregister all projects, a user deselects all checkboxes and submits the form. You may think the following code would then clear the property (setting it to null):

```
<jsp:setProperty name="validUser" property="projects"
  param="projects" />
```

Yet it doesn't. Without any checkbox selections, the projects parameter is not sent and the corresponding property setter method is not called. The workaround used in Chapter 10 is to use a request-time attribute expression to explicitly set the property to either the array of selected checkboxes or null if none is selected:

```
<jsp:setProperty name="validUser" property="projects"
  value='<%= request.getParameterValues("projects") %>' />
```

If you have been developing web applications for a while, you may not think this is so surprising. The <jsp:setProperty> action behaves the same way, however, even when a parameter matching a property is received but its value is an empty string. This happens for text fields that the user leaves empty.

If you have properties matching text fields, make sure the code that uses the values of the corresponding properties can deal with null values, or initialize them to empty strings. If you keep a bean like this in a scope other than the page and request scopes (where a new instance is created for each request), also be aware that the user cannot clear the property by erasing the field in a form. One possible workaround is to define a reset property, with a setter method that clears all properties. Then call it explicitly in the JSP page before setting the other properties, like this:

```
<jsp:setProperty name="validUser" property="reset"
  value="any value" />
<jsp:setProperty name="validUser" property="*" />
```

This way, all properties are first reset by the first <jsp:setProperty> action, and then all properties matching request parameters are set by the second action.

16

Developing JSP
Custom Actions

Custom actions let you encapsulate logic and make it available to page authors in a familiar format. Throughout this book, a number of generic custom actions are used for such tasks as accessing a database, including localized content, encoding URLs, and much more. Using these actions, the amount of Java code in the JSP pages can be kept to a minimum, making the application easier to debug and maintain. However, for a complex application, the generic actions presented in this book are not enough. Perhaps you want to develop application-specific actions to access the database instead of putting SQL statements in the JSP pages. Or you may want to present complex data as a set of nested HTML tables with cells formatted differently depending on their values. Instead of using conditional scripting code in the JSP page to generate this table, an application-specific custom action can be used.

Custom actions know about their environment. They automatically get access to all information about the request, the response, and all the variables in the JSP scopes. Another common use for a custom action is as an HTTP-specific adapter to a bean. JavaBeans components are frequently used in a JSP application, and a bean is easier to reuse if it doesn't know about the environment where it's used.

To develop a custom action, you use a set of classes and interfaces referred to in the JSP 1.1 specification as the *tag extension mechanism*. The simplest custom action implementation is just a class with bean-like accessor methods plus a couple of other well-defined methods. But it's a very powerful mechanism, letting you develop custom actions to do pretty much anything. As always, with increased power comes some amount of complexity. For more advanced actions you need to implement additional methods, and in some cases an extra class. But it's still not rocket science. We'll take it step by step, starting with the most common and simple cases, and then work through some examples of the advanced features in the later sections of this chapter.

Tag Extension Basics

A custom action—actually a *tag handler* class for a custom action—is basically a bean with property setter methods corresponding to the custom action element's attributes. In addition, the tag handler class must implement one of two Java interfaces defined by the JSP specification.

All the interfaces and classes you need to implement a tag handler are defined in the javax.servlet.jsp.tagext package. The two primary interfaces are named Tag and BodyTag. The Tag interface defines the methods you need to implement for any action. The BodyTag interface extends the Tag interface and adds methods used to access the body of an action element. To make it easier to develop a tag handler, two support classes are defined by the API: TagSupport and BodyTagSupport, as shown in Figure 16-1. These classes provide default implementations for the methods in the corresponding interface.

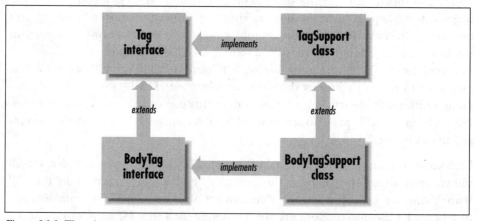

Figure 16-1. The primary tag extension interfaces and support classes

The reason the specification defines both interfaces and the support classes that implement those interfaces is simply to cover all the bases. If you already have a class with functionality that you want to access as a custom action, you can specify that it implements the appropriate interface and add the few methods defined by that interface. In practice, though, I recommend that you implement your tag handlers as extensions to the support classes. This way, you get most of the methods implemented for free, and you can still reuse the existing classes by calling them from the tag handler.

A *tag library* is a collection of custom actions. For instance, all custom actions used in this book are packaged as one tag library. Besides the tag handler class files, a tag library must contain a *Tag Library Descriptor* (TLD) file. This is an XML file that maps all custom action names to the corresponding tag handler classes, and describes all attributes supported by each custom action. The class files and the TLD can be packaged in a JAR file to make it easy to install. We look at the TLD syntax and packaging details at the end of this chapter.

Before we get into all the intricate details, let's take a brief look at what it takes to develop, deploy, and use a custom action. First, you implement a tag handler class, like the following:

```
package com.mycompany;

import java.io.*;
import javax.servlet.jsp.*;
import javax.servlet.jsp.tagext.*;

public class HelloTag extends TagSupport {
    private String name = "World";

    public void setName(String name) {
        this.name = name;
    }

    public int doEndTag() {
        try {
            pageContext.getOut().println("Hello " + name);
        }
        catch (IOException e) {} // Ignore it
        return EVAL_PAGE;
    }
}
```

The tag handler class contains a setter method for an attribute named name. The doEndTag() method (defined by the Tag interface) simply writes "Hello" plus the name attribute value to the response. You compile the class and place the result-ing class file in the *WEB-INF/classes* directory for the application.

Next, you create the TLD file. The following is a minimal TLD file for a library with just one custom action element:

```
<?xml version="1.0" encoding="ISO-8859-1" ?>
<!DOCTYPE taglib
  PUBLIC "-//Sun Microsystems, Inc.//DTD JSP Tag Library 1.1//EN"
  "http://java.sun.com/j2ee/dtds/web-jsptaglibrary_1_1.dtd">

<taglib>
  <tlibversion>1.0</tlibversion>
```

```
    <jspversion>1.1</jspversion>
    <shortname>test</shortname>

    <tag>
      <name>hello</name>
      <tagclass>com.mycompany.HelloTag</tagclass>
      <bodycontent>empty</bodycontent>
      <attribute>
        <name>name</name>
      </attribute>
    </tag>
  </tablib>
```

The TLD maps the custom action name `hello` to the tag handler class `com.mycompany.HelloTag`, and defines the `name` attribute. Place the TLD file in the application's *WEB-INF/tlds* directory, for instance with the filename *mylib.tld*.

Now you're ready to use the custom action in a JSP page, like this:

```
<%@ taglib uri="/WEB-INF/mylib.tld" prefix="test" %>
<html>
  <body bgcolor="white">
    <test:hello name="Hans" />
  </body>
</html>
```

When the page is requested, the JSP container uses the TLD to figure out which class to execute for the custom action. It then calls all the appropriate methods, resulting in the text "Hello Hans" being added to the response. That's all there's to it for the most simple case. In the remainder of this chapter, we go through all of this in greater detail.

Developing a Simple Action

As you have seen in the previous chapters, a custom action element in a JSP page consists of a start tag (possibly with attributes), a body, and an end tag:

```
<prefix:actionName attr1="value1" attr2="value2">
  The body
</prefix:actionName>
```

If the action element doesn't have a body, the following shorthand notation can be used instead of the start tag and the end tag:

```
<prefix:actionName attr1="value1" attr2="value2" />
```

A tag handler is the object invoked by the JSP container when a custom action is found in a JSP page. In order for the tag handler to do anything interesting, it needs access to all information about the request and the page, as well as the action element's attribute values (if any). At a minimum, the tag handler must implement the `Tag` interface, which contains methods for giving it access to the request and page information, as well as methods called when the start tag and end tag are encountered. Note that an action element supported by a tag handler that implements the `Tag` interface may have a body, but the tag handler has more limited control over the body content than a tag handler that implements the `BodyTag` interface. For the attribute values, the JSP container treats the tag handler as a bean and calls a property setter method corresponding to each attribute, as shown in Figure 16-2.

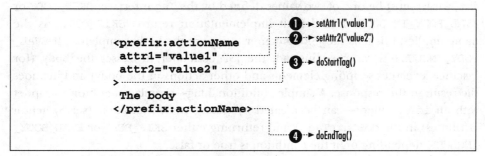

Figure 16-2. Tag interface methods and property setter methods

Here are the most important methods of the `Tag` interface:

```
public void setPageContext(PageContext pageContext);
public int doStartTag() throws JspException;
public int doEndTag() throws JspException;
```

To be complete, let's first look at the implementation of these methods provided by the `TagSupport` class. This is the class that most simple tag handlers extend, so it's important to know how `TagSupport` implements the methods a tag handler inherits.

The first method of interest is the `setPageContext()` method:

```
public class TagSupport implements Tag, Serializable {
    ...
    protected PageContext pageContext;
    ...
    public void setPageContext(PageContext pageContext) {
        this.pageContext = pageContext;
    }
}
```

This method is called by the JSP container before the tag handler is used. The `TagSupport` implementation simply sets an instance variable to the current `PageContext` object. The `PageContext` provides access to the request and response objects and all the JSP scope variables, and it implements a number of utility methods that the tag handler may use. Appendix B, *JSP API Reference*, includes a complete list of all `PageContext` methods.

When the start tag is encountered, the JSP container calls the `doStartTag()` method, implemented like this in the `TagSupport` class:

```
public int doStartTag() throws JspException {
    return SKIP_BODY;
}
```

This method gives the tag handler a chance to initialize itself, perhaps verifying that all attributes have valid values. Another use for this method is to decide what to do with the element's body content, if a body exists. The method returns an `int`, which must be one of two values defined by the `Tag` interface: `SKIP_BODY` or `EVAL_BODY_INCLUDE`. The default implementation returns `SKIP_BODY`. As the name implies, this tells the JSP container to ignore the body completely. If `EVAL_BODY_INCLUDE` is returned instead, the JSP container processes the body (for instance, executes scripting elements and other actions in the body) and includes the result in the response. A simple conditional tag—a replacement for a scriptlet with an `if` statement—can be created by testing some condition (set by action attributes) in the `doStartTag()` and returning either `SKIP_BODY` or `EVAL_BODY_INCLUDE`, depending on if the condition is true or false.

No matter which value the `doStartTag()` method returns, the JSP container calls `doEndTag()` when it encounters the end tag:

```
public int doEndTag() throws JspException {
    return EVAL_PAGE;
}
```

This is the method that most tag handlers override to do the real work. It can also return one of two `int` values defined by the `Tag` interface. The `TagSupport` class returns `EVAL_PAGE`, telling the JSP container to continue to process the rest of the page. But a tag handler can also return `SKIP_PAGE`, which aborts the processing of the rest of the page. This is appropriate for a tag handler that forwards processing to another page or that sends a redirect response to the browser, like the `<ora:redirect>` custom action introduced in Chapter 8, *Sharing Data Between JSP Pages, Requests, and Users*.

An example of a custom action that can be implemented as a simple tag handler is the `<ora:addCookie>` action, introduced in Chapter 10, *Authentication and Personalization*. The tag handler class is called `com.ora.jsp.tags.generic.AddCookieTag` and extends the `TagSupport` class to inherit most of the `Tag` interface method implementations:

```
package com.ora.jsp.tags.generic;

import javax.servlet.http.*;
import javax.servlet.jsp.*;
import javax.servlet.jsp.tagext.*;
```

```
import com.ora.jsp.util.*;

public class AddCookieTag extends TagSupport {
```

The `<ora:addCookie>` action has two mandatory attributes, `name` and `value`, and one optional attribute, `maxAge`. Each attribute is represented by an instance variable and a standard property setter method:

```
private String name;
private String value;
private String maxAgeString;

public void setName(String name) {
    this.name = name;
}

public void setValue(String value) {
    this.value = value;
}

public void setMaxAge(String maxAgeString) {
    this.maxAgeString = maxAgeString;
}
```

The purpose of the custom action is to create a new `javax.servlet.Cookie` object, with the name, value, and max age values specified by the attributes, and to add the cookie to the response. The tag handler class overrides the `doEndTag()` method to carry out this work:

```
public int doEndTag() throws JspException {
    int maxAge = -1;
    if (maxAgeString != null) {
        try {
            maxAge = Integer.valueOf(maxAgeString).intValue();
        }
        catch (NumberFormatException e) {
            throw new JspException("Invalid maxAge: " +
                e.getMessage());
        }
    }
    CookieUtils.sendCookie(name, value, maxAge,
        (HttpServletResponse) pageContext.getResponse());
    return EVAL_PAGE;
}
```

The `maxAge` attribute is optional, so before the corresponding `String` value is converted into an `int`, a test is performed to see if it is set or not. You may wonder why similar tests are not done for the `name` and `value` variables. The reason is that the JSP container verifies that all mandatory attributes are set in the custom action. If a mandatory attribute is not set, the JSP container refuses to process the page, so you can always be sure that a variable corresponding to a mandatory attribute has a value. I describe how to specify a mandatory attribute at the end of this chapter.

The code that actually creates the `Cookie` object and adds it to the response object is executed by the `sendCookie()` method in the `com.ora.jsp.util.CookieUtils` class. This is a pretty common practice; the tag handler is just a simple adapter for logic that's implemented in another class, providing a JSP-specific interface to the reusable class.

One last thing to note in this example is that the property setter method for the `maxAge` attribute, and the corresponding instance variable, is of type `String`, even though it's later converted to an `int` before it's used. In a regular bean, you would likely make it a property of type `int` to begin with instead. Using a `String` property and converting it to an `int` in the tag handler is not necessarily the best implementation strategy, but it's the safest. A JSP 1.1–compliant container should automatically convert a literal string attribute value to the appropriate type, as shown in Table 16-1.

Table 16-1. Conversion of String Value to Property Type

Property Type	Conversion Method
boolean or Boolean	Boolean.valueOf(String)
byte or Byte	Byte.valueOf(String)
char or Character	String.charAt(int)
double or Double	Double.valueOf(String)
int or Integer	Integer.valueOf(String)
float or Float	Float.valueOf(String)
long or Long	Long.valueOf(String)

This is a very recent clarification of the specification, documented in the specification errata document available at *http://java.sun.com/products/jsp/*. Even though Tomcat 3.2 works according to the updated specification, other early implementations may not. If the conversion from a `String` to the appropriate type is not done by the container, a page author has to use a request-time attribute expression to set a non-`String` attribute value:

```
<ora:addCookie name="myCookie"
  value="myValue"
  maxAge="<%= 2592000 %>" />
```

That's likely to cause at least some confusion; it can be avoided by taking care of the conversion in the tag handler instead.

Whether to count on the container to do the conversion or to do it in the tag handler depends on how mature container implementations are when you read this.
Letting the container take care of it is easiest, of course, but if the containers you
plan to deploy with your application are still first-generation JSP 1.1 implementations, you should test to make sure they handle the conversion correctly.

The tag handler class should also implement the `release()` method, to release
all references to objects that it has acquired:

```
public void release() {
    name = null;
    value = null;
    maxAgeString = null;
    super.release();
}
```

The `release()` method is called when the tag handler is no longer needed. The
`AddCookieTag` class sets all its properties to `null` and calls `super.release()` to
let the `TagSupport` class do the same. This makes all property objects available for
garbage collection.

Processing the Action Body

As you can see, it's easy to develop a tag handler that doesn't need to do anything
with the action element's body. For a tag handler that does need to process the
body, however, just a few more methods are needed. They are defined by the
`BodyTag` interface, which extends the `Tag` interface.

The action element's body has many possible uses. It can be used for input values
spanning multiple lines; the SQL custom actions introduced in Chapter 9, *Database Access*, use the body this way. The SQL statement is often large, so it's better to
let the page author write it in the action body instead of forcing it to fit on one
line, which is a requirement for an attribute value. The body can also contain
nested actions that rely on the enclosing action in some way. The `<ora:
sqlTransaction>` action, also from Chapter 9, provides the nested SQL actions
with the `DataSource` object they use to communicate with the database, and
ensures that the SQL statements in all actions are treated as one transaction that
either fails or succeeds.

A third example is an action that processes the body content in one way or
another before it's added to the response. Chapter 12, *Bits and Pieces*, contains an
example of an action that processes its XML body using the XSL stylesheet specified as an attribute. Later in this section we look at an action that replaces characters that have special meanings in HTML with the corresponding HTML character
entities.

As with the `Tag` interface, there's a `BodyTagSupport` class that implements all the methods of the `BodyTag` interface, plus a few utility methods:

```
public class BodyTagSupport extends TagSupport implements BodyTag {
```

A tag handler that implements the `BodyTag` interface is at first handled the same way as a tag handler implementing the `Tag` interface: the container calls all property setter methods and the `doStartTag()` method. But then things divert, as illustrated in Figure 16-3.

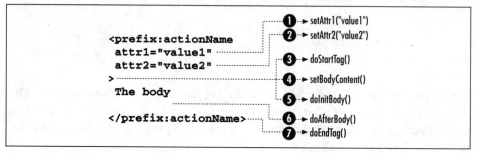

Figure 16-3. BodyTag interface methods

First of all, the `BodyTagSupport` class overrides the `doStartTag()` method inherited from the `TagSupport` class:

```
public int doStartTag() throws JspException {
    return EVAL_BODY_TAG;
}
```

Instead of returning `SKIP_BODY`, like the `TagSupport` class does, it returns `EVAL_BODY_TAG`. The `EVAL_BODY_TAG` value is valid only for a tag handler that implements the `BodyTag` interface. It means that not only should the action's body be processed, but the container must also make the result available to the tag handler.

To satisfy this requirement, the container uses a `BodyContent` object. This is a subclass of the `JspWriter`, the class used to write text to the response body. In addition to the inherited methods for writing to the object, the `BodyContent` class has methods that the tag handler can use to read the content.

This is how it works. The JSP container assigns a reference to a `JspWriter` to the implicit out variable at the top of the page. Everything that's added to the response body—either explicitly by JSP elements or implicitly by the JSP container (template text)—is written to out, so it ends up in the `JspWriter` before it's sent to the browser. When the JSP container encounters a custom action with a tag handler that implements the `BodyTag` interface, it temporarily reassigns out to a `BodyContent` object until the action's end tag is encountered. The content produced when the element body is processed is therefore buffered in the BodyContent object where the tag handler can read it.

The tag handler gets a reference to the BodyContent object through the setBodyContent() method:

```
...
protected BodyContent    bodyContent;
...
public void setBodyContent(BodyContent b) {
    this.bodyContent = b;
}
```

The BodyTagSupport class simply saves the reference to the BodyContent object in an instance variable.

Next, the container gives the tag handler a chance to initialize itself before the body is processed by calling doInitBody():

```
public void doInitBody() throws JspException {
}
```

The implementation in BodyTagSupport does nothing. A tag handler can, however, use this method to prepare for the first pass through the action body, perhaps initializing scripting variables that it makes available to the body. We look at this in more detail later. A tag handler that doesn't introduce variables rarely overrides this method.

When the body has been processed, the doAfterBody() method is invoked:

```
public int doAfterBody() throws JspException {
    return SKIP_BODY;
}
```

A tag handler can use this method to read the buffered body content and process it in some way. This method also gives the tag handler a chance to decide whether the body should be processed again. If so, it returns the EVAL_BODY_TAG value. We'll look at an example of an iteration action that takes advantage of this later. The BodyTagSupport implementation returns SKIP_BODY to let the processing continue to the doEndTag() method. As with a tag handler implementing the Tag interface, this method returns either EVAL_PAGE or SKIP_PAGE.

Let's look at a tag handler class that extends the BodyTagSupport class. The EncodeHTMLTag class is the tag handler class for a custom action called <ora:encodeHTML>. This action reads its body, replaces all characters with special meanings in HTML (single quotes, double quotes, less-than and greater-than symbols, and ampersands) with their corresponding HTML character entities (', ", <, >, and &) and inserts the result in the response body.

Example 16-1 shows how the action can be used in a JSP page, and Figure 16-4 what the processed result looks like in a browser.

Example 16-1. A JSP Page Using the <ora:encodeHTML> Action

```
<%@ page language="java" %>
<%@ taglib uri="/orataglib" prefix="ora" %>
<html>
  <head>
    <title>Encoded HTML Example</title>
  </head>
  <body>
    <h1>Encoded HTML Example</h1>
    The following text is encoded by the &lt;ora:encodeHTML&gt;
    custom action:
    <pre>
      <ora:encodeHTML>
        HTML 3.2 Documents start with a <!DOCTYPE>
        declaration followed by an HTML element containing
        a HEAD and then a BODY element:

        <!DOCTYPE HTML PUBLIC "-//W3C//DTD HTML 3.2 Final//EN">
        <HTML>
        <HEAD>
        <TITLE>A study of population dynamics</TITLE>
        ... other head elements
        </HEAD>
        <BODY>
        ... document body
        </BODY>
        </HTML>
      </ora:encodeHTML>
    </pre>
  </body>
</html>
```

Note how the body of the <ora:encodeHTML> action in Example 16-1 contains HTML elements. Unless the special characters were converted to HTML character entities, the browser would interpret the HTML and show the result instead of the elements themselves. Besides static text, the action body can contain any JSP element. A more realistic example of the use of this action is to insert text from a database into a JSP page, without having to worry about how special characters in the text are interpreted by the browser.

The tag handler class is very trivial, as shown in Example 16-2.

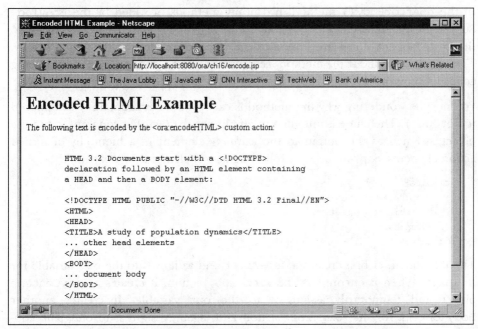

Figure 16-4. A JSP page with HTML source processed by the <ora:encodeHTML> action

Example 16-2. The EncodeHTMLTag Class

```
package com.ora.jsp.tags.generic;

import java.io.*;
import javax.servlet.jsp.*;
import javax.servlet.jsp.tagext.*;
import com.ora.jsp.util.*;

public class EncodeHTMLTag extends BodyTagSupport {

    public int doAfterBody() throws JspException {
        BodyContent bc = getBodyContent();
        JspWriter out = getPreviousOut();
        try {
            out.write(StringFormat.toHTMLString(bc.getString()));
        }
        catch (IOException e) {} // Ignore
        return SKIP_BODY;
    }
}
```

The action doesn't have any attributes, so the tag handler doesn't need any
instance variables and property access methods. The tag handler can reuse all
BodyTag methods implemented by the BodyTagSupport class except for the
doAfterBody() method.

In the `doAfterBody()` method, two utility methods provided by the `BodyTag-Support` class are used. The `getBodyContent()` method returns a reference to the `BodyContent` object that contains the result of processing the action's body. The `getPreviousOut()` method returns the `BodyContent` of the enclosing action (if any) or the main `JspWriter` for the page if the action is at the top level.

You may be wondering why the method is called `getPreviousOut()` as opposed to `getOut()`. The name is intended to emphasize the fact that you want to use the object assigned as the output to the *enclosing* element in a hierarchy of nested action elements. Say you have the following action elements in a page:

```
<xmp:foo>
    <xmp:bar>
        Some template text
    </xmp:bar>
</xmp:foo>
```

The JSP container first creates a `JspWriter` and assigns it to the out variable for the page. When it encounters the `<xmp:foo>` action, it creates a `BodyContent` object and temporarily assigns it to the out variable. It creates another `BodyContent` for the `<xmp:bar>` action and, again, assigns it to out. The container keeps track of this hierarchy of output objects. Template text and output produced by the standard JSP elements end up in the current output object. Each element can get access to its own `BodyContent` object by calling the `getBodyContent()` method and reading the content. For the `<xmp:bar>` element, the content is the template text. After processing the content, it can write it to the `<xmp:foo>` body by getting the `BodyContent` for this element through the `getPreviousOut()` method. Finally, the `<xmp:foo>` element can process the content provided by the `<xmp:bar>` element and add it to the top-level output object: the `JspWriter` object it gets by calling the `getPreviousOut()` method.

The tag handler in Example 16-2 converts all the special characters it finds in its `BodyContent` object using the `toHTMLString()` method in the `com.ora.jsp.utils.StringFormat` class, introduced in Chapter 6, *Using Scripting Elements*. It gets the content of the `BodyContent` by using the `getString()` method, and uses it as the argument to the `toHTMLString()` method. The result is written to the `JspWriter` obtained by calling `getPreviousOut()`. The `doAfterBody()` method then returns `SKIP_BODY`, since no iteration is needed.

Letting Actions Cooperate

Now that you've seen how to develop basic tag handlers, let's discuss some more advanced features. In this section, we look at tag handlers that let a page author use custom actions that cooperate with each other.

You have seen examples of this throughout this book. For instance, in Chapter 9, various types of value actions are nested within the body of an <ora:sqlQuery> action to set the values of place holders in the SQL statement. Another example is the <ora:encodeURL> action with nested <ora:param> actions, which are used in Chapter 8:

```
<ora:encodeURL url="product1.jsp">
  <ora:param name="id" value="<%= product.getId()%>" />
</ora:encodeURL>
```

How does the <ora:param> action tell the enclosing <ora:encodeURL> action about the parameter it defines? The answer to this question lies in a couple of Tag interface methods and a utility method implemented by the TagSupport class that I skipped earlier.

The Tag interface methods are setParent() and getParent(), implemented like this by the TagSupport class:

```
    ...
    private Tag parent;
    ...
    public void setParent(Tag t) {
        parent = t;
    }

    public Tag getParent() {
        return parent;
    }
```

These two methods are standard accessor methods for the parent instance variable. For a nested action element, the setParent() method is always called on the tag handler with the value of the enclosing Tag as its value. This way, a nested tag handler always has a reference to its parent. So a tag handler at any nesting level can ask for its parent using getParent(), and then ask for the parent's parent, and so on until it reaches a Tag that doesn't have a parent (that is, getParent() returns null). This means it has reached the top level.

This is part of the puzzle. However, a tag handler is usually interested only in finding a parent it's been designed to work with. It would be nice to have a method that works its way up the hierarchy until it finds the parent of interest. That's exactly what the findAncestorWithClass() method implemented by the Tag-Support class does:

```
    public static final Tag findAncestorWithClass(Tag from, Class klass) {
        boolean isInterface = false;

        if (from == null ||
            klass == null ||
```

```
        (!Tag.class.isAssignableFrom(klass) &&
           !(isInterface = klass.isInterface())))) {
        return null;
    }

    for (;;) {
        Tag tag = from.getParent();
        if (tag == null) {
            return null;
        }
        if ((isInterface && klass.isInstance(tag)) ||
            klass.isAssignableFrom(tag.getClass()))
                return tag;
        else
            from = tag;
    }
}
```

First of all, note that this is a static method. Consequently, it can be used even by tag handlers that implement the `Tag` interface directly, instead of extending the `TagSupport` class. The method takes two arguments: the tag handler instance to start searching from, and the class or interface of the parent. After making sure that all parameters are valid, it starts working its way up the nested tag handlers. It stops when it finds a tag handler of the specified class or interface and returns it. If the specified parent type is not found, the method returns `null`.

This is all that's needed to let a nested action communicate with its parent: the `parent` accessor methods, and the method that walks the action hierarchy to find the parent of interest. Example 16-3 shows how the `ParamTag` class uses this mechanism to find the enclosing `EncodeURLTag` instance.

Example 16-3. The ParamTag Class

```
package com.ora.jsp.tags.generic;

import java.net.*;
import javax.servlet.jsp.*;
import javax.servlet.jsp.tagext.*;

public class ParamTag extends TagSupport {
    private String name;
    private String value;

    public void setName(String name) {
        this.name = name;
    }

    public void setValue(String value) {
        this.value = value;
```

Example 16-3. The ParamTag Class (continued)

```
    }

    public int doEndTag() throws JspException {
        Tag parent = findAncestorWithClass(this, ParamParent.class);
        if (parent == null) {
            throw new JspException("The param action is not " +
                "enclosed by a supported action type");
        }
        ParamParent paramParent = (ParamParent) parent;
        paramParent.setParam(name, URLEncoder.encode(value));
        return EVAL_PAGE;
    }
}
```

The class has two instance variables, `name` and `value`, and the corresponding set-ter methods. The most interesting method is the `doEndTag()` method. This method first uses the `findAncestorWithClass()` method to try to locate the enclosing `EncodeURLTag` instance. Note that this is not the class name used as the argument value. Instead, the `ParamParent` interface is used. The reason is that the `<ora:param>` action is supported in the body of other actions besides `<ora:encodeURL>`, such as the `<ora:redirect>` action. The `ParamParent` interface is implemented by all tag handlers for actions that can contain nested `<ora:param>` actions:

```
package com.ora.jsp.tags.generic;

public interface ParamParent {
    void setParam(String name, String value);
}
```

The interface defines one method: the `setParam()` method. This is the method the nested `ParamTag` tag handler uses to communicate with its parent. For each nested `<ora:param>` action, the `setParam()` method gets called when the parent's action body is processed. The name and value for each `<ora:param>` action are accumulated in the parent tag handler, ready to be used when the parent's `doEndTag()` method is called. Example 16-4 shows the `setParam()` and `doEndTag()` methods implemented by the `EncodeURLTag` class.

Example 16-4. EncodeURLTag

```
    ...
    private Vector params;
    ...
    public void setParam(String name, String value) {
        if (params == null) {
            params = new Vector();
        }
```

Example 16-4. EncodeURLTag (continued)

```
    Param param = new Param(name, value);
    params.addElement(param);
}

public int doEndTag() throws JspException {
    StringBuffer encodedURL = new StringBuffer(url);
    if (params != null && params.size() > 0) {
        encodedURL.append('?');
        boolean isFirst = true;
        Enumeration e = params.elements();
        while (e.hasMoreElements()) {
            Param p = (Param) e.nextElement();
            if (!isFirst) {
                encodedURL.append('&');
            }
            encodedURL.append(p.getName()).append('=').
                append(p.getValue());
            isFirst = false;
        }
    }
    try {
        HttpServletResponse res =
            (HttpServletResponse) pageContext.getResponse();
        JspWriter out = pageContext.getOut();
        out.print(res.encodeURL(encodedURL.toString()));
    }
    catch (IOException e) {}
    return SKIP_BODY;
}
```

In `setParam()`, the parameter name and value are saved as instances of a simple value holder class named `Param`, held in a `Vector`. In the `doEndTag()` method, each parameter's name/value pair is added to the URL before the complete URL is encoded to support session tracking through URL rewriting. If you don't remember what all of this means, you can refresh your memory by looking at Chapter 8 again.

Creating New Variables Through Actions

Actions can also cooperate through objects available in the standard JSP scopes (page, request, session, and application). One example of this type of cooperation is illustrated by the three standard JSP actions: `<jsp:useBean>`, `<jsp:setProperty>`, and `<jsp:getProperty>`. The `<jspUseBean>` action creates a new object and makes it available in one of the JSP scopes. The other two actions can then access the properties of the object by searching for it in the scopes. Besides making the object available in one of the scopes, the <jsp:useBean> action also makes it available as a scripting variable, so it can be accessed by scripting elements in the page.

The JSP 1.1 specification defines that an attribute named id typically is used to name a variable created by an action.* The value of the id attribute must be unique within the page. Because it's used as a scripting variable name, it must also follow the variable name rules for the scripting language. For Java, this means it must start with a letter followed by a combination of letters and digits, and must not contain special characters, such as a dot or a plus sign. The attribute used in another action to refer to the variable can be named anything, but the convention established by the standard actions is to call it name.

When a custom action creates a variable, it must cooperate with the JSP container to make it happen. To understand how this works, recall that the JSP page is turned into a servlet by the JSP container. The JSP container needs to generate code that declares the scripting variable in the generated servlet and assigns the variable a value. Before getting into how the tag handler and the container cooperate, let's look at the kind of code that is generated for the <ora:useProperty> custom action introduced in Chapter 8. Here's a JSP page fragment:

```
<jsp:useBean id="catalog"
  class="com.ora.jsp.beans.shopping.CatalogBean" />

<ora:useProperty name="catalog" id="prod"
  property="product" arg="1"
  className="com.ora.jsp.beans.shopping.ProductBean" />

<jsp:getProperty name="prod" property="name" />

<% prod.getName(); %>
```

The <jsp:useBean> action creates an instance of the CatalogBean (or locates an existing instance) and saves it in the page scope with the name catalog. It also declares a scripting variable named catalog and sets it to the same CatalogBean instance. The <ora:useProperty> custom action retrieves the product property from the CatalogBean and introduces it as a page scope object named prod and a scripting variable with the same name, in the same manner as the <jsp:useBean> action. Finally, the value of prod is added to the response twice: first using the <jsp:getProperty> action, and then again using a JSP expression.

This JSP page fragment results in code similar to Example 16-5 in the generated servlet.

---

* If an action creates more than one variable, the id attribute is typically used to name one of them.

Example 16-5. Code Generated for JSP Actions

```
// Code for <jsp:useBean>
com.ora.jsp.beans.shopping.CatalogBean catalog = null;
catalog= (com.ora.jsp.beans.shopping.CatalogBean)
  pageContext.getAttribute("catalog",PageContext.PAGE_SCOPE);
if ( catalog == null ) {
  try {
    catalog = (com.ora.jsp.beans.shopping.CatalogBean)
      Beans.instantiate(getClassLoader(),
        "com.ora.jsp.beans.shopping.CatalogBean");
  } catch (Exception exc) {
    throw new ServletException ("Cannot create bean of class "+
      "com.ora.jsp.beans.shopping.CatalogBean");
  }
  pageContext.setAttribute("catalog", catalog, PageContext.PAGE_SCOPE);
}
...
// Code for <ora:useProperty>
com.ora.jsp.tags.generic.UsePropertyTag _jspx_th_ora_useProperty_1 =
  new com.ora.jsp.tags.generic.UsePropertyTag();
_jspx_th_ora_useProperty_1.setPageContext(pageContext);
_jspx_th_ora_useProperty_1.setParent(null);
_jspx_th_ora_useProperty_1.setId("prod");
_jspx_th_ora_useProperty_1.setName("catalog");
_jspx_th_ora_useProperty_1.setProperty("product");
_jspx_th_ora_useProperty_1.setArg("1");
_jspx_th_ora_useProperty_1.setClassName(
  "com.ora.jsp.beans.shopping.ProductBean");
try {
  _jspx_th_ora_useProperty_1.doStartTag();
  if (_jspx_th_ora_useProperty_1.doEndTag() == Tag.SKIP_PAGE)
    return;
} finally {
  _jspx_th_ora_useProperty_1.release();
}
com.ora.jsp.beans.shopping.ProductBean prod = null;
prod = (com.ora.jsp.beans.shopping.ProductBean)
  pageContext.findAttribute("prod");
...
// Code for <jsp:getProperty>
out.print(pageContext.findAttribute("prod"), "name")));
...
// Code for <%= prod.getName() %>
out.print( prod.getName() );
```

The `<jsp:useBean>` action results in code for locating or creating the CatalogBean, and declaring and assigning a Java variable named catalog. But since we're talking about custom actions here, let's focus on the code generated for the `<ora:useProperty>` action.

First, a tag handler instance is created and initialized with the standard properties (pageContext and parent) plus all properties corresponding to the action attributes. Next, the doStartTag() and doEndTag() methods are called. Then comes the code that makes the object created by the action available as a scripting variable. Note how a variable with the name specified by the id attribute (prod) is declared, using the type specified by the className attribute. Also note that the variable is declared at the top level of the method. This means that it's available to scripting elements anywhere on the page after the action element. The variable is then assigned the value of the object with same name located in one of the standard JSP scopes, using the findAttribute() method. This method searches through the scopes, in the order page, request, session, and application, until it finds the specified object.

With the object available in the JSP page scope, the code generated for the <jsp: getProperty> action can find it. Since it's also assigned to a Java variable, the JSP expression works correctly as well.

At least two things are required for a tag handler to create a new object and make it accessible for other actions and JSP scripting code:

1. The JSP container must know the name and the Java type for the object, so it can generate the code for the variable declaration.

2. The object must be placed in one of the JSP scopes, so it can be found by findAttribute() and assigned to the variable.

The first requirement is fulfilled by a class called TagExtraInfo. When you develop a tag handler for an action that introduces an object, you must also create a subclass of the TagExtraInfo class. The JSP container consults an instance of this class when it generates the code. Example 16-6 shows the class associated with the <ora:useProperty> action.

Example 16-6. UsePropertyTagExtraInfo Class

```
package com.ora.jsp.tags.generic;

import javax.servlet.jsp.tagext.*;

public class UsePropertyTagExtraInfo extends TagExtraInfo {
    public VariableInfo[] getVariableInfo(TagData data) {
        return new VariableInfo[]
        {
            new VariableInfo(data.getAttributeString("id"),
                data.getAttributeString("className"),
                true,
                VariableInfo.AT_END)
        };
    }
}
```

The method used by the JSP container during code generation is called getVariableInfo(). It returns an array of VariableInfo objects, one per variable introduced by the tag handler.

The VariableInfo class is a simple bean with four properties, all of them initialized to the values passed as arguments to the constructor: varName, className, declare, and scope. The meaning of the first two is not hard to guess: the name of the variable and the name of its class. The declare property is a boolean, in which true means that a new variable is created by the action. In other words, a declaration of the variable must be added to the generated servlet. A value of false means that the variable has already been created by another action or by another occurrence of the same action, so the generated code already contains the declaration. This is all the information the JSP container needs to generate the code for the variable declaration; the first requirement is satisfied.

The scope property has nothing to do with the JSP scopes we have seen so far (page, request, session, and application). Instead, it defines where the new variable is available to JSP scripting elements. A value of AT_BEGIN means that it is available from the action's start tag and stays available after the action's end tag. AT_END means it is not available until after the action's end tag. A variable with scope NESTED is available only in the action's body, between the start and the end tags. The scope therefore controls where the variable declaration and value assignment code is generated, and the tag handler class must make sure the variable is available in one of the JSP scopes at the appropriate time.

The UsePropertyTagExtraInfo class sets the scope to AT_END. As you can see in Example 16-5, this results in the variable declaration and assignment code being added after the doEndTag() call. To satisfy the second requirement, the tag handler must therefore give the variable a value and save it in one of the JSP scopes at the very latest in the doEndTag() method. Example 16-7 shows the doEndTag() method for the UsePropertyTag class.

Example 16-7. Saving the New Object in a JSP Scope

```
public int doEndTag() throws JspException {
    Object obj = pageContext.findAttribute(name);
    if (obj == null) {
        throw new JspException("Variable " + name + " not found");
    }
    Object propObj = getProperty(obj, property, className);
    pageContext.setAttribute(id, propObj);
    return SKIP_BODY;
}
```

The value is added to the page scope by calling the setAttribute() method on the current PageContext object, using the name specified by the id attribute.

If the scope is specified as AT_BEGIN instead, the declaration is added before the doStartTag() call and the assignment code is added right after the call. In this case, the tag handler must save the variable in a JSP scope in the doStartTag() method. If the tag handler implements BodyTag, assignment code is also added so that it is executed for every evaluation of the body, and after the call to doAfterBody(). This allows the tag handler to modify the variable value in the doAfterBody() method, so each evaluation of the body has a new value. When we look at an iteration action later, you'll see why this is important.

Finally, if the scope is set to NESTED, both the declaration and the value assignment code are inserted in the code block representing the action body. The tag handler must therefore make the variable available in either the doStartTag() method or the doInitBody() method, and can also modify the value in the doAfterBody() method.

The UsePropertyTagExtraInfo class sets the varName and className properties of the VariableInfo bean to the values of the id and className attributes specified by the page author in the JSP page. This is done using another simple class named TagData, passed as the argument to the getVariableInfo() method, as shown in Example 16-6. The TagData instance is created by the JSP container and contains information about all action attributes that the page author specified in the JSP page. It has two methods of interest. First, the getAttributeString() method, used in Example 16-6, simply returns the specified attribute as a String. But some attribute values may be specified by a JSP expression instead of a string literal, so-called request-time attributes. Since these values are not known during the translation phase, the TagData class also provides the getAttribute() method to indicate if an attribute value is a literal string, a request-time attribute, or not set at all. The getAttribute() method returns an Object. If the attribute is specified as a request-time value, the special REQUEST_TIME_VALUE object is returned. Otherwise, a String is returned, or null if the attribute is not set.

Developing an Iterating Action

As I alluded to earlier, a tag handler can iterate over the element's body until some condition is true. The evaluation of the body may be different for each iteration, since the tag handler can introduce a variable (used in the body) that changes its value. An example of an iterating action is the <ora:loop> used in this book. It can be used to iterate over the element body once for each value in an array, a java.util.Vector, a java.util.Dictionary, or a java.util. Enumeration. Here's an example of how the <ora:loop> action can be used:

```
<%@ page language="java" contentType="text/html" %>
<%@ taglib uri="/orataglib" prefix="ora" %>
```

```
<html>
  <body bgcolor="white">
    <%
       String[] test = new String[4];
       test[0] = "first";
       test[1] = "second";
       test[2] = "third";
       test[3] = "fourth";
       pageContext.setAttribute("test", test);
    %>

    <pre>
       <ora:loop name="test" loopId="x" className="java.lang.String">
         Current value: <%= x %>
       </ora:loop>
    </pre>
  </body>
</html>
```

Here, the `<ora:loop>` tag iterates over the elements of a `String` array, adding the current value to the response using a JSP expression in the action's body.

The `com.ora.jsp.tags.generic.LoopTag` class is the tag handler class for the `<ora:loop>` action. It extends `BodyTag` support and has four properties:

```
public class LoopTag extends BodyTagSupport {
    private String name;
    private String loopId;
    private String className;
    private String property;
    ...
```

A standard property setter method is provided for each property. This is no different than in previous examples, so it's not shown here. The `name`, `loopId`, and `className` properties are mandatory. The `name` is the name of a JSP scope variable of one of the types listed earlier. The current value of the data structure is made available in the element body through a variable with the name specified by `loopId`, of the type specified by `className`. Optionally, `property` can be specified. If it is, it's used to get the data structure from the specified property of the bean named by `name`, instead of using the `name` object itself as the data structure.

To make the `loopId` variable available in the element's body, a `TagExtraInfo` subclass is needed, as described in the previous section. The `LoopTagExtraInfo` class looks like this:

```
public class LoopTagExtraInfo extends TagExtraInfo {
    public VariableInfo[] getVariableInfo(TagData data) {
        return new VariableInfo[]
        {
```

```
                    new VariableInfo(data.getAttributeString("loopId"),
                        data.getAttributeString("className"),
                        true,
                        VariableInfo.NESTED)
            };
        }
    }
```

It introduces a variable named by the `loopId` attribute, with the type specified by the `className` attribute. The scope is specified as `NESTED`, meaning the variable is available only within the action element's body.

In addition to the property variables, the tag handler class has an `Enumeration` instance variable:

```
    private Enumeration enum;
```

This variable is initiated by the `doStartTag()` method:

```
    public int doStartTag() throws JspException {
        Object obj = pageContext.findAttribute(name);
        if (obj == null) {
            throw new JspException("Variable " + name + " not found");
        }

        Object mvObj = obj;
        try {
            // Get the multi-value object using the specified property
            // getter method, if any
            if (property != null) {
                mvObj = getProperty(obj, property);
            }

            enum = getEnumeration(mvObj);
        }
        catch (JspException e) {
            throw new JspException("Error getting loop data from " +
                name + ": " + e.getMessage());
        }

        // Set the first loop value, if any
        if (enum != null && enum.hasMoreElements()) {
            Object currValue = enum.nextElement();
            pageContext.setAttribute(loopId, currValue);
            return EVAL_BODY_TAG;
        }
        else {
            return SKIP_BODY;
        }
    }
```

After verifying that there really is an object with the specified name, a test is done to see if a property name is specified. If it is, the getProperty() method is called to retrieve the property value from the specified object so it can be used for the iteration. If a property name is not specified, the object itself is used. All the supported data structure types can be turned into an Enumeration. That's done by calling the getEnumeration() method. The getProperty() method and the getEnumeration() method are not shown here, because this code is just plain Java code that has nothing to do with implementing iteration in a tag handler. You can look at the source code to see how they work.

When the Enumeration has been created, the doStartTag() method initializes the loopId variable and places it in the JSP page scope. As you learned in the previous section, the code generated for the page uses the information gained from the LoopTagExtraInfo class to declare a Java variable and assign it the value it finds in one of the JSP scopes, right after the doStartTag() call.

When the body has been evaluated, the doAfterBody() method is called:

```
public int doAfterBody() throws JspException {
    if (enum.hasMoreElements()) {
        Object currValue = enum.nextElement();
        pageContext.setAttribute(loopId, currValue);
        return EVAL_BODY_TAG;
    }
    else {
        return SKIP_BODY;
    }
}
```

The Enumeration is tested to see if it contains any more values. If it does, the loopId page scope variable is reassigned to the new value, and EVAL_BODY_TAG is returned to evaluate the body again. When the end of the Enumeration is reached, SKIP_BODY is returned to break the iteration.

When the doAfterBody() method returns SKIP_BODY, the doEndTag() method is called:

```
public int doEndTag() throws JspException {
    // Test if bodyContent is set, since it will be null if the
    // body was never evaluated (doStartTag returned SKIP_BODY)
    if (getBodyContent() != null) {
        try {
            getPreviousOut().print(getBodyContent().getString());
        }
        catch (IOException e) {}
    }
    return EVAL_PAGE;
}
```

For every iteration, the content of the evaluated body is buffered in the BodyContent instance assigned to the tag handler. In the doEndTag(), the content is simply moved to the parent's BodyContent instance or the main JspWriter instance for the page. An alternative to accumulating the content until the doEndTag() method is called is to write it to the parent's output stream already in the doAfterBody() method, using the same code as shown here.

---

class Versus className

You may have noticed that all the custom actions in this book use an attribute named className to specify a class name, while all the standard JSP actions use an attribute named class for the same purpose.

The reason for this inconsistency is the fact that tag handlers are handled as JavaBeans components with regards to the attributes, combined with an unfortunate name clash.

The attribute is used to specify a class name, in other words a String. If the attribute name class is used, the corresponding property setter method must be named setClass(), with a String as its argument. The Object class, however, implements a method named getClass() that returns a Class object. The java.beans.Introspector class, used to figure out which properties a bean supports by looking for accessor methods, doesn't approve of what it sees as a type mismatch between the setter and getter methods for the class property. It therefore refuses to accept that class is a valid bean property.

To work around this problem, all custom actions in this book use an attribute called className instead of class.

Creating the Tag Library Descriptor

Now you have a good idea about what the code for a tag handler looks like. But when the JSP container converts custom action elements into code that creates and calls the correct tag handler, it needs information about which tag handler implements which custom action element. It gets this information from the Tag Library Descriptor (TLD). As you will see in the next section, the JSP container also uses the TLD information to verify that the attribute list for an action element is correct.

The TLD is an XML file with information about all custom actions in one library. A JSP page that uses custom actions must identify the corresponding TLD and the namespace prefix used for the actions in the page with the taglib directive (this is described in more detail later).

```
<%@ taglib uri="/WEB-INF/tlds/orataglib_1_0.tld" prefix="ora" %>
...
<ora:redirect page="main.jsp" />
```

The JSP page then uses the TLD to find the information it needs when it encounters an action element with a matching prefix.

Example 16-8 shows a part of the TLD for the custom actions in this book.

Example 16-8. Tag Library Descriptor (TLD)

```
<?xml version="1.0" encoding="ISO-8859-1" ?>
<!DOCTYPE taglib
  PUBLIC "-//Sun Microsystems, Inc.//DTD JSP Tag Library 1.1//EN"
  "http://java.sun.com/j2ee/dtds/web-jsptaglibrary_1_1.dtd">

<taglib>
  <tlibversion>1.0</tlibversion>
  <jspversion>1.1</jspversion>
  <shortname>ora</shortname>
  <uri>
    /orataglib
  </uri>
  <info>
    A tab library for the examples in the O'Reilly JSP book
  </info>

  <tag>
    <name>redirect</name>
    <tagclass>com.ora.jsp.tags.generic.RedirectTag</tagclass>
    <bodycontent>JSP</bodycontent>
    <info>
      Encodes the url attribute and possible param tags in the body
      and sets redirect headers.
    </info>
    <attribute>
      <name>page</name>
      <required>true</required>
      <rtexprvalue>true</rtexprvalue>
    </attribute>
  </tag>
  ...
</taglib>
```

At the top of the TLD file, you find a standard XML declaration and a DOCTYPE declaration, specifying the Document Type Definition (DTD) for this file. A DTD defines the rules for how elements in an XML file must be used, such as the order of the elements, which elements are mandatory and which are optional, if an element can be included multiple times, etc. If you're not familiar with XML, don't worry about this. Just accept the fact that you need to copy the first two elements of Example 16-8 faithfully into your own TLD files. Regarding the order of the elements, just follow the same order as in Example 16-8. Whether an element is mandatory or optional is spelled out in the following descriptions of each element.

After the two declarations, the first element in the TLD file must be the <taglib> element. This is the main element for the TLD, enclosing all more specific elements that describe the library. Within the body of the <taglib> element, you can specify elements that describe the library as such, as well as each individual tag handler. Let's start with the five elements that describe the library itself.

The <tlibversion> element is mandatory and is used to specify the tag library version. The version should be specified as a series of numbers separated by dots. In other words, the normal conventions for software version numbers, such as 1.1 or 2.0.3, should be used.

The <jspversion> element, specifying the version of the JSP specification that the library depends on, is optional. The default value is 1.1.

The <shortname> element is intended to be used by page authoring tools. It's a mandatory element that should contain the default prefix for the action elements. In Example 16-8 the value is ora, meaning that an authoring tool by default generates custom action elements using the ora prefix, for instance <ora: redirect page="main.jsp">. This element value can also be used by a tool as the value of the prefix attribute if it generates the taglib directive in the JSP page. The element value must not include whitespace or other special characters, or start with a digit or underscore.

The <uri> element is also intended to benefit authoring tools. The value can be used as the default value for the uri attribute in a taglib directive. It's an optional element, following the same character rules as the <shortname> element.

The last element that describes the library as such is the optional <info> element. It can be used to provide a short description of the library, perhaps something a tool might display to help users decide if the library is what they are looking for.

Besides the general elements, the TLD must include at least one <tag> element. The <tag> element contains other elements that describe different aspects of the custom action: <name>, <tagclass>, <teiclass>, <bodycontent>, <info>, and <attribute>.

The <name> element is mandatory and contains the unique name for the corresponding custom action element.

The `<tagclass>` element, also mandatory, contains the fully qualified class name for the tag handler class.

If the action introduces variables or needs to do additional syntax validation as described in the next section, the optional `<teiclass>` element is used to specify the fully qualified class name for the `TagExtraInfo` subclass.

Another optional element is `<bodycontent>`. It can contain one of three values. A value of `empty` means that the action body must be empty. If the body can contain JSP elements, such as standard or custom actions or scripting elements, the JSP value should be used. All JSP elements in the body are processed, and the result is handled as specified by the tag handler (i.e., processed by the tag handler or sent through to the response body). This is also the default value, in case you omit the `<bodycontent>` element. The third alternative is `tagdependent`. This value means that possible JSP elements in the body are not processed. Typically, this value is used when the body is processed by the tag handler and the content may contain characters that could be confused with JSP elements, for example, `SELECT * FROM MyTable WHERE Name LIKE '<%>'`. If a tag that expects this kind of body content is declared as JSP, the `<%>` is likely to confuse the JSP container. The `tagdependent` value can be used to avoid this risk for confusion.

The `<info>` element can optionally be used to describe the purpose of the action.

The `<tag>` element must also contain an `<attribute>` element for each action attribute. Each element in turn contains other elements that describe the attribute: `<name>`, `<required>`, and `<rtexprvalue>`.

The mandatory `<name>` element contains the attribute name. The optional `<required>` element tells if the attribute is required or not. The values `true`, `false`, `yes`, and `no` are valid, with `false` being the default. Finally, the `<rtexprvalue>` element is an optional element that can have the same values as the `<required>` element. If the value is `true` or `yes`, a request-time attribute expression can be used to specify the attribute value, for instance `'attr="<%= request.getParameter("par") %>'`. The default value is `false`.

Validating Syntax

The TLD for a tag library contains information about the attributes each action element supports. Therefore, the JSP container can help by verifying that the custom action is used correctly by the page author, at least with respect to the attributes.

When the JSP container converts a JSP page to a servlet, it compares each custom action element to the specification of the action element in the TLD. First, it makes sure that the action name matches the name of an action specified in the

TLD corresponding to the action element's prefix. It then looks at the attribute list in the page and compares it to the attribute specification in the TLD. If a required attribute is missing, or an attribute is used in the page but not specified in the TLD, it reports it as an error so the page author can correct the mistake.

But for some actions, it's not that simple. Some attributes may depend on the presence of other attributes. Attributes may be mutually exclusive, so that if one is used, the other must not be used. Or an optional attribute may require that another optional attribute is used as well. To be able to verify these kinds of dependencies, the JSP container asks the tag handler's `TagExtraInfo` subclass for assistance.

After the JSP container has checked everything it can on its own, it looks for a `TagExtraInfo` subclass, defined by the `<teiclass>` element, for the action. If one is defined, it puts all attribute information in an instance of the `TagData` class and calls the `TagExtraInfo` `isValid()` method:

```
public boolean isValid(TagData data) {
    // Mutually exclusive attributes
    if (data.getAttribute("attr1") != null &&
        data.getAttribute("attr2" != null) {
        return false;
    }

    // Dependent optional attributes
    if (data.getAttribute("attr3") != null &&
        data.getAttribute("attr4" == null) {
        return false;
    }
    return true;
}
```

A `TagExtraInfo` subclass can use the `TagData` instance to verify that all attribute dependencies are okay, as in this example. In JSP 1.1, unfortunately, there's no way to generate an appropriate error message; the method can only return `false` to indicate that something is not quite right. This will hopefully be rectified in a future version of JSP.

How Tag Handlers May Be Reused

Creating new objects is a relatively expensive operation in Java. For high-performance applications, it's common to try to minimize the number of objects created and reuse the same objects instead. The JSP 1.1 specification describes how a tag handler instance can be reused within the code generated for a JSP page if the same type of custom action appears more than once. The reuse is subject to a number of restrictions and relies on tag handler classes dealing with their internal state as specified. It's important to understand the reuse rules, so your tag handler classes behave as expected in a JSP implementation that takes advantage of this mechanism.

As discussed in the previous sections of this chapter, a tag handler's state is initiated through property setter methods corresponding to the action element's attributes. The tag handler is then offered a chance to do its thing in various stages, represented by the doStartTag(), doInitBody(), doAfterBody(), and doEndTag() methods. It's clear that the property values must be kept at least until the tag handler has done what it intends to do. But when can it safely reset its state? If a tag handler implements all logic in the doStartTag() method, can it reset all instance variables before it returns from this method? Or should it wait until the doEndTag() method is called? The answer is that it must not reset the state until the release() method is called. Let's use a JSP page fragment to discuss why:

```
<test:myAction attr1="one" attr2="two" />
<test:myAction attr1="one" attr2="new" />
```

In this case, a JSP container is allowed to use one instance of the tag handler for both <test:myAction> action elements, with generated code similar to this:

```
// Code for first occurrence
MyActionTag _jspx_th_test_myAction_1 = new MyActionTag();
_jspx_th_test_myAction_1.setPageContext(pageContext);
_jspx_th_test_myAction_1.setParent(null);
_jspx_th_test_myAction_1.setAttr1("one");
_jspx_th_test_myAction_1.setAttr2("two");
_jspx_th_test_myAction_1.doStartTag();
if (_jspx_th_test_myAction_1.doEndTag() == Tag.SKIP_PAGE)
  return;

// Code for second occurrence
_jspx_th_test_myAction_1.setAttr2("new");
_jspx_th_test_myAction_1.doStartTag();
if (_jspx_th_test_myAction_1.doEndTag() == Tag.SKIP_PAGE)
  return;

_jspx_th_test_myAction_1.release();
```

As you can see, all the property setter methods are called to initialize the instance for the first occurrence of the element. But for the second occurrence, only the setter method for the property with a different value is called. The release() method is called when the tag handler has been used for both occurrences. If the tag handler class resets all property variables in any method other than release(), the processing of the second action element fails.

The only scenario in which a tag handler can be reused in JSP 1.1 is the one described above. If the same action element is used multiple times on the same page but with different sets of attributes, the state of the tag handler is not guaranteed to be correct if the same instance is reused.

Reuse between pages, using a tag handler object pool, is not explicitly supported in JSP 1.1. For this reason, most JSP containers do not implement tag handler pooling today. To get your tag handler classes to work with the few that do, you must reset all properties before the tag handler is used to handle a new request. I recommend that you do this in the `release()` method, as shown in the examples in this chapter. Note that if some properties must have a default value set instead of `null`, you must set it in the `release()` method as well. A typical example is a primitive type property, such as an `int` property:

```
public void release() {
    aStringProperty = null;
    anIntProperty = -1;
}
```

To make it easier for a container to reuse tag handlers, both within a page and between pages, a future version of JSP will likely introduce a method that resets all properties in a controlled manner.

Packaging and Installing a Tag Library

During development, you may want to let the tag library classes and the TLD file reside as-is in the filesystem, since it makes it easy to change the TLD and modify and recompile the classes. Just make sure the class files are stored in a directory that's part of the classpath for the JSP container, such as the *WEB-INF/classes* directory for the web application. The TLD must also be in a directory where the JSP container can find it. The recommended location is the *WEB-INF/tlds* directory. To identify the library with the TLD stored in this location, use a `taglib` directive in the JSP pages like this:

```
<%@ taglib uri="/WEB-INF/tlds/orataglib_1_0.tld" prefix="ora" %>
```

Here the `uri` attribute refers directly to the TLD file's location.

When you're done with the development, you may want to package all tag handler classes, `TagExtraInfo` classes, beans used by the tag handler classes, and the TLD in a JAR file. This makes it easier to install the library in an application. The TLD must be saved as */META-INF/taglib.tld* within the JAR file.

To create the JAR file, first arrange the files in a directory with a structure like this:

```
META-INF/
  taglib.tld
```

```
com/
  ora/
    jsp/
      tags/
        generic/
          EncodeHTMLTag.class
          ...
      util/
        StringFormat.class
        ...
```

The structure for the class files must match the package names for your classes. Here a few of the classes in the tag library for this book are shown as an example.

With the file structure in place, use the *jar* command to create the JAR file:

```
jar cvf orataglib_1_0.jar META-INF com
```

This command creates a JAR file named *orataglib_1_0.jar* containing the files in the *META-INF* and *com* directories. Use any JAR filename that makes sense for your own tag library. Including the version number for the library is also a good idea, since it lets the users know which version of the library they are using.

You can now use the packaged tag library in any application. Just copy the JAR file to the application's *WEB-INF/lib* directory and use a `taglib` directive like this in the JSP pages:

```
<%@ taglib uri="/WEB-INF/lib/orataglib_1_0.jar" prefix="ora" %>
```

Note that the `uri` attribute now refers to the JAR file instead of the TLD file. A JSP 1.1 container is supposed to be able to find the TLD file in the JAR file, but this is a fairly recent clarification of the specification. If the JSP container you use doesn't support this notation yet, you have to extract the TLD file from the JAR file, save it somewhere else, for instance in *WEB-INF/tlds,* and let the `uri` attribute refer to the TLD file instead.

Instead of letting the `taglib` directive point directly to the TLD or JAR file, you can specify a symbolic name as the `uri` attribute value, and provide a mapping between this name and the real location in the *WEB-INF/web.xml* file for the application:

```
<%@ taglib uri="/orataglib" prefix="ora" %>
```

The *WEB-INF/web.xml* file must then contain the following elements:

```
<web-app>
  ...
  <taglib>
    <taglib-uri>
      /orataglib
```

```
      </taglib-uri>
      <taglib-location>
        /WEB-INF/lib/orataglib_1_0.jar
      </taglib-location>
    </taglib>
    ...
  </web-app>
```

The `<taglib-uri>` element contains the symbolic name, and the `<taglib-location>` element contains the path to either the JAR file or the extracted TLD file.

17

Developing Database Access Components

In this final chapter, we look at more examples of how to develop custom actions, namely the database custom actions introduced in Chapter 9, *Database Access*.

Before digging into the code for these actions, a number of fundamental Java database access features are discussed. First, we take a look at the JDBC Connection class, and how pooling Connection objects helps solve a number of common problems. We look at two ways to provide connection pooling capabilities to an application: with JDBC 2.0, and by letting a JDBC 1.0 connection pool simulate a JDBC 2.0 pool. The purpose of a connection pool is to be able to share database connections between all components of an application. The approach discussed in this chapter is to use an application initialization servlet that makes the pool available to all servlets and JSP pages.

No matter if you use a servlet or a custom action in a JSP page to access the database, there are a number of things to think about. We look at a generic database access bean and related classes that take care of datatype issues and make the result of a query easy to access. Next, we look at how the bean is used by the database access custom actions described in Chapter 9. You can also use the bean directly in servlets, as described in Chapter 15, *Developing JavaBeans for JSP*, or in your own application-specific database access actions. The last section contains an example of an application-specific custom action using the bean.

To really appreciate the material in this chapter, you should already be familiar with JDBC. If this is not the case, I recommend that you look at the JDBC documentation online at *http://java.sun.com/products/jdbc/* or read a book about JDBC, such as George Reese's *Database Programming with JDBC and Java* (O'Reilly).

Using Connections and Connection Pools

In a JDBC-based application, a lot revolves around the `java.sql.Connection` interface. Before any database operations can take place, the application must create a `Connection` to the database. It then acts as the communication channel between the application and the database, carrying the SQL statements sent by the application and the results returned by the database. A `Connection` is associated with a database user account, to allow the database to enforce access control rules for the SQL statements submitted through the `Connection`. Finally, the `Connection` is also the boundary for database transactions. Only SQL statements executed through the same `Connection` can make up a transaction. A transaction consists of a number of SQL statements that must either all succeed or all fail as one atomic operation. A transaction can be committed (the changes resulting from the statements are permanently saved) or rolled back (all changes are ignored) by calling `Connection` methods.

In a standalone application, a `Connection` is typically created once and kept open until the application is shut down. This is not surprising, since a standalone application serves only one user at a time, and all database operations initiated by a single user are typically related to each other. In a server application that deals with unrelated requests from many different users, it's not so obvious how to deal with connections. There are three things to consider: a `Connection` is time-consuming to create, it must be used for only one user at a time to avoid transaction clashes, and it is expensive to keep open.

Creating a `Connection` is an operation that can actually take a second or two to perform. Besides establishing a network connection to the database, the database engine must authenticate the user and create a context with various data structures to keep track of transactions, cached statements, results, and so forth. Creating a new `Connection` for each request received by the server, while simple to implement, is far too time-consuming in a high-traffic server application.

One way to minimize the number of times a connection needs to be created is to keep one `Connection` per servlet or JSP page that need access to the database. A `Connection` can be created when the web resource is initialized, and kept in an instance variable until the application is shut down. As you will discover when you deploy an application based on this approach, this route will lead to numerous multithreading issues. Each request executes as a separate thread through the same servlet or JSP page. Many JDBC drivers do not support multiple threads accessing the same `Connection`, causing all kinds of runtime errors. Others support it by serializing all calls, leading to poor scalability. An even more serious problem with this approach is that requests from multiple users, all using the same `Connection`, operate within the same transaction. If one request leads to a rollback, all other database operations using the same `Connection` are also rolled back.

A connection is expensive to keep open in terms of server resources such as memory. Many commercial database products also use licenses that are priced based on the number of simultaneously open connections, so a connection can also be expensive in terms of real money. Therefore, it's wise to try to minimize the number of connections the application needs. An alternative to the "one `Connection` per resource" approach is to create a `Connection` for each user when the first request is received and keep it as a session scope object. However, a drawback with this approach is that the `Connection` will be inactive most of the time, since the user needs time to look at the result of one request before making the next.

The best alternative is to use a *connection pool*. A connection pool contains a number of `Connection` objects shared by all servlets and JSP pages. For each request, one `Connection` is checked out, used, and checked back in. Using a pool solves the problems described for the other alternatives:

It's time-consuming to create a Connection.
> A pooled `Connection` is created only once and then reused. Most pool implementations let you specify an initial number of `Connection` objects to create at startup, as well as a max number. New `Connection` objects are created as needed up to the max number. Once the max number has been reached, the pool clients wait until an existing `Connection` object becomes available instead of creating a new one.

There are multithreading problems with a shared Connection.
> Each request gets its own `Connection`, so it's used by only one thread at a time, eliminating any potential multithreading issues.

A Connection is a limited resource.
> With a pool, each `Connection` is used efficiently. It never sits idle if there are requests pending. If the pool allows you to specify a max number of `Connection` objects, you can also balance a license limit for the number of simultaneous connections against acceptable response times.

A connection pool, however, doesn't solve all problems. Since all users are using the same `Connection` objects, you cannot rely on the database engine to limit access to protected data on a per-user basis. Instead, you have to define data access rules in terms of roles (groups of users with the same access rights). You can then use separate pools for different roles, each pool creating `Connection` objects with a user account that represents the role.

Using a JDBC 2.0 Optional Package Connection Pool

Connection pools exist in many forms. You can find them in books, articles, and on the Web. Yet prior to JDBC 2.0, there was no standard defined for how a Java application would interact with a connection pool. The JDBC 2.0 Optional

Package (formerly known as a Standard Extension) changes this by introducing a set of interfaces that connection pools should implement:

javax.sql.DataSource

A DataSource represents a database. This is the interface the application always uses to get a Connection. The class that implements the interface can provide connection pooling capabilities or hand out regular, unpooled Connection objects; the application code is identical for both cases, as described later.

javax.sql.ConnectionPoolDataSource

A DataSource implementation that provides pooling capabilities uses a class that implements the ConnectionPoolDataSource interface. A Connection-PoolDataSource is a factory for PooledConnection objects.

javax.sql.PooledConnection

The objects that a DataSource keeps in its pool implement the Pooled-Connection interface. When the application asks the DataSource for a Connection, it locates an available PooledConnection object, or gets a new one from its ConnectionPoolDataSource if the pool is empty.

The PooledConnection provides a getConnection() method that returns a Connection object. The DataSource calls this method and returns the Connection to the application. This Connection object behaves like a regular Connection with one exception: when the application calls the close() method, instead of closing the connection to the database, it informs the PooledConnection it belongs to that it's no longer being used. The PooledConnection relays this information to the DataSource, which returns the PooledConnection to the pool.

Figure 17-1 outlines how an application uses implementations of these interfaces to obtain a pooled connection and how to return that connection to the pool.

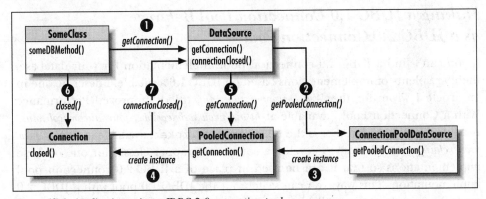

Figure 17-1. Application using a JDBC 2.0 connection pool

The application calls the DataSource getConnection() method. The Data-Source looks for an available PooledConnection object in its pool. If it doesn't find one, it uses its ConnectionPoolDataSource object to create a new one. It then calls the getConnection() method on the PooledConnection object and returns the Connection object associated with the PooledConnection. The application uses the Connection, and calls its close() method when it's done. This results in a notification event being sent to the DataSource, which puts the corresponding PooledConnection object back in the pool. If you would like to learn more about the JDBC 2.0 connection pool model, you can download the JDBC 2.0 Optional Package specification from *http://java.sun.com/products/jdbc/*.

The real beauty of these interfaces is that the application doesn't have to be aware that it's using a connection pool. All configuration data, such as which JDBC driver and JDBC URL to use, the initial and maximum numbers of pooled connections, and the database account name and password, can be set by a server administrator. The completely configured DataSource object is registered as a JNDI resource, and the application can obtain a reference to it with the following code:

```
Context ctx = new InitialContext();
DataSource ds = (DataSource) ctx.lookup("jdbc/EmployeeDB");
```

It then gets a Connection, uses it, and returns it with the following code:

```
Connection conn = ds.getConnection();
// Uses the Connection
conn.close(); // Returns the Connection to the pool
```

By implementing these JDBC 2.0 interfaces, JDBC driver and middleware vendors can offer portable connection pooling implementations. Sun's JDBC driver list contains roughly ten different companies that claim to either offer implementations of connection pools today or have announced products to be delivered during 2000.

Making a JDBC 1.0 Connection Pool Behave as a JDBC 2.0 Connection Pool

If you can't find a JDBC 2.0 connection pool implementation for your database, there are plenty of implementations based on JDBC 1.0 available. I describe one in an article I wrote for the *Web Developer's Journal*, titled "Improved Performance With a Connection Pool," available at *http://www.webdevelopersjournal.com/columns/connection_pool.html*. Another is the DBConnectionBroker, available at *http://www.javaexchange.com*. It's easy to develop a couple of wrapper classes for one of these implementations so that it can be used in place of a JDBC 2.0 connection pool implementation. This way, you can switch out the JDBC 1.0 pool with a JDBC 2.0 pool when one becomes available from your database vendor or a third party.

The interaction between the wrapper classes and a connection pool implementation is illustrated in Figure 17-2.

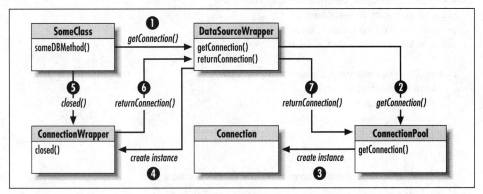

Figure 17-2. A JDBC 1.0 connection pool wrapped with JDBC 2.0 interface classes

Figure 17-2 can be explained like this: the application calls the `DataSource-Wrapper getConnection()` method. The `DataSourceWrapper` obtains a `Connection` object from its `ConnectionPool` object. The `ConnectionPool` either finds an available `Connection` in its pool or creates a new one. The `DataSource-Wrapper` creates a new `ConnectionWrapper` object for the `Connection` it obtained, and returns the `ConnectionWrapper` to the application. The application uses the `ConnectionWrapper` object as a regular `Connection`. The `ConnectionWrapper` relays all calls to the corresponding method in the `Connection` it wraps, except for the `close()` method. When the application calls the `close()` method, the `ConnectionWrapper` returns its `Connection` to the `DataSourceWrapper`, which in turn returns it to its `ConnectionPool`.

In this example, I show you how to wrap the connection pool described in Jason Hunter and William Crawford's *Java Servlet Programming* (O'Reilly). It's a simple implementation, intended only to illustrate the principles of connection pooling. The source code for the connection pool is included with the code for this book, but I will not discuss the implementation of the pool itself, only how to make it look like a JDBC 2.0 connection pool. For production use, I recommend that instead of this code, you use a pool intended for real use, such as one of the implementations mentioned earlier. The first wrapper class is called `com.ora.jsp.sql.ConnectionWrapper`, shown in Example 17-1.

Example 17-1. The ConnectionWrapper Class

```
package com.ora.jsp.sql;

import java.sql.*;
import java.util.*;
```

Example 17-1. The ConnectionWrapper Class (continued)

```java
class ConnectionWrapper implements Connection {
    private Connection realConn;
    private DataSourceWrapper dsw;
    private boolean isClosed = false;

    public ConnectionWrapper(Connection realConn,
        DataSourceWrapper dsw) {
        this.realConn = realConn;
        this.dsw = dsw;
    }

    /**
     * Inform the DataSourceWrapper that the ConnectionWrapper
     * is closed.
     */
    public void close() throws SQLException {
        isClosed = true;
        dsw.returnConnection(realConn);
    }

    /**
     * Returns true if the ConnectionWrapper is closed, false
     * otherwise.
     */
    public boolean isClosed() throws SQLException {
        return isClosed;
    }

    /*
     * Wrapped methods.
     */
    public void clearWarnings() throws SQLException {
        if (isClosed) {
            throw new SQLException("Pooled connection is closed");
        }
        realConn.clearWarnings();
    }
    ...
}
```

An instance of this class is associated with a real `Connection` object, retrieved from a connection pool, through the constructor. The constructor also provides a reference to the `DataSourceWrapper` instance that creates it, described next.

The `ConnectionWrapper` class implements the `Connection` interface. The implementations of all the methods except two simply relay the call to the real

Connection object so it can perform the requested database operation. The implementation of the close() method, however, doesn't call the real Connect object's method. Instead, it calls the DataSourceWrapper object's return-Connection() method, to return the Connection to the pool. The isClosed() method, finally, returns the state of the ConnectionWrapper object as opposed to the real Connection object.

Example 17-2 shows how the com.ora.jsp.sql.DataSourceWrapper gets a connection from a pool, and returns it when the pool client is done with it.

Example 17-2. The DataSourceWrapper Class

```
package com.ora.jsp.sql;

import java.io.*;
import java.sql.*;
import javax.sql.*;

public class DataSourceWrapper implements DataSource {
    private ConnectionPool pool;

    public DataSourceWrapper(String driverClass, String url,
        String user, String pw)
        throws ClassNotFoundException, InstantiationException,
        SQLException, IllegalAccessException {
        pool = new ConnectionPool(url, user, pw, driverClass, 1, 1);
    }

    /**
     * Gets a connection from the pool and returns it wrapped in
     * a ConnectionWrapper.
     */
    public Connection getConnection() throws SQLException {
        return new ConnectionWrapper(pool.getConnection(), this);
    }

    /**
     * Returns a Connection to the pool. This method is called by
     * the ConnectionWrapper's close() method.
     */
    public void returnConnection(Connection conn) {
        pool.returnConnection(conn);
    }

    /**
     * Always throws a SQLException. Username and password are set
     * in the constructor and can not be changed.
     */
```

Example 17-2. The DataSourceWrapper Class (continued)

```
    public Connection getConnection(String username, String password)
            throws SQLException {
        throw new SQLException("Not supported");
    }

    public int getLoginTimeout() throws SQLException {
        throw new SQLException("Not supported");
    }

    public PrintWriter getLogWriter() throws SQLException {
        throw new SQLException("Not supported");
    }

    public void setLoginTimeout(int seconds) throws SQLException {
        throw new SQLException("Not supported");
    }

    public synchronized void setLogWriter(PrintWriter out)
            throws SQLException {
        throw new SQLException("Not supported");
    }
}
```

The DataSourceWrapper class implements the DataSource interface, so that it can be used in place of a pure JDBC 2.0 connection pool implementation. The constructor creates an instance of the real connection pool class, using the provided JDBC driver, URL, user and password information. Besides the constructor, the two most interesting methods are getConnection() and returnConnection().

The pool client application calls the getConnection() method, and the Data-SourceWrapper relays the call to the connection pool class. It then wraps the Connection object it receives in a ConnectionWrapper object and returns it to the client application.

As described earlier, the ConnectionWrapper object calls the return-Connection() method when the pool client calls close() on the Connection-Wrapper object. The returnConnection() method hands over the Connection to the real connection pool so it can be returned to the pool.

All other DataSource interface methods are implemented to throw an SQL-Exception. If you use the wrapper classes presented here to wrap a more sophisticated connection pool, you may be able to relay some of these method calls to the real connection pool instead.

Making a Connection Pool Available to Application Components

Through a `DataSource` object, the servlets and JSP pages in an application can get the `Connection` they need to access a database. What's missing is how they get access to the `DataSource`. I touched on this in Chapter 14, *Combining Servlets and JSP*, but let's recap and add a few details.

The place for resources that all components in an application need access to is the application scope, corresponding to `ServletContext` attributes in the servlet world. The current versions of the servlet and JSP specifications, 2.2 and 1.1 respectively, do not provide a specific mechanism for automatic creation and release of application scope objects when the application starts and stops (but this is being discussed as a feature for future versions of the specifications). A regular servlet can, however, fill this need nicely.*

As described in Chapter 14, the container can be configured to load and initialize a servlet when the application starts. Such a servlet can create objects and make them available to other application components in its `init()` method before any user requests are received. The servlet is also informed when the application is shut down by a call to its `destroy()` method, allowing it to release all shared objects. Finally, a servlet can read configuration data, defined as servlet initialization parameters, so that it can work in different settings. In this section, we look at how all of this can be used to make a `DataSource` object available to all components of an application.

The servlet used to manage the shared `DataSource` can be defined like this in the application's *WEB-INF/web.xml* file:

```
<web-app>
  <servlet>
    <servlet-name>appInit</servlet-name>
    <servlet-class>com.mycompany.AppInitServlet</servlet-class>
    <init-param>
      <param-name>jdbcDriverClassName</param-name>
      <param-value>sun.jdbc.odbc.JdbcOdbcDriver</param-value>
    </init-param>
    <init-param>
      <param-name>jdbcURL</param-name>
      <param-value>jdbc:odbc:example</param-value>
    </init-param>
```

---

* Theoretically, a web container is allowed to unload a servlet at any time, for instance to preserve memory. This could cause the shared resources to be removed while other parts of the application are still active and need access to them. In practice, though, none of the major web containers unloads a servlet before the application as such is shut down.

```
    <init-param>
      <param-name>dbUserName</param-name>
      <param-value>foo</param-value>
    </init-param>
    <init-param>
      <param-name>dbUserPassword</param-name>
      <param-value>bar</param-value>
    </init-param>
    <load-on-startup>1</load-on-startup>
  </servlet>
  ...
```

The servlet class, defined by the `<servlet-class>` element, is given a name
through the `<servlet-name>` element. A number of `<init-param>` elements,
with nested `<param-name>` and `<param-value>` elements, are used to define the
following initialization parameters: `jdbcDriverClassName`, `jdbcURL`, `dbUser-`
`Name`, and `dbUserPassword`. If you use a JDBC 2.0 connection pool, you need to
define the URL used to get a reference from JNDI to it instead of all these parameters. The last servlet element, `<load-on-startup>`, tells the container that this
servlet should be initialized when the web application is started. The container initializes servlets in the relative order specified by this element, from the lowest
number to the highest. If two servlets have the same value, their relative start order
is undefined.

The servlet reads all the initialization parameters in its `init()` method, creates a
`DataSourceWrapper` instance, and sets it as a `ServletContext` attribute named
`exampleDS`:

```
public void init() throws ServletException {
    ServletConfig config = getServletConfig();
    String jdbcDriverClassName =
        config.getInitParameter("jdbcDriverClassName");
    String jdbcURL = config.getInitParameter("jdbcURL");
    String dbUserName = config.getInitParameter("dbUserName");
    String dbUserPassword = config.getInitParameter("dbUserPassword");

    // Make sure a driver class and JDBC URL is specified
    if (jdbcDriverClassName == null || jdbcURL == null) {
        throw new UnavailableException("Init params missing");
    }

    DataSource ds = null;
    try {
      ds = new DataSourceWrapper(jdbcDriverClassName, jdbcURL,
          dbUserName, dbUserPassword);
    }
    catch (Exception e) {
        throw new UnavailableException("Cannot create connection pool"
```

```
                + ": " + e.getMessage());
        }
        getServletContext().setAttribute("exampleDS", ds);
    }
```

All servlets and JSP pages in the application can now obtain a reference to the
DataSource. Servlets use the `ServletContext` `getAttribute()` method to
accomplish this. For JSP pages, the DataSource appears as an application scope
object. All the database custom actions introduced in Chapter 9 look for a
DataSource in the application scope, so all you have to do to use the one created
by the initialization servlet is to provide the name:

```
<%@ page language="java" contentType="text/html" %>
<%@ taglib uri="/orataglib" prefix="ora" %>

<ora:sqlQuery id="empList" dataSource="exampleDS" scope="request">
  SELECT * FROM Employee
    WHERE FirstName LIKE ?
      AND LastName LIKE ?
      AND Dept LIKE ?
    ORDER BY LastName
  <ora:sqlStringValue param="firstName" prefix="%" suffix="%" />
  <ora:sqlStringValue param="lastName" prefix="%" suffix="%" />
  <ora:sqlStringValue param="dept" prefix="%" suffix="%" />
</ora:sqlQuery>

<jsp:forward page="list.jsp" />
```

Note how the `dataSource` attribute value matches the name of the `Servlet-
Context` attribute holding the reference to the DataSource, set by the initializa-
tion servlet.

It's much better to let an initialization servlet create the DataSource, as described
here, than to use the `<ora:useDataSource>` custom action described in
Chapter 9. With a servlet, all information about the JDBC driver class, URL, user
and password is in one place (the *WEB-INF/web.xml* file), as opposed to being
repeated in every JSP page that uses the database custom actions. This makes it
easier to change the information when needed. Also, if you decide at some point
to use another connection pool implementation, such as a true JDBC 2.0 connection pool available from your JDBC driver or database vendor, you can easily
change the servlet's `init()` method. So even for a pure JSP application, I recommend that you use an application initialization servlet like the one described here.

The initialization servlet should also clean up when the application is shut down.
The web container calls the `destroy()` method:

```
public void destroy() {
    getServletContext().removeAttribute("exampleDS");
}
```

Most connection pools used in production provide a method that should be called at shutdown to let it close all connections. If you use such a pool, you need to call this method in the servlet's destroy() method as well. The example pool used here doesn't provide a shutdown method.

Using a Generic Database Bean

All the database custom action tag handler classes described later in this chapter are based on a generic database bean named com.ora.jsp.sql.SQLCommand-Bean. This bean uses a number of other classes. Figure 17-3 shows the relationship between all these classes.

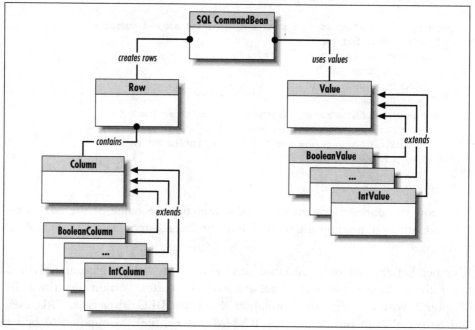

Figure 17-3. The SQLCommandBean and related classes

The SQLCommandBean takes care of setting all values in a JDBC java.sql.PreparedStatement and executing the statement. For SELECT statements, it also processes the result by creating com.ora.jsp.sql.Row objects containing a com.ora.jsp.sql.Column object for each column in the result. The rows returned by the SELECT statement are returned to the caller as a java.util.Vector with Row objects. The EmployeeRegistryBean described in Chapter 15 is one example of how to use this bean, and other examples follow in this chapter. Let's look at each class in detail, starting with the SQLCommandBean itself.

The SQLCommandBean and Value Classes

The SQLCommandBean has three write-only properties. Example 17-3 shows the beginning of the class file with the setter methods.

Example 17-3. SQLCommandBean Property Setter Methods

```
package com.ora.jsp.sql;

import java.util.*;
import java.sql.*;
import com.ora.jsp.sql.value.*;

public class SQLCommandBean {
    private Connection conn;
    private String sqlValue;
    private Vector values;
    private boolean isExceptionThrown = false;

    public void setConnection(Connection conn) {
        this.conn = conn;
    }

    public void setSqlValue(String sqlValue) {
        this.sqlValue = sqlValue;
    }

    public void setValues(Vector values) {
        this.values = values;
    }
    ...
```

The connection property holds the Connection to use, and the sqlValue property is set to the SQL statement to execute, with question marks as placeholders for variable values, if any. The placeholders are then replaced with the values defined by the values property, a Vector with one com.ora.jsp.sql.Value object per placeholder. Before we look at the other SQLCommandBean methods, let's look at the Value class.

The Value class is an abstract class used as a superclass for classes representing specific Java types, as shown in Figure 17-3. It contains default implementations of methods for getting the specific type of value a subclass represents. Example 17-4 shows two of the methods.

Example 17-4. Two Value Class Methods

```
public abstract class Value {

    public BigDecimal getBigDecimal()
        throws UnsupportedConversionException {
```

Example 17-4. Two Value Class Methods (continued)

```
            throw new UnsupportedConversionException(
                "No conversion to BigDecimal");
    }

    public boolean getBoolean()
        throws UnsupportedConversionException {
        throw new UnsupportedConversionException(
            "No conversion to boolean");
    }
    ...
```

The default implementation for each method simply throws a com.ora.jsp.sql. UnsupportedConversionException. Each subclass implements the method that returns the value of the type it represents, as well as the getString() method. The getString() method returns the value converted to a String. Example 17-5 shows the com.ora.jsp.sql.value.IntValue subclass.

Example 17-5. The IntValue Class

```
package com.ora.jsp.sql.value;

import com.ora.jsp.sql.Value;

public class IntValue extends Value {
    private int value;

    public IntValue(int value) {
        this.value = value;
    }

    public int getInt() {
        return value;
    }

    public String getString() {
        return String.valueOf(value);
    }
}
```

An application that uses the SQLCommandBean can create Value objects and set the bean's properties like this:

```
SQLCommandBean sqlBean = new SQLCommandBean();
sqlBean.setConnection(ds.getConnection());
String sqlValue =
    "SELECT * FROM MyTable WHERE IntCol = ? AND TextCol = ?";
sqlBean.setSqlValue(sqlValue);
Vector values = new Vector();
```

```
values.addElement(new IntValue(10));
values.addElement(new StringValue("Hello!"));
sqlBean.setValues(values);
```

One of two methods in the SQLCommandBean is used to execute the SQL statement: the executeQuery() method for a SELECT statement, and the executeUpdate() method for all other types of statements. Example 17-6 shows the executeQuery() method.

Example 17-6. The SQLCommandBean's executeQuery( ) Method

```
public Vector executeQuery() throws SQLException,
    UnsupportedTypeException {
    Vector rows = null;
    ResultSet rs = null;
    PreparedStatement pstmt = null;
    Statement stmt = null;
    try {
        if (values != null && values.size() > 0) {
            // Use a PreparedStatement and set all values
            pstmt = conn.prepareStatement(sqlValue);
            setValues(pstmt, values);
            rs = pstmt.executeQuery();
        }
        else {
            // Use a regular Statement.
            stmt = conn.createStatement();
            rs = stmt.executeQuery(sqlValue);
        }
        // Save the result in a Vector of Row object
        rows = toVector(rs);
    }
    finally {
        try {
            if (rs != null) {
                rs.close();
            }
            if (stmt != null) {
                stmt.close();
            }
            if (pstmt != null) {
                pstmt.close();
            }
        }
        catch (SQLException e) {
            // Ignore. Probably caused by a previous
            // SQLException thrown by the outer try block
```

Example 17-6. The SQLCommandBean's executeQuery( ) Method (continued)

```
        }
    }
    return rows;
}
```

If the `values` property is set, a JDBC `PreparedStatement` is needed to associate the values with the question mark placeholders in the SQL statement. A method named `setValues()` takes care of setting all values, using the appropriate JDBC method for the datatype represented by each `Value` object. If the `values` property is not set, a regular JDBC `Statement` is created instead. In both cases, the JDBC driver is asked to execute the statement, and the resulting `ResultSet` is turned into a `Vector` with `Row` objects by the `toVector()` method. The `Vector` is then returned to the caller.

You may wonder why the `ResultSet` is not returned directly instead of creating a `Vector` with `Row` objects. The reason is that a `ResultSet` is tied to the `Connection` that was used to generate it. When the `Connection` is closed or used to execute a new SQL statement, all open `ResultSet` objects for the `Connection` are released. You must therefore make sure to save the information from the `ResultSet` in a new data structure before reusing the `Connection` or returning it to the pool.

The code for creating the `PreparedStatement` or `Statement` object and executing the statement is enclosed in a `try/finally` block. This is important, because if something fails (due to an invalid SQL statement, for instance), the JDBC methods throw an `SQLException`. You want the exception to be handled by the application using the `SQLCommandBean`, but first you must make sure that all JDBC resources are released and the `Connection` object is returned to the pool. Using a `try` block with a `finally` clause but no `catch` clause gives this behavior. If an exception is thrown, the `finally` clause is executed, and then the exception is automatically thrown to the object that called the `executeQuery()` method. In the `finally` clause, the `ResultSet` object and either the `PreparedStatement` or `Statement` object are closed. It should be enough to close the statement object according to the JDBC specification (closing the statement should also close the `ResultSet` associated with the statement), but doing it explicitly doesn't hurt and makes the code work even with a buggy JDBC driver.

Example 17-7 shows a part of the `setValues()` method.

Example 17-7. The SQLCommandBean's setValues( ) Method

```
private void setValues(PreparedStatement pstmt, Vector values)
    throws SQLException {
    for (int i = 0; i < values.size(); i++) {
        try {
```

Example 17-7. The SQLCommandBean's setValues( ) Method (continued)

```
                Value v = (Value) values.elementAt(i);
                // Set the value using the method corresponding to
                // the type.
                // Note! Set methods are indexed from 1, so we add
                // 1 to i
                if (v instanceof BigDecimalValue) {
                    pstmt.setBigDecimal(i + 1, v.getBigDecimal());
                }
                else if (v instanceof BooleanValue) {
                    pstmt.setBoolean(i + 1, v.getBoolean());
                }
                ...
            }
        catch (UnsupportedConversionException e) {
            // Can not happen here since we test the type first
        }
    }
}
```

The setValue() method loops through all elements in the Vector with values. For each element, it tests which Value subclass it is and uses the corresponding JDBC method to set the value for the PreparedStatement object. You may wonder why a PreparedStatement is used here, since it's used only once. It's true that a PreparedStatement is intended to be reused over and over again to execute the same SQL statement with new values. But it offers a convenient solution to the problem of different syntax for values of type date/time and numbers when represented by a string literal. When a PreparedStatement is used, the variable values in the SQL statement can be represented by Java variables of the appropriate types without worrying about what literal representation a certain JDBC driver supports. So even though it's used only once, a PreparedStatement still has an advantage over a regular Statement.

The toVector() method is shown in Example 17-8.

Example 17-8. The SQLCommandBean's toVector( ) Method

```
    private Vector toVector(ResultSet rs) throws SQLException,
        UnsupportedTypeException {
        Vector rows = new Vector();
        while (rs.next()) {
            Row row = new Row(rs);
            rows.addElement(row);
        }
        return rows;
    }
```

This method simply walks through the ResultSet and adds a new Row object for each row to a Vector that it then returns. As you will see later, the Row constructor reads all column values and creates a Column object for each.

The executeUpdate() method, shown in Example 17-9, is very similar to the executeQuery() method.

Example 17-9. The SQLCommandBean's executeUpdate( ) Method

```
public int executeUpdate() throws SQLException, UnsupportedTypeException {
        int noOfRows = 0;
        ResultSet rs = null;
        PreparedStatement pstmt = null;
        Statement stmt = null;
        try {
            if (values != null && values.size() > 0) {
                // Use a PreparedStatement and set all values
                pstmt = conn.prepareStatement(sqlValue);
                setValues(pstmt, values);
                noOfRows = pstmt.executeUpdate();
            }
            else {
                // Use a regular Statement
                stmt = conn.createStatement();
                noOfRows = stmt.executeUpdate(sqlValue);
            }
        }
        finally {
            try {
                if (rs != null) {
                    rs.close();
                }
                if (stmt != null) {
                    stmt.close();
                }
                if (pstmt != null) {
                    pstmt.close();
                }
            }
            catch (SQLException e) {
                // Ignore. Probably caused by a previous
                // SQLException thrown by the outer try block.
            }
        }
        return noOfRows;
    }
```

The main difference is that the executeUpdate() method is used to execute SQL statements that do not return rows, only the number of rows affected by the statement. Examples of such statements are UPDATE, INSERT, and DELETE. In the same way as the executeQuery() method, a PreparedStatement is created and initialized with the values defined by the values property, if set. Otherwise a regular Statement is used. The statement is executed and the number of affected rows is returned to the caller.

The Row and Column Classes

Let's now look at the Row and Column classes. Example 17-10 shows a part of the Row class constructor.

Example 17-10. The Row Class Constructor

```
package com.ora.jsp.sql;

import java.util.*;
import java.sql.*;
import java.sql.Date;
import java.math.*;
import com.ora.jsp.sql.column.*;

public class Row {
    private Column[] columns;

    public Row(ResultSet rs) throws SQLException,
        UnsupportedTypeException {
        ResultSetMetaData rsmd = rs.getMetaData();
        int cols = rsmd.getColumnCount();
        columns = new Column[cols];
        // Note! Columns are numbered from 1 in the ResultSet
        for (int i = 1; i <= cols; i++) {
            int type = rsmd.getColumnType(i);
            switch (type) {
                case Types.DATE:
                    columns[i - 1] =
                        new DateColumn(rsmd.getColumnName(i),
                            rs.getDate(i));
                    break;
                case Types.TIME:
                    columns[i - 1] =
                        new TimeColumn(rsmd.getColumnName(i),
                            rs.getTime(i));
                    break;
                ...
                default:
                    throw new
                        UnsupportedTypeException("Unsupported SQL " +
```

Example 17-10. The Row Class Constructor (continued)

```
                             "data type: " + type);
        }
    }
}
```

The Row class keeps all column values as an array of Column objects. The constructor is called with a ResultSet that has been positioned at a new row by the caller using the next() method. It loops through all columns in the row and creates a Column subclass instance for each. The column's datatype, retrieved from the ResultSetMetaData object, is used to decide which Column subclass to create. Similarly to the Value class structure, the Column class structure contains subclasses corresponding to JDBC column datatypes, as shown in Figure 17-3.

Two methods provide access to the number of columns and the array of Column objects, shown in Example 17-11.

Example 17-11. The Row's getColumnCount( ) and getColumns( ) Methods

```
public int getColumnCount() {
    return columns.length;
}


public Column[] getColumns() {
    return columns;
}
```

Another set of methods can be used to retrieve the value of an individual column, given its name or index. This set of methods contains one pair per supported datatype. Example 17-12 shows the methods for the BigDecimal, boolean, and String types.

Example 17-12. The Row's Column Value Access Methods

```
public BigDecimal getBigDecimal(int columnIndex)
    throws NoSuchColumnException, UnsupportedConversionException {
    Column col = null;
    try {
        col = columns[columnIndex - 1];
    }
    catch (ArrayIndexOutOfBoundsException e) {
        throw
            new NoSuchColumnException(String.valueOf(columnIndex));
    }
    return col.getBigDecimal();
}


public BigDecimal getBigDecimal(String columnName)
```

Example 17-12. The Row's Column Value Access Methods (continued)

```
        throws NoSuchColumnException, UnsupportedConversionException {
        return getBigDecimal(getIndex(columnName));
    }

    public boolean getBoolean(int columnIndex)
        throws NoSuchColumnException, UnsupportedConversionException {
        Column col = null;
        try {
            col = columns[columnIndex - 1];
        }
        catch (ArrayIndexOutOfBoundsException e) {
            throw
                new NoSuchColumnException(String.valueOf(columnIndex));
        }
        return col.getBoolean();
    }

    public boolean getBoolean(String columnName)
        throws NoSuchColumnException, UnsupportedConversionException {
        return getBoolean(getIndex(columnName));
    }
    ...
    public String getString(int columnIndex)
        throws NoSuchColumnException {
        Column col = null;
        try {
            col = columns[columnIndex - 1];
        }
        catch (ArrayIndexOutOfBoundsException e) {
            throw
                new NoSuchColumnException(String.valueOf(columnIndex));
        }
        return col.getString();
    }

    public String getString(String columnName)
        throws NoSuchColumnException {
        return getString(getIndex(columnName));
    }
```

All these methods locate the Column subclass instance specified by the argument and call the corresponding method on the instance. Except for the getString() method, this call results in an UnsupportedConversionException if the column is not of the requested type. All types can be converted to a String, however, so a getString() call is successful provided that the requested column exists.

The Column class is an abstract class, very similar to the Value class shown in Example 17-4. It contains access methods for all datatypes, with default implementations that throw an UnsupportedConversionException. Each subclass provides a real implementation of the access method corresponding to its type, plus the getString() method. Example 17-13 shows the IntColumn class.

Example 17-13. The IntColumn Class

```
package com.ora.jsp.sql.column;

import com.ora.jsp.sql.Column;

public class IntColumn extends Column {
    private int value;

    public IntColumn(String name, int value) {
        super(name);
        this.value = value;
    }

    public int getInt() {
        return value;
    }

    public String getString() {
        return String.valueOf(value);
    }
}
```

The constructor takes the column name and value as arguments. The name is used to initialize the Column superclass and is returned by its getName() method.

Developing Generic Database Custom Actions

The database custom actions introduced in Chapter 9 can be used like this in a JSP page:

```
<ora:sqlTransaction dataSource="example">

    <ora:sqlUpdate>
    UPDATE Account SET Balance = Balance - ?
      WHERE AccountNumber = ?
      <ora:floatValue param="amount" />
      <ora:intValue param="account" />
    </ora:sqlUpdate>
    <ora:sqlUpdate>
      UPDATE Account SET Balance = Balance + ?
```

```
        WHERE AccountNumber = ?
      <ora:floatValue param="amount" />
      <ora:intValue param="account" />
    </ora:sqlUpdate>

  </ora:sqlTransaction>
```

The database custom actions use all of the classes described previously in this chapter. A DataSource available in the application scope is used to get a Connection, and an SQLCommandBean is used to execute the SQL statement specified in the database action element body. The nested value actions create Value subclass instances and add them to a list held by the parent action tag handler. The <ora:sqlQuery> action saves the result as a Vector of Row objects in the scope specified by the page author. In this section, we first look at how the tag handlers for the <ora:sqlQuery>, <ora:sqlUpdate>, and <ora:sqlIntValue> actions are implemented. All value actions follow the same pattern as <ora:sqlIntValue>, so they are not described here. At the end of this section, we also look at the tag handler for the <ora:sqlTransatction> action to see how it provides a transaction scope for the database actions nested in its body.

The <ora:sqlQuery> and <ora:sqlUpdate> Actions

The <ora:sqlQuery> and <ora:sqlUpdate> actions both need access to the action body to read the SQL statement. Hence, the corresponding tag handlers extend the BodyTagSupport class described in Chapter 16, *Developing JSP Custom Actions*. They also implement an interface called com.ora.jsp.sql. ValueParent, which is used by the nested value actions to find the correct parent, following the pattern described for cooperating actions in Chapter 16.

These two actions share the same set of attributes and have almost the same behavior, so a common superclass called com.ora.jsp.tags.sql.DBTag implements most of the tag handler functionality for both actions. Example 17-14 shows the top part of the DBTag class, with the class declaration and all property setter methods.

Example 17-14. The DBTag Declaration and Properties

```
package com.ora.jsp.tags.sql;

import java.util.*;
import java.sql.*;
import javax.sql.*;
import javax.servlet.jsp.*;
import javax.servlet.jsp.tagext.*;
import com.ora.jsp.sql.*;
import com.ora.jsp.sql.value.*;
```

Example 17-14. The DBTag Declaration and Properties (continued)

```
public abstract class DBTag extends BodyTagSupport
    implements ValueTagParent {
    private SQLCommandBean sqlCommandBean = new SQLCommandBean();
    private String dataSourceName;
    private String id;
    private int scope = PageContext.PAGE_SCOPE;
    private String sqlValue;
    private Vector values;
    private boolean isExceptionThrown = false;
    private boolean isPartOfTransaction = false;

    public void setDataSource(String dataSourceName) {
        this.dataSourceName = dataSourceName;
    }

    public void setId(String id) {
        this.id = id;
    }

    public void setScope(String scopeName) {
        if ("page".equals(scopeName)) {
            scope = PageContext.PAGE_SCOPE;
        }
        else if ("request".equals(scopeName)) {
            scope = PageContext.REQUEST_SCOPE;
        }
        else if ("session".equals(scopeName)) {
            scope = PageContext.SESSION_SCOPE;
        }
        else if ("application".equals(scopeName)) {
            scope = PageContext.APPLICATION_SCOPE;
        }
    }
}
```

An instance of the SQLCommandBean is kept as a private instance variable. The bean is used to perform all database operations; the tag handler just provides an easy-to-use interface to the bean for page authors. The setter methods for the dataSource and id properties set the corresponding instance variables. The setter method for the scope property converts the String value to the corresponding scope int value defined by the PageContext class before saving the value, since the int value is later needed in the doEndTag() method.

The page author specifies the SQL statement to execute in the action element's body. Because the tag handler implements the BodyTag interface (by extending the BodyTagSupport class), it can read the SQL statement in the doAfterBody() method as shown in Example 17-15.

Example 17-15. The DBTag's doAfterBody( ) Method

```
public int doAfterBody() throws JspException {
    sqlValue = bodyContent.getString();
    return SKIP_BODY;
}
```

The SQL statement may contain question marks as placeholders for values set by nested value actions. As you will see later, the value actions create the appropriate Value subclass and call the DBTag's addValue() method, shown in Example 17-16.

Example 17-16. The DBTag's addValue( ) Method

```
public void addValue(Value value) {
    if (values == null) {
        values = new Vector();
    }
    values.addElement(value);
}
```

This method creates a Vector to hold all values the first time it's called, and then adds the Value object to the Vector. When called by subsequent value action tag handlers, the Value objects are simply added to the list.

The real processing happens in the doEndTag() method, shown in Example 17-17. This method is called by the container when the action element's body has been processed and the end tag is encountered.

Example 17-17. The DBTag's doEndTag( ) Method

```
public int doEndTag() throws JspException {
    Connection conn = getConnection();
    sqlCommandBean.setConnection(conn);
    sqlCommandBean.setSqlValue(sqlValue);
    sqlCommandBean.setValues(values);
    Object result = null;
    try {
        result = execute(sqlCommandBean);
    }
    catch (SQLException e) {
        ...
    }
    catch (UnsupportedTypeException e) {
        ...
    }
    finally {
        ...
    }
    // Save the result with the specified id in the specified scope
    if (id != null) {
```

Example 17-17. The DBTag's doEndTag( ) Method (continued)

```
            pageContext.setAttribute(id, result, scope);
        }
        return EVAL_PAGE;
    }
```

The private getConnection() method is used to get a Connection. The Connection is retrieved either from the DataSource specified by the data-Source attribute value for the <ora:sqlQuery> or the <ora:sqlUpdate> action itself, or from an enclosing <ora:sqlTransaction> element. We'll return to getConnection() and the exception handling code later when we look at trans-action support. The Connection, the SQL statement, and all values (if any) are passed to the bean. Then, the abstract execute() method is called to ask the bean to execute the SQL statement. The Object returned by execute() is saved in the scope specified by the scope attribute, using the name specified by the id attribute.

The implementation of the execute() method is the only thing that differs between the tag handlers for the <ora:sqlQuery> action and the <ora:sqlUpdate> action. The corresponding tag handler classes, QueryTag and UpdateTag, extend the DBTag class and implement the execute() method. Example 17-18 shows the implementation in the QueryTag tag handler.

Example 17-18. The QueryTag's execute( ) Method

```
    public Object execute(SQLCommandBean sqlCommandBean)
        throws SQLException, UnsupportedTypeException {
        return sqlCommandBean.executeQuery();
    }
```

This method simply calls the bean's executeQuery() method.

The UpdateTag tag handler uses the bean's executeUpdate() method instead, and wraps the returned int in an Integer object, as shown in Example 17-19.

Example 17-19. The UpdateTag's execute( ) Method

```
    public Object execute(SQLCommandBean sqlCommandBean)
        throws SQLException, UnsupportedTypeException {
        return new Integer(sqlCommandBean.executeUpdate());
    }
```

The reason for wrapping the int in an Integer is that only real objects can be saved as JSP scope objects; primitive types are not supported.

The <ora:sqlQuery> and the <sql:Update> actions define separate TagExtra-Info classes, named QueryTagExtraInfo and UpdateTagExtraInfo, respectively. They both extend a class called com.ora.jsp.tags.sql.DBTagExtraInfo. The isValid() method for the DBTagExtraInfo class makes sure a valid value is specified for the scope attribute. It's shown in Example 17-20.

Example 17-20. The DBTagExtraInfo Class

```
package com.ora.jsp.tags.sql;

import javax.servlet.jsp.tagext.*;

public class DBTagExtraInfo extends TagExtraInfo {
    /**
     * Returns true only if a valid scope value is specified:
     * page, request, session or application.
     */
    public boolean isValid(TagData data) {
        boolean isValid = false;
        String scope = data.getAttributeString("scope");

        if (scope == null || scope.equals("page") ||
            scope.equals("request") ||
            scope.equals("session") || scope.equals("application")) {
            isValid = true;
        }
        return isValid;
    }
}
```

The QueryTagExtraInfo and UpdateTagExtraInfo classes implement the getVariableInfo() method to tell the container about the result variables they create. Here's the UpdateTagExtraInfo class:

```
package com.ora.jsp.tags.sql;

import javax.servlet.jsp.tagext.*;
public class UpdateTagExtraInfo extends DBTagExtraInfo {
    public VariableInfo[] getVariableInfo(TagData data) {
        if (data.getAttributeString("id") == null) {
            return new VariableInfo[0];
        }
        else {
            return new VariableInfo[]
            {
                new VariableInfo(data.getAttributeString("id"),
                    "java.lang.Integer",
                    true,
                    VariableInfo.AT_END)
            };
        }
    }
}
```

The `QueryTagExtraInfo` class is almost identical. The only difference is that it sets the class name to `com.ora.jsp.sql.Row` instead of `java.lang.Integer`.

The <ora:intValue> Action

A set of value actions can be used inside the body of an `<ora:sqlQuery>` or `<ora:sqlUpdate>` action to set the values for placeholders in the SQL statement. The example tag library contains value actions for date/time values as well as for numeric and string values. The tag handlers for all these actions have a great deal in common, so they all extend a common superclass called `com.ora.jsp.tags.sql.value.ValueTag`. This superclass contains instance variables and property setter methods for the attributes shared by all value actions: `stringValue`, `pattern`, `param`, `name`, and `property`. In addition, it contains methods used by the subclasses to get the value when it's specified as a parameter name or a bean name plus a property name.

Let's look at the tag handler class for the `<ora:intValue>` action as an example. All other value actions follow the same pattern. The `com.ora.jsp.tags.sql.IntValueTag` class extends the `ValueTag` class as shown in Example 17-21.

Example 17-21. The IntValueTag Class

```
package com.ora.jsp.tags.sql.value;

import java.lang.reflect.*;
import java.text.*;
import javax.servlet.jsp.*;
import javax.servlet.jsp.tagext.*;
import com.ora.jsp.sql.value.*;
import com.ora.jsp.tags.sql.ValueTagParent;
import com.ora.jsp.util.*;

public class IntValueTag extends ValueTag {
    private int value;

    public void setValue(int value) {
        this.value = value;
    }

    public int doEndTag() throws JspException {
        if (stringValue != null) {
            value = toInt(stringValue, pattern);
        }
        else if (param != null) {
            String paramValue = getParameter(param);
            value = toInt(paramValue, pattern);
        }
```

Example 17-21. The IntValueTag Class (continued)

```
        else if (name != null) {
            value = getInt(name, property, pattern);
        }
        ValueTagParent parent =
            (ValueTagParent) findAncestorWithClass(this,
                ValueTagParent.class);
        if (parent == null) {
            throw new JspException("The sqlIntValue action is not " +
                "enclosed by a supported action type");
        }
        parent.addValue(new IntValue(value));
        return EVAL_PAGE;
    }
    ...
}
```

The Java datatype is different for each value action, so all subclasses implement their own value property setter methods to store the value in an instance variable. The value property for the `IntValueTag` is of course an `int`.

Besides the value attribute, all value actions support three other ways to set the value: as a `String` value specified by the `stringValue` attribute, as a request parameter specified by the `param` attribute, or as a bean property specified by the `name` and `property` attributes. The `ValueTag` superclass contains the setter methods and instance variables for these attributes, and the `ValueTagExtraInfo` class makes sure that a page author uses only one of these alternatives to specify the value. The `doEndTag()` method finds out which alternative is used by looking at all property instance variables in turn. If it's a `String` value, defined by the `stringValue` or `param` attributes, the method converts the value to an `int` using a private `toInt()` method. If it's specified as a bean property, another private method, `getInt()`, is used to invoke the bean to get the value. These private methods are not shown here, but you can look at the source code if you want to see how they work.

The enclosing `<ora:sqlQuery>` or `<ora:sqlUpdate>` action's tag handler is then located, as described in Chapter 16, *Developing JSP Custom Actions*, using the `findAncestorWithClass()` method. The tag handlers for the enclosing actions implement the `ValueTagParent` interface used as the parent class argument. If an enclosing action is found, its `addValue()` method is called to add the `int` value wrapped in an `IntValue` object to the parent's value list.

The `<ora:sqlTransaction>` Action

The final database action in the example tag library is the `<ora:sql-Transaction>` action. A database transaction consists of the execution of a number of SQL statements on the same Connection; they either all succeed or all fail. As you may recall, the data changes resulting from executing all statements are then either permanently saved by committing the transaction, or ignored by rolling back the transaction. The task for the <ora:sqlTransaction> action is to provide a Connection to all database actions enclosed in its body, and commit the transaction when they have all been executed. The nested database actions must cooperate with the <ora:sqlTransaction> action tag handler by retrieving the shared Connection and rolling back the transaction if they fail.

Let's look at how the Connection is handled first. Example 17-22 shows the TransactionTag class declaration, the dataSource property setter method, and the doStartTag() method.

Example 17-22. Part of the TransactionTag Class

```
package com.ora.jsp.tags.sql;

import java.io.*;
import java.util.*;
import java.sql.*;
import javax.sql.*;
import javax.servlet.jsp.*;
import javax.servlet.jsp.tagext.*;

public class TransactionTag extends TagSupport {
    private String dataSourceName;
    private Connection conn;

    public void setDataSource(String dataSourceName) {
        this.dataSourceName = dataSourceName;
    }

    public int doStartTag() throws JspException {
        conn = getTransactionConnection();
        return EVAL_BODY_INCLUDE;
    }
```

The TransactionTag class extends the TagSupport class. It doesn't need to access its body content; it only needs to tell the JSP container to execute all actions and possible scripting elements in the body, so the TagSupport class is the proper choice. The dataSource property corresponds to the attribute with the same name. The page author sets it to the name of the DataSource object in the application scope to use for all nested database actions.

The doStartTag() method, invoked by the container before the actions in the body are processed, sets the conn instance variable by calling the get-TransactionConnection() method, shown in Example 17-23.

Example 17-23. The TransactionTag's getTransactionConnection( ) and getConnection( ) Methods

```
    private Connection getTransactionConnection() throws JspException {
        DataSource dataSource = (DataSource)
            pageContext.getAttribute(dataSourceName,
                PageContext.APPLICATION_SCOPE);
        if (dataSource == null) {
            throw new JspException("dataSource " + dataSourceName +
                " not found");
        }
        try {
            conn = dataSource.getConnection();
            conn.setAutoCommit(false);
        }
        catch (SQLException e) {
            throw new JspException("SQL error: " + e.getMessage());
        }
        return conn;
    }

    Connection getConnection() {
        return conn;
    }
```

This method retrieves the `DataSource` object from the application scope and gets a `Connection`. A `Connection` automatically commits each SQL statement by default. In order to use the `Connection` to execute more than one statement within the same transaction, the `setAutoCommit()` method is called with the value `false`.

The package scope `getConnection()` method, also shown in Example 17-23, is used by the tag handlers for the `<ora:sqlQuery>` and `<ora:sqlUpdate>` actions. To see how it's used, let's look at the method with the same name in the `DBTag` class that we skipped earlier. The `DBTag`'s `getConnection()` method is shown in Example 17-24.

Example 17-24. The DBTag's getConnection( ) Method

```
private Connection getConnection() throws JspException {
        Connection conn = null;
        TransactionTag transactionTag = (TransactionTag)
            findAncestorWithClass(this, TransactionTag.class);
        if (transactionTag != null) {
            conn = transactionTag.getConnection();
            isPartOfTransaction = true;
            if (dataSourceName != null) {
                throw new JspException("A dataSource must not be " +
                    "specified when the action is part of a " +
                    "transaction");
```

Example 17-24. The DBTag's getConnection( ) Method (continued)

```
            }
        }
        else {
            DataSource dataSource = (DataSource)
                pageContext.getAttribute(dataSourceName,
                    PageContext.APPLICATION_SCOPE);
            if (dataSource == null) {
                throw new JspException("dataSource " +
                    dataSourceName + " not found");
            }
            try {
                conn = dataSource.getConnection();
            }
            catch (SQLException e) {
                throw new JspException("SQL error: " + e.getMessage());
            }
        }
        return conn;
    }
```

The `findAncestorWithClass()` is used to find out whether or not the action is nested in the body of an `<ora:sqlTransaction>` tag. If a `TransactionTag` is found, the action is part of a transaction, so the `TransactionTag`'s `get-Connection()` is used to retrieve the shared `Connection`, and a `boolean` flag is set to remember that the action is part of a transaction. If a parent tag handler is not found, the action is not part of a transaction. In this case, the `DBTag`'s `dataSource` property value is used instead to locate the `DataSource` in the application scope and get a `Connection`.

The `doEndTag()` method in the `DBTag` class contains some details related to database transactions that we also skipped earlier. Let's revisit this method, shown in Example 17-25.

Example 17-25. The DBTag's doEndTag( ) Method

```
public int doEndTag() throws JspException {
    Connection conn = getConnection();
    sqlCommandBean.setConnection(conn);
    sqlCommandBean.setSqlValue(sqlValue);
    sqlCommandBean.setValues(values);
    Object result = null;
    try {
        result = execute(sqlCommandBean);
    }
    catch (SQLException e) {
        try {
            isExceptionThrown = true;
```

Example 17-25. The DBTag's doEndTag( ) Method (continued)

```
              conn.rollback();
        }
        catch (SQLException se) {
            // Ignore, probably a result of the main exception
        }
        throw new JspException("SQL error: " + e.getMessage());
    }
    catch (UnsupportedTypeException e) {
        try {
            isExceptionThrown = true;
            conn.rollback();
        }
        catch (SQLException se) {
            // Ignore, probably caused by the main exception
        }
        throw new JspException("Query result error: " +
            e.getMessage());
    }
    finally {
        try {
            if (isPartOfTransaction && isExceptionThrown) {
                // Reset auto commit in case the connection is
                // pooled before it's returned to the pool by close
                conn.setAutoCommit(true);
                conn.close();
            }
            else if (!isPartOfTransaction) {
                // If we're not part of a transaction, the
                // connection is in auto commit mode so we only
                // close it
                conn.close();
            }
        }
        catch (SQLException e) {
            e.printStackTrace(System.err);
        }
    }
    // Save the result with the specified id in the specified scope
    if (id != null) {
        pageContext.setAttribute(id, result, scope);
    }
    return EVAL_PAGE;
}
```

The interesting code is in the catch and finally clauses of the try block. If the
execution of the SQL statement causes an exception to be thrown, the transaction

is rolled back and a `JspException` is thrown. This aborts the processing of the rest of the page and informs the user about the error. A `boolean` flag is also set to be able to handle this case in the `finally` clause. The `finally` clause is executed whether or not an exception is thrown. If this action is part of a transaction and an exception is thrown by the `execute()` method, the `Connection` is returned to the pool by calling the `close()` method after auto commit is turned on again to reset it to its default state. If the action is not part of a transaction, there's no need to reset the auto commit since it has never been changed; the `Connection` is just returned to the pool by calling the `close()` method. If the action is part of a transaction and no exception is thrown, the result is saved in the specified scope, and processing continues with the next nested database action. Note that the `Connection` is not closed in this case, as the same `Connection` must be used for all SQL statements in the transaction.

If all actions execute successfully, the `TransactionTag`'s `doEndTag()`, shown in Example 17-26, is invoked.

Example 17-26. The TransactionTag's doEndTag( ) Method

```
public int doEndTag() throws JspException {
    try {
        conn.commit();
        conn.setAutoCommit(true);
        conn.close();
    }
    catch (SQLException e) {
        throw new JspException("SQL error: " + e.getMessage());
    }
    return EVAL_PAGE;
}
```

The `doEndTag()` method commits the transaction, resets the auto commit for the `Connection`, and returns the `Connection` to the pool by calling the `close()` method.

Developing Application-Specific Database Components

The classes described in this chapter can also be used for application-specific components that access a database. Chapter 15 includes one example of an application-specific bean, the `EmployeeRegisterBean`, that uses the `SQLCommandBean` to execute its SQL statements.

You can also use these classes in your application-specific custom actions. One example is the custom action that's mentioned in Chapter 9 as an alternative to the generic database actions for inserting or updating employee information:

```
<%@ page language="java" contentType="text/html" %>
<%@ taglib uri="/orataglib" prefix="ora" %>
<%@ taglib uri="/mytaglib" prefix="myLib" %>


<myLib:saveEmployeeInfo dataSource="example" />


<%-- Get the new or updated data from the database --%>
<ora:sqlQuery id="newEmpDbInfo" dataSource="example" scope="session">
  SELECT * FROM Employee
    WHERE UserName = ?
  <ora:sqlStringValue param="userName" />
</ora:sqlQuery>


<%-- Redirect to the confirmation page --%>
<ora:redirect page="confirmation.jsp" />
```

Example 17-27 shows one way to implement this custom action.

Example 17-27. SaveEmployeeInfoTag Class

```
package com.mycompany.tags;

import java.sql.*;
import java.text.*;
import java.util.Vector;
import javax.sql.*;
import javax.servlet.*;
import javax.servlet.jsp.*;
import javax.servlet.jsp.tagext.*;
import com.ora.jsp.sql.*;
import com.ora.jsp.sql.value.*;
import com.ora.jsp.util.*;

public class SaveEmployeeInfoTag extends TagSupport {
    private String dataSourceName;

    public void setDataSource(String dataSourceName) {
        this.dataSourceName = dataSourceName;
    }

    public int doEndTag() throws JspException {
        // Get all request parameters
        ServletRequest request = pageContext.getRequest();
        String userName = request.getParameter("userName");
        String password = request.getParameter("password");
```

Example 17-27. SaveEmployeeInfoTag Class (continued)

```
String firstName = request.getParameter("firstName");
String lastName = request.getParameter("lastName");
String dept = request.getParameter("dept");
String empDate = request.getParameter("empDate");
String emailAddr = request.getParameter("emailAddr");
if (userName == null || password == null ||
    firstName == null || lastName == null ||
    dept == null || empDate == null ||
    emailAddr == null) {
    throw new JspException("Missing a mandatory parameter");
}

SQLCommandBean sqlCommandBean = new SQLCommandBean();
DataSource dataSource = (DataSource)
    pageContext.getAttribute(dataSourceName,
        PageContext.APPLICATION_SCOPE);
if (dataSource == null) {
    throw new JspException("The data source " + dataSource +
        " is not found in the application scope");
}

Connection conn = null;
try {
    conn = dataSource.getConnection();
    sqlCommandBean.setConnection(conn);

    // See if the user exists
    String sqlValue =
        "SELECT * FROM Employee WHERE UserName = ?";
    Vector values = new Vector();
    values.addElement(new StringValue(userName));
    sqlCommandBean.setSqlValue(sqlValue);
    sqlCommandBean.setValues(values);
    Vector rows = sqlCommandBean.executeQuery();

    // Create values for insert/update
    values.removeAllElements();
    values.addElement(new StringValue(password));
    values.addElement(new StringValue(firstName));
    values.addElement(new StringValue(lastName));
    values.addElement(new StringValue(dept));
    values.addElement(new DateValue(
        new Date(StringFormat.toDate(empDate,
            "yyyy-MM-dd").getTime())));
    values.addElement(new StringValue(emailAddr));
    values.addElement(new TimestampValue(
        new Timestamp(System.currentTimeMillis())));
    values.addElement(new StringValue(userName));
```

Example 17-27. SaveEmployeeInfoTag Class (continued)

```
            if (rows.size() == 0) {
                // New user. Insert
                StringBuffer sb = new StringBuffer();
                sb.append("INSERT INTO Employee ").
                    append("(Password, FirstName, LastName, Dept, ").
                    append("EmpDate, EmailAddr, ModDate, UserName) ").
                    append("VALUES(?, ?, ?, ?, ?, ?, ?, ?)");
                sqlCommandBean.setSqlValue(sb.toString());
            }
            else {
                // Existing user. Update
                StringBuffer sb = new StringBuffer();
                sb.append("UPDATE Employee ").
                    append("SET Password = ?, FirstName = ?, ").
                    append("LastName = ?, Dept = ?, EmpDate = ?, ").
                    append("EmailAddr = ?, ModDate = ? ").
                    append("WHERE UserName = ?");
                sqlCommandBean.setSqlValue(sb.toString());
            }
            sqlCommandBean.executeUpdate();
        }
        catch (SQLException e) {
            throw new JspException("SQL error: " + e.getMessage());
        }
        catch (UnsupportedTypeException e) {
            throw new JspException("Query result error: " +
                e.getMessage());
        }
        catch (ParseException e) {
            throw new JspException("Invalid empDate format: " +
                e.getMessage());
        }
        finally {
            try {
                if (conn != null) {
                    conn.close();
                }
            }
            catch (SQLException e) {
                // Ignore
            }
        }
        return EVAL_PAGE;
    }

    public void release() {
```

Example 17-27. SaveEmployeeInfoTag Class (continued)

```
        dataSourceName = null;
        super.release();
    }
}
```

This tag handler has one property, named `dataSource`. It's marked as required in the TLD for the tag, so it will always be set:

```
    ...
    <tag>
      <name>saveEmployeeInfo</name>
      <tagclass>com.mycompany.tags.SaveEmployeeInfoTag</tagclass>
      <bodycontent>empty</bodycontent>
      <info>
      </info>

      <attribute>
        <name>dataSource</name>
        <required>true</required>
      </attribute>
    </tag>
    ...
```

In the `doEndTag()` method, all request parameters with information about the employee are first retrieved. If a parameter is missing, an exception is thrown. Then an `SQLCommandBean` instance is created, the `DataSource` object fetched from the application scope, and a `Connection` created and provided to the bean.

The bean is used to execute a `SELECT` statement to find out if the specified employee is already defined in the database. If not, the bean is used to execute an `INSERT` statement with all the information provided through the request parameters. Otherwise, the bean is used to execute an `UPDATE` statement.

The tag handler class described here is intended only to show how you can use the database access classes to implement your own custom actions. The tag handler class could be improved in several ways. For instance, it could provide default values for missing parameters, such as the current date for a missing employment date, or an email address based on the employee's first and last names if the email address is missing. You could also use a bean as input to the action instead of reading request parameters directly. This would allow the bean to be used as described in Chapter 6, *Using Scripting Elements*, and Chapter 8, *Sharing Data Between JSP Pages, Requests, and Users,* to capture and validate the user input until all information is valid, and then pass it on to the custom action for permanent storage of the information in a database.

IV

APPENDIXES

In this part of the book, you find reference material, such as descriptions of JSP elements and classes, all book example components, the web application deployment descriptor, and more.

- Appendix A, *JSP Elements Syntax Reference*
- Appendix B, *JSP API Reference*
- Appendix C, *Book Example Custom Actions and Classes Reference*
- Appendix D, *Web-Application Structure and Deployment Descriptor Reference*
- Appendix E, *JSP Resource Reference*

A

JSP Elements Syntax Reference

JSP defines three types of elements: directives, scripting elements, and action elements. In addition, you can define your own custom actions. This appendix contains descriptions of all JSP elements as well as the general syntax rules for custom actions.

Directive Elements

Directive elements are used to specify information about the page itself, especially information that doesn't differ between requests for the page. The general directive syntax is:

```
<%@ directiveName attr1="value1" attr2="value2" %>
```

The attribute values can be enclosed with single quotes instead of double quotes. The directive name and all attribute names are case-sensitive.

include Directive

The `include` directive includes a static file, merging its content with the including page before the combined result is converted to a JSP page implementation class. The `include` directive supports the attribute described in Table A-1.

Table A-1. include Directive Attribute

Attribute Name	Default	Description
file	No default	A page-relative or context-relative URI path for the file to include

A page can contain multiple `include` directives. The including page and all included pages together form what is called a *JSP translation unit*.

Example:

```
<%@ include file="header.html" %>
```

page Directive

The page directive defines page-dependent attributes, such as scripting language, error page, and buffering requirements. It supports the attributes described in Table A-2.

Table A-2. page Directive Attributes

Attribute Name	Default	Description
autoFlush	true	Set to true if the page buffer should be flushed automatically when it's full, or to false if an exception should be thrown when it's full.
buffer	8kb	Specifies the buffer size for the page. The value must be expressed as the size in kilobytes followed by kb, or be the keyword none to disable buffering.
contentType	text/html	The MIME type for the response generated by the page, and optionally the charset for the source page as well as the response; e.g., text/html;charset=Shift_JIS.
errorPage	No default	A page-relative or context-relative URI path for the JSP page to forward to if an exception is thrown by code in the page.
extends	No default	The fully qualified name of a Java class that the generated JSP page implementation class extends. The class must implement the JspPage or HttpJspPage interface in the javax.servlet.jsp package. Note that the recommendation is to *not* use this attribute. Specifying your own superclass restricts the JSP container's ability to provide a specialized, high-performance superclass.
import	No default	A Java import declaration, i.e., a comma-separated list of fully qualified class names or package names followed by .* (for all public classes in the package).
info	No default	Text that a web container may use as a description of the page in its administration user interface.
isErrorPage	false	Set to true for a page that is used as an error page, to make the implicit exception variable available to scripting elements. Use false for regular JSP pages.
isThreadSafe	true	Set to true if the container is allowed to run multiple threads through the page (i.e., lets the page serve parallel requests). If set to false, the container serializes all requests for the page. It may also use a pool of page implementation class instances to serve more than one request at a time. The recommendation is to always use true, and handle multithread issues by avoiding JSP declarations and ensuring that all objects used by the page are thread-safe.

Table A-2. page Directive Attributes (continued)

Attribute Name	Default	Description
language	java	Defines the scripting language used in the page.
session	true	Set to true if the page should participate in a user session. If set to false, the implicit session variable is not available to scripting elements in the page.

A translation unit (the JSP source file and any files included via the include directive) can contain more than one page directive, as long as there is only one occurrence of an attribute, with the exception of the import attribute. If multiple import attribute values are used, they are combined into one list of import definitions.

Example:

```
<%@ page language="java" contentType="text/html;charset=Shift_JIS"%>
<%@ page import="java.util.*, java.text.*" %>
<%@ page import="java.sql.Date" %>
```

taglib Directive

Declares a tag library, containing custom actions, that is used in the page. The taglib directive supports the attributes described in Table A-3.

Table A-3. taglib Directive Attributes

Attribute Name	Default	Description
prefix	No default	Mandatory. The prefix to use in the action element names for all actions in the library.
uri	No default	Mandatory. Either a symbolic name for the tag library defined in the *web.xml* file for the application, or a page-relative or context-relative URI path for the library's TLD file or JAR file.

Example:

```
<%@ taglib uri="/orataglib" prefix="ora" %>
```

Scripting Elements

Scripting elements let you add small pieces of code to a JSP page, such as an if statement that generates different HTML depending on some condition. The scripting code must be written in the language defined by the page directive. It is executed when the JSP page is requested.

Declaration

A declaration starts with <%! and ends with %>. The content between the start and the end characters must be a complete, valid declaration in the scripting language defined by the page directive. The JSP implicit variables are not visible in a declaration element.

A declaration can be used to declare a scripting language variable or method. When the scripting language is Java, a variable declared by a declaration element ends up as an instance variable in the JSP page implementation class. It is therefore visible to parallel threads (requests) processing the page, and needs to be handled in a thread-safe manner. A thread-safe alternative is to declare variables within a scriptlet element instead. It then becomes a local variable of the method in the page implementation class used to process each request, and is not shared by parallel threads.

Example:

```
<%! int globalCounter = 0; %>
```

Expression

An expression starts with <%= and ends with %>. The content between the start and the end characters must be a complete, valid expression in the scripting language defined by the page directive that results in or can be converted to a string. All JSP implicit variables are visible in an expression element.

Example:

```
<%= globalCounter++ %>
```

Scriptlet

A scriptlet starts with <% and ends with %>. The content between the start and the end characters must be a code fragment in the scripting language defined by the page directive. Scriptlet code fragments are combined with code for sending the template data between them to the browser. The combination of all scriptlets in a page must form valid scripting language statements. All JSP implicit variables are visible in a scripting element.

Example:

```
<% java.util Date clock = new java.util.Date() %>

<% if (clock.getHours() < 12) { %>
  Good morning!
<% } else if (clock.getHours() < 17) { %>
  Good day!
```

```
<% } else { %>
  Good evening!
<% } %>
```

Action Elements

Actions are executed when the JSP page is requested by a client. They are inserted in a page using XML element syntax, and encapsulate functionality such as input validation using beans, database access, or passing control to another page. The JSP specification defines a few standard action elements, described in this section, and also includes a framework for developing custom action elements.

An action element consists of a start tag (optionally with attributes), a body, and an end tag. Other elements can be nested in the body. Here's an example:

```
<jsp:forward page="nextPage.jsp">
  <jsp:param name="aParam" value="aValue" />
</jsp:forward>
```

If the action element doesn't have a body, a shorthand notation can be used in which the start tag ends with /> instead of >, as shown by the <jsp:param> action in this example. The action element name and attribute names are case-sensitive.

Some action attributes accept a request-time attribute value, using the JSP expression syntax:

```
<% String headerPage = currentTemplateDir + "/header.jsp"; %>
<jsp:include page="<%= headerPage %>" />
```

The attribute descriptions for each action in this section define whether a request-time attribute value is accepted or not.

<jsp:fallback>

The <jsp:fallback> action can only be used in the body of a <jsp:plugin> action. Its body is used to specify the template text to use for browsers that do not support the HTML <embed> or <object> elements. This action supports no attributes.

Example:

```
<jsp:plugin type="applet" code="Clock2.class"
  codebase="applet"
  jreversion="1.2" width="160" height="150" >
  <jsp:fallback>
    Plugin tag OBJECT or EMBED not supported by browser.
  </jsp:fallback>
</jsp:plugin>
```

<jsp:forward>

The `<jsp:forward>` action passes the request processing control to another JSP page or servlet in the same web application. The execution of the current page is terminated, giving the target resource full control over the request.

If any response content has been buffered when the `<jsp:forward>` action is executed, the buffer is cleared first. If the response has already been committed (i.e., partly sent to the browser), the forwarding fails with an `IllegalStateException`.

The URI path information available through the implicit `request` object is adjusted to reflect the URI path information for the target resource. All other request information is left untouched, so the target resource has access to all the original parameters and headers passed with the request. Additional parameters can be passed to the target resource through `<jsp:param>` elements in the `<jsp:forward>` element's body.

The `<jsp:forward>` action supports the attributes described in Table A-4.

Table A-4. <jsp:forward> Attributes

Attribute Name	Java Type	Request-Time Value Accepted	Description
page	String	Yes	Mandatory. A page-relative or context-relative URI path for the resource to forward to.

Example:

```
<jsp:forward page="list.jsp" />
```

<jsp:getProperty>

The `<jsp:getProperty>` action adds the value of a bean property, converted to a string, to the response generated by the page. The attributes described in Table A-5 are supported.

Table A-5. <jsp:getProperty> Attributes

Attribute Name	Java Type	Request-Time Value Accepted	Description
name	String	No	Mandatory. The name assigned to a bean in one of the JSP scopes.
property	String	No	Mandatory. The name of the bean's property to include in the page.

Example:

```
<jsp:getProperty name="clock" property="hours" />
```

<jsp:include>

The `<jsp:include>` action includes the response from another JSP page, servlet, or static file in the same web application. The execution of the current page continues after including the response generated by the target resource.

If any response content has been buffered when the `<jsp:include>` action is executed, the buffer is flushed first. Even though this behavior can be controlled by the flush attribute, the only valid value in JSP 1.1 is `true`. This limitation will likely be lifted in a future version of JSP.

The URI path information available through the implicit `request` object reflects the URI path information for the source JSP page even in the target resource. All other request information is also left untouched, so the target resource has access to all the original parameters and headers passed with the request. Additional parameters can be passed to the target resource through `<jsp:param>` elements in the `<jsp:include>` element's body.

The `<jsp:include>` action supports the attributes described in Table A-6.

Table A-6. <jsp:include> Attributes

Attribute Name	Java Type	Request-Time Value Accepted	Description
page	String	Yes	Mandatory. A page-relative or context-relative URI path for the resource to include.
flush	boolean	No	Mandatory in JSP 1.1 with true as the only accepted value.

Example:

```
<jsp:include page="navigation.jsp" />
```

<jsp:param>

The `<jsp:param>` action can be used in the body of a `<jsp:forward>` or `<jsp:include>` action to specify additional request parameters for the target resource, as well as in the body of a `<jsp:params>` action to specify applet parameters. The attributes described in Table A-7 are supported.

Table A-7. <jsp:param> Attributes

Attribute Name	Java Type	Request-Time Value Accepted	Description
name	String	No	Mandatory. The parameter name.
value	String	Yes	Mandatory. The parameter value.

Example:

```
<jsp:include page="navigation.jsp">
    <jsp:param name="bgColor" value="<%= currentBGColor %>" />
</jsp:include>
```

<jsp:params>

The `<jsp:params>` action can only be used in the body of a `<jsp:plugin>` action to enclose a set of `<jsp:param>` actions that are used to specify applet parameters. This action supports no attributes.

Example:

```
<jsp:plugin type="applet" code="Clock2.class"
    codebase="applet"
    jreversion="1.2" width="160" height="150" >
    <jsp:params>
        <jsp:param name="bgcolor" value="ccddff" />
    </jsp:params>
</jsp:plugin>
```

<jsp:plugin>

The `<jsp:plugin>` action generates HTML `<embed>` or `<object>` elements (depending on the browser type) that result in the download of the Java Plugin software (if required) and subsequent execution of the specified Java Applet or JavaBeans component. The body of the action can contain a `<jsp:params>` element to specify applet parameters, and a `<jsp:fallback>` element to specify the text shown in browsers that do not support the `<embed>` or `<object>` HTML elements. For more information about the Java Plugin, see *http://java.sun.com/products/plugin/*.

The attributes described in Table A-8 are supported.

Table A-8. <jsp:plugin> Attributes

Attribute Name	Java Type	Request-Time Value Accepted	Description
align	String	No	Optional. Alignment of the applet area. One of bottom, middle, or top.
archive	String	No	Optional. A comma-separated list of URIs for archives containing classes and other resources that will be preloaded. The classes are loaded using an instance of an AppletClassLoader with the given codebase. Relative URIs for archives are interpreted with respect to the applet's codebase.

Table A-8. <jsp:plugin> Attributes (continued)

Attribute Name	Java Type	Request-Time Value Accepted	Description
code	String	No	Mandatory. The fully qualified class name for the object.
codebase	String	No	Mandatory. The relative URL for the directory that contains the class file. The directory must be a subdirectory to the directory holding the page, according to the HTML 4.0 specification.
height	String	No	Optional. The height of the applet area, in pixels or percentage.
hspace	String	No	Optional. The amount of whitespace to be inserted to the left and right of the applet area, in pixels.
iepluginurl	String	No	Optional. The URL for the location of the Internet Explorer Java Plugin. The default is implementation-dependent.
jreversion	String	No	Optional. Identifies the spec version number of the JRE the component requires in order to operate. The default is 1.1.
name	String	No	Optional. The applet name, used by other applets on the same page that need to communicate with it.
nspluginurl	String	No	Optional. The URL for the location of the Netscape Java Plugin. The default is implementation-dependent.
title	String	No	Optional. Text to be rendered by the browser for the applet in a some way, for instance as a "tool tip."
type	String	No	Mandatory. The type of object to embed, one of applet or bean.
vspace	String	No	Optional. The amount of whitespace to be inserted above and below the applet area, in pixels.
width	String	No	Optional. The width of the applet area, in pixels or percentage.

Example:

```
<jsp:plugin type="applet" code="Clock2.class"
  codebase="applet"
  jreversion="1.2" width="160" height="150" >
  <jsp:params>
    <jsp:param name="bgcolor" value="ccddff" />
  </jsp:params>
  <jsp:fallback>
    Plugin tag OBJECT or EMBED not supported by browser.
```

```
    </jsp:fallback>
  </jsp:plugin>
```

<jsp:setProperty>

The `<jsp:setProperty>` action sets the value of one or more bean properties. The attributes described in Table A-9 are supported.

Table A-9. <jsp:setProperty> Attributes

Attribute Name	Java Type	Request-Time Value Accepted	Description
name	String	No	Mandatory. The name assigned to a bean in one of the JSP scopes.
property	String	No	Mandatory. The name of the bean's property to set, or an asterisk (*) to set all properties with names matching request parameters.
param	String	No	Optional. The name of a request parameter that holds the value to use for the specified property. If omitted, the parameter name and the property name must be the same.
value	See below	Yes	Optional. An explicit value to assign to the property. This attribute cannot be combined with the param attribute.

The property type can be any valid Java type, including primitive types and arrays (i.e., an indexed property). If a runtime attribute value is specified by the value attribute, the type of the expression must match the property's type.

If the value is a string, either in the form of a request parameter value or explicitly specified by the value attribute, it is converted to the property's type as described in Table A-10.

Table A-10. Conversion of String Value to Property Type

Property Type	Conversion Method
boolean or Boolean	Boolean.valueOf(String)
byte or Byte	Byte.valueOf(String)
char or Character	String.charAt(int)
double or Double	Double.valueOf(String)
int or Integer	Integer.valueOf(String)
float or Float	Float.valueOf(String)
long or Long	Long.valueOf(String)

Example:

```
<jsp:setProperty name="user" property="*" />
<jsp:setProperty name="user" property="modDate"
  value="<%= new java.util.Date() %>" />
```

<jsp:useBean>

The <jsp:useBean> action associates a Java bean with a name in one of the JSP scopes and also makes it available as a scripting variable. An attempt is first made to find a bean with the specified name in the specified scope. If it's not found, a new instance of the specified class is created. The attributes described in Table A-11 are supported.

Table A-11. <jsp:useBean> Attributes

Attribute Name	Java Type	Request-Time Value Accepted	Description
beanName	String	Yes	Optional. The name of the bean, as expected by the instantiate() method of the Beans class in the java.beans package.
class	String	No	Optional. The fully qualified class name for the bean.
id	String	No	Mandatory. The name to assign to the bean in the specified scope, as well as the name of the scripting variable.
scope	String	No	Optional. The scope for the bean, one of page, request, session, or application. The default is page.
type	String	No	Optional. The fully qualified type name for the bean (i.e., a superclass or an interface implemented by the bean's class).

Of the optional attributes, at least one of class or type must be specified. If both are specified, class must be assignable to type. The beanName attribute must be combined with the type attribute, and is not valid with the class attribute.

The action is processed in these steps:

1. Attempt to locate an object based on the id and scope attribute values.

2. Define a scripting language variable with the given id of the specified type or class.

3. If the object is found, the variable's value is initialized with a reference to the located object, cast to the specified type or class. This completes the processing of the action. If the action element has a nonempty body, it is ignored.

4. If the object is not found in the specified scope and neither `class` nor `beanName` is specified, a `InstantiationException` is thrown. This completes the processing of the action.

5. If the object is not found in the specified scope, and the `class` attribute specifies a nonabstract class with a public no-arg constructor, a new instance of the class is created and associated with the scripting variable and with the specified name in the specified scope. After this, Step 7 is performed.

   If the object is not found and the specified class doesn't fulfill the requirements, a `InstantiationException` is thrown. This completes the processing of the action.

6. If the object is not found in the specified scope and the `beanName` attribute is specified, the `instantiate()` method of the `java.beans.Beans` class is invoked, with the `ClassLoader` of the JSP implementation class instance and the `beanName` as arguments. If the method succeeds, the new object reference is associated with the scripting variable and with the specified name in the specified scope. After this, Step 7 is performed.

7. If the action element has a nonempty body, the body is processed. The scripting variable is initialized and available within the scope of the body. The text of the body is treated as elsewhere: any template text is passed through to the response, and scriptlets and action tags are evaluated.

   A common use of a nonempty body is to complete initializing the created instance; in that case, the body typically contains `<jsp:setProperty>` actions and scriptlets. This completes the processing of the action.

Example:

```
<jsp:useBean id="clock" class="java.util.Date" />
```

Custom Actions

A custom action element can be developed by a programmer to extend the JSP language. The examples in this book use custom actions for database access, internationalization, access control, and more. They are described in Appendix C, *Book Example Custom Actions and Classes Reference*. The general syntax for custom actions is the same as for the JSP standard actions: a start tag (optionally with attributes), a body, and an end tag. Other elements and template text can be nested in the body. Here's an example:

```
<ora:loop name="anArray" loopId="current" className="String">
  <li><%= current %>
</ ora:loop >
```

The tag library containing the custom actions must be declared by the `taglib` directive, assigning a prefix for the custom action elements (`ora` in this example) before a custom action can be used in a JSP page.

Comments

You can use JSP comments in JSP pages to describe what a scripting element or action is doing:

```
<%-- This is a comment --%>
```

All text between the start and stop tags is ignored by the JSP container and is not included in the response. The comment text can be anything except the character sequence representing the closing tag: --%>.

Besides describing what's going on in the JSP page, comments can also be used to "comment out" portions of the JSP page, for instance during testing:

```
<jsp:useBean id="user" class="com.mycompany.UserBean" />
<%--
<jsp:setProperty name="user" property="*" />
<jsp:setProperty name="user" property="modDate"
  value="<%= new java.util.Date() %>" />
<% boolean isValid = user.isValid(); %>
--%>
```

The action and scripting elements within the comment are not executed.

Escape Characters

Since certain character sequences are used to represent start and stop tags, you sometimes need to escape a character so the container doesn't interpret it as part of a special character sequence.

In a scripting element, if you need to use the characters %> literally, you must escape the greater-than character with a backslash:

```
<% String msg = "Literal %\> must be escaped"; %>
```

To avoid the character sequence <% in template text being interpreted as the start of a scripting element, you must escape the percent sign:

```
This is template text, and <\% is not a start of a scriptlet.
```

In an attribute value, you must use the following escapes:

```
attr='a value with an escaped \' single quote'
attr="a value with an escaped \" double quote"
attr="a value with an escaped \\ backslash"
attr="a value with an escaped %\> scripting end tag"
attr="a value with an escaped <\% scripting start tag"
```

B

JSP API Reference

Besides the JSP elements described in Appendix A, *JSP Elements Syntax Reference*, the JSP specification also defines a number of Java classes and interfaces. Instances of some of these classes are assigned to the implicit variables available to scripting elements in a JSP page. Others are used for development of custom actions and to allow JSP container vendors to encapsulate internal implementations. This appendix describes the classes and interfaces in all these categories.

Implicit Variables

The JSP specification defines a number of implicit variables. Most of the implicit variables have types defined by classes and interfaces in the servlet specification's `javax.servlet.http` package, but two are part of the JSP `javax.servlet.jsp` package and one is part of the Java core API. Scripting elements in a JSP page can use these objects to access request and response information as well as objects saved in one of the JSP scopes: page, request, session, and application.

application

Synopsis

Variable Name:	application
Interface Name:	javax.servlet.ServletContext
Extends:	None
Implemented by:	Internal container-dependent class
JSP Page Type:	Available in both regular JSP pages and error pages

Description

The ServletContext provides resources shared within a web application. It holds attribute values representing the JSP application scope. An attribute value can be an instance of any valid Java class. It also defines a set of methods that a JSP page or a servlet uses to communicate with its container, for example, to get the MIME type of a file, dispatch requests, or write to a log file. The web container is responsible for providing an implementation of the ServletContext interface.

A ServletContext is assigned a specific URI path prefix within a web server. For example, a context could be responsible for all resources under *http://www.mycorp. com/catalog*. All requests that start with the */catalog* request path, which is known as the *context path*, are routed to this servlet context.

Only one instance of a ServletContext may be available to the servlets and JSP pages in a web application. If the web application indicates that it is distributable, there must be only one instance of the ServletContext object in use per application per Java Virtual Machine.

Interface Declaration

```
public interface ServletContext {

    public Object getAttribute(String name);
    public Enumeration getAttributeNames();
    public ServletContext getContext(String uripath);
    public String getInitParameter(String name);
    public Enumeration getInitParameterNames();
    public int getMajorVersion();
    public String getMimeType(String filename);
    public int getMinorVersion();
    public RequestDispatcher getNamedDispatcher(String name);
    public String getRealPath(String path);
    public RequestDispatcher getRequestDispatcher(String path);
    public URL getResource(String path) throws MalformedURLException;
    public InputStream getResourceAsStream(String path);
    public String getServerInfo();
    public void log(String message);
    public void log(String message, Throwable cause);
    public void removeAttribute(String name);
    public void setAttribute(String name, Object attribute);

    // Deprecated methods
    public Servlet getServlet(String name) throws ServletException;
    public Enumeration getServlets();
    public Enumeration getServletNames();
    public void log(Exception exception, String message);
}
```

Methods

`public Object getAttribute(String name)`

Returns the servlet context attribute with the specified name, or `null` if there is no attribute by that name. Context attributes can be set by a servlet or a JSP page, representing the JSP application scope. A container can also use attributes to provide information that is not already available through methods in this interface.

`public java.util.Enumeration getAttributeNames()`

Returns an `Enumeration` of `String` objects containing the attribute names available within this servlet context.

`public ServletContext getContext(String uripath)`

Returns a `ServletContext` object that corresponds to a specified URI in the web container. This method allows servlets and JSP pages to gain access to contexts other than its own. The URI path must be absolute (beginning with /) and is interpreted based on the container's document root. In a security-conscious environment, the container may return `null` for a given URI.

`public String getInitParameter(String name)`

Returns a `String` containing the value of the named context-wide initialization parameter, or `null` if the parameter does not exist. Context initialization parameters can be defined in the web application deployment descriptor.

`public java.util.Enumeration getInitParameterNames()`

Returns the names of the context's initialization parameters as an `Enumeration` of `String` objects, or an empty `Enumeration` if the context has no initialization parameters.

`public int getMajorVersion()`

Returns the major version of the Java servlet API that this web container supports. For example, a container that complies with the Servlet 2.3 API returns 2.

`public String getMimeType(String filename)`

Returns the MIME type of the specified file, or `null` if the MIME type is not known. The MIME type is determined by the configuration of the web container, and may be specified in a web application deployment descriptor.

`public int getMinorVersion()`

Returns the minor version of the Java servlet API that this web container supports. For example, a container that complies with the Servlet 2.3 API returns 3.

`public RequestDispatcher getNamedDispatcher(String name)`

Returns a `RequestDispatcher` object that acts as a wrapper for the named servlet or JSP page. Names can be defined for servlets and JSP pages in the web application deployment descriptor.

`public String getRealPath(String path)`

Returns a `String` containing the filesystem path for a specified context-relative path. This method returns `null` if the web container cannot translate the path to a filesystem path for any reason (such as when the content is being made available from a WAR archive).

`public RequestDispatcher getRequestDispatcher(String path)`

Returns a `RequestDispatcher` object that acts as a wrapper for the resource located at the specified context-relative path. The resource can be dynamic (servlet or JSP) or static (for instance, a regular HTML file).

`public java.net.URL getResource(String path) throws`
`MalformedURLException`

Returns a URL to the resource that is mapped to the specified context-relative path. This method allows the web container to make a resource available to servlets and JSP pages from other sources than a local filesystem, such as a database or a WAR file.

The URL provides access to the resource content directly, so be aware that requesting a JSP page returns a URL for the JSP source code as opposed to the processed result. Use a `RequestDispatcher` instead to include results of an execution.

This method returns `null` if no resource is mapped to the pathname.

`public java.io.InputStream getResourceAsStream(String path)`

Returns the resource mapped to the specified context-relative path as an `InputStream` object. See `getResource()` for details.

`public String getServerInfo()`

Returns the name and version of the servlet container on which the servlet or JSP page is running as a `String` with the format "servername/versionnumber" (for example, "Tomcat/3.2"). Optionally, a container may include other information, such as the Java version and operating system information, within parentheses.

`public void log(String message)`

Writes the specified message to a container log file. The name and type of the log file is container-dependent.

`public void log(String message, Throwable cause)`

Writes the specified message and a stack trace for the specified `Throwable` to the servlet log file. The name and type of the log file is container-dependent.

`public void removeAttribute(String name)`

Removes the attribute with the specified name from the servlet context.

`public void setAttribute(String name, Object attribute)`
Binds an object to the specified attribute name in this servlet context. If the specified name is already used for an attribute, this method removes the old attribute and binds the name to the new attribute.

The following methods are deprecated:

`public Servlet getServlet(String name) throws ServletException`
This method was originally defined to retrieve a servlet from a Servlet-Context. As of the Servlet 2.1 API, this method always returns `null`, and remains only to preserve binary compatibility. This method will be permanently removed in a future version of the Java servlet API.

`public Enumeration getServlets()`
This method was originally defined to return an `Enumeration` of all the servlets known to this servlet context. As of the Servlet 2.1 API, this method always returns an empty `Enumeration`, and remains only to preserve binary compatibility. This method will be permanently removed in a future version of the Java servlet API.

`public Enumeration getServletNames()`
This method was originally defined to return an `Enumeration` of all the servlet names known to this context. As of the Servlet 2.1 API, this method always returns an empty `Enumeration`, and remains only to preserve binary compatibility. This method will be permanently removed in a future version of the Java servlet API.

`public void log(Exception exception, String message)`
This method was originally defined to write an exception's stack trace and an explanatory error message to the web container log file. As of the Servlet 2.1 API, the recommendation is to use `log(String, Throwable)` instead.

config

Synopsis

Variable Name:	config
Interface Name:	javax.servlet.ServletConfig
Extends:	None
Implemented by:	Internal container-dependent class
JSP Page Type:	Available in both regular JSP pages and error pages

Description

A `ServletConfig` instance is used by a web container to pass information to a servlet or JSP page during initialization. The configuration information contains initialization parameters (defined in the web application deployment descriptor) and the `ServletContext` object representing the web application the servlet or JSP page belongs to.

Interface Declaration

```
public interface ServletConfig {
    public String getInitParameter(String name);
    public Enumeration getInitParameterNames();
    public ServletContext getServletContext();
    public String getServletName();
}
```

Methods

`public String getInitParameter(String name)`

Returns a `String` containing the value of the specified servlet or JSP page initialization parameter, or `null` if the parameter does not exist.

`public java.util.Enumeration getInitParameterNames()`

Returns the names of the servlet's or JSP page's initialization parameters as an `Enumeration` of `String` objects, or an empty `Enumeration` if the servlet has no initialization parameters.

`public ServletContext getServletContext()`

Returns a reference to the `ServletContext` that the servlet or JSP page belongs to.

`public String getServletName()`

Returns the name of the servlet instance or JSP page. The name may be assigned in the web application deployment descriptor. For an unregistered (and thus unnamed) servlet instance or JSP page, the servlet's class name is returned.

exception

Synopsis

Variable Name:	`exception`
Class Name:	`java.lang.Throwable`
Extends:	None

Implements:	java.io.Serializable
Implemented by:	Part of the standard Java library
JSP Page Type:	Available only in a page marked as an error page using the page directive isErrorPage attribute

Description

The exception variable is assigned to the subclass of Throwable that caused the error page to be invoked. The Throwable class is the superclass of all errors and exceptions in the Java language. Only objects that are instances of this class (or of one of its subclasses) are thrown by the Java Virtual Machine or by the Java throw statement. See the Java documentation at *http://java.sun.com/docs/index.html* for a description of the Throwable class.

out

Synopsis

Variable Name:	out
Class Name:	javax.servlet.jsp.JspWriter
Extends:	java.io.Writer
Implements:	None
Implemented by:	A concrete subclass of this abstract class is provided as an internal container-dependent class
JSP Page Type:	Available in both regular JSP pages and error pages

Description

The out variable is assigned to a concrete subclass of the JspWriter abstract class by the web container. JspWriter emulates some of the functionality found in the java.io.BufferedWriter and java.io.PrintWriter classes. It differs, however, in that it throws a java.io.IOException from the print methods, while the PrintWriter does not.

If the page directive attribute autoflush is set to true, all the I/O operations on this class automatically flush the contents of the buffer when it's full. If autoflush is set to false, all the I/O operations on this class throw an IOException when the buffer is full.

Class Summary

```
public abstract class JspWriter extends java.io.Writer {
    // Constructor
    protected JspWriter(int bufferSize, boolean autoFlush);
```

```
    // Methods
    public abstract void clear() throws java.io.IOException;
    public abstract void clearBuffer() throws java.io.IOException;
    public abstract void close()throws java.io.IOException;
    public abstract void flush() throws java.io.IOException;
    public int getBufferSize();
    public abstract int getRemaining();
    public boolean isAutoFlush();
}
```

Constructor

`protected JspWriter(int bufferSize, boolean autoFlush)`

Creates an instance with at least the specified buffer size and auto-flush behavior.

Methods

`public abstract void clear() throws java.io.IOException`

Clears the contents of the buffer. If the buffer has already been flushed, throws an `IOException` to signal that some data has already been irrevocably written to the client response stream.

`public abstract void clearBuffer() throws java.io.IOException`

Clears the current contents of the buffer. Unlike `clear()`, this method does not throw an `IOException` if the buffer has already been flushed. It just clears the current content of the buffer and returns.

`public abstract void close() throws java.io.IOException`

Closes the `JspWriter` after flushing it. A call to `flush()` or `write()` after a call to `close()` results in an `IOException` being thrown. If `close()` is called on a previously closed `JspWriter`, it is ignored.

`public abstract void flush() throws java.io.IOException`

Flushes the current contents of the buffer to the underlying writer, and flushes the underlying writer as well. This means the buffered content is delivered to the client immediately.

`public int getBufferSize()`

Returns the size of the buffer in bytes, or 0 if it is not buffered.

`public abstract int getRemaining()`

Returns the number of bytes unused in the buffer.

`public boolean isAutoFlush()`

Returns `true` if this `JspWriter` is set to auto-flush the buffer, `false` otherwise.

page

Synopsis

Variable Name:	page
Class Name:	Object
Extends:	None
Implements:	None
Implemented by:	Part of the standard Java library
JSP Page Type:	Available in both regular JSP pages and error pages

Description

The page variable is assigned to the instance of the JSP implementation class declared as an Object. This variable is rarely, if ever, used. See the Java documentation at *http://java.sun.com/docs/index.html* for a description of the Object class.

pageContext

Synopsis

Variable Name:	pageContext
Class Name:	javax.servlet.jsp.PageContext
Extends:	None
Implements:	None
Implemented by:	A concrete subclass of this abstract class is provided as an internal container-dependent class
JSP Page Type:	Available in both regular JSP pages and error pages

Description

A PageContext instance provides access to all the JSP scopes and several page attributes, and offers a layer above the container implementation details to enable a container to generate portable JSP implementation classes. The JSP page scope is represented by PageContext attributes. A unique instance of this object is created by the web container and assigned to the pageContext variable for each request.

Class Summary

```
public abstract class PageContext {
    // Constants
    public static final int APPLICATION_SCOPE;
```

```
public static final int PAGE_SCOPE;
public static final int REQUEST_SCOPE;
public static final int SESSION_SCOPE;

// Constructor
public PageContext();

// Methods
public abstract java.lang.Object findAttribute(String name);
public abstract void forward(String relativeUrlPath)
   throws ServletException, java.io.IOException;
public abstract Object getAttribute(String name);
public abstract Object getAttribute(String name,
   int scope);
public abstract
   java.util.Enumeration getAttributeNamesInScope(int scope);
public abstract int getAttributesScope(String name);
public abstract Exception getException();
public abstract JspWriter getOut();
public abstract Object getPage();
public abstract ServletRequest getRequest();
public abstract ServletResponse getResponse();
public abstract ServletConfig getServletConfig();
public abstract ServletContext getServletContext();
public abstract HttpSession getSession();
public abstract void handlePageException(Exception e)
   throws ServletException, java.io.IOException;
public abstract void include(String relativeUrlPath)
   throws ServletException, java.io.IOException;
public abstract void initialize(Servlet servlet,
   ServletRequest request, ServletResponse response,
   String errorPageURL, boolean needsSession, int bufferSize,
   boolean autoFlush) throws java.io.IOException,
   IllegalStateException, IllegalArgumentException;
public JspWriter popBody();
public BodyContent pushBody();
public abstract void release();
public abstract void removeAttribute(String name);
public abstract void removeAttribute(String name, int scope);
public abstract void setAttribute(String name, Object attribute);
public abstract void setAttribute(String name, Object o, int scope);
}
```

Constructor

`public PageContext()`

Creates an instance of the `PageContext` class. Typically, an instance is created and initialized by the `JspFactory` class.

Methods

`public abstract Object findAttribute(String name)`

Searches for the named attribute in page, request, session (if valid), and application scopes, in order, and returns the associated value, or `null` if the attribute is not found.

`public abstract void forward(String relativeUrlPath) throws`
`ServletException, java.io.IOException`

This method is used to forward the current request to another active component, such as a servlet or JSP page, in the application. If the specified URI starts with a slash, it's interpreted as a context-relative path; otherwise, it's interpreted as a page-relative path.

The response must not be modified after calling this method, since the response is committed before this method returns.

`public abstract Object getAttribute(String name)`

Returns the object associated with the specified attribute name in the page scope, or `null` if the attribute is not found.

`public abstract Object getAttribute(String name, int scope)`

Returns the object associated with the specified attribute name in the specified scope, or `null` if the attribute is not found. The `scope` argument must be one of the `int` values specified by the `PageContext` static scope variables.

`public abstract java.util.Enumeration`
`getAttributeNamesInScope(int scope)`

Returns an `Enumeration` of `String` objects containing all attribute names for the specified scope. The `scope` argument must be one of the `int` values specified by the `PageContext` static scope variables.

`public abstract int getAttributesScope(String name)`

Returns one of the `int` values specified by the `PageContext` static scope variables for the scope of the object associated with the specified attribute name, or 0 if the attribute is not found.

`public abstract Exception getException()`

Returns the `Exception` that caused the current page to be invoked if its `page` directive `isErrorPage` is set to `true`.

`public abstract JspWriter getOut()`

Returns the current `JspWriter` for the page. When this method is called by a tag handler that implements `BodyTag` or is nested in the body of another action element, the returned object may be an instance of the `BodyContent` subclass.

```
public abstract Object getPage()
```
Returns the object that represents the JSP page implementation class instance that this PageContext is associated with.

```
public abstract ServletRequest getRequest()
```
Returns the current ServletRequest.

```
public abstract ServletResponse getResponse()
```
Returns the current ServletResponse.

```
public abstract ServletConfig getServletConfig()
```
Returns the ServletConfig for this JSP page implementation class instance.

```
public abstract ServletContext getServletContext()
```
Returns the ServletContext for this JSP page implementation class instance.

```
public abstract HttpSession getSession()
```
Returns the current HttpSession, or null if the page directive session attribute is set to false.

```
public abstract void handlePageException(Exception e) throws
ServletException, java.io.IOException
```
This method is intended to be called by the JSP page implementation class only to process unhandled exceptions by forwarding the request exception to either the error page specified by the page directive's errorPage attribute, or to perform an implementation-dependent action if no error page is specified.

```
public abstract void include(String relativeUrlPath) throws
ServletException, java.io.IOException
```
Causes the specified resource to be processed as part of the current request. The current JspWriter is flushed before invoking the target resource, and the output of the target resource's processing of the request is written directly to the current ServletResponse object's writer. If the specified URI starts with a slash, it's interpreted as a context-relative path, otherwise as a page-relative path.

```
public abstract void initialize(Servlet servlet,
ServletRequest request, ServletResponse response,
String errorPageURL, boolean needsSession,
int bufferSize, boolean autoFlush)
throws java.io.IOException, IllegalStateException,
IllegalArgumentException
```
This method is called to initialize a PageContext object so that it can be used by a JSP implementation class to service an incoming request. This method is typically called from the JspFactory.getPageContext() method.

`public JspWriter popBody()`

> This method is intended to be called by the JSP page implementation class only to reassign the previous `JspWriter`, saved by the matching `pushBody()` method, as the current `JspWriter`.

`public BodyContent pushBody()`

> This method is intended to be called by the JSP page implementation class only to get a new `BodyContent` object, and to save the current `JspWriter` on the `PageContext` object's internal stack.

`public abstract void release()`

> Resets the internal state of a `PageContext`, releasing all internal references and preparing the `PageContext` for potential reuse by a later invocation of `initialize()`. This method is typically called from the `JspFactory.releasePageContext()` method.

`public abstract void removeAttribute(String name)`

> Removes the object reference associated with the specified attribute name in the page scope.

`public abstract void removeAttribute(String name, int scope)`

> Removes the object reference associated with the specified attribute name in the specified scope. The `scope` argument must be one of the `int` values specified by the `PageContext` static scope variables.

`public abstract void setAttribute(String name, Object attribute)`

> Saves the specified attribute name and object in the page scope.

`public abstract void setAttribute(String name, Object o, int scope)`

> Saves the specified attribute name and object in the specified scope. The `scope` argument must be one of the `int` values specified by the `PageContext` static scope variables.

request

Synopsis

Variable Name:	`request`
Interface Name:	`javax.servlet.http.HttpServletRequest`
Extends:	`javax.servlet.ServletRequest`
Implemented by:	Internal container-dependent class
JSP Page Type:	Available in both regular JSP pages and error pages

Description

The request variable is assigned a reference to an internal container-dependent class that implements a protocol-dependent interface extending the javax. servlet.ServletRequest. Since HTTP is the only protocol supported by JSP 1.1, the class always implements the javax.servlet.http.HttpServletRequest interface. The method descriptions in this section include all methods from both interfaces.

Interface Declarations

```
public interface ServletRequest {

  public Object getAttribute(String name);
  public java.util.Enumeration getAttributeNames();
  public String getCharacterEncoding();
  public int getContentLength();
  public String getContentType();
  public ServletInputStream getInputStream()
    throws java.io.IOException;
  public java.util.Locale getLocale();
  public java.util.Enumeration getLocales();
  public String getParameter(String name);
  public java.util.Enumeration getParameterNames();
  public String[] getParameterValues();
  public String getProtocol();
  public java.io.BufferedReader getReader()
    throws java.io.IOException;
  public String getRemoteAddr();
  public String getRemoteHost();
  public RequestDispatcher getRequestDispatcher(String path);
  public String getScheme();
  public String getServerName();
  public int getServerPort();
  public boolean isSecure();
  public void removeAttribute(String name);
  public Object setAttribute(String name, Object attribute);

  // Deprecated methods
  public String getRealPath();
}

public interface HttpServletRequest extends ServletRequest {

  public String getAuthType();
  public String getContextPath();
  public Cookie[] getCookies();
  public long getDateHeader(String name);
  public String getHeader(String name);
```

```
    public java.util.Enumeration getHeaderNames();
    public java.util.Enumeration getHeaders(String name);
    public int getIntHeader(String name);
    public String getMethod();
    public String getPathInfo();
    public String getPathTranslated();
    public String getQueryString();
    public String getRequestedSessionId();
    public String getRequestURI();
    public String getRemoteUser();
    public String getServletPath();
    public HttpSession getSession();
    public HttpSession getSession(boolean create);
    public java.security.Principal getUserPrincipal();
    public boolean isRequestedSessionIdFromCookie();
    public boolean isRequestedSessionIdFromURL();
    public boolean isRequestedSessionIdValid();
    public boolean isUserInRole(String role);

    // Deprecated methods
    public boolean isRequestSessionIdFromUrl();
}
```

Methods

`public Object getAttribute(String name)`

Returns the value of the named attribute as an `Object`, or `null` if no attribute of the given name exists.

`public java.util.Enumeration getAttributeNames()`

Returns an `Enumeration` containing the names of the attributes available to this request. The `Enumeration` is empty if the request doesn't have any attributes.

`public String getAuthType()`

Returns the name of the authentication scheme used to protect the servlet, for example BASIC or SSL, or `null` if the servlet is not protected.

`public String getCharacterEncoding()`

Returns the name of the character encoding used in the body of this request, or `null` if the request does not specify a character encoding.

`public int getContentLength()`

Returns the length, in bytes, of the request body made available by the input stream, or −1 if the length is not known.

`public String getContentType()`

Returns the MIME type of the body of the request, or `null` if the type is not known.

`public String getContextPath()`

Returns the portion of the request URI that indicates the context of the request.

`public Cookie[] getCookies()`

Returns an array containing all of the `Cookie` objects the client sent with this request, or `null` if the request contains no cookies.

`public long getDateHeader(String name)`

Returns the value of the specified request header as a `long` value that represents a date value, or –1 if the header is not included in the request.

`public String getHeader(String name)`

Returns the value of the specified request header as a `String`, or `null` if the header is not included with the request.

`public java.util.Enumeration getHeaderNames()`

Returns all the header names contained by this request as an `Enumeration` of `String` objects. The `Enumeration` is empty if the request doesn't have any headers.

`public java.util.Enumeration getHeaders(String name)`

Returns all the values of the specified request header as an `Enumeration` of `String` objects. The `Enumeration` is empty if the request doesn't contain the specified header.

`public ServletInputStream getInputStream() throws java.io.`
`   IOException`

Retrieves the body of the request as binary data using a `ServletInputStream`.

`public int getIntHeader(String name)`

Returns the value of the specified request header as an `int`, or –1 if the header is not included in the request.

`public java.util.Locale getLocale()`

Returns the preferred `Locale` in which the client accepts content, based on the `Accept-Language` header.

`public java.util.Enumeration getLocales()`

Returns an `Enumeration` of `Locale` objects indicating, in decreasing order and starting with the preferred locale, the locales that are acceptable to the client based on the `Accept-Language` header.

`public String getMethod()`

Returns the name of the HTTP method with which this request was made, for example GET, POST, or PUT.

`public String getParameter(String name)`

Returns the value of a request parameter as a `String`, or `null` if the parameter does not exist.

`public java.util.Enumeration getParameterNames()`
Returns an `Enumeration` of `String` objects containing the names of the parameters contained in this request.

`public String[] getParameterValues()`
Returns an array of `String` objects containing all of the values the given request parameter has, or `null` if the parameter does not exist.

`public String getPathInfo()`
Returns any extra path information associated with the URI the client sent when it made this request, or `null` if there is no extra path information. For a JSP page, this method always returns `null`.

`public String getPathTranslated()`
Returns the result of `getPathInfo()` translated into the corresponding file-system path. Returns `null` if `getPathInfo()` returns `null`.

`public String getProtocol()`
Returns the name and version of the protocol the request uses in the form *protocol/majorVersion.minorVersion*, for example, `HTTP/1.1`.

`public String getQueryString()`
Returns the query string that is contained in the request URI after the path.

`public java.io.BufferedReader getReader()`
  `throws java.io.IOException`
Retrieves the body of the request as character data using a `BufferedReader`.

`public String getRemoteAddr()`
Returns the Internet Protocol (IP) address of the client that sent the request.

`public String getRemoteHost()`
Returns the fully qualified name of the client host that sent the request, or the IP address of the client if the hostname cannot be determined.

`public String getRemoteUser()`
Returns the login name of the user making this request if the user has been authenticated, or `null` if the user has not been authenticated.

`public RequestDispatcher getRequestDispatcher(String path)`
Returns a `RequestDispatcher` object that acts as a wrapper for the resource located at the given path. The path must be context-relative or relative to the current URL.

`public String getRequestedSessionId()`
Returns the session ID specified by the client.

`public String getRequestURI()`
Returns the part of this request's URL from the protocol name up to the query string in the first line of the HTTP request.

public String getScheme()
>   Returns the name of the scheme (protocol) used to make this request, for
>   example, http, https, or ftp.

public String getServerName()
>   Returns the hostname of the server that received the request.

public int getServerPort()
>   Returns the port number on which this request was received.

public String getServletPath()
>   Returns the part of this request's URI that calls the servlet. For a JSP page, this
>   is the complete context-relative path for the JSP page.

public HttpSession getSession()
>   Returns the current HttpSession associated with this request. If the request
>   does not have a session, a new HttpSession object is created, associated with
>   the request, and returned.

public HttpSession getSession(boolean create)
>   Returns the current HttpSession associated with this request. If there is no
>   current session and create is true, a new HttpSession object is created,
>   associated with the request, and returned. If create is false and the request
>   is not associated with a session, this method returns null.

public java.security.Principal getUserPrincipal()
>   Returns a Principal object containing the name of the current authenti-
>   cated user, or null if the user is not authenticated.

public boolean isRequestedSessionIdFromCookie()
>   Checks whether the requested session ID came in as a cookie.

public boolean isRequestedSessionIdFromURL()
>   Checks whether the requested session ID came in as part of the request URL.

public boolean isRequestedSessionIdValid()
>   Checks whether the requested session ID is still valid.

public boolean isSecure()
>   Returns a boolean indicating whether this request was made using a secure
>   channel, such as HTTPS.

public boolean isUserInRole(String role)
>   Returns a boolean indicating whether the authenticated user is included in
>   the specified logical "role."

public void removeAttribute(String name)
>   Removes the specified attribute from this request.

public Object setAttribute(String name, Object attribute)
>   Stores the specified attribute in this request.

The following methods are deprecated:

`public String getRealPath()`

 As of the Servlet 2.1 API, use `ServletContext.getRealPath(String)` instead.

`public boolean isRequestSessionIdFromUrl()`

 As of the Servlet 2.1 API, use `isRequestedSessionIdFromURL()` instead.

---

response

Synopsis

Variable Name:	response
Interface Name:	javax.servlet.http.HttpServletResponse
Extends:	javax.servlet.ServletResponse
Implemented by:	Internal container-dependent class
JSP Page Type:	Available in both regular JSP pages and error pages

Description

The `response` variable is assigned a reference to an internal container-dependent class that implements a protocol-dependent interface extending the `javax.servlet.ServletResponse`. Since HTTP is the only protocol supported by JSP 1.1, the class always implements the `javax.servlet.http.HttpServlet-Response` interface. The method descriptions in this section include all methods from both interfaces.

Interface Declarations

```
public interface ServletResponse {

    public void flushBuffer() throws IOException;
    public int getBufferSize();
    public String getCharacterEncoding();
    public Locale getLocale();
    public ServletOutputStream getOutputStream() throws IOException
    public PrintWriter getWriter throws IOException
    public boolean isCommitted();
    public void reset();
    public void setBufferSize(int size);
    public void setContentLength(int length);
    public void setContentType(String type);
    public void setLocale(Locale locale);
}
```

```
public interface HttpServletResponse extends ServletResponse {
  public void addCookie(Cookie cookie);
  public void addDateHeader(String headername, long date);
  public void addHeader(String headername, String value);
  public void addIntHeader(String headername, int value);
  public boolean containsHeader(String name);
  public String encodeRedirectURL(String url);
  public String encodeURL(String url);
  public void sendError(int status) throws IOException;
  public void sendError(int status, String message)
     throws IOException;
  public void sendRedirect(String location) throws IOException;
  public void setDateHeader(String headername, long date);
  public void setHeader(String headername, String value);
  public void setIntHeader(String headername, int value);
  public void setStatus(int statuscode);

  // Deprecated methods
  public String encodeRedirectUrl(String url);}
  public String encodeUrl(String url);
  public void setStatus(int statuscode, String message);
}
```

Methods

`public void addCookie(Cookie cookie)`
> Adds the specified cookie to the response.

`public void addDateHeader(String headername, long date)`
> Adds a response header with the given name and date value. The date is specified in terms of milliseconds since the epoch (January 1, 1970, 00:00:00 GMT).

`public void addHeader(String headername, String value)`
> Adds a response header with the specified name and value.

`public void addIntHeader(String headername, int value)`
> Adds a response header with the given name and integer value.

`public boolean containsHeader(String name)`
> Returns a `boolean` indicating whether the named response header has already been set.

`public String encodeRedirectURL(String url)`
> Encodes the specified URL for use in the `sendRedirect()` method by including the session ID in it. If encoding (URL rewriting) is not needed, it returns the URL unchanged.

`public String encodeURL(String url)`
> Encodes the specified URL for use in a reference element (e.g., `<a>`) by including the session ID in it. If encoding (URL rewriting) is not needed, it returns the URL unchanged.

`public void flushBuffer() throws IOException`
 Forces any content in the response body buffer to be written to the client.

`public int getBufferSize()`
 Returns the actual buffer size (in bytes) used for the response. If no buffering is used, this method returns 0.

`public String getCharacterEncoding()`
 Returns the name of the charset used for the MIME body sent in this response.

`public Locale getLocale()`
 Returns the locale assigned to the response. This is either a `Locale` object for the server's default locale, or the `Locale` set with `setLocale()`.

`public ServletOutputStream getOutputStream() throws IOException`
 Returns a `ServletOutputStream` suitable for writing binary data in the response. It's recommended that this method is not used in a JSP page, since JSP pages are intended for text data.

`public PrintWriter getWriter throws IOException`
 Returns a `PrintWriter` object that can send character text to the client. It's recommended that this method is not used in a JSP page, since it may interfere with the container's writer mechanism. Use the `PageContext` methods instead to get the current `JspWriter`.

`public boolean isCommitted()`
 Returns a `boolean` indicating if the response has been committed.

`public void reset()`
 Clears any data that exists in the buffer as well as the status code and headers. If the response has been committed, this method throws an `IllegalState-Exception`.

`public void sendError(int status) throws IOException`
 Sends an error response to the client using the specified status. If the response has already been committed, this method throws an `IllegalState-Exception`. After using this method, the response should be considered to be committed and should not be written to.

`public void sendError(int status, String message) throws IOException`
 Sends an error response to the client using the specified status code and a descriptive message. If the response has already been committed, this method throws an `IllegalStateException`. After using this method, the response should be considered to be committed and should not be written to.

`public void sendRedirect(String location) throws IOException`

Sends a temporary redirect response to the client using the specified redirect location URL. This method can accept relative URLs; the servlet container converts the relative URL to an absolute URL before sending the response to the client. If the response is already committed, this method throws an `IllegalStateException`. After using this method, the response should be considered to be committed and should not be written to.

`public void setBufferSize(int size)`

Sets the preferred buffer size (in bytes) for the body of the response. The servlet container uses a buffer at least as large as the size requested. The actual buffer size used can be found using `getBufferSize()`.

`public void setContentLength(int length)`

Sets the length (in bytes) of the content body in the response. In HTTP servlets, this method sets the HTTP `Content-Length` header. It's recommended that this method is not used in a JSP page, since it may interfere with the container's writer mechanism.

`public void setContentType(String type)`

Sets the content type of the response being sent to the client.

`public void setDateHeader(String headername, long date)`

Sets a response header with the given name and date value. The date is specified in terms of milliseconds since the epoch (January 1, 1970, 00:00:00 GMT). If the header is already set, the new value overwrites the previous one.

`public void setHeader(String headername, String value)`

Sets a response header with the given name and value. If the header is already set, the new value overwrites the previous one.

`public void setIntHeader(String headername, int value)`

Sets a response header with the given name and integer value. If the header is already set, the new value overwrites the previous one.

`public void setLocale(Locale locale)`

Sets the locale of the response, setting the headers (including the `Content-Type` header's charset) as appropriate.

`public void setStatus(int statuscode)`

Sets the status code for this response. As opposed to the `sendError()` method, this method only sets the status code; it doesn't add a body or commit the response.

The following methods are deprecated:

`public String encodeRedirectUrl(String url)`

As of the Servlet 2.1 API, use `encodeRedirectURL(String url)` instead.

`public String encodeUrl(String url)`

   As of the Servlet 2.1 API, use `encodeURL(String url)` instead.

`public void setStatus(int statuscode, String message)`

   Due to ambiguous meaning of the message parameter, different methods should be used as of the Servlet 2.1 API. To set a status code, use `setStatus(int)`; to send an error with a description, use `sendError(int, String)`.

session

Synopsis

Variable Name:	session
Interface Name:	javax.servlet.http.HttpSession
Extends:	None
Implemented by:	Internal container-dependent class
JSP Page Type:	Available in both regular JSP pages and error pages, unless the page directive session attribute is set to false

Description

The `session` variable is assigned a reference to the `HttpSession` object that represents the current client session. Information stored as `HttpSession` attributes corresponds to objects in the JSP session scope.

By default, the session persists for a time period specified in the web application deployment descriptor, across more than one page request from the user. The container can maintain a session in many ways, such as using cookies or rewriting URLs.

Interface Declarations

```
public interface HttpSession {

    public Object getAttribute(String name);
    public java.util.Enumeration getAttributeNames();
    public long getCreationTime();
    public String getId();
    public long getLastAccessedTime();
    public int getMaxInactiveInterval();
    public void invalidate();
    public boolean isNew();
    public void removeAttribute(String name);
    public void setAttribute(String name, Object attribute);
    public void setMaxInactiveInterval(int interval);
```

```
        // Deprecated methods
        public HttpSessionContext getSessionContext();
        public Object getValue(String name);
        public String[] getValueNames();
        public void putValue(String name, Object value);
        public void removeValue(String name);
    }
```

Methods

public Object getAttribute(String name)

Returns the object associated with the specified name in this session, or null if the object is not found.

public java.util.Enumeration getAttributeNames()

Returns an Enumeration of String objects containing the names of all the objects in this session.

public long getCreationTime()

Returns the time when this session was created, measured in milliseconds since the epoch (January 1, 1970, 00:00:00 GMT).

public String getId()

Returns a string containing the unique identifier assigned to this session.

public long getLastAccessedTime()

Returns the last time the client sent a request associated with this session, measured in milliseconds since the epoch (January 1, 1970, 00:00:00 GMT).

public int getMaxInactiveInterval()

Returns the maximum time interval, in seconds, that the servlet container will keep this session active between client accesses.

public void invalidate()

Invalidates this session and unbinds any objects bound to it, calling the valueUnbound() methods of all objects in the session implementing the HttpSessionBindingListener interface.

public boolean isNew()

Returns true if a request for this session has not yet been received from the client.

public void removeAttribute(String name)

Removes the object bound with the specified name from this session.

public void setAttribute(String name, Object attribute)

Associates the specified object with this session using the name specified.

public void setMaxInactiveInterval(int interval)

Specifies the time, in seconds, between client requests before the servlet container invalidates this session.

The following methods are deprecated:

public HttpSessionContext getSessionContext()
> As of the Servlet 2.1 API, this method is deprecated and has no replacement.

public Object getValue(String name)
> As of the Servlet 2.2 API, this method is replaced by getAttribute(String).

public String[] getValueNames()
> As of the Servlet 2.2 API, this method is replaced by getAttributeNames().

public void putValue(String name, Object value)
> As of the Servlet 2.2 API, this method is replaced by setAttribute(String, Object).

public void removeValue(String name)
> As of the Servlet 2.2 API, this method is replaced by setAttribute(String, Object).

Servlet Classes Accessible Through Implicit Variables

This section contains descriptions of the servlet API classes that methods on the objects assigned to the implicit variables can return.

Cookie

Synopsis

Class Name:	javax.servlet.http.Cookie
Extends:	None
Implements:	Cloneable
Implemented by:	Internal container-dependent class. Most containers use the reference implementation of the class (developed in the Apache Jakarta project).

Description

A Cookie object represents an HTTP cookie: a small amount of information sent by a servlet to a web browser, saved by the browser, and later sent back to the server with new requests. A cookie's value can uniquely identify a client, so cookies are commonly used for session management. A cookie has a name, a single value, and optional attributes such as comments, path and domain qualifiers, a maximum age, and a version number.

This class supports both the Version 0 (the informal specification first introduced by Netscape) and the Version 1 (formally defined by RFC 2109) cookie specifications. By default, cookies are created using Version 0 to ensure the best interoperability.

Class Summary

```
public class Cookie implements Cloneable {
    // Constructor
    public Cookie(String name, String value);

    // Methods
    public Object clone();
    public String getComment();
    public String getDomain();
    public int getMaxAge();
    public String getName();
    public String getPath();
    public boolean getSecure();
    public String getValue();
    public int getVersion();
    public void setComment(String comment);
    public void setDomain(String domain);
    public void setMaxAge(int expiry);
    public void setPath(String uriPath);
    public void setSecure();
    public void setValue(String value);
    public void setVersion(int version);
}
```

Constructor

public Cookie(String name, String value)
    Creates a new instance with the specified name and value.

Methods

public Object clone()
    Overrides the standard Object.clone() method to return a copy of this cookie.

public String getComment()
    Returns the comment describing the purpose of this cookie, or null if the cookie has no comment.

public String getDomain()
    Returns the domain name set for this cookie.

public int getMaxAge()
    Returns the maximum age of the cookie, specified in seconds. A value of −1 indicates that the cookie will persist until browser shutdown.

`public String getName()`
> Returns the name of the cookie.

`public String getPath()`
> Returns the server path to which the browser returns this cookie.

`public boolean getSecure()`
> Returns `true` if the browser is sending cookies only over a secure protocol, or `false` if the browser can send cookies using any protocol.

`public String getValue()`
> Returns the value of the cookie.

`public int getVersion()`
> Returns the version of the protocol this cookie complies with. A value of 0 means that the cookie should comply with the original Netscape specification; 1 means that it should comply with RFC 2109.

`public void setComment(String comment)`
> Specifies a comment that describes a cookie's purpose.

`public void setDomain(String domain)`
> Specifies the domain within which this cookie should be presented.

`public void setMaxAge(int expiry)`
> Sets the maximum age of the cookie in seconds.

`public void setPath(String uriPath)`
> Specifies a server path to which the client should return the cookie.

`public void setSecure()`
> Indicates to the browser whether the cookie should be sent only using a secure protocol, such as HTTPS.

`public void setValue(String value)`
> Assigns a new value to a cookie after the cookie is created.

`public void setVersion(int version)`
> Sets the version of the cookie protocol this cookie complies with.

RequestDispatcher

Synopsis

Interface Name:	`javax.servlet.RequestDispatcher`
Extends:	None
Implemented by:	Internal container-dependent class

Description

The RequestDispatcher class defines an object that receives requests from the client and sends them to any resource (such as a servlet, HTML file, or JSP file) in the same web container. The container creates the RequestDispatcher object, which is used as a wrapper around a resource located at a particular URI path or identified by a particular name.

Interface Declarations

```
public interface RequestDispatcher {
  public void forward(ServletRequest req, ServletResponse res);
  public void include(ServletRequest req, ServletResponse res);
}
```

Methods

public void forward(ServletRequest req, ServletResponse res)

Forwards a request from a servlet to another resource (servlet, JSP file, or static file) on the server. For a RequestDispatcher obtained via the getRequestDispatcher() method, the ServletRequest object has its path elements and parameters adjusted to match the path of the target resource.

This method must be called before the response has been committed to the client (before response body output has been flushed). If the response has already been committed, this method throws an IllegalStateException. Uncommitted output in the response buffer is automatically cleared before the forward.

The request and response parameters must be the same objects that were passed to the calling servlet's service method.

public void include(ServletRequest req, ServletResponse res)

Includes the response generated by a resource (servlet, JSP page, static file) in the response.

The ServletRequest object's path elements and parameters remain unchanged from the caller's. The included servlet cannot change the response status code or set headers; any attempt to make a change is ignored.

The request and response parameters must be the same objects that were passed to the calling servlet's service method.

Tag Extension Classes

The JSP specification defines a number of classes and interfaces in the javax. servlet.jsp.tagext package. These classes are used to develop tag handler classes for JSP custom actions. This section contains descriptions of each class and interface. Chapters 16, *Developing JSP Custom Actions*, and 17, *Developing Database-Access Components*, show examples of how you can use these classes and interfaces to develop custom actions.

BodyContent

Synopsis

Class Name:	`javax.servlet.jsp.tagext.BodyContent`
Extends:	`javax.servlet.jsp.JspWriter`
Implements:	None
Implemented by:	Internal container-dependent class

Description

The container creates an instance of the `BodyContent` class to encapsulate the element body of a custom action element if the corresponding tag handler implements the `BodyTag` interface. The container makes the `BodyContent` instance available to the tag handler by calling the `setBodyContent()` method, so the tag handler can process the body content.

Class Summary

```
public abstract class BodyContent extends JspWriter {
   // Constructor
   protected BodyContent(JspWriter e);

   // Methods
   public void clearBody();
   public void flush() throws java.io.IOException;
   public JspWriter getEnclosingWriter();
   public abstract java.io.Reader getReader();
   public abstract String getString();
   public abstract void writeOut(java.io.Writer out)
      throws java.io.IOException;
}
```

Constructor

`protected BodyContent(JspWriter e)`

Creates a new instance with the specified `JspWriter` as the enclosing writer.

Methods

`public void clearBody()`

Removes all buffered content for this instance.

public void flush() throws java.io.IOException
> Overwrites the behavior inherited from JspWriter to always throw an IOException, since it's invalid to flush a BodyContent instance.

public JspWriter getEnclosingWriter()
> Returns the enclosing JspWriter, which is either the top level JspWriter or the JspWriter (BodyContent subclass) of the parent tag handler.

public abstract java.io.Reader getReader()
> Returns the value of this BodyContent as a Reader with the content produced by evaluating the element's body.

public abstract String getString()
> Returns the value of this BodyContent as a String with the content produced by evaluating the element's body.

public abstract void writeOut(java.io.Writer out) throws java.io.IOException
> Writes the content of this BodyContent into a Writer.

BodyTag

Synopsis

Interface Name:	javax.servlet.jsp.tagext.BodyTag
Extends:	javax.servlet.jsp.tagext.Tag
Implemented by:	Custom action tag handler classes and javax.servlet.jsp.tagext.BodyTagSupport

Description

The BodyTag interface must be implemented by tag handler classes that need access to the body contents of the corresponding custom action element, perhaps to perform a transformation of the contents before it's included in the response. This interface must also be implemented by tag handlers that need to iterate over the body of a custom action element.

Interface Declarations

```
public interface BodyTag extends Tag {
    // Constants
    public static final int EVAL_BODY_TAG;

    // Methods
    public int doAfterBody() throws JspException;
    public void doInitBody() throws JspException;
    public void setBodyContent(BodyContent b);
}
```

Methods

`public int doAfterBody() throws JspException`

> Performs actions after the body has been evaluated. It is invoked after every body evaluation. If this method returns `EVAL_BODY_TAG`, the body is evaluated again, typically after changing the value of variables used in the body. If it returns `SKIP_BODY`, the processing continues with a call to `doEndTag()`.
>
> If the element body is empty, or if `doStartTag()` returns `SKIP_BODY`, this method is not invoked.

`public void doInitBody() throws JspException`

> Prepares for evaluation of the body. This method is invoked once per action invocation by the page implementation, after a new `BodyContent` has been obtained and set on the tag handler via the `setBodyContent()` method, just before the evaluation of the element's body.
>
> If the element body is empty, or if `doStartTag()` returns `SKIP_BODY`, this method is not invoked.

`public void setBodyContent(BodyContent b)`

> Sets the `BodyContent` created for this tag handler. If the element body is empty, or if `doStartTag()` returns `SKIP_BODY`, this method is not invoked.

BodyTagSupport

Synopsis

Class Name:	`javax.servlet.jsp.tagext.BodyTagSupport`
Extends:	`javax.servlet.jsp.tagext.TagSupport`
Implements:	`BodyTag`
Implemented by:	Internal container-dependent class. Most containers use the reference implementation of the class (developed in the Apache Jakarta project).

Description

`BodyTagSupport` is a support class that provides default implementations of all `BodyTag` interface methods. It's intended to be used as a superclass for tag handlers that need access to the body contents of the corresponding custom action element.

Class Summary

```
public class BodyTagSupport extends TagSupport implements BodyTag {
    // Constructor
    public BodyTagSupport();
```

```
// Methods
public int doAfterBody() throws JspException;
public int doEndTag() throws JspException;
public void doInitBody();
public BodyContent getBodyContent();
public JspWriter getPreviousOut();
public void release();
public void setBodyContent(BodyContent b);
}
```

Constructor

public BodyTagSupport()

Creates a new BodyTagSupport instance.

Methods

public int doAfterBody() throws JspException

Returns SKIP_BODY.

public int doEndTag() throws JspException

Returns EVAL_PAGE.

public void doInitBody()

This method currently does nothing. You should override this method in a class that extends BodyTagSupport to perform initialization.

public BodyContent getBodyContent()

Returns the BodyContent object assigned to this instance.

public JspWriter getPreviousOut()

Returns the enclosing writer of the BodyContent object assigned to this instance.

public void release()

Removes the references to all objects held by this instance.

public void setBodyContent(BodyContent b)

Saves a reference to the assigned BodyContent as an instance variable.

Tag

Synopsis

Interface Name:	javax.servlet.jsp.tagext.Tag
Extends:	None
Implemented by:	Custom action tag handler classes and javax.servlet.jsp.tagext. TagSupport

Description

The Tag interface should be implemented by tag handler classes that do not need access to the body contents of the corresponding custom action element, and that do not need to iterate over the body of a custom action element.

Interface Declarations

```
public interface Tag {
   // Constants
   public static final int EVAL_BODY_INCLUDE;
   public static final int EVAL_PAGE;
   public static final int SKIP_BODY;
   public static final int SKIP_PAGE;

   // Methods
   public int doEndTag() throws JspException;
   public int doStartTag() throws JspException;
   public Tag getParent();
   public void release();
   public void setPageContext(PageContext pc);
   public void setParent(Tag t)
}
```

Methods

public int doEndTag() throws JspException

Performs actions when the end tag is encountered. If this method returns SKIP_ PAGE, execution of the rest of the page is aborted and the _jspService() method of JSP page implementation class returns. If EVAL_PAGE is returned, the code following the custom action in the _jspService() method is executed.

public int doStartTag() throws JspException

Performs actions when the start tag is encountered. This method is called by the JSP container after all property setter methods have been called. The return value from this method controls how the action's body is handled, if there is one. If it returns EVAL_BODY_INCLUDE, the JSP container evaluates the body and processes possible JSP elements. The result of the evaluation is then added to the response. If SKIP_BODY is returned, the body is ignored.

A tag handler class that implements the BodyTag interface (extending the Tag interface) can return EVAL_BODY_TAG instead of EVAL_BODY_INCLUDE. The JSP container then creates a BodyContent instance and makes it available to the tag handler for special processing.

public Tag getParent()

Returns the tag handler's parent (the Tag instance for the enclosing action element, if any) or null if the tag handler doesn't have a parent.

```
public void release()
```
Removes the references to all objects held by this instance.

```
public void setPageContext(PageContext pc)
```
Saves a reference to the current `PageContext`.

```
public void setParent(Tag t)
```
Saves a reference to the tag handler's parent (the `Tag` instance for the enclosing action element).

TagAttributeInfo

Synopsis

Class Name:	`javax.servlet.jsp.tagext.TagAttributeInfo`
Extends:	None
Implements:	None
Implemented by:	Internal container-dependent class. Most containers use the reference implementation of the class (developed in the Apache Jakarta project).

Description

`TagAttributeInfo` instances are created by the JSP container to provide information found in the Tag Library Descriptor (TLD) about each attribute supported by a custom action. It's primarily intended to be used by the JSP container itself during the translation phase.

Class Summary

```
public class TagAttributeInfo {
  // Constructor
  public TagAttributeInfo(String name, boolean required,
    boolean rtexprvalue, String type, boolean reqTime);

  // Methods
  public boolean canBeRequestTime();
  public static TagAttributeInfo getIdAttribute(TagAttributeInfo[] a);
  public String getName();
  public String getTypeName();
  public boolean isRequired();
  public String toString();
}
```

Constructor

public TagAttributeInfo(String name, boolean required,
    boolean rtexprvalue, String type, boolean reqTime)
    Creates a new instance with the specified information from the TLD. Instances
    of this class should be created only by the JSP container.

Methods

public boolean canBeRequestTime()
    Returns true if a request time attribute value can be used for this attribute.

public static TagAttributeInfo
    getIdAttribute(TagAttributeInfo[] a)
    Convenience method that returns the TagAttributeInfo instance in the
    specified array that represents an attribute named id, or null if not found.

public String getName()
    Returns the attribute name.

public String getTypeName()
    Returns the attribute's Java type (a fully qualified class or interface name).

public boolean isRequired()
    Returns true if this attribute is required, false otherwise.

public String toString()
    Returns a String representation of the attribute info.

TagData

Synopsis

Class Name:	javax.servlet.jsp.tagext.TagData
Extends:	None
Implements:	Cloneable
Implemented by:	Internal container-dependent class. Most containers use the reference implementation of the class (developed in the Apache Jakarta project).

Description

TagData instances are created by the JSP container during the translation phase,
and provide information about the attribute values specified for a custom action to
the TagExtraInfo subclass for the corresponding tag handler, if any.

Class Summary

```
public class TagData implements Cloneable {
    // Constants
    public static final Object REQUEST_TIME_VALUE;

    // Constructor
    public TagData(Object[][] atts);
    public TagData(java.util.Hashtable attrs);

    // Methods
    public Object getAttribute(String attName);
    public String getAttributeString(String attName);
    public String getId();
    public void setAttribute(String attName, Object value);
}
```

Constructors

`public TagData(Object[][] atts)`

Creates a new instance with the attribute name/value pairs specified by the `Object[][]`. Element 0 of each `Object[]` contains the name, and Element 1 contains the value or `REQUEST_TIME_VALUE`, if the attribute value is defined as a request time value (a JSP expression).

`public TagData(java.util.Hashtable attrs)`

Creates a new instance with the attribute name/value pairs specified by the `Hashtable`.

Methods

`public Object getAttribute(String attName)`

Returns the specified attribute value as a `String` or as the `REQUEST_TIME_VALUE` Object, if the attribute value is defined as a request time value (a JSP expression).

`public String getAttributeString(String attName)`

Returns the specified attribute value as a `String`. A `ClassCastException` is thrown if the attribute value is defined as a request time value (a JSP expression).

`public String getId()`

Returns the attribute named `id` as a `String`, or `null` if not found.

`public void setAttribute(String attName, Object value)`

Sets the specified attribute to the specified value.

TagExtraInfo

Synopsis

Class Name:	`javax.servlet.jsp.tagext.TagExtraInfo`
Extends:	None
Implements:	None
Implemented by:	Internal container-dependent class. Most containers use the reference implementation of the class (developed in the Apache Jakarta project).

Description

For custom actions that create scripting variables or require additional translation time validation of the tag attributes, a subclass of the `TagExtraInfo` class must be developed for the custom action and declared in the Tag Library Descriptor. The JSP container creates an instance of the `TagExtraInfo` subclass during the translation phase.

Class Summary

```
public abstract class TagExtraInfo {
    // Constructor
    public TagExtraInfo();

    // Methods
    public TagInfo getTagInfo();
    public VariableInfo[] getVariableInfo(TagData data);
    public boolean isValid(TagData data);
    public void setTagInfo(TagInfo tagInfo);
}
```

Constructor

`public TagExtraInfo()`
    Creates a new `TagExtraInfo` instance.

Methods

`public TagInfo getTagInfo()`
    Returns the `TagInfo` instance for the custom action associated with this `TagExtraInfo` instance. The `TagInfo` instance is set by the `setTagInfo()` method (called by the container).

`public VariableInfo[] getVariableInfo(TagData data)`
    Returns a `VariableInfo[]` with information about scripting variables created by the tag handler class associated with this `TagExtraInfo` instance. The

default implementation returns an empty array. A subclass must override this method if the corresponding tag handler creates scripting variables.

public boolean isValid(TagData data)

Returns true if the set of attribute values specified for the custom action associated with this TagExtraInfo instance is valid, false otherwise. The default implementation returns true. A subclass can override this method if the validation performed by the JSP container based on the Tag Library Descriptor information is not enough.

public void setTagInfo(TagInfo tagInfo)

Sets the TagInfo for this instance. This method is called by the JSP container before any of the other methods are called.

TagInfo

Synopsis

Class Name:	javax.servlet.jsp.tagext.TagInfo
Extends:	None
Implements:	None
Implemented by:	Internal container-dependent class. Most containers use the reference implementation of the class (developed in the Apache Jakarta project).

Description

TagInfo instances are created by the JSP container to provide information found in the Tag Library Descriptor (TLD) about a custom action, as well as information about the attribute values used in a JSP page for an instance of the custom action. It's primarily intended to be used by the JSP container itself during the translation phase.

Class Summary

```
public class TagInfo {
    // Constants
    public static final String BODY_CONTENT_EMPTY;
    public static final String BODY_CONTENT_JSP;
    public static final String BODY_CONTENT_TAG_DEPENDENT;

    // Constructor
    public TagInfo(String tagName, String tagClassName,
        String bodycontent, String infoString, TagLibraryInfo taglib,
        TagExtraInfo tagExtraInfo, TagAttributeInfo[] attributeInfo);
```

```
// Methods
public TagAttributeInfo[] getAttributes();
public String getBodyContent();
public String getInfoString();
public String getTagClassName();
public TagExtraInfo getTagExtraInfo();
public TagLibraryInfo getTagLibrary();
public String getTagName();
public VariableInfo[] getVariableInfo(TagData data);
public boolean isValid(TagData data);
public String toString();
}
```

Constructor

```
public TagInfo(String tagName, String tagClassName,
  String bodycontent, String infoString, TagLibraryInfo taglib,
  TagExtraInfo tagExtraInfo, TagAttributeInfo[] attributeInfo)
```
Creates a new instance with the specified values.

Methods

`public TagAttributeInfo[] getAttributes()`
Returns information from the TLD about all attribute values, or null if no attributes are declared.

`public String getBodyContent()`
Returns one of BODY_CONTENT_EMPTY, BODY_CONTENT_JSP, or BODY_CONTENT_TAG_DEPENDENT, based on the value in the TLD.

`public String getInfoString()`
Returns the tag information string from the TLD, or null if there is no info.

`public String getTagClassName()`
Returns the tag handler class name declared in the TLD.

`public TagExtraInfo getTagExtraInfo()`
Returns an instance of the TagExtraInfo subclass for the tag, or null if no class is declared in the TLD.

`public TagLibraryInfo getTagLibrary()`
Returns a TagLibraryInfo instance for the library the tag is part of.

`public String getTagName()`
Returns the name for the tag declared in the TLD.

`public VariableInfo[] getVariableInfo(TagData data)`
Returns information about scripting variables created by the tag handler, or null if no variables are created. This information is obtained from the TagExtraInfo for the tag, if any.

```
public boolean isValid(TagData data)
```
Returns true if the set of attributes specified for the custom action associated with this TagExtraInfo instance is valid, false otherwise. This information is obtained from the TagExtraInfo for the tag, if any.

```
public String toString()
```
Returns a String representation of all information held by the instance.

TagLibraryInfo

Synopsis

Class Name:	javax.servlet.jsp.tagext.TagLibraryInfo
Extends:	None
Implements:	None
Implemented by:	Internal container-dependent class. Most containers use the reference implementation of the class (developed in the Apache Jakarta project).

Description

TagLibraryInfo instances are created by the JSP container to provide information found in the Tag Library Descriptor (TLD) about a tag library, as well as information from the taglib directive used in a JSP page. It's primarily intended to be used by the JSP container itself during the translation phase.

Class Summary

```
public abstract class TagLibraryInfo {
   // Constructor
   protected TagLibraryInfo(String prefix, String uri);

   // Methods
   public String getInfoString();
   public String getPrefixString();
   public String getReliableURN();
   public String getRequiredVersion();
   public String getShortName();
   public TagInfo getTag(String shortname);
   public TagInfo[] getTags();
   public String getURI();
}
```

Constructor

`protected TagLibraryInfo(String prefix, String uri)`
    Creates a new instance with the specified prefix and URI (from the `taglib` directive in the JSP page).

Methods

`public java.lang.String getInfoString()`
    Returns the information string from the TLD for the library.

`public String getPrefixString()`
    Returns the prefix assigned by the `taglib` directive for the library.

`public String getReliableURN()`
    Returns the URI value from the TLD for the library.

`public String getRequiredVersion()`
    Returns the required JSP version from the TLD for the library.

`public String getShortName()`
    Returns the short name from the TLD for the library.

`public TagInfo getTag(String shortname)`
    Returns a `TagInfo` instance for the specified tag in the library.

`public TagInfo[] getTags()`
    Returns a `TagInfo[]` for all tags in the library.

`public String getURI()`
    Returns the URI assigned by the `taglib` directive for the library.

TagSupport

Synopsis

Class Name:	`javax.servlet.jsp.tagext.TagSupport`
Extends:	None
Implements:	`Tag, java.io.Serializable`
Implemented by:	Internal container-dependent class. Most containers use the reference implementation of the class (developed in the Apache Jakarta project).

Description

`TagSupport` is a support class that provides default implementations of all `Tag` interface methods. It's intended to be used as a superclass for tag handlers that do not need access to the body contents of the corresponding custom action element.

Class Summary

```
public class TagSupport implements Tag, java.io.Serializable {
  // Constructor
  public TagSupport();

  // Methods
  public int doEndTag() throws JspException;
  public int doStartTag() throws JspException;
  public static final Tag findAncestorWithClass(Tag from, Class klass);
  public String getId();
  public Tag getParent();
  public Object getValue(String k);
  public java.util.Enumeration getValues();
  public void release();
  public void removeValue(String k);
  public void setPageContext(PageContext pageContext);
  public void setId(String id);
  public void setParent(Tag t);
  public void setValue(String k, Object o);
}
```

Constructor

public TagSupport()
  Creates a new instance with the specified name and value.

Methods

public int doEndTag() throws JspException
  Returns EVAL_PAGE.

public int doStartTag() throws JspException
  Returns SKIP_BODY.

public static final Tag findAncestorWithClass(Tag from, Class
klass)
  Returns the instance of the specified class, found by testing for a match of
  each parent in a tag handler nesting structure (corresponding to nested
  action elements) starting with the specified Tag instance, or null if not
  found.

public String getId()
  Returns the id attribute value, or null if not set.

public Tag getParent()
  Returns the parent of this Tag instance (representing the action element that
  contains the action element corresponding to this Tag instance), or null if
  the instance has no parent (at the top level in the JSP page).

`public Object getValue(String k)`

Returns the value for the specified attribute that has been set with the `setValue()` method, or `null` if not found.

`public java.util.Enumeration getValues()`

Returns an `Enumeration` of all attribute names for values set with the `setValue()` method.

`public void release()`

Removes the references to all objects held by this instance.

`public void removeValue(String k)`

Removes a value set with the `setValue()` method.

`public void setPageContext(PageContext pageContext)`

Saves a reference to the current `PageContext`.

`public void setId(String id)`

Sets the `id` attribute value.

`public void setParent(Tag t)`

Saves a reference to the parent for this instance.

`public void setValue(String k, Object o)`

Saves the specified attribute with the specified value. Subclasses can use this method to save attribute values as an alternative to instance variables.

VariableInfo

Synopsis

Class Name:	`javax.servlet.jsp.tagext.VariableInfo`
Extends:	None
Implements:	None
Implemented by:	Internal container-dependent class. Most containers use the reference implementation of the class (developed in the Apache Jakarta project).

Description

`VariableInfo` instances are created by `TagExtraInfo` subclasses to describe each scripting variable that the corresponding tag handler class creates.

Class Summary

```
public class VariableInfo {
  // Constants
  public static final int AT_BEGIN;
```

```
        public static final int AT_END;
        public static final int NESTED;

        // Constructor
        public VariableInfo(String varName, String className,
          boolean declare, int scope);

        // Methods
        public String getClassName();
        public boolean getDeclare();
        public int getScope();
        public String getVarName();
    }
```

Constructor

public VariableInfo(String varName, String className,
  boolean declare, int scope)

Creates a new instance with the specified values.

Methods

public String getClassName()

Returns the scripting variable Java type.

public boolean getDeclare()

Returns true if the JSP container should create a declaration statement for a scripting variable, and otherwise returns false (used if the variable has already been declared by another tag handler, and is updated only by the tag handler corresponding to the TagExtraInfo subclass creating this VariableInfo instance).

public int getScope()

Returns one of AT_BEGIN (make the scripting variable available from the start tag to the end of the JSP page), AT_END (make the variable available after the end tag to the end of the JSP page) or NESTED (make the variable available only between the start and stop tags).

public String getVarName()

Returns the variable name.

Other JSP Classes

The JSP specification defines a number of other classes and interfaces that don't fit into the categories already covered. The exception classes, the interface for JSP page implementation classes, and the classes that let a JSP container vendor hide implementation details are described in this section.

HttpJspPage

Synopsis

Interface Name:	`javax.servlet.jsp.HttpJspPage`
Extends:	`javax.servlet.jsp.JspPage`
Implemented by:	JSP page implementation classes serving HTTP requests

Description

The `HttpJspPage` interface must be implemented by the generated JSP page implementation classes when HTTP is used.

Interface Declarations

```
public interface HttpJspPage extends JspPage {
    public void _jspService(javax.servlet.http.HttpServletRequest request,
      javax.servlet.http.HttpServletResponse response)
      throws javax.servlet.ServletException, java.io.IOException;
}
```

Methods

`public void _jspService(javax.servlet.http.HttpServletRequest request,`
`javax.servlet.http.HttpServletResponse response)`
`throws javax.servlet.ServletException, java.io.IOException`
This method corresponds to the body of the JSP page. It is defined automatically by the JSP processor and should never be defined by the JSP page author.

JspEngineInfo

Synopsis

Class Name:	`javax.servlet.jsp.JspEngineInfo`
Extends:	None
Implements:	None
Implemented by:	Internal container-dependent class. Most containers use the reference implementation of the class (developed in the Apache Jakarta project).

Description

`JspEngineInfo` is an abstract class that provides information about the JSP container. Each specific JSP container provides a concrete subclass.

Class Summary

```
public abstract class JspEngineInfo {
  // Constructor
  public JspEngineInfo();

  // Methods
  public abstract String getSpecificationVersion();
}
```

Constructor

`public JspEngineInfo()`

Creates a new `JspEngineInfo` instance.

Methods

`public abstract String getSpecificationVersion()`

Returns the version of the JSP specification implemented by the container, for instance, "1.1" for a JSP 1.1–compliant container.

JspException

Synopsis

Class Name:	`javax.servlet.jsp.JspException`
Extends:	`java.lang.Exception`
Implements:	None
Implemented by:	Internal container-dependent class. Most containers use the reference implementation of the class (developed in the Apache Jakarta project).

Description

The `JspException` class is the superclass for all JSP-related exceptions.

Class Summary

```
public class JspException extends Exception {
  // Constructors
  public JspException();
  public JspException(String msg);
}
```

Constructors

`public JspException()`

Creates a new `JspException` instance.

```
public JspException(String msg)
```
Creates a new JspException instance with the specified message.

JspFactory

Synopsis

Class Name:	javax.servlet.jsp.JspFactory
Extends:	None
Implements:	None
Implemented by:	Internal container-dependent class. Most containers use the reference implementation of the class (developed in the Apache Jakarta project).

Description

The JspFactory is an abstract class that defines a number of factory methods available to a JSP page at runtime, for the purpose of creating instances of various interfaces and classes used to support the JSP implementation.

A JSP container creates an instance of a concrete subclass during its initialization phase and makes it globally available for use by JSP implementation classes by registering the instance created with this class via the static setDefaultFactory() method.

Class Summary

```
public abstract class JspFactory {
    // Constructor
    public JspFactory()

    // Methods
    public static JspFactory getDefaultFactory();
    public abstract JspEngineInfo getEngineInfo();
    public abstract PageContext
      getPageContext(javax.servlet.Servlet servlet,
        javax.servlet.ServletRequest request,
        javax.servlet.ServletResponse response,
        String errorPageURL, boolean needsSession,
        int buffer, boolean autoflush);
    public abstract void releasePageContext(PageContext pc);
    public static void setDefaultFactory(JspFactory deflt);
}
```

Constructor

`public JspFactory()`

Creates a new `JspFactory` instance.

Methods

`public static JspFactory getDefaultFactory()`

Returns the default `JspFactory` for the container.

`public abstract JspEngineInfo getEngineInfo()`

Returns the `JspEngineInfo` for the container.

```
public abstract PageContext
  getPageContext(javax.servlet.Servlet servlet,
  javax.servlet.ServletRequest request,
  javax.servlet.ServletResponse response,
  String errorPageURL, boolean needsSession, int buffer,
  boolean autoflush)
```

Returns a properly initialized instance of an implementation-dependent `PageContext` subclass. This method is typically called early in the processing of the `_jspService()` method of a JSP implementation class to get a `PageContext` object for the request being processed. Calling this method results in the `PageContext.initialize()` method being invoked.

`public abstract void releasePageContext(PageContext pc)`

Releases a previously allocated `PageContext` object. Calling this method results in `PageContext.release()` being invoked. This method should be invoked prior to returning from the `_jspService()` method of a JSP implementation class.

`public static void setDefaultFactory(JspFactory deflt)`

Sets the default factory for this implementation. It is illegal for anything other than the JSP container to call this method.

JspPage

Synopsis

Interface Name:	`javax.servlet.jsp.JspPage`
Extends:	None
Implemented by:	JSP page implementation classes

Description

The `JspPage` interface must be implemented by the generated JSP page implementation classes. The interface defines a protocol with three methods; only two of them, `jspInit()` and `jspDestroy()`, are part of this interface. The signature of the third method, `_jspService()`, depends on the specific protocol used and cannot be expressed in a generic way in Java. See also `HttpJspPage`.

A class implementing this interface is responsible for invoking these methods at the appropriate time, based on the corresponding servlet-based method invocations.

The `jspInit()` and `jspDestroy()` methods can be defined by a JSP page author, but the `_jspService()` method is defined automatically by the JSP container, based on the contents of the JSP page.

Interface Declarations

```
public interface JspPage {
  public void jspDestroy();
  public void jspInit();
}
```

Methods

public void jspDestroy()

This method is invoked when the JSP page implementation instance is about to be destroyed. It can be used to perform cleanup, such as saving the state kept in instance variables to permanent storage.

public void jspInit()

This method is invoked when the JSP page implementation instance is initialized. It can be used to perform tasks such as restoring the state kept in instance variables from permanent storage.

JspTagException

Synopsis

Class Name:	`javax.servlet.jsp.JspTagException`
Extends:	`javax.servlet.jsp.JspException`
Implements:	None
Implemented by:	Internal container-dependent class. Most containers use the reference implementation of the class (developed in the Apache Jakarta project).

Description

The JspTagException is intended to be used by a tag handler to indicate some unrecoverable error. This exception is caught by the top level of the JSP page and results in an error page.

Class Summary

```
public class JspTagException extends JspException {
    // Constructors
    public JspTagException();
    public JspTagException(String msg);
}
```

Constructors

public JspTagException()

Creates a new JspTagException instance.

public JspTagException(String msg)

Creates a new JspTagException instance with the specified message.

C

Book Example Custom Actions and Classes Reference

This appendix contains reference material for all custom actions, utility classes, and beans described in this book that can be used as-is in other applications.

Example code in this book that is not intended to be reused directly is not included in this appendix. All source code for the book can, however, be downloaded either from the O'Reilly web site at *http://www.oreilly.com/catalog/jserverpages/* or from the web site dedicated to this book at *http://www.TheJSPBook.com.*

Generic Custom Actions

The following are generic custom actions defined in the ora custom tag library.

<ora:addCookie>

The <ora:addCookie> action sets response headers for creating or deleting a cookie. It must be used before the response is committed, for instance before a <jsp:include> action. The attributes supported by this action are described in Table C-1.

Table C-1. <ora:addCookie> Attributes

Attribute Name	Java Type	Request-Time Value Accepted	Description
maxAge	String	Yes	Optional. The number of seconds before the cookie expires. Default is –1, meaning that the cookie expires when the browser is closed. Use 0 to delete the cookie from the browser.
name	String	Yes	Mandatory. The cookie name.
value	String	Yes	Mandatory. The cookie value.

Example:

```
<%--
   Add a cookie named "userName", using the value from a
   request parameter with the same name, that expires in
   30 days.
--%>
<ora:addCookie name="userName"
   value='<%= request.getParameter("userName") %>'
   maxAge="2592000"
/>

<%--
   Delete a cookie named "userName".
--%>
<ora:addCookie name="userName"
   value="ignored"
   maxAge="0"
/>
```

< ora:encodeHTML >

The <ora:encodeHTML> action replaces all HTML special characters (', ", <, >, &) found in the body text with the corresponding HTML character entities (', ", <, >, &) and writes the result to the current JspWriter. This action doesn't have any attributes.

Example:

```
<%--
   Encode special characters in a bean property value.
--%>
<ora:encodeHTML>
   <jsp:getProperty name="someBean" property="someTextValue" />
</ora:encodeHTML>
```

< ora:encodeURL >

The <ora:encodeURL> action encodes the specified URL for session tracking using URL rewriting (which embeds the session ID if needed) and URL encoding (which replaces special characters with hex code) parameters specified by nested <ora:param> actions, and adds them to the URL. The resulting URL is written to the current JspWriter. The attribute supported by this action is described in Table C-2.

Table C-2. <ora:encodeURL> Attribute

Attribute Name	Java Type	Request-Time Value Accepted	Description
url	String	Yes	Mandatory. The URL to be encoded.

Example:

```
<%--
   Encode a URL and add a parameter with a value from a
   bean property.
--%>
<ora:encodeURL url="product.jsp">
   <ora:param name="id" value="<%= product.getId() %>" />
</ora:encodeURL>
```

<ora:getCookieValue>

The `<ora:getCookieValue>` action writes the value of the specified cookie to the current `JspWriter`, or writes a blank string (`""`) if the cookie is not found in the current request. The attribute supported by this action is described in Table C-3.

Table C-3. <ora:getCookieValue>Attribute

Attribute Name	Java Type	Request-Time Value Accepted	Description
name	String	Yes	Mandatory. The cookie name.

Example:

```
<%--
   Add a cookie value to the response body.
--%>
Hello <ora:getCookieValue name="userName" />
```

<ora:loop>

The `<ora:loop>` action iterates through the elements of the specified object or the elements represented by the specified property of the specified bean, and evaluates the body once for each element. The current element is made available as a scripting variable within the action element's body. The attributes supported by this action are described in Table C-4.

Table C-4. <ora:loop> Attributes

Attribute Name	Java Type	Request-Time Value Accepted	Description
name	String	No	Mandatory. The name of a data structure object or bean. The object must be of type `Object[]`, `Vector`, `Dictionary`, or `Enumeration`, or be a bean with a property of one of these types. The object or bean can be located in any JSP scope.

Table C-4. <ora:loop> Attributes (continued)

Attribute Name	Java Type	Request-Time Value Accepted	Description
property	String	No	Optional. The name of a bean property. The property type must be one of Object[], Vector, Dictionary, or Enumeration.
loopId	String	No	Mandatory. The name of the variable that holds a reference to the current element when the action's body is evaluated.
className	String	No	Mandatory. The class name for the elements of the bean or property.

Example:

```
<%--
   Make a bean with an indexed property available in a page.
--%>
<jsp:useBean id="catalog" scope="application"
   class="com.ora.jsp.beans.shopping.Catalog" />
<%--
   Loop over all elements of the index productList property.
--%>
<ora:loop name="catalog" property="productList" loopId="product"
   className="com.ora.jsp.beans.shopping.ProductBean">
   <%-- Use the current element as a bean in an action. --%>
   <jsp:getProperty name="product" property="name" />
   <%-- Use the current element as a scripting variable. --%>
   <%= product.getId() %>
</ora:loop>
```

<ora:menuItem>

The <ora:menuItem> action writes its body contents to the current JSPWriter. If the specified page is the currently requested page, the content is used as-is; otherwise, it's embedded in an HTML link element (<a>), using the specified page as the link target and the body contents as the link text. This action is intended to be used in navigation bars to generate links for all page menu items except the current page. The attribute supported by this action is described in Table C-5.

Table C-5. <ora:menuItem> Attribute

Attribute Name	Java Type	Request-Time Value Accepted	Description
page	String	Yes	Mandatory. The page name for the menu item as a page-relative or context-relative URI path.

Example:

```
<%--
   Generate a navigation menu table with two page menu items.
--%>
<table bgcolor="lightblue">
  <tr>
    <td>
      <ora:menuItem page="page1.jsp">
        <b>Page 1</b>
      </ora:menuItem>
    </td>
  </tr>
  <tr>
    <td>
      <ora:menuItem page="page2.jsp">
        <b>Page 2</b>
      </ora:menuItem>
    </td>
  </tr>
</table>
```

<ora:noCache>

The <ora:noCache> action sets response headers that prevent the page from being cached by a browser or proxy server. It must be used before the response is committed, for instance before a <jsp:include> action. This action doesn't have any attributes.

Example:

```
<%--
   Set headers to prevent caching.
--%>
<ora:noCache />
```

<ora:param>

The <ora:param> action can be used only in the body of the <ora:encodeURL> and <ora:redirect> actions to set parameter values. The specified parameter value is URL encoded; that is, all special characters are replaced with the corresponding URL code for the character (e.g., a plus sign for a space). The attributes supported by this action are described in Table C-6.

Table C-6. <ora:param> Attributes

Attribute Name	Java Type	Request-Time Value Accepted	Description
name	String	Yes	Mandatory. The parameter name.
value	String	Yes	Mandatory. The parameter value.

Example:

```
<%--
    Encode a URL and add one parameter with a value from a
    bean property and one parameter with a static string value.
--%>
<ora:encodeURL url="process.jsp">
    <ora:param name="id" value="<%= product.getId() %>" />
    <ora:param name="action" value="list" />
</ora:encodeURL>
```

<ora:redirect>

The <ora:redirect> action sets response headers to redirect the browser to the specified page and aborts the processing of the rest of the JSP page. It encodes the specified URL for session tracking using URL rewriting (embedding the session ID if needed) and URL encodes (replacing special characters with hex code) parameters specified by nested <ora:param> actions, and adds the parameters to the URL. This action must be used before the response is committed, for instance before a <jsp:include> action. The attribute supported by this action is described in Table C-7.

Table C-7. <ora:redirect> Attribute

Attribute Name	Java Type	Request-Time Value Accepted	Description
page	String	Yes	Mandatory. The URL of the page to redirect to, relative to the current page, or if it starts with a slash (/), relative to the context path.

Example:

```
<%--
    Redirect to a new page and include a parameter with a value
    from a bean property.
--%>
<ora:redirect page="productdescr.jsp">
    <ora:param name="id" value="<%= product.getId() %>" />
</ora:encodeURL>
```

<ora:useProperty>

The <ora:useProperty> action associates a bean property value with a variable name. The property is retrieved from the specified bean in the specified scope by calling the corresponding property getter method. If an argument is specified by the arg attribute, a getter method that takes a String argument is used instead. The attributes supported by this action are described in Table C-8.

Table C-8. <ora:useProperty> Attributes

Attribute Name	Java Type	Request-Time Value Accepted	Description
arg	String	Yes	Optional. The argument value used as the argument for the property getter method, typically to identify one specific property value.
className	String	No	Mandatory. The class name for the retrieved bean property.
id	String	No	Mandatory. The name of the variable to hold the retrieved bean. The bean is placed in the page scope.
name	String	No	Mandatory. The name of the object with the bean to retrieve. The object must be available in one of the standard scopes.
property	String	No	Mandatory. The name of the property holding the bean.

Example:

```
<%--
  Make a bean with the appropriate access methods available in
  the application scope.
--%>
<jsp:useBean
  id="catalog"
  scope="application"
  className="com.ora.jsp.beans.shopping.CatalogBean"
/>

<%--
  Make one of the bean's properties available in the default scope
  (page scope) using a request parameter value as the argument.
--%>
<ora:useProperty id="product" name="catalog" property="product"
  arg='<%= request.getParameter("id") %>'
  className="com.ora.jsp.beans.shopping.ProductBean" />
```

<ora:validateSession>

The <ora:validateSession> action is used to protect JSP pages in an application that implements its own authentication and authorization. The action looks for a bean in the session scope that signifies proof of authentication. If the bean is not found, it forwards the request to the specified page (typically a login page), adding the request parameters origURL (containing the URL for the requested page) and errorMsg (containing the text specified by the attribute with the same name, URL encoded). The attributes supported by this action are described in Table C-9.

Table C-9. <ora:validateSession> Attributes

Attribute Name	Java Type	Request-Time Value Accepted	Description
errorMsg	String	Yes	Mandatory. The error message to pass to the login page.
loginPage	String	Yes	Mandatory. A page-relative or context-relative URI for the login page.
name	String	No	Mandatory. The name of the authentication proof bean in the session scope.

Example:

```
<%--
   Check if the page is requested by an authenticated user by
   looking for the specified bean in the session scope.
   Forward to the login page if not.
--%>
<ora:validateSession name="validUser" loginPage="login.jsp"
   errorMsg="Please log in first" />
```

Internationalization Custom Actions

<ora:getLocalDate>

The <ora:getLocalDate> action writes the specified date, formatted according to the currently selected locale (see <ora:useLocaleBundle>), to the current JspWriter. The attributes supported by this particular action are described in Table C-10.

Table C-10. <ora:getLocalDate> Attributes

Attribute Name	Java Type	Request-Time Value Accepted	Description
date	java.util. Date	Yes	Mandatory. The date to format.
name	String	No	Mandatory. The name of the LocaleBean created by <ora: useLocaleBean>.

Example:

```
<%--
   Create a LocaleBean (see <ora:useLocaleBean> for details.
--%>
<ora:useLocaleBean id="locale" bundleName="poll"
   supportedLangs="en, sv, de" />
```

```
<%--
  Add a localized date to the response body.
--%>
<ora:getLocalDate name="locale" date="<%= new java.util.Date() %>" />
```

<ora:getLocalNumber>

The <ora:getLocalNumber> action writes the specified number, formatted according to the currently selected locale (see <ora:useLocaleBundle>), to the current JspWriter. The attributes supported by this action are described in Table C-11.

Table C-11. <ora:getLocalNumber> Attributes

Attribute Name	Java Type	Request-Time Value Accepted	Description
name	String	No	Mandatory. The name of the LocaleBean created by <ora: useLocaleBean>.
value	double	Yes	Mandatory. The number to format.

Example:

```
<%--
  Create a LocaleBean (see <ora:useLocaleBean> for details).
--%>
<ora:useLocaleBean id="locale" bundleName="poll"
  supportedLangs="en, sv, de" />


<%--
  Add a localized number to the response body.
--%>
<ora:getLocalDate name="locale" value="1000.67" />
```

<ora:getLocalPageName>

The <ora:getLocalPageName> action writes the localized name of the specified page base name for the currently selected locale (see <ora:useLocaleBundle>) to the current JspWriter. The page base name is converted to the localized page name according to the same rules that the java.util.PropertyResourceBundle uses to find a localized *.properties* file, i.e., by appending country and language codes to the base name (excluding the extension). Unlike PropertyResourceBundle, this action does not verify that the file exists; it just creates a page name corresponding to the currently selected locale. The attributes supported by this action are described in Table C-12.

Table C-12. <ora:getLocalPageName> Attributes

Attribute Name	Java Type	Request-Time Value Accepted	Description
name	String	No	Mandatory. The name of the LocaleBean created by <ora: useLocaleBean>.
pageName	String	Yes	Mandatory. The page base name.

Example:

```
<%--
   Create a LocaleBean (see <ora:useLocaleBean> for details).
--%>
<ora:useLocaleBean id="locale" bundleName="poll"
   supportedLangs="en, sv, de" />

<%--
   Add a localized page name (as a link) to the response body.
--%>
<a href="<ora:getLocalPageName name="locale"
   pageName="details.jsp" />">some link</a>
```

<ora:getLocalText>

The <ora:getLocalText> action writes the value of the specified key for the currently selected locale (see <ora:useLocaleBundle>), backed by localized properties files, to the current JspWriter. The attributes supported by this action are described in Table C-13.

Table C-13. <ora:getLocalText> Attributes

Attribute Name	Java Type	Request-Time Value Accepted	Description
key	String	Yes	Mandatory. The property key for the localized text.
name	String	No	Mandatory. The name of the LocaleBean created by <ora: useLocaleBean>.

Example:

```
<%--
   Create a LocaleBean (see <ora:useLocaleBean> for details).
--%>
<ora:useLocaleBean id="locale" bundleName="poll"
   supportedLangs="en, sv, de" />
```

```
<%--
   Add localized text to the response body.
--%>
<ora:getLocalText name="locale" key="poll.title" />
```

<ora:useLocaleBundle>

The `<ora:useLocaleBundle>` action creates and initializes a `com.ora.jsp.` `beans.locale.LocaleBean` instance that can then be used with the `<ora:` `getLocalDate>`, `<ora:getLocalNumber>`, `<ora:getLocalPageName>`, and `<ora:getLocalText>` actions. The `LocaleBean` is created as a session scope bean the first time a page with the `<ora:useLocaleBundle>` action is requested within a user session. From then on, the properties of the bean are adjusted based on the current request information. The `LocaleBean` properties are described in Table C-14, and the attributes supported by the `<ora:useLocaleBundle>` action are described in Table C-15.

Table C-14. com.ora.jsp.beans.locale.LocaleBean Properties

Property Name	Java Type	Access	Description
bundleName	String	write	The base name for the properties files used for localized text
charset	String	write	The charset used to decode request parameters
language	String	read/write	The language code for the selected locale
locale	java.util. Locale	read	The locale, selected based on other properties
requestLocales	java.util. Locale[]	write	The locales received with the request
supportedLangs	String	write	A comma-separated list of language codes

Table C-15. <ora:useLocaleBean> Attributes

Attribute Name	Java Type	Request-Time Value Accepted	Description
bundleName	String	Yes	Mandatory. The base name for text resource properties files.
id	String	No	Mandatory. The name used to reference the `LocaleBean` instance.
supportedLangs	String	Yes	Mandatory. A comma-separated list of language/country codes. The first code is used as the default language.

The `<ora:useLocaleBean>` action sets the bean's `language` and `charset` properties to the values of the request parameters with the same names, if present, and the `requestLocales` property to the locale information found in the `Accept-Language` request header. The `supportedLangs` and `bundleName` properties are set to the action attributes with the same names. The bean selects the most appropriate locale by comparing the `language` attribute value, if present, or the `requestLocales` in priority order with the languages specified by the `supportedLangs` property. See Chapter 11, *Internationalization*, for more details.

Besides accessing the `LocaleBean` through action elements, the bean also provides these regular methods, which you can use with scripting code in a JSP page:

`public java.util.Date getDate(String date) throws java.text.`
  `ParseException`
  Returns the specified date `String` converted to a `Date`, parsed as defined by the currently selected locale.

`public String getDateString(java.util.Date date)`
  Returns the specified `Date` converted to a `String`, formatted as defined by the currently selected locale.

`public double getDouble(String number) throws java.text.`
  `ParseException`
  Returns the specified number `String` converted to a `double`, parsed as defined by the currently selected locale.

`public float getFloat(String number) throws java.text.`
  `ParseException`
  Returns the specified number `String` converted to a `float`, parsed as defined by the currently selected locale.

`public int getInt(String number) throws java.text.ParseException`
  Returns the specified number `String` converted to an `int`, parsed as defined by the currently selected locale.

`public String getLanguage()`
  Returns the language code for the currently selected locale.

`public java.util.Locale getLocale()`
  Returns a `Locale`. The `Locale` is constructed based on the `language` property, if set. If not, the `Locale` is determined based on the `Accept-Language` header (the `requestLocales` property), if set. If the `Locale` found this way matches one of the supported languages, it's returned. Otherwise, the `Locale` for the first language in the list of supported languages is returned.

`public long getLong(String number) throws java.text.`
  `ParseException`
  Returns the specified number `String` converted to a `long`, parsed as defined by the currently selected locale.

`public String getNumberString(double number)`

Returns the specified number converted to a `String`, formatted as defined by the currently selected locale.

`public String getPageName(String basePageName)`

Returns a version of the specified page name with a language/country suffix for the currently selected locale.

`public String getParameter(String parameter)`
`    throws java.io.UnsupportedEncodingException`

Returns the first all value for the specified parameter, parsed using the currently specified charset.

`public java.util.Enumeration getParameterNames()`

Returns an `Enumeration` of all parameter names.

`public String[] getParameterValues(String parameter)`
`    throws java.io.UnsupportedEncodingException`

Returns an array of all values for the specified parameter, parsed using the currently specified charset.

`public java.lang.String getText(String resourceName)`

Returns the text resource for the specified key, with the best match for the currently selected locale.

`public void setBundleName(String bundleName)`

Sets the bundle name. Resets the current `ResourceBundle` so that a new one will be created with the new bundle name the next time the `ResourceBundle` is retrieved.

`public void setCharset(String charset)`

Sets the charset used to parse request parameters.

`public void setLanguage(String language)`

Sets the user-selected language/country code. Resets the currently selected locale if the new language is different from the current one. This is done so that all possible locale sources will be evaluated again the next time the locale property is retrieved.

`public void setParameters(java.util.Hashtable parameters)`

Sets the parameter list.

`public void setRequestLocales(java.util.Locale[] locales)`

Sets the set of locales received with the request, and resets the currently selected locale if the new set is different from the current set. This is done so that all possible locale sources will be evaluated again the next time the locale property is retrieved.

```
public void setSupportedLangs(String supportedLangs)
```
Sets the set of supported languages, provided as a comma-separated list of country/language codes. This is a mandatory property. Resets the currently selected locale if the new set is different from the current set. This is done so that all possible locale sources will be evaluated again the next time the locale property is retrieved.

Example:

```
<%--
  Create and initialize a LocaleBean.
--%>
<ora:useLocaleBean id="locale" bundleName="poll"
  supportedLangs="en, sv, de" />

<%--
  Add localized text to the response body using action element.
--%>
<ora:getLocalText name="locale" key="poll.title" />
<%--
  Add localized number to the response body using scripting elements
--%>
<% int aNumber = 10000; %>
<%= locale.getNumberString(aNumber) %>
```

Database Custom Actions

<ora:sqlQuery>

The <ora:sqlQuery> action executes a SQL SELECT statement and makes the result available as a java.util.Vector of com.ora.jsp.sql.Row objects. The SQL statement is specified in the body of the action element. Placeholder characters (question marks) can be used in the statement and given values dynamically by nested value action elements (see the section "Value Action Elements" later in this appendix for details). The attributes supported by the <ora:sqlQuery> action are described in Table C-16.

Table C-16. <ora:sqlQuery> Attributes

Attribute Name	Java Type	Request-Time Value Accepted	Description
dataSource	String	No	Mandatory, unless used with <ora: sqlTransaction>. The name of the data source.
id	String	No	Mandatory. The name of the vector to hold the result.

Table C-16. <ora:sqlQuery> Attributes (continued)

Attribute Name	Java Type	Request-Time Value Accepted	Description
scope	String	No	Optional. The scope for the result, one of page, request, session, or application. Default is page.

Example:

```
<%--
  Get all rows from a table where a column matches the value
  of a request parameter.
--%>
<ora:sqlQuery id="empDbInfo" dataSource="example">
  SELECT * FROM Employee
    WHERE UserName = ?
  <ora:sqlStringValue param="userName" />
</ora:sqlQuery>
```

<ora:sqlTransaction>

The <ora:sqlTransaction> action is used to enclose other database action elements that together make up a database transaction: a set of database operations where all operations either fail or succeed. The attribute supported by this action is described in Table C-17.

Table C-17. <ora:sqlTransaction>Attribute

Attribute Name	Java Type	Request-Time Value Accepted	Description
dataSource	String	No	Mandatory. The name of the data source to use for all nested database access actions.

Example:

```
<%--
  Execute two database operations as one database transaction.
--%>
<ora:sqlTransaction dataSource="example">

  <ora:sqlUpdate>
    UPDATE Account SET Balance = Balance - 1000
      WHERE AccountNumber = 1234
  </ora:sqlUpdate>
  <ora:sqlUpdate>
    UPDATE Account SET Balance = Balance + 1000
      WHERE AccountNumber = 5678
  </ora:sqlUpdate>

</ora:sqlTransaction>
```

`<ora:sqlUpdate>`

The `<ora:sqlUpdate>` action executes SQL INSERT, UPDATE, and DELETE statements, as well as so-called Data Definition Language (DDL) statements, such as the CREATE TABLE statement. This action optionally makes the number of affected rows available as an Integer object. The SQL statement is specified in the body of the action element. Placeholder characters (question marks) can be used in the statement and given values dynamically by nested value action elements (see the next section, "Value Action Elements," for details). The attributes supported by the `<ora:sqlUpdate>` action are described in Table C-18.

Table C-18. `<ora:sqlUpdate>` Attributes

Attribute Name	Java Type	Request-Time Value Accepted	Description
dataSource	String	No	Mandatory, unless used with `<ora:sqlTransaction>`. The name of the data source.
id	String	No	Optional. The name of the Integer to hold the number of rows affected by the statement.
scope	String	No	Optional. The scope for the result, one of page, request, session, or application. Default is page.

Example:

```
<%--
    Insert a row in a table using the value of a request parameter.
--%>
<ora:sqlUpdate dataSource="example">
  INSERT INTO Employee
    (UserName) VALUES(?)
  <ora:sqlStringValue param="userName" />
</ora:sqlQuery>
```

`<ora:useDataSource>`

The `<ora:useDataSource>` action creates a javax.sql.DataSource object in the application scope that supports connection pooling and can be used with the other database actions. Note that this action is intended only for prototyping and examples. A better approach is to use a servlet loaded at startup to make a DataSource available as an application scope object, as described in Chapter 17, *Developing Database Access Components*. The attributes supported by the `<ora:sqlUpdate>` action are described in Table C-19.

Table C-19. <ora:useDataSource> Attributes

Attribute Name	Java Type	Request-Time Value Accepted	Description
className	String	No	Mandatory. The name of the JDBC driver class used to access the database.
id	String	No	Mandatory. The name used to reference the data source from other actions.
pw	String	No	Optional. The password for the database user account name.
url	String	No	Mandatory. The JDBC URL for the database.
user	String	No	Optional. The database user account name.

Example:

```
<%--
   Make a DataSource available for other database actions.
--%>
<ora:useDataSource id="example"
   className="sun.jdbc.odbc.JdbcOdbcDriver" url="jdbc:odbc:example" />
```

Value Action Elements

The SQL statements specified in the body of the <ora:sqlQuery> and <ora:sqlUpdate> elements may contain placeholder characters (question marks) that are given values dynamically by nested value action elements. Most of the Java datatypes supported by the JDBC are represented by specific action elements. They support the attributes described in Table C-20 according to the matrix in Table C-21.

Table C-20. Value Action Attributes

Attribute Name	Java Type	Request-Time Value Accepted	Description
name	String	No	Optional. The name of a bean with a property holding the value.
param	String	Yes	Optional. The name of a request parameter holding the String value.
pattern	String	Yes	The pattern used to interpret a String specified by the stringValue, param, or name/property attributes.
property	String	No	Mandatory if name is specified. The name of the bean property holding the value.
stringValue	String	Yes	Optional. The String to use as the value.

Table C-20. Value Action Attributes (continued)

Attribute Name	Java Type	Request-Time Value Accepted	Description
value	See Table C-21	Yes	Optional. The value to use for a place-holder in the enclosing database action.

Table C-21. Value Action Attribute Matrix

Action Name	name	param	pattern	property	stringValue	value
bigDecimal Value	✗	✗	✗	✗	✗	java.math. BigDecimal
booleanValue	✗	✗		✗	✗	boolean
bytesValue	✗	✗		✗	✗	byte[]
byteValue	✗	✗		✗	✗	byte
dateValue	✗	✗	✗	✗	✗	java.util. Date
doubleValue	✗	✗	✗	✗	✗	double
floatValue	✗	✗	✗	✗	✗	float
intValue	✗	✗	✗	✗	✗	int
longValue	✗	✗	✗	✗	✗	long
objectValue	✗	✗		✗	✗	Object
shortValue	✗	✗	✗	✗	✗	short
stringValue	✗	✗		✗		String
timestamp Value	✗	✗	✗	✗	✗	java.util. Date
timeValue	✗	✗	✗	✗	✗	java.util. Date

The patterns that can be used as values for the pattern attribute are the same as for `java.text.SimpleDateFormat` and `java.text.NumberFormat`. See the Java API documentation for details.

The `<ora:stringValue>` action supports two additional attributes, described in Table C-22.

Table C-22. Additional <ora:stringValue> Attributes

Attribute Name	Java Type	Request-Time Value Accepted	Description
prefix	String	Yes	Optional. A `String` to be concatenated to the beginning of the value.
suffix	String	Yes	Optional. A `String` to be concatenated to the end of the value.

Example:

```
<%--
  Use dynamic values in an UPDATE statment.
--%>
<ora:sqlUpdate dataSource="example">
  UPDATE Employee
    SET Password = ?,
        FirstName = ?,
        LastName = ?,
        Dept = ?,
        EmpDate = ?,
        EmailAddr = ?,
        ModDate = ?
        Salary = ?
    WHERE UserName = ?
  <ora:sqlStringValue param="password" />
  <ora:sqlStringValue param="firstName" />
  <ora:sqlStringValue param="lastName" />
  <ora:sqlStringValue param="dept" />
  <ora:sqlDateValue param="empDate" pattern="yyyy-MM-dd" />
  <ora:sqlStringValue param="emailAddr" />
  <ora:sqlTimestampValue value="<%= new java.util.Date() %>" />
  <ora:sqlIntValue stringValue="95000" />
  <ora:sqlStringValue param="userName" />
</ora:sqlUpdate>
```

Utility Classes

ArraySupport

Synopsis

Class Name:	com.ora.jsp.util.ArraySupport
Extends:	None
Implements:	None

Description

The ArraySupport class contains static methods for working with arrays.

Class Summary

```
public class ArraySupport {
  // Methods
  public static boolean contains(String[] array, String value);
}
```

Methods

`public static boolean contains(String[] array, String value)`
> Returns true if the specified value matches one of the elements in the specified array.

CookieUtils

Synopsis

Class Name:	`com.ora.jsp.util.CookieUtils`
Extends:	None
Implements:	None

Description

The `CookieUtils` class contains a number of static methods that can be used to work with `javax.servlet.http.Cookie` objects.

Class Summary

```
public class CookieUtils {
  // Methods
  public static String getCookieValue(String name,
    javax.servlet.http.HttpServletRequest req);
  public static boolean isCookieSet(String name,
    javax.servlet.http.HttpServletRequest req);
  public static void sendCookie(String name, String value,
    int maxAge, javax.servlet.http.HttpServletResponse res);
}
```

Methods

`public static String getCookieValue(String name,`
`  javax.servlet.http.HttpServletRequest req)`
> Returns the value of the cookie with the specified name, or null if not found.

`public static boolean isCookieSet(String name,`
`  javax.servlet.http.HttpServletRequest req)`
> Returns true if a cookie with the specified name is present in the request.

`public static void sendCookie(String name, String value,`
`  int maxAge, javax.servlet.http.HttpServletResponse res)`
> Creates a cookie with the specified name, value, and max age, and adds it to the response.

DebugBean

Synopsis

Class Name:	com.ora.jsp.util.DebugBean
Extends:	None
Implements:	None

Description

The DebugBean class is a bean that can be used to extract debug information from a JSP PageContext. The debug info is sent to the browser, System.out, and the servlet log file, depending on the value of the debug request parameter sent with the request for the JSP page: resp, stdout, and log, respectively. These parameter values can be combined to get the information directed to multiple targets. The bean properties are described in Table C-23.

Table C-23. com.ora.jsp.util.DebugBean Properties

Property Name	Java Type	Access	Description
applicationScope	String	read	A string, formatted as a table, with the names and values of all application scope variables.
cookies	String	read	A string, formatted as a table, with the names and values of all cookies received with the request.
elapsedTime	String	read	A string with the number of milliseconds elapsed since the bean was created or this property was last read.
headers	String	read	A string, formatted as a table, with the names and values of all headers received with the request.
pageContext	javax.servlet. jsp.PageContext	write	Mandatory. Must be set for the bean to find the value of its other properties.
pageScope	String	read	A string, formatted as a table, with the names and values of all page scope variables.
parameters	String	read	A string, formatted as a table, with the names and values of all parameters received with the request.

Table C-23. com.ora.jsp.util.DebugBean Properties (continued)

Property Name	Java Type	Access	Description
requestInfo	String	read	A string, formatted as a table, with information about the request, such as authentication type, content length and encoding, path information, remote host and user, etc.
requestScope	String	read	A string, formatted as a table, with the names and values of all request scope variables.
sessionScope	String	read	A string, formatted as a table, with the names and values of all session scope variables.

StringFormat

Synopsis

Class Name:	com.ora.jsp.util.StringFormat
Extends:	None
Implements:	None

Description

The StringFormat class contains a number of static methods that can be used to validate the format of strings, typically received as input from a user, and to format values as strings that can be used in HTML output without causing browser interpretation problems.

Class Summary

```
public class StringFormat {
    // Methods
    public static boolean isValidDate(String dateString,
        String dateFormatPattern);
    public static boolean isValidEmailAddr(String emailAddrString);
    public static boolean isValidInteger(String numberString,
        int min, int max);
    public static boolean isValidString(String value,
        String[] validStrings, boolean ignoreCase);
    public static String replaceInString(String in, String from,
        String to);
    public static java.util.Date toDate(String dateString,
        String dateFormatPattern) throws java.text.ParseException;
```

```
    public static String toHTMLString(String in);
    public static Number toNumber(String numString,
       String numFormatPattern) throws java.text.ParseException;
}
```

Methods

public static boolean isValidDate(String dateString,
    String dateFormatPattern)
> Returns true if the specified date string represents a valid date in the speci-
> fied format. The dateFormatPattern is a String specifying the format to be
> used when parsing the dateString. The pattern is expressed with the pat-
> tern letters defined for the java.text.SimpleDateFormat class.

public static boolean isValidEmailAddr(String emailAddrString)
> Returns true if the email string contains an @ sign and at least one dot; i.e.,
> hans@gefionsoftware.com is accepted but hans@gefionsoftware is not.
> Note! This rule is not always correct (e.g., on an intranet it may be okay with
> just a name) and it does not guarantee a valid Internet email address, but it
> takes care of the most obvious Internet mail address format errors.

public static boolean isValidInteger(String numberString,
    int min, int max)
> Returns true if the specified number string represents a valid integer in the
> specified range.

public static boolean isValidString(String value,
    String[] validStrings, boolean ignoreCase)
> Returns true if the specified string matches a string in the set of provided
> valid strings, ignoring case if specified.

public static String replaceInString(String in, String from,
    String to)
> Replaces one String with another throughout a source String.

public static java.util.Date toDate(String dateString,
    String dateFormatPattern) throws java.text.ParseException
> Converts a String to a Date, using the specified pattern (see java.text.
> SimpleDateFormat for pattern description).

public static String toHTMLString(String in)
> Returns the specified string converted to a format suitable for HTML: All sin-
> gle-quote, double-quote, greater-than, less-than, and ampersand characters are
> replaced with their corresponding HTML character entity code.

public static Number toNumber(String numString,
    String numFormatPattern) throws java.text.ParseException
> Converts a String to a Number, using the specified pattern (see java.text.
> NumberFormat for pattern description).

Database Access Classes

ConnectionPool

Synopsis

Class Name:	com.ora.jsp.sql.ConnectionPool
Extends:	None
Implements:	None

Description

This class implements a connection pool. It's the same class as the Connection-Pool class described in *Java Servlet Programming* (O'Reilly), and is copied with permission from Jason Hunter. It's used by the DataSourceWrapper class to provide a JDBC 2.0 DataSource interface to the pool.

Class Summary

```
public class ConnectionPool {
    // Constructor
    public ConnectionPool(String dbURL, String user, String password,
        String driverClassName, int initialConnections, int increment)
        throws java.sql.SQLException, ClassNotFoundException;

    // Methods
    public java.sql.Connection getConnection()
        throws java.sql.SQLException;
    public void returnConnection(java.sql.Connection returned);
}
```

Constructor

public ConnectionPool(String dbURL, String user, String password,
    String driverClassName, int initialConnections, int increment)
    throws java.sql.SQLException, ClassNotFoundException
Creates a connection pool for the specified JDBC URL using the specified JDBC driver class and database user ID and password. The specified number of connections is created initially, and the pool is expanded in the specified increments if the pool is empty when a new request is received.

Methods

public java.sql.Connection getConnection()
    throws java.sql.SQLException
Returns a Connection from the pool.

`public void returnConnection(java.sql.Connection returned)`
  Used by the connection pool client to return a `Connection` to the pool.

ConnectionWrapper

Synopsis

Class Name:	`com.ora.jsp.sql.ConnectionWrapper`
Extends:	None
Implements:	`java.sql.Connection`

Description

This class is a wrapper around a `Connection`, with a `close()` method that informs its `DataSourceWrapper` that it's available for reuse again, and an `isClosed()` method to return the state of the wrapper instead of the wrapped `Connection`. All other methods just relay the call to the wrapped `Connection`.

Class Summary

```
public class ConnectionWrapper implements java.sql.Connection {
  // Constructor
  public ConnectionWrapper(Connection realConn,
    DataSourceWrapper dsw);

  // Methods
  public void close() throws SQLException;
  public boolean isClosed() throws SQLException;

  // Wrapped methods
  public void clearWarnings() throws SQLException;
  public void commit() throws SQLException;
  public Statement createStatement() throws SQLException;
  public boolean getAutoCommit() throws SQLException;
  public String getCatalog() throws SQLException;
  public DatabaseMetaData getMetaData() throws SQLException;
  public int getTransactionIsolation() throws SQLException;
  public SQLWarning getWarnings() throws SQLException;
  public boolean isReadOnly() throws SQLException;
  public String nativeSQL(String sql) throws SQLException;
  public CallableStatement prepareCall(String sql)
    throws SQLException;
  public PreparedStatement prepareStatement(String sql)
    throws SQLException;
  public void rollback() throws SQLException;
  public void setAutoCommit(boolean autoCommit) throws SQLException;
  public void setCatalog(String catalog) throws SQLException;
```

```
        public void setReadOnly(boolean readOnly) throws SQLException;
        public void setTransactionIsolation(int level) throws SQLException;
    }
```

Constructor

```
public ConnectionWrapper(Connection realConn,
    DataSourceWrapper dsw);
```
Creates a new ConnectionWrapper around the specified Connection owned by the specified DataSourceWrapper.

Methods

```
public void close() throws SQLException;
```
Informs the DataSourceWrapper that this ConnectionWrapper is closed by calling its returnConnection() method.

```
public boolean isClosed() throws SQLException;
```
Returns true if the close() method has been called, false otherwise.

All wrapped methods simply call the corresponding method on the wrapped Connection. See the Java documentation at *http://java.sun.com/docs/index.html* for details about these methods.

DataSourceWrapper

Synopsis

Class Name: com.ora.jsp.sql.DataSourceWrapper
Extends: None
Implements: javax.sql.DataSource

Description

This class is a wrapper implementing the JDBC 2.0 SE DataSource interface, used to make the ConnectionPool class look like a JDBC 2.0 DataSource. It can easily be modified to be used as a wrapper for any JDBC 1.0 connection pool implementation.

Class Summary

```
public class DataSourceWrapper implements javax.sql.DataSource {
    // Constructor
    public DataSourceWrapper(String driverClass, String url,
        String user, String pw)
        throws ClassNotFoundException, InstantiationException,
        java.sql.SQLException, IllegalAccessException;
```

```
    // Methods
    public java.sql.Connection getConnection()
       throws java.sql.SQLException;
    public void returnConnection(java.sql.Connection conn);

    // Methods with dummy implementations
    public java.sql.Connection getConnection(String username,
       String password) throws java.sql.SQLException;
    public int getLoginTimeout() throws java.sql.SQLException;
    public java.io.PrintWriter getLogWriter()
       throws java.sql.SQLException;
    public void setLoginTimeout(int seconds)
       throws java.sql.SQLException;
    public void setLogWriter(java.io.PrintWriter out)
       throws java.sql.SQLException;
}
```

Constructor

**public DataSourceWrapper(String driverClass, String url,
    String user, String pw)
    throws ClassNotFoundException, InstantiationException,
    java.sql.SQLException, IllegalAccessException**
Creates a connection pool for the specified JDBC URL using the specified
JDBC driver class and database user ID and password. One connection is created initially, and the pool is expanded in increments of one if the pool is
empty when a new request is received.

Methods

**public java.sql.Connection getConnection()
    throws java.sql.SQLException**
Returns a ConnectionWrapper from the pool.

public void returnConnection(java.sql.Connection conn)
Used by the ConnectionWrapper to return a Connection to the pool when
the client calls close().

Row

Synopsis

Class Name:	com.ora.jsp.sql.Row
Extends:	None
Implements:	None

Description

The Row class represents a row in a database query result. It contains a collection of com.ora.jsp.sql.Column objects.

Class Summary

```
public class Row {
  // Constructor
  public Row(java.sql.ResultSet rs)
    throws java.sql.SQLException, UnsupportedTypeException

  // Methods
  public java.math.BigDecimal getBigDecimal(int columnIndex)
    throws NoSuchColumnException, UnsupportedConversionException;
  public java.math.BigDecimal getBigDecimal(String columnName)
    throws NoSuchColumnException, UnsupportedConversionException;
  public boolean getBoolean(int columnIndex)
    throws NoSuchColumnException, UnsupportedConversionException;
  public boolean getBoolean(String columnName)
    throws NoSuchColumnException, UnsupportedConversionException;
  public byte getByte(int columnIndex)
    throws NoSuchColumnException, UnsupportedConversionException;
  public byte getByte(String columnName)
    throws NoSuchColumnException, UnsupportedConversionException;
  public byte[] getBytes(int columnIndex)
    throws NoSuchColumnException, UnsupportedConversionException;
  public byte[] getBytes(String columnName)
    throws NoSuchColumnException, UnsupportedConversionException;
  public int getColumnCount();
  public Column[] getColumns();
  public java.sql.Date getDate(int columnIndex)
    throws NoSuchColumnException, UnsupportedConversionException;
  public java.sql.Date getDate(String columnName)
    throws NoSuchColumnException, UnsupportedConversionException;
  public double getDouble(int columnIndex)
    throws NoSuchColumnException, UnsupportedConversionException;
  public double getDouble(String columnName)
    throws NoSuchColumnException, UnsupportedConversionException;
  public float getFloat(int columnIndex)
    throws NoSuchColumnException, UnsupportedConversionException;
  public float getFloat(String columnName)
    throws NoSuchColumnException, UnsupportedConversionException;
  public int getInt(int columnIndex)
    throws NoSuchColumnException, UnsupportedConversionException;
  public int getInt(java.lang.String columnName)
    throws NoSuchColumnException, UnsupportedConversionException;
  public long getLong(int columnIndex)
    throws NoSuchColumnException, UnsupportedConversionException;
  public long getLong(String columnName)
```

```
    throws NoSuchColumnException, UnsupportedConversionException;
  public Object getObject(int columnIndex)
    throws NoSuchColumnException, UnsupportedConversionException;
  public Object getObject(String columnName)
    throws NoSuchColumnException, UnsupportedConversionException;
  public short getShort(int columnIndex)
    throws NoSuchColumnException, UnsupportedConversionException;
  public short getShort(java.lang.String columnName)
    throws NoSuchColumnException, UnsupportedConversionException;
  public String getString(int columnIndex)
    throws NoSuchColumnException;
  public String getString(String columnName)
    throws NoSuchColumnException;
  public java.sql.Time getTime(int columnIndex)
    throws NoSuchColumnException, UnsupportedConversionException;
  public java.sql.Time getTime(String columnName)
    throws NoSuchColumnException, UnsupportedConversionException;
  public java.sql.Timestamp getTimestamp(int columnIndex)
    throws NoSuchColumnException, UnsupportedConversionException;
  public java.sql.Timestamp getTimestamp(String columnName)
    throws NoSuchColumnException, UnsupportedConversionException;
}
```

Constructor

```
public Row(java.sql.ResultSet rs)
    throws java.sql.SQLException, UnsupportedTypeException
```
Reads the columns from the current row in the specified ResultSet, and creates the corresponding Column objects.

Methods

```
public java.math.BigDecimal getBigDecimal(int columnIndex)
    throws NoSuchColumnException, UnsupportedConversionException
public java.math.BigDecimal getBigDecimal(String columnName)
    throws NoSuchColumnException, UnsupportedConversionException
```
Returns the specified column value (by column name or index) as a BigDecimal.

```
public boolean getBoolean(int columnIndex)
    throws NoSuchColumnException, UnsupportedConversionException
public boolean getBoolean(String columnName)
    throws NoSuchColumnException, UnsupportedConversionException
```
Returns the specified column value (by column name or index) as a boolean.

```
public byte getByte(int columnIndex)
    throws NoSuchColumnException, UnsupportedConversionException
public byte getByte(String columnName)
    throws NoSuchColumnException, UnsupportedConversionException
```
Returns the specified column value (by column name or index) as a byte.

```
public byte[] getBytes(int columnIndex)
    throws NoSuchColumnException, UnsupportedConversionException
public byte[] getBytes(String columnName)
    throws NoSuchColumnException, UnsupportedConversionException
```
Returns the specified column value (by column name or index) as a byte[].

```
public int getColumnCount()
```
Returns the number of columns in the row.

```
public Column[] getColumns()
```
Returns all columns as a Column[].

```
public java.sql.Date getDate(int columnIndex)
    throws NoSuchColumnException, UnsupportedConversionException
public java.sql.Date getDate(String columnName)
    throws NoSuchColumnException, UnsupportedConversionException
```
Returns the specified column value (by column name or index) as a Date.

```
public double getDouble(int columnIndex)
    throws NoSuchColumnException, UnsupportedConversionException
public double getDouble(String columnName)
    throws NoSuchColumnException, UnsupportedConversionException
```
Returns the specified column value (by column name or index) as a double.

```
public float getFloat(int columnIndex)
    throws NoSuchColumnException, UnsupportedConversionException
public float getFloat(String columnName)
    throws NoSuchColumnException, UnsupportedConversionException
```
Returns the specified column value (by column name or index) as a float.

```
public int getInt(int columnIndex)
    throws NoSuchColumnException, UnsupportedConversionException
public int getInt(java.lang.String columnName)
    throws NoSuchColumnException, UnsupportedConversionException
```
Returns the specified column value (by column name or index) as an int.

```
public long getLong(int columnIndex)
    throws NoSuchColumnException, UnsupportedConversionException
public long getLong(String columnName)
    throws NoSuchColumnException, UnsupportedConversionException
```
Returns the specified column value (by column name or index) as a long.

```
public Object getObject(int columnIndex)
    throws NoSuchColumnException, UnsupportedConversionException
public Object getObject(String columnName)
    throws NoSuchColumnException, UnsupportedConversionException
```
Returns the specified column value (by column name or index) as an Object.

```
public short getShort(int columnIndex)
    throws NoSuchColumnException, UnsupportedConversionException
public short getShort(java.lang.String columnName)
    throws NoSuchColumnException, UnsupportedConversionException
```
Returns the specified column value (by column name or index) as a short.

```
public String getString(int columnIndex)
    throws NoSuchColumnException
public String getString(String columnName)
    throws NoSuchColumnException
```
Returns the specified column value (by column name or index) as a String.

```
public java.sql.Time getTime(int columnIndex)
    throws NoSuchColumnException, UnsupportedConversionException
public java.sql.Time getTime(String columnName)
    throws NoSuchColumnException, UnsupportedConversionException
```
Returns the specified column value (by column name or index) as a Time.

```
public java.sql.Timestamp getTimestamp(int columnIndex)
    throws NoSuchColumnException, UnsupportedConversionException
public java.sql.Timestamp getTimestamp(String columnName)
    throws NoSuchColumnException, UnsupportedConversionException
```
Returns the specified column value (by column name or index) as a Timestamp.

SQLCommandBean

Synopsis

Class Name:	com.ora.jsp.sql.SQLCommandBean
Extends:	None
Implements:	None

Description

The SQLCommandBean class is a bean for executing SQL statements, and is used by the database custom actions. It can also be used in a servlet to simplify the database access code. The bean has three properties that can be set: connection, sqlValue, and values. The connection and sqlValue properties must always be set before calling one of the execute methods. If the values property is set, the sqlValue property must be a SQL statement with question marks as placeholders for the value objects in the values property. The bean properties are described in Table C-24.

Table C-24. com.ora.jsp.SQLCommandBean Properties

Property Name	Java Type	Access	Description
connection	java.sql.Connection	write	The database Connection to use.
sqlValue	String	write	The SQL statement to execute, optionally with question marks as placeholders for values.
values	java.util.Vector	write	A Vector with Value objects (see the next section, "Value Classes").

The SQLCommandBean class also provides the following regular methods for executing the SQL statement.

public java.util.Vector executeQuery()
    throws java.sql.SQLException, UnsupportedTypeException
    Returns a Vector with Row objects as the result of executing a SELECT statement.

public int executeUpdate()
    throws java.sql.SQLException, UnsupportedTypeException
    Returns the number of rows affected by a DELETE, INSERT, or UPDATE statement.

Value Classes

The SQLCommandBean class has a property named values, which is a java.util. Vector with com.ora.jsp.sql.Value subclass instances. The subclasses are defined in the com.ora.jsp.sql.value package, with subclasses corresponding to most of the JDBC column datatypes.

All subclasses provide a constructor with an argument of the Java datatype that the class represents. The Value superclass contains access methods for all datatypes (that just throw an UnsupportedConversionException), and each subclass overrides the method for its datatype:

```
com.ora.jsp.sql.value.BigDecimalValue:
    public BigDecimalValue(java.math.BigDecimal value);
    public java.math.BigDecimal getBigDecimal()
      throws UnsupportedConversionException;

com.ora.jsp.sql.value.BooleanValue:
    public BooleanValue(boolean value);
    public boolean getBooleanValue()
      throws UnsupportedConversionException;

com.ora.jsp.sql.value.BytesValue:
    public BytesValue(byte[] value);
    public byte[] getBytesValue() throws UnsupportedConversionException;
```

```
com.ora.jsp.sql.value.ByteValue:
   public ByteValue(byte value);
   public byte getByte() throws UnsupportedConversionException;

com.ora.jsp.sql.value.DateValue:
   public DateValue(java.sql.Date value);
   public java.sql.Date getDate()
     throws UnsupportedConversionException;

com.ora.jsp.sql.value.DoubleValue:
   public DoubleValue(double value);
   public double getDouble() throws UnsupportedConversionException;

com.ora.jsp.sql.value.FloatValue:
   public FloatValue(float value);
   public float getFloat() throws UnsupportedConversionException;

com.ora.jsp.sql.value.IntValue:
   public IntValue(int value);
   public int getInt() throws UnsupportedConversionException;

com.ora.jsp.sql.value.LongValue:
   public LongValue(long value);
   public long getLong() throws UnsupportedConversionException;

com.ora.jsp.sql.value.ObjectValue:
   public ObjectValue(Object value);
   public Object getObject() throws UnsupportedConversionException;

com.ora.jsp.sql.value.ShortValue:
   public ShortValue(short value);
   public short getShort() throws UnsupportedConversionException;

com.ora.jsp.sql.value.StringValue:
   public StringValue(String value);
   public String getString();

com.ora.jsp.sql.value.TimestampValue:
   public TimestampValue(java.sql.Timestamp value);
   public java.sql.Timestamp getTimestamp()
     throws UnsupportedConversionException;

com.ora.jsp.sql.value.TimeValue:
   public TimeValue(java.sql.Time value);
   public java.sql.Time getTime()
     throws UnsupportedConversionException;
```

All subclasses also override the method that returns the value converted to a String:

```
public String getString();
```

Column Classes

The Row class contains com.ora.jsp.sql.Column subclass instances. The subclasses are defined in the com.ora.jsp.sql.column package, with subclasses corresponding to most of the JDBC column datatypes.

All subclasses provide a constructor with a String argument for the column name, and a value argument of the Java datatype the class represents. The Column superclass contains access methods for all datatypes (that just throws an UnsupportedConversionException), and each subclass overrides the method for its datatype:

```
com.ora.jsp.sql.column.BigDecimalColumn:
  public BigDecimalColumn(String name, BigDecimal value);
  public java.math.BigDecimal getBigDecimal()
    throws UnsupportedConversionException;

com.ora.jsp.sql.column.BooleanColumn:
  public BooleanColumn(String name, boolean value);
  public boolean getBooleanValue()
    throws UnsupportedConversionException;

com.ora.jsp.sql.column.ByteColumn:
  public ByteColumn(String name, byte value);
  public byte getByte() throws UnsupportedConversionException;

com.ora.jsp.sql.column.BytesColumn:
  public BytesColumn(String name, byte[] value);
  public byte[] getBytesValue() throws UnsupportedConversionException;

com.ora.jsp.sql.column.DateColumn:
  public DateColumn(String name, java.sql.Date value);
  public java.sql.Date getDate()
    throws UnsupportedConversionException;

com.ora.jsp.sql.column.DoubleColumn:
  public DoubleColumn(String name, double value);
  public double getDouble() throws UnsupportedConversionException;

com.ora.jsp.sql.column.FloatColumn:
  public FloatColumn(String name, float value);
  public float getFloat() throws UnsupportedConversionException;

com.ora.jsp.sql.column.IntColumn:
  public IntColumn(String name, int value);
  public int getInt() throws UnsupportedConversionException;

com.ora.jsp.sql.column.LongColumn:
  public LongColumn(String name, long value);
  public long getLong() throws UnsupportedConversionException;
```

```
com.ora.jsp.sql.column.ObjectColumn:
  public ObjectColumn(String name, Object value);
  public Object getObject() throws UnsupportedConversionException;

com.ora.jsp.sql.column.ShortColumn:
  public ShortColumn(String name, short value);
  public short getShort() throws UnsupportedConversionException;

com.ora.jsp.sql.column.StringColumn:
  public StringColumn(String name, String value);
  public String getString();

com.ora.jsp.sql.column.TimeColumn:
  public TimeColumn(String name, java.sql.Time value);
  public java.sql.Time getTime()
    throws UnsupportedConversionException;

com.ora.jsp.sql.column.TimestampColumn:
  public TimestampColumn(String name, java.sql.Timestamp value);
  public java.sql.Timestamp getTimestamp()
    throws UnsupportedConversionException;
```

All subclasses also override the method that returns the value converted to a
String. A method for returning the column name is provided by the Value
superclass:

```
public String getString();
public String toString();
public String getName();
```

D

Web-Application Structure and Deployment Descriptor Reference

A complete web application may consist of several different resources: JSP pages, servlets, applets, static HTML pages, custom tag libraries, and other Java class files. Version 2.2 of the servlet specification defines a portable way to package all these resources together with a deployment descriptor that contains configuration information, such as how all the resources fit together, security requirements, etc. This appendix describes the standard file structure for a web application, and how to use the deployment descriptor to configure the application.

Web Application File Structure

The portable distribution and deployment format for a web application defined by the servlet specification is the Web Archive (WAR). All Servlet 2.2–compliant servers provide tools for installing a WAR file and associate the application with a servlet context.

A WAR file has a *.war* file extension and can be created with the Java *jar* command or a ZIP utility program, such as *WinZip*, as described at the end of this appendix. The internal structure of the WAR file is defined by the servlet specification:

```
/index.html
/company/index.html
/company/contact.html
/company/phonelist.jsp
/products/searchform.html
/products/list.jsp
/images/banner.gif
/WEB-INF/web.xml
/WEB-INF/lib/bean.jar
/WEB-INF/lib/actions.jar
/WEB-INF/classes/com/mycorp/servlets/PurchaseServlet.class
```

```
/WEB-INF/classes/com/mycorp/util/MyUtils.class
/WEB-INF/tlds/actions.tld
```

The top level in this structure is the document root for all application web page files. This is where you place all your HTML pages, JSP pages, and image files. All these files can be accessed with a URI starting with the context path. For instance, if the application has been assigned the context path */sales*, the URI */sales/ products/list.jsp* is used to access the JSP page named *list.jsp* in the *products* directory in this example.

Placing Java Class Files in the Right Directory

The *WEB-INF* directory contains files and subdirectories for other types of resources. Two *WEB-INF* subdirectories have special meanings: *lib* and *classes*. The *lib* directory contains JAR files with Java class files, for instance JavaBeans classes, custom action handler classes, and utility classes. The *classes* directory contains class files that are not packaged in JAR files. The servlet container automatically has access to all class files in the *lib* and *classes* directories; in other words, you do *not* have to add them to the CLASSPATH environment variable.

If you store class files in the *classes* directory, they must be stored in subdirectories mirroring the package structure. For instance, if you have a class named com. mycorp.util.MyUtils, you must store the class file in *WEB-INF/classes/com/ mycorp/util/MyUtils.class*. Another type of file that can be stored in the *classes* directory is a resource properties file used by the PropertyResourceBundle class, as described in Chapter 11, *Internationalization*.

The *WEB-INF* directory can also contain other directories. For instance, a directory named *tlds* is by convention used for tag library Tag Library Descriptor (TLD) files. Files under the *WEB-INF* directory can't be accessed directly by a browser, so it's a good place for all types of configuration files.

During development, it's more convenient to work with the web application files in a regular filesystem structure instead of creating a new WAR file every time something changes. Most containers therefore support the WAR structure in an open filesystem as well. The book example application is distributed as an open filesystem structure to make it easier for you to see all the files.

Web Application Deployment Descriptor

The *WEB-INF/web.xml* file is a very important file. It is the application deployment descriptor that contains all configuration information for the application. If your application consists only of JSP and HTML files, you typically do not need to worry about this file at all. But if the application also contains servlets, tag libraries, or uses the container-provided security mechanisms, you often need to define some configuration information in the *web.xml* file.

The deployment descriptor is an XML file. A standard XML Document Type Definition (DTD) defines the elements it can contain and how they must be arranged. Example D-1 shows a version of the complete DTD* without the comments. All elements are instead described after the example.

Example D-1. Java Web Application Descriptor DTD

```
<!ELEMENT web-app (icon?, display-name?, description?, distributable?,
context-param*, servlet*, servlet-mapping*, session-config?,
mime-mapping*, welcome-file-list?, error-page*, taglib*,
resource-ref*, security-constraint*, login-config?, security-role*,
env-entry*, ejb-ref*)>

<!ELEMENT icon (small-icon?, large-icon?)>
<!ELEMENT small-icon (#PCDATA)>
<!ELEMENT large-icon (#PCDATA)>
<!ELEMENT display-name (#PCDATA)>
<!ELEMENT description (#PCDATA)>

<!ELEMENT distributable EMPTY>

<!ELEMENT context-param (param-name, param-value, description?)>
<!ELEMENT param-name (#PCDATA)>
<!ELEMENT param-value (#PCDATA)>

<!ELEMENT servlet (icon?, servlet-name, display-name?, description?,
(servlet-class|jsp-file), init-param*, load-on-startup?,
security-role-ref*)>
<!ELEMENT servlet-name (#PCDATA)>
<!ELEMENT servlet-class (#PCDATA)>
<!ELEMENT jsp-file (#PCDATA)>
<!ELEMENT init-param (param-name, param-value, description?)>
<!ELEMENT load-on-startup (#PCDATA)>

<!ELEMENT servlet-mapping (servlet-name, url-pattern)>
<!ELEMENT url-pattern (#PCDATA)>

<!ELEMENT session-config (session-timeout?)>
<!ELEMENT session-timeout (#PCDATA)>

<!ELEMENT mime-mapping (extension, mime-type)>
<!ELEMENT extension (#PCDATA)>
<!ELEMENT mime-type (#PCDATA)>
```

---

* The ID attribute declarations are not included, since they are of interest only to tool developers who need to extend the DTD.

Example D-1. Java Web Application Descriptor DTD (continued)

```
<!ELEMENT welcome-file-list (welcome-file+)>
<!ELEMENT welcome-file (#PCDATA)>

<!ELEMENT taglib (taglib-uri, taglib-location)>
<!ELEMENT taglib-uri (#PCDATA)>
<!ELEMENT taglib-location (#PCDATA)>

<!ELEMENT error-page ((error-code | exception-type), location)>
<!ELEMENT error-code (#PCDATA)>
<!ELEMENT exception-type (#PCDATA)>
<!ELEMENT location (#PCDATA)>

<!ELEMENT resource-ref (description?, res-ref-name, res-type,
res-auth)>
<!ELEMENT res-ref-name (#PCDATA)>
<!ELEMENT res-type (#PCDATA)>
<!ELEMENT res-auth (#PCDATA)>

<!ELEMENT security-constraint (web-resource-collection+,
auth-constraint?, user-data-constraint?)>
<!ELEMENT web-resource-collection (web-resource-name, description?,
url-pattern*, http-method*)>
<!ELEMENT web-resource-name (#PCDATA)>
<!ELEMENT http-method (#PCDATA)>
<!ELEMENT user-data-constraint (description?, transport-guarantee)>
<!ELEMENT transport-guarantee (#PCDATA)>
<!ELEMENT auth-constraint (description?, role-name*)>
<!ELEMENT role-name (#PCDATA)>

<!ELEMENT login-config (auth-method?, realm-name?,
form-login-config?)>
<!ELEMENT realm-name (#PCDATA)>
<!ELEMENT form-login-config (form-login-page, form-error-page)>
<!ELEMENT form-login-page (#PCDATA)>
<!ELEMENT form-error-page (#PCDATA)>
<!ELEMENT auth-method (#PCDATA)>

<!ELEMENT security-role (description?, role-name)>
<!ELEMENT security-role-ref (description?, role-name, role-link)>
<!ELEMENT role-link (#PCDATA)>

<!ELEMENT env-entry (description?, env-entry-name, env-entry-value?,
env-entry-type)>
<!ELEMENT env-entry-name (#PCDATA)>
<!ELEMENT env-entry-value (#PCDATA)>
<!ELEMENT env-entry-type (#PCDATA)>
```

Example D-1. Java Web Application Descriptor DTD (continued)

```
<!ELEMENT ejb-ref (description?, ejb-ref-name, ejb-ref-type, home,
remote, ejb-link?)>
<!ELEMENT ejb-ref-name (#PCDATA)>
<!ELEMENT ejb-ref-type (#PCDATA)>
<!ELEMENT home (#PCDATA)>
<!ELEMENT remote (#PCDATA)>
<!ELEMENT ejb-link (#PCDATA)>
```

If you're not familiar with DTD syntax, don't worry. This DTD contains only element declarations, and the rules are simple. The `<!ELEMENT ... >` declaration contains two parts: the element name and the element syntax rules within parentheses. The rules in this DTD contain the following types:

- A comma-separated list of elements. The named elements must appear in the same order as in the XML document. For example, the `taglib` declaration says that a `<taglib>` element must contain first a `<taglib-uri>` element, and then a `<taglib-location>` element:

```
<!ELEMENT taglib (taglib-uri, taglib-location)>
```

- An element name followed by a question mark. This means that the named element is optional. For instance, an `<init-param>` element must contain a `<param-name>` and a `<param-value>` element, optionally followed by a `<description>` element:

```
<!ELEMENT init-param (param-name, param-value, description?)>
```

- An element name followed by a plus sign. This means that the named element can be used one or more times. A `<welcome-file-list>` can contain one or more `<welcome-file>` elements; for instance:

```
<!ELEMENT welcome-file-list (welcome-file+)>
```

- An element name followed by an asterisk. This means the element can be used zero or more times. That's the case for the `<role-name>` element in an `<auth-constraint>` element:

```
<!ELEMENT auth-constraint (description?, role-name*)>
```

- Two element names separated by a vertical bar. This means that one, but not both, of the elements must be used. An example of this is found in the `<servlet>` element declaration, which says that it must contain either a `<servlet-class>` element or a `<jsp-file>` element:

```
<!ELEMENT servlet (icon?, servlet-name, display-name?, description?,
(servlet-class|jsp-file), init-param*, load-on-startup?,
security-role-ref*)>
```

- The `#PCDATA` keyword. This means *parsed character data*, i.e., ordinary text as opposed to nested subelements.

The first element declaration in the DTD shown in Example D-1 is the main element for the *web.xml* file, named the <web-app> element:

```
<!ELEMENT web-app (icon?, display-name?, description?, distributable?,
context-param*, servlet*, servlet-mapping*, session-config?,
mime-mapping*, welcome-file-list?, error-page*, taglib*,
resource-ref*, security-constraint*, login-config?, security-role*,
env-entry*, ejb-ref*)>
```

It contains a comma-separated list of all the top-level elements that the <web-app> element can contain. All of them are optional (marked with question marks or asterisks). The rest of this section describes all these elements in more detail.

<icon>, <display-name>, and <description>

The first three elements are used to provide information a web container deployment tool can use to describe the application. The <icon> element can contain a <small-icon> and a <large-icon> element, each with a context-relative path to an image file (GIF and JPEG formats are supported). The <display-name> element can be used to specify a name for the application, and the <description> element for a longer description:

```
<icon>
   <small-icon>/images/small.gif</small-icon>
   <large-icon>/images/large.gif</large-icon>
</icon>
<display-name>The application name</display-name>
<description>
   A longer description of
   the application.
</description>
```

<distributable>

The <distributable> element is used to tell the web container that the application is designed to run in a distributed web container. This element does not contain a body:

```
<distributable/>
```

A distributable application does not rely on servlet instance variables, static classes or variables, servlet context attributes, or any other mechanism for shared information that is restricted to one Java VM. It also means that all objects placed in the session scope are serializable, so that the container can move the session data from one JVM to another. For more information about distributed applications, see Chapter 13, *Web Application Models*.

<context-param>

Using the <context-param> element, you can define initialization parameters that are available to all components of the application (both servlets and JSP pages). The <param-name> subelement is used to specify the name, and the <param-value> element the value. Optionally, the <description> element can be used for a description that can be displayed by a deployment tool:

```
<context-param>
  <param-name>jdbcURL</param-name>
  <param-value>jdbc:idb:/usr/local/db/mydb.prp</param-value>
</context-param>
```

The value of a context initialization parameter can be retrieved with code like this in a servlet:

```
ServletContext context = getServletContext();
String jdbcURL = context.getInitParameter("jdbcURL");
```

In a JSP page, a reference to the context is always assigned to the application implicit variable, so scriptlet code like this can be used:

```
<%
  String jdbcURL = application.getInitParameter("jdbcURL");
%>
```

<servlet>

The <servlet> element can be used to describe a servlet class or a JSP page, giving it a short name and specifying initialization parameters:

```
<servlet>
  <servlet-name>
    purchase
  </servlet-name>
  <servlet-class>
    com.mycorp.servlets.PurchaseServlet
  </servlet-class>
  <init-param>
    <param-name>maxAmount</param-name>
    <param-value>500.00</param-value>
  </init-param>
</servlet>

<servlet>
  <servlet-name>
    order-form
  </servlet-name>
  <jsp-file>
    /po/orderform.jsp
```

```
  </jsp-file>
  <init-param>
    <param-name>bgColor</param-name>
    <param-value>blue</param-value>
  </init-param>
</servlet>
```

The same servlet class (or JSP page) can be defined with multiple names, typically with different initialization parameters. The container creates one instance of the class for each name.

An initialization parameter value is retrieved like this in a servlet:

```
ServletConfig config = getServletConfig();
String maxAmount = config.getInitParameter("maxAmount");
```

A reference to the servlet configuration object is assigned to the config implicit variable in a JSP page, so scriptlet code like this can be used:

```
<%
    String bgColor = config.getInitParameter("bgColor");
%>
```

The <load-on-startup> subelement can be used to tell the container to load the servlet when the application is started. The value is a positive integer, indicating when the servlet is to be loaded relative to other servlets. A servlet with a low value is loaded before a servlet with a higher value:

```
<servlet>
  <servlet-name>
    controller
  </servlet-name>
  <servlet-class>
    com.mycorp.servlets.ControllerServlet
  </servlet-class>
  <load-on-startup>1</load-on-startup>
</servlet>
```

The <icon>, <display-name>, and <description> elements can be used to describe the servlet or JSP page, the same way as these elements can used to describe the application.

Finally, <security-role-ref> elements, combined with <security-role> elements, can be used to link a security role name used in a servlet as the argument to the HttpServletRequest.isUserInRole() method to a role name known by the web container:

```
<servlet>
  <servlet-name>
    controller
  </servlet-name>
```

```
    <servlet-class>
      com.mycorp.servlets.ControllerServlet
    </servlet-class>
    <security-role-ref>
      <role-name>administrator</role-name>
      <role-link>admin</role-link>
    </security-role-ref>
  </servlet>
  ...
  <security-role>
    <role-name>admin</role-name>
  </security-role>
```

All role names defined by `<security-role>` elements must be mapped to users and/or groups known by the web container. How this is done is container-dependent. The `<security-role-ref>` element allows you to use a servlet that uses a role name in the `isUserInRole()` method that is not defined by a `<security-role>` element. A typical scenario where this can be useful is when combining servlets from different sources into one application, where the servlets use different role names for the same logical role.

<servlet-mapping>

Most containers support a special URI prefix (*/servlet*) that can be used to invoke any servlet class that the container has access to; for instance, the URI */servlet/com. mycompany.MyServlet* can be used to invoke the servlet class `com.mycompany.MyServlet`. This is not mandated by the specification, however, so to ensure that the application is portable it's better to map a unique path to a servlet instead. Explicit mapping also simplifies references between servlets and JSP pages, as described in Chapter 14, *Combining Servlets and JSP*. The `<servlet-mapping>` element is used for this purpose. The `<servlet-name>` subelement contains a name defined by a `<servlet>` element, and the `<url-pattern>` contains the pattern that should be mapped to the servlet (or JSP page):

```
<servlet-mapping>
  <servlet-name>purchase</servlet-name>
  <url-pattern>/po/*</url-pattern>
</servlet-mapping>

<servlet-mapping>
  <servlet-name>sales-report</servlet-name>
  <url-pattern>/report</url-pattern>
</servlet-mapping>

<servlet-mapping>
  <servlet-name>XMLProcessor</servlet-name>
  <url-pattern>*.xml</url-pattern>
</servlet-mapping>
```

A pattern can take one of four forms:

- A *path prefix pattern* starts with a slash (/) and ends with /*, for instance /po/*.

- An *extension mapping pattern* starts with *., for instance *.xml.

- A *default servlet pattern* consists of just the / character.

- All other patterns are *exact match patterns*.

When the container receives a request, it strips off the context path and then tries to find a pattern that matches a servlet mapping. Exact match patterns are analyzed first, then the path prefix patterns starting with the longest one, and then the extension mapping patterns. If none of these patterns match, the default servlet pattern is used, if specified. As a last resort, the request is handled by the container's default request processor.

With the mappings defined here, a URI such as */po/supplies* invokes the purchase servlet, */report* invokes the *sales-report* servlet (but note that */report/spring* does not, since an exact match pattern is used), and */eastcoast/forecast.xml* invokes the XMLProcessor servlet.

<session-config>

The <session-config> element contains just one subelement, the <session-timeout> element used to specify the default session timeout value in minutes:

```
<session-config>
  <session-timout>30</session-timeout>
</session-config>
```

<mime-mapping>

A servlet may need to know which MIME type a file extension corresponds to. The <mime-mapping> element can be used to define the mappings an application requires:

```
<mime-mapping>
  <extension>wml</extension>
  <mime-type>text/vnd.wap.wml</mime-type>
</mime-mapping>
```

Most containers provide default mappings for the most commonly used extensions, such as *.html*, *.htm*, *.gif*, *.jpg*, and so on, but if you need to be absolutely sure that a mapping is defined for your application, put it in the *web.xml* file.

<welcome-file-list>

A welcome file is a file that the container serves when it receives a request URI that identifies a directory as opposed to a web page or a servlet. The <welcome-file-

list> element can be used to define an ordered list of files to look for in the directory and serve if present:

```
<welcome-file-list>
  <welcome-file>index.html</welcome-file>
  <welcome-file>index.htm</welcome-file>
  <welcome-file>default.html</welcome-file>
  <welcome-file>default.htm</welcome-file>
</welcome-file-list>
```

When a request is received that does not match a servlet mapping, the container appends each welcome filename, in the order specified in the deployment descriptor, to the request URI, and checks whether a resource in the WAR is mapped to the new URI. If it is, the request is passed to the resource. If no matching resource is found, the behavior is container-dependent. The container may, for instance, return a directory listing or a 404 status code (Not Found).

<error-page>

The <error-page> element can be used to define pages that inform the user about various errors. A page can be specified for an HTTP error status code, such as 404 (Not Found), using the <error-code> sub-element. As an alternative, the <exception-type> subelement can be used to specify a Java exception class name, in order to use a special page to handle exceptions thrown by servlets and JSP pages. The <location> subelement contains the context-relative path for the error page:

```
<error-page>
  <error-code>404</error-code>
  <location>/errors/404.html</location>
</error-page>
<error-page>
  <exception-type>javax.servlet.ServletException</exception-type>
  <location>/errors/exception.jsp</location>
</error-page>
```

<taglib>

The <taglib> element maps the symbolic name for a tag library specified by the taglib directive in a JSP page to the location of the Tag Library Descriptor (TLD) file or JAR file. The <taglib-uri> element value must match the uri attribute value used in the JSP page, and the <taglib-location> subelement contains the context-relative path to the library file:

```
<taglib>
  <taglib-uri>/orataglib</taglib-uri>
  <taglib-location>/WEB-INF/lib/orataglib_1_0.jar</taglib-location>
</taglib>
```

For more details, see Chapter 16, *Developing JSP Custom Actions.*

<security-constraint>, <security-role>, and <login-config>

The <security-constraint> element contains a subelement called <web-resource-collection> that defines the resources to be protected, and an <auth-constraint> subelement that defines who has access to the protected resources. It can also contain a <user-data-constraint> subelement that describes security requirements for the connection used to access the resource:

```
<security-constraint>
  <web-resource-collection>
    <web-resource-name>admin</web-resource-name>
    <url-pattern>/admin/*</url-pattern>
    <http-method>GET</http-method>
  </web-resource-collection>
  <auth-constraint>
    <role-name>admin</role-name>
  </auth-constraint>
  <user-data-constraint>
    <transport-guarantee>CONFIDENTIAL</ transport-guarantee>
  </user-data-constraint>
</security-constraint>
```

Within the <web-resource-collection> element, the resource is given a name with the <web-resource-name> subelement, and the URI patterns for the protected resources are specified with <url-pattern> elements. <http-method> subelements can also be used to restrict the types of accepted requests. This example protects all resources accessed with URIs that starts with */admin* and indicates that only the GET method can be used to access these resources.

The <role-name> subelements within the <auth-constraint> element specify the roles that the current user must have to get access to the resource. The value should be a role name defined by a <security-role> element, but some containers (like Tomcat) accept role names that are not defined by <security-role> elements as well. In this example, the user must belong to the admin role in order to access resources under */admin.* How the role names are mapped to user and/or group names in the container's security system is container-dependent.

A <transport-guarantee> element can contain one of three values:

- NONE. No special requirements. This is the default.

- INTEGRAL. Data must be sent between the client and server in such a way that it cannot be changed in transit. Typically this means that an SSL connection is required.

- CONFIDENTIAL. Data must be sent in such a way that it cannot be observed by others. This is also typically satisfied by an SSL connection.

<security-role> elements are used to define the role names that the application uses in isUserInRole() calls, in <security-role-ref> elements, and in <auth-constraint> elements:

```
<security-role>
  <role-name>admin</role-name>
</security-role>
```

Each role must be mapped to a user and/or group in the container's security domain in a container-dependent way.

For an application that uses the <security-constraint> element to protect resources, you must also define how to authenticate users with a <login-config> element. It can contain three subelements: <auth-method>, <realm-name>, and <form-login-config>:

```
<login-config>
  <auth-method>BASIC</auth-method>
  <realm-name>Protected pages</realm-name>
</login-config>
```

The <auth-method> element can have one of the values BASIC, DIGEST, FORM, or CLIENT-CERT, corresponding to the four container-provided authentication methods described in Chapter 10, *Authentication and Personalization*. When the BASIC or DIGEST authentication is used, the <realm-name> element can be used to specify the name shown by the browser when it prompts for a password.

If FORM authentication is used, the <form-login-config> element defines the login page and an error page (used for invalid login attempts):

```
<login-config>
  <auth-method>FORM</auth-method>
  <realm-name>Protected pages</realm-name>
  <form-login-config>
    <form-login-page>/login/login.html</form-login-page>
    <form-error-page>/login/error.html</form-error-page>
  </form-login-config>
</login-config>
```

For more about authentication, see Chapter 10.

<resource-ref>, <env-entry>, and <ejb-ref>

The <resource-ref>, <env-entry>, and <ejb-ref> elements are supported only by containers that provide a complete Java 2 Enterprise Edition (J2EE) environment. They are all used to declare names that the web components (servlets and JSP pages) use to access external resources, such as Enterprise JavaBeans (EJB) and JDBC DataSource objects. The <resource-ref> element is used to declare the connection factories (such as a DataSource) used by the web application, the <env-entry> element is used to define simple objects, such as a String or Boolean, and the <ejb-ref> element is used to declare EJB objects. All resources must be set up by the deployer, and the container makes them available to the web application through JNDI. For more about these elements, please see the J2EE documentation at *http://java.sun.com/j2ee/docs.html.*

Example Application Deployment Descriptor

Example D-2 shows an example of a *web.xml* file.

Example D-2. Example web.xml File

```
<?xml version="1.0" encoding="ISO-8859-1"?>

<!DOCTYPE web-app
  PUBLIC "-//Sun Microsystems, Inc.//DTD Web Application 2.2//EN"
  "http://java.sun.com/j2ee/dtds/web-app_2.2.dtd">

<web-app>
  <servlet>
    <servlet-name>
      purchase
    </servlet-name>
    <servlet-class>
      com.mycorp.servlets.PurchaseServlet
    </servlet-class>
  </servlet>

  <servlet-mapping>
    <servlet-name>
      purchase
    </servlet-name>
    <url-pattern>
      /po/*
    </url-pattern>
  </servlet-mapping>
</web-app>
```

At the top of the file, you find a standard XML declaration and a DOCTYPE declaration, specifying the Document Type Definition (DTD) for this file. Then follows the <web-app> element with a <servlet> element that defines a servlet named purchase, and a <servlet-mapping> element that maps the servlet to the /po/* path prefix pattern.

Creating a WAR File

A WAR file is an archive file, used to group all application files into a convenient package. A WAR file can be created with the *jar* command, included in the Java runtime environment, or a ZIP utility program such as *WinZip*. To create a WAR file, you first need to create the file structure as directories in the filesystem and place all files in the correct location as described earlier.

With the file structure in place, *cd* to the top-level directory for the application in the filesystem. You can then use the *jar* command to create the WAR file:

```
C:\> cd myapp
C:\myapp> jar cvf myapp_1_0.war *
```

This command creates a WAR file named *myapp_1_0.war* containing all files in the *myapp* directory. You can use any filename that makes sense for your application, but avoid spaces in the filename since they can cause problems on many platforms. Including the version number of the application in the filename is a good idea, since it is helpful for the users to know which version of the application the file contains.

E

JSP Resource Reference

This appendix contains references to JSP-related products, web hosting services, and sites where you can learn more about JSP and related technologies.

JSP-Related Products

Syntax-Aware Editors

A syntax-aware editor is a text editor that color-codes programming language elements, provides automatic indentation and element completion, and more. Some examples are listed here. Most of them do not specifically support JSP syntax, but can be configured to handle JSP elements as well, and are frequently recommended on the *jsp-interest* mailing list:

Emacs (GNU Project), http://www.gnu.org/software/emacs/emacs.html
> A powerful editor that can do almost anything and runs on pretty much any platform. Emacs can be configured for mixed HTML and Java mode using the *html-helper-mode.el* and *multi-mode.el* modules. The *jsp-interest* mailing list archive has more details about this: *http://archives.java.sun.com/archives/jsp-interest.html*.

HomeSite (Allaire), http://www.allaire.com/products/homesite/index.cfm
> An HTML editor with support for JSP, ASP, JavaScript, VBScript, and more. Available for Windows only.

JPad Pro (Modelworks Software), http://www.modelworks.com
> A Java IDE with support for editing customized HTML, for Windows only.

SlickEdit (MicroEdge, Inc.), http://www.slickedit.com
> Supports syntax for customized HTML and many programming languages, on Windows, OS/2, and most Unix flavors, including Linux.

Web Page Authoring Tools

Web page authoring tools are What-You-See-Is-What-You-Get (WYSIWYG) tools for web page development (or as close as is possible with HTML). They provide a graphic user interface that hides all HTML details and lets you drag-and-drop components such as HTML form elements, images, etc., to the location you want them to appear on the screen. The products listed here support JSP to varying degrees:

GoLive (Adobe), http://www.adobe.com/products/golive/
> GoLive 5.0 supports only ASP elements, but JSP support has been announced and may be available when you read this. Available on Windows and Mac platforms.

Dreamweaver UltraDev (Macromedia), http://www.macromedia.com
> Supports integration of JSP, ASP, and ColdFusion elements in the web pages. Available on Windows and Mac platforms.

Unify eWave Studio (Unify), http://www.unify.com/products/ewave/studio.htm
> A web application development tool that helps you create JSP pages without extensive coding. Includes features such as DataForm Wizard to create web interfaces to databases, and Studio Asset Center for collaboration and centralized management of all web application resources.

WebSphere Studio (IBM), http://www-4.ibm.com/software/
> Includes a page designer tool for visual development of HTML and JSP pages. Available only for Windows platforms.

Java IDEs with JSP support

A number of Java Interactive Development Environments (IDEs) include varying degrees of support for JSP development, such as syntax-aware editors and debugging capabilities. Here are some examples:

Forte, Forte for Java (Sun), http://www.sun.com/forte/ffj/ce/
> A Java IDE that includes a JSP module providing a JSP page editor, templates, and execution of JSP pages. Forte is a Java application, so it runs on any platform with a Java runtime environment.

JRun Studio (Allaire), http://www.allaire.com
> An IDE for server-side Java development, including a JSP page editor with color-coding and a custom action property sheet editor.

Kawa (TEK-TOOLS), http://www.tek-tools.com
> An IDE with support for EJB, JSP, and servlet debugging. Kawa is a Java application, so it runs on any platform with a Java runtime environment.

Oracle, JDeveloper http://www.oracle.com/java/
    A development environment for Java-based database applications with support for JSP-based user interfaces.

VisualAge for Java (IBM), http://www-4.ibm.com/software/ad/vajava/
    An IDE with support for servlet and JSP debugging as well as a wizard for generation of template code. Available for Windows and Linux.

JSP Component Suites

More and more JSP components, such as tag libraries and server-side JavaBeans, are being offered by commercial companies as well as open source organizations. Here are a few examples:

BEA WebLogic Portal JSP Tag Libraries (BEA), http://edocs.beasys.com/wlac/portals/docs/ tagscontents.html
    A tag library for building web portals plus a set of utility actions.

InstantOnline Basic (Gefion software*), http://www.gefionsoftware.com
    A tag library and JavaBeans for accessing databases, sending email, uploading files, validating input, conditional processing, and more. This library lets you use a simple variable syntax to access request information, JavaBeans properties, query results, etc., eliminating the need for Java code in the JSP pages.

IN 16 JSP Tag Library (SourceForge), http://sourceforge.net/projects/jsptags/
    An open source project working on various tag libraries, currently in the areas of HTML generation, database access, EJB access, and XML.

Jakarta taglibs (Apache Software Foundation), http://jakarta.apache.org
    Tag libraries for database access, processing XML data with an XSL stylesheet, using the Bean Scripting Framework (BSF) to embed scriptlets written in Rhino (JavaScript), VBScript, Perl, Tcl, Python, NetRexx and Rexx, as well as an implementation of the example tags described in the JSP specification.

JRun components (Allaire), http://www.allaire.com
    A tag library included with the JRun product, with support for database access, message services, email, XML transformations, and JNDI access.

Orion Taglibs (Evermind), http://www.orionserver.com
    A tag library for accessing EJB resources and utility actions for conditional processing, localized number and date formatting, and sending email.

Pager Tag Library (JSPtags.com), http://jsptags.com/tags/navigation/pager/
    A tag library for generation of Google- and AltaVista-style search result navigators.

---

* For full disclosure, I am the founder of Gefion software.

Web and Application Servers with JSP 1.1 Support

Most of the major web and application servers support JSP 1.1 out of the box. For servers without native support, add-on containers can be used. This is just a short sample of the most popular servers and add-on containers:

BEA WebLogic (BEA), http://www.bea.com
A family of application servers with support for EJB, servlets, JSP, JDBC, and JNDI.

iPlanet (iPlanet), http://www.iplanet.com
A web server with support for servlets and JSP, and an application server with support for the full J2EE platform.

JRun (Allaire), http://www.allaire.com/products/jrun/
An application server with support for the complete J2EE specification.

LiteWebServer (Gefion software), http://www.gefionsoftware.com
A web server with a very small footprint and support for servlets and JSP, suitable as an embedded server and for development, demos, and small work groups.

Oracle8i JServer (Oracle), http://www.oracle.com/java/
A Java server integrated in the Oracle 8i database with support for servlets and JSP.

Orion (Evermind), http://www.orionserver.com
A high-performance application server with support for the complete J2EE platform.

Resin (Caucho), http://www.caucho.com
An open source, standalone servlet and JSP-enabled web server that can also be used as an add-on container for Apache, IIS, and iPlanet web servers.

SilverStream (SilverStream), http://www.silverstream.com
An application server with support for the J2EE specification.

Tomcat (Apache Software Foundation), http://jakarta.apache.org
Tomcat is the official reference implementation for the servlet and JSP specifications, developed as an open source product in the Apache Jakarta project.

Unify eWave ServletExec (Unify), http://www.unify.com
An add-on container for Apache, IIS, Netscape, and other web servers, with support for servlets and JSP.

WebSphere (IBM), http://www.software.ibm.com
An application server with support for servlets and JSP.

Web Hosting

If you want to host your web site on an external site, a growing number of hosting companies offer servlet and JSP support. This information changes frequently, so instead of including references to companies here, I suggest that you look at an up-to-date list on one of these web sites:

http://www.servlets.com/resources/urls/isps.html
> A list of web hosting companies with servlet support, on the web site of Jason Hunter's *Java Servlet Programming* book.

http://www.TheJSPBook.com
> The web site for this book, where you can find a list of web hosting companies with JSP support, as well as a lot of other JSP-related information.

Information and Specifications

If you would like to find out more about JSP, servlets and related technologies such as the other parts of the J2EE platform and HTTP, here are some sites you can visit:

- Sun's JSP site, *http://java.sun.com/products/jsp/*

- Sun's servlet site, *http://java.sun.com/products/servlet/*

- Sun's mailing list archives, *http://archives.java.sun.com/archives/*

- Developing Enterprise Applications With the Java 2 Platform, Enterprise Edition, *http://java.sun.com/j2ee/blueprints/*

- jGuru JSP FAQ, *http://www.jguru.com/jguru/faq/faqpage.jsp?name=JSP*

- Esperanto JSP FAQ, *http://www.esperanto.org.nz/jsp/jspfaq.html*

- JSPTags.com, *http://jsptags.com*

- The JSP Resource Index, *http://www.jspin.com*

- JSPInsider, *http://www.jspinsider.com*

- ServerPages.com, *http://www.serverpages.com/Java_Server_Pages/*

- HTTP/1.1 specification, *ftp://ftp.isi.edu/in-notes/rfc2616.txt*

- HTML 3.2 specification, *http://www.w3.org/TR/REC-html32.html*

- HTML 4.0 specification, *http://www.w3.org/TR/REC-html40/*

As you know, things move extremely fast in this industry, so by the time you read this there may be many more products and sites available. For the latest news, I suggest that you take a look at Sun's JSP site at *http://java.sun.com/products/jsp/*. The web site for this book, *http://www.TheJSPBook.com*, also contains up-to-date references to a number of JSP resources, in addition to the source code for all examples, and other information about this book.

Index

Symbols

<%! %>, enclosing declarations, 402
<%@ %>, enclosing directives, 58
<%= %>, enclosing expressions, 402
<%- -%>, enclosing JSP comments, 70, 411
<% %>, enclosing scriptlets, 402
? (question mark)
  beginning string queries, 17
  conditional operator, 82
  SQL statement placeholder, 167
/ (slash)
  /* */, enclosing block comments, 79
  // beginning end-of-line comments, 79
  /* wildcard sequence, ending path
    patterns, 292
  in context path, 118

A

<a> HTML link element, 465
absolute path, URIs, 265
Accept headers, 14
Accept-Language header, 215
access control, 184
  application-controlled
    requirements for, 191
  applications, adding to
    (main.jsp), 202–204
  connection pools, role in, 360

  for JSP pages, 294
  SQL statements submitted through
    Connection interface, 359
Access database, 159
  System DSN, creating for, 164
accessor methods, 302
  beans, naming of, 86
  Column, for all datatypes, 380
  getter, no-argument, 133
  for parent instance variable, 337
action elements, 5, 33, 60, 403–410
  body, processing, 331–336
  code generated for, 342
  custom, 410
    database access, features of, 156
    developing, 323–357
    for databases, 162
    prefixes for, 140
    using, 138–143
    (see also custom actions)
  in JSP pages, attributes for, 345
  <jsp:fallback>, 260, 403
  <jsp:forward>, 124, 404
    forward() vs., 290
  <jsp:getProperty>, 298, 404
    counters, use with, 135
  <jsp:include>, 243, 405, 466
    include directive vs., 244, 248
  <jsp:param>, 124, 405

About the Author

Hans Bergsten is the founder of Gefion Software, whose main product is a JSP-based component suite for developing web applications. Hans has been an active participant in the working groups for both the servlet and JSP specifications from the time they were formed, and contributes to the development of the Apache Tomcat reference implementation for both specifications as a member of the Apache Jakarta Project Management Committee.

Colophon

Our look is the result of reader comments, our own experimentation, and feedback from distribution channels. Distinctive covers complement our distinctive approach to technical topics, breathing personality and life into potentially dry subjects.

Nicole Arigo was the production editor, and Emily Quill was the copyeditor for *JavaServer Pages*™. Leanne Soylemez proofread the book, and Darren Kelly and Rachel Wheeler provided quality control. Ellen Troutman wrote the index.

The animal on the cover of *JavaServer Pages*™ is a grey wolf. Pam Spremulli designed the cover of this book, based on a series design by Edie Freedman. The image is a 19th-century engraving from the Dover Pictorial Archive. Emma Colby produced the cover layout with QuarkXPress 4.1 using Adobe's ITC Garamond font.

David Futato designed the interior layout based on a series design by Nancy Priest. Mike Sierra implemented the design in FrameMaker 5.5.6. The heading font is Bodoni BT, the text font is New Baskerville, and the code font is Constant Willison. The illustrations that appear in the book were produced by Robert Romano using Macromedia FreeHand 9 and Adobe Photoshop 5.5.

Whenever possible, our books use a durable and flexible lay-flat binding. If the page count exceeds this binding's limit, perfect binding is used.

How to stay in touch with O'Reilly

1. Visit Our Award-Winning Web Site

http://www.oreilly.com/

★ "Top 100 Sites on the Web" —*PC Magazine*
★ "Top 5% Web sites" —*Point Communications*
★ "3-Star site" —*The McKinley Group*

Our web site contains a library of comprehensive product information (including book excerpts and tables of contents), downloadable software, background articles, interviews with technology leaders, links to relevant sites, book cover art, and more. File us in your Bookmarks or Hotlist!

2. Join Our Email Mailing Lists

New Product Releases

To receive automatic email with brief descriptions of all new O'Reilly products as they are released, send email to:
listproc@online.oreilly.com
Put the following information in the first line of your message (*not* in the Subject field):
subscribe oreilly-news

O'Reilly Events

If you'd also like us to send information about trade show events, special promotions, and other O'Reilly events, send email to:
listproc@online.oreilly.com
Put the following information in the first line of your message (*not* in the Subject field):
subscribe oreilly-events

3. Get Examples from Our Books via FTP

There are two ways to access an archive of example files from our books:

Regular FTP
- ftp to:
  ftp.oreilly.com
  (login: anonymous
  password: your email address)
- Point your web browser to:
  ftp://ftp.oreilly.com/

FTPMAIL
- Send an email message to:
  ftpmail@online.oreilly.com
  (Write "help" in the message body)

4. Contact Us via Email

order@oreilly.com
To place a book or software order online. Good for North American and international customers.

subscriptions@oreilly.com
To place an order for any of our newsletters or periodicals.

books@oreilly.com
General questions about any of our books.

software@oreilly.com
For general questions and product information about our software. Check out O'Reilly Software Online at **http://software.oreilly.com/** for software and technical support information. Registered O'Reilly software users send your questions to: **website-support@oreilly.com**

cs@oreilly.com
For answers to problems regarding your order or our products.

booktech@oreilly.com
For book content technical questions or corrections.

proposals@oreilly.com
To submit new book or software proposals to our editors and product managers.

international@oreilly.com
For information about our international distributors or translation queries. For a list of our distributors outside of North America check out:
http://www.oreilly.com/www/order/country.html

5. Work with Us

Check out our website for current employment opportunites:
www.jobs@oreilly.com
Click on "Work with Us"

O'Reilly & Associates, Inc.
101 Morris Street, Sebastopol, CA 95472 USA
TEL   707-829-0515 or 800-998-9938
      (6am to 5pm PST)
FAX   707-829-0104

O'REILLY®

International Distributors

UK, EUROPE, MIDDLE EAST AND AFRICA (EXCEPT FRANCE, GERMANY, AUSTRIA, SWITZERLAND, LUXEMBOURG, AND LIECHTENSTEIN)

INQUIRIES
O'Reilly UK Limited
4 Castle Street
Farnham
Surrey, GU9 7HS
United Kingdom
Telephone: 44-1252-711776
Fax: 44-1252-734211
Email: information@oreilly.co.uk

ORDERS
Wiley Distribution Services Ltd.
1 Oldlands Way
Bognor Regis
West Sussex PO22 9SA
United Kingdom
Telephone: 44-1243-843294
UK Freephone: 0800-243207
Fax: 44-1243-843302 (Europe/EU orders)
or 44-1243-843274 (Middle East/Africa)
Email: cs-books@wiley.co.uk

FRANCE

INQUIRIES & ORDERS
Éditions O'Reilly
18 rue Séguier
75006 Paris, France
Tel: 33-1-40-51-52-30
Fax: 33-1-40-51-52-31
Email: france@oreilly.fr

GERMANY, SWITZERLAND, AUSTRIA, LUXEMBOURG, AND LIECHTENSTEIN

INQUIRIES & ORDERS
O'Reilly Verlag
Balthasarstr. 81
D-50670 Köln, Germany
Telephone: 49-221-973160-91
Fax: 49-221-973160-8
Email: anfragen@oreilly.de (inquiries)
Email: order@oreilly.de (orders)

CANADA (FRENCH LANGUAGE BOOKS)

Les Éditions Flammarion ltée
375, Avenue Laurier Ouest
Montréal (Québec) H2V 2K3
Tel: 00-1-514-277-8807
Fax: 00-1-514-278-2085
Email: info@flammarion.qc.ca

HONG KONG

City Discount Subscription Service, Ltd.
Unit A, 6th Floor, Yan's Tower
27 Wong Chuk Hang Road
Aberdeen, Hong Kong
Tel: 852-2580-3539
Fax: 852-2580-6463
Email: citydis@ppn.com.hk

KOREA

Hanbit Media, Inc.
Chungmu Bldg. 210
Yonnam-dong 568-33
Mapo-gu
Seoul, Korea
Tel: 822-325-0397
Fax: 822-325-9697
Email: hant93@chollian.dacom.co.kr

PHILIPPINES

Global Publishing
G/F Benavides Garden
1186 Benavides Street
Manila, Philippines
Tel: 632-254-8949/632-252-2582
Fax: 632-734-5060/632-252-2733
Email: globalp@pacific.net.ph

TAIWAN

O'Reilly Taiwan
1st Floor, No. 21, Lane 295
Section 1, Fu-Shing South Road
Taipei, 106 Taiwan
Tel: 886-2-27099669
Fax: 886-2-27038802
Email: mori@oreilly.com

INDIA

Shroff Publishers & Distributors Pvt. Ltd.
12, "Roseland", 2nd Floor
180, Waterfield Road, Bandra (West)
Mumbai 400 050
Tel: 91-22-641-1800/643-9910
Fax: 91-22-643-2422
Email: spd@vsnl.com

CHINA

O'Reilly Beijing
SIGMA Building, Suite B809
No. 49 Zhichun Road
Haidian District
Beijing, China PR 100080
Tel: 86-10-8809-7475
Fax: 86-10-8809-7463
Email: beijing@oreilly.com

JAPAN

O'Reilly Japan, Inc.
Yotsuya Y's Building
7 Banch 6, Honshio-cho
Shinjuku-ku
Tokyo 160-0003 Japan
Tel: 81-3-3356-5227
Fax: 81-3-3356-5261
Email: japan@oreilly.com

THAILAND

TransQuest Publishers (Thailand)
535/49 Kasemsuk Yaek 5
Soi Pracharat-Bampen 15
Huay Kwang, Bangkok
Thailand 10310
Tel: 662-6910421 or 6910638
Fax: 662-6902235
Email: puripat@.inet.co.th

ALL OTHER ASIAN COUNTRIES

O'Reilly & Associates, Inc.
101 Morris Street
Sebastopol, CA 95472 USA
Tel: 707-829-0515
Fax: 707-829-0104
Email: order@oreilly.com

AUSTRALIA

Woodslane Pty., Ltd.
7/5 Vuko Place
Warriewood NSW 2102
Australia
Tel: 61-2-9970-5111
Fax: 61-2-9970-5002
Email: info@woodslane.com.au

NEW ZEALAND

Woodslane New Zealand, Ltd.
21 Cooks Street (P.O. Box 575)
Waganui, New Zealand
Tel: 64-6-347-6543
Fax: 64-6-345-4840
Email: info@woodslane.com.au

ARGENTINA

Distribuidora Cuspide
Suipacha 764
1008 Buenos Aires
Argentina
Phone: 5411-4322-8868
Fax: 5411-4322-3456
Email: libros@cuspide.com

O'REILLY®